# SIR WALTER MILDMAY
## AND TUDOR GOVERNMENT

Portrait of Sir Walter Mildmay, about 1584, in the
Old Library, Emmanuel College, Cambridge.

# Sir Walter Mildmay and Tudor Government

*Stanford E. Lehmberg*

UNIVERSITY OF TEXAS PRESS, AUSTIN

## PREFACE

Historians have long recognized Sir Walter Mildmay as one of the three or four great figures in Tudor financial administration. Rising by his diligence and ability from a clerkship in the Court of Augmentations, he became Chancellor of the Exchequer at the beginning of Elizabeth's reign and continued to direct financial operations for thirty years. His other activities have been less well known, perhaps because of the inaccessibility of materials necessary for understanding them, but recent acquisitions of family papers by the Northamptonshire Record Office at last render assessment possible. Mildmay now appears as a towering parliamentary figure, leading the House of Commons from 1576 to 1589; as a skilled negotiator, involved particularly in attempts to reach an accommodation between Elizabeth and Mary, Queen of Scots; as a shrewd analyst of foreign affairs, especially relations with Scotland and the Netherlands; and as a dutiful member of the Privy Council. He was deeply concerned for education and religion, as his work in the Exchequer and Parliament, together with his foundation of Emmanuel College, Cambridge, testifies. His contributions in all these areas of Tudor government form the subject of this study.

The reader may wonder at the scant attention to Mildmay's private life and at the extensive quotations from his letters and papers. The first is inevitable; little information about personal affairs survives. The loss may not, however, be great, for like Lord Burghley Mildmay devoted nearly all his time and energy to his public duties. The quotations are a result of my conviction that Mildmay's biographer has an obligation to make available a good selection of his writings, virtually none of which have been printed. No paraphrase can convey his thoughts and manner of expressing them so well as his own words. In quoted matter I have preserved the original spelling, except for the treatment of *i*'s and *j*'s, *u*'s and *v*'s, but I have altered punctuation and capitalization to conform to modern practice.

My researches into Mildmay's career were facilitated by generous grants from the Johnson Fund of the American Philosophical Society and from the University of Texas Research Institute. Dr. F. H. Stubbings, librarian of Emmanuel College; Mr. P. I. King, of the Northamptonshire Record Office; and Mr. F. G. Emmison, Miss Hilda Grieve, and Mr. A. C. Edwards, of the Essex Record Office, were unusually helpful in placing at my disposal the materials in their charge. Dr. Stubbings excised several incorrect statements from Chapter 14, and Dr. G. R. Elton and Professor W. C. Richardson were good enough to comment on the entire work. The Master and Fellows of Emmanuel College, the librarian of the University Library, Cambridge, the editors of *Country Life,* and the director of the Cleveland Museum of Art kindly permitted the reproduction of portraits, prints, and photographs in their possession. My colleagues at the University of Texas, my friend Dr. D. E. D. Beales, of Sidney Sussex College, Cambridge, my parents, and my wife assisted me in various ways. To all I express my gratitude, while accepting sole responsibility for such flaws as remain.

S. E. L.

*Austin, Texas*

# CONTENTS

# ILLUSTRATIONS

## LIST OF ABBREVIATIONS

Add. MSS: Additional Manuscripts, British Museum

*APC*: *Acts of the Privy Council*

BM: British Museum

Bod. Lib.: Bodleian Library, Oxford

C: Chancery Papers, Public Record Office

*Cal. Salisbury MSS*: Historical Manuscripts Commission, *Calendar of the Manuscripts of the Marquis of Salisbury*

*CJ*: *Journals of the House of Commons*

Cot. MSS: Cottonian Manuscripts, British Museum

*CPR, Edw. VI*: *Calendar of Patent Rolls, Edward VI*

*CPR, Eliz.*: *Calendar of Patent Rolls, Elizabeth*

*CPR, P&M*: *Calendar of Patent Rolls, Philip and Mary*

Crom. d.: Thomas Cromwell's diary, MS N. 2. 12, Trinity College Library, Dublin

*CSP, Dom.*: *Calendar of State Papers, Domestic*

*CSP, For.*: *Calendar of State Papers, Foreign*

*CSP, Ire.*: *Calendar of State Papers, Ireland*

*CSP, Scot.*: *Calendar of State Papers Relating to Scotland and Mary, Queen of Scots*

*CSP, Spn.*: *Calendar of State Papers, Spanish*

*DNB*: *Dictionary of National Biography*

E: Exchequer Papers, Public Record Office

EC Lib.: Emmanuel College Library, Cambridge

*EHR*: *English Historical Review*

ERO: Essex Record Office, Chelmsford

Fitz. jour.: William Fitzwilliam's journal, F(M)P 2, Northampton-shire Record Office, Northampton

F(M)P: Fitzwilliam of Milton Papers, Northamptonshire Record Office, Northampton

Harl. MSS: Harleian Manuscripts, British Museum

HMC: Historical Manuscripts Commission

Lans. MSS: Lansdowne Manuscripts, British Museum

*LJ*: *Journals of the House of Lords*

*LP*: *Letters and Papers, Foreign and Domestic, Henry VIII*

NRO: Northamptonshire Record Office, Northampton

PRO: Public Record Office, London

SP: State Papers, Public Record Office

Westm. MSS: Westmorland Manuscripts, Northamptonshire Record Office

SIR WALTER MILDMAY
AND TUDOR GOVERNMENT

# 1. YOUTH, 1520–1540

W ALTER MILDMAY was born in Chelmsford, Essex, the son of
Thomas Mildmay, a mercer. No record of the exact date remains,
for the Chelmsford parish registers begin only in 1538; but 1520, the
year traditionally accepted, cannot be far wrong.[1]

The origins of the Mildmay family are shrouded in a mist partially
of Sir Walter's own making. In 1583, desiring a grant of arms from
Robert Cooke, Clarenceux herald, he produced "auntient credible and
authenticall deedes, charters, recordes, wrytinges, evidences and letters"
which purported to show that "the said Sir Walter is by fourtene
discentes (from father to sonne) lineally and lawfully extracted of the
body of a very auncient gentleman of this land called Hugh de
Mildemay, whoe . . . lyved about Kinge Stephens tyme, now foure
hundreth and thirtie yeares past." Having examined the documents,
Cooke proceeded to "restore, ratify and confirme" the ancient arms of
the Mildmay family, "that is to say, the feild argent, three lyons
rampynge asure." In passing he expressed his pleasure that time, which
so often casts down noble families, also "bringeth to light and dis-
covereth to be gentlemen of longe and auncient contynuance dyvers
whose auncestores (sondry yeares beffore) were not reputed of such
antiquitie, that therby . . . Gods mercy may be sene and his bounty
praysed."[2]

These arms were not, however, the first obtained by Mildmay.
Thirty-one years earlier, in 1552, he had been granted the use of a coat
showing a winged horse on a silver bend. His ancestors were not
mentioned in the grant; it said merely that Sir Walter was "descended

---

[1] One of the portraits of Mildmay at Emmanuel College is dated 1574,
*aetatis* 53. See Plate 4.

[2] Harl. MS 245, fols. 142–144.

3

of a howse unedefemyd, and hath of longe tyme used hymself in feats of armes and warks vertuous, so that he is well worthie to beare the tokens and ensignes of honnoure, that is to say, armes."[3] It seems curious that Mildmay should have sought arms without producing whatever genealogical documents he might possess and even less likely that in 1583 he should have unearthed a complete series of hitherto unknown family papers. These improbabilities, together with certain discrepancies in the documents cited in the grant of 1583, led J. H. Round some years ago to surmise that the papers were forgeries and the ancestral arms "rediscovered" in 1583 a fake.[4] Although Round was unable to examine the documents himself, they can now be studied at the Northamptonshire Record Office, and they fully confirm his suspicions.[5] The genealogy in Cooke's grant to Mildmay, as indeed in a number of his other grants, is fabrication, utterly unreliable. Why Mildmay, an old man by 1583, should have wanted new arms and suppositious ancestors remains a mystery.

Sources more reliable than Cooke permit the family to be traced to Sir Walter's great-grandfather, Thomas Mildmay, probably a yeoman farmer of Great Waltham, Essex, who married Margaret Cornish about 1465.[6] A deed of 1484 refers to their son, Walter, as keeper of the park of Morlewood, with fees of 30s. 4d. a year,[7] and Cooke's genealogy, which may perhaps be trusted at this point, calls Walter an officer in the household of Anne Neville, Duchess of Buckingham, at Writtle, Essex.[8] He married Margaret Everard of Great Waltham about 1483.[9]

---

[3] Cot. MS Faustina E. 1, quoted in *Genealogical Memoranda Relating to the Family of Mildmay.*

[4] J. H. Round, "The Mildmay Mystery," in his *Family Origins and Other Studies,* pp. 60–72.

[5] Westm. MSS, 1, I, 4; 1, I, 158.

[6] See the genealogical table.

[7] Round, *Family Origins,* p. 67.

[8] Harl. MS 245, fols. 142–143.

[9] H. A. St. John Mildmay, *A Brief Memoir of the Mildmay Family,* pp. 237–238; pedigree, compiled ca. 1780, ERO MSS, D/DM F 8. The Mildmay family had probably lived in Essex for generations and may have taken its name from the "mildemet" manor recorded in the Domesday Book, now represented by the hamlet of Middlemead in Little Baddow.

More is known of Walter's son Thomas Mildmay, the first member of the family to settle in Chelmsford. He seems to have taken over a mercer's business already established by the Cornish family, which had migrated earlier from Great Waltham; a document of 1507 relates that one Anne Cornish, a widow, had illegally sold a stall in "le Shoprow" to "a certain Thomas Mildmay," a phrase implying that he was new and not well known in the city. Since this practice was contrary to the custom of the manor, the stall was seized, but it was probably restored to Mildmay after the payment of a fine.[10] Thomas Mildmay also obtained a house from the Cornish family: in 1515 he leased "Mayes," a rather small dwelling opposite the fish stalls in the center of Chelmsford, from John Cornish, and the lease, with option to purchase, was subsequently renewed.[11] It was probably at Mayes that Thomas's son, the future Chancellor of the Exchequer, was born; but the house was not large enough for Thomas's seven children, nor did it accord with his acquired wealth. He therefore purchased in 1530 the commodious dwelling which had been erected half a century before by Guy Harling, an ancestor of the Cornishes.[12] In this pleasant house facing the parish church and surrounded by ample gardens Walter with his brothers and sisters grew to maturity.

Thomas and his wife, the former Agnes Read of High Easter, provided well for their children. The eldest son, Edward, was apprenticed to Christopher Campion, a London mercer, and was admitted to the liberty of the City in 1541. He predeceased his father, dying in 1549 in the parish of St. Botolph without Aldersgate; his younger brother Walter served as executor of his estate.[13] The second son, and heir to most of Thomas Mildmay's estates, bore his father's name. Thomas II, as it will be convenient to call him, married Avicia Gunson, daughter of the royal treasurer of marine causes. Considerable wealth and in-

[10] ERO MSS, D/DM M 6, membrane 39ᵛ.

[11] ERO MSS, D/DAV 14–16. Thomas Mildmay is specifically called a mercer in D/DAV 14.

[12] ERO MSS, D/DV 23/24–25. The present house on this site is still called Guy Harlings; it appears to be of the eighteenth century but may incorporate some fifteenth-century work.

[13] St. John Mildmay, *Memoir,* p. 14; Westm. MSS, 2, X, 2, B4. See also the genealogical table.

fluence came to Thomas II through his post as auditor of the Court of Augmentations; it was probably through his patronage that Walter Mildmay, Thomas I's fifth son, first obtained governmental office. Thomas the Auditor died in 1566.[14]

Thomas I's third and fourth sons, William and John, were probably mercers in Chelmsford, for their father's will granted them both stalls in the market place. They later acquired estates in Essex, William at Springfield Barnes and John at Terling. It may be of interest to note that William's son, Thomas, married Agnes Winthrop, a relative of the first governor of Massachusetts. William died in 1570, his brother a decade later.

Two girls, Margery and Joanne, also grew to maturity at Guy Harlings. Margery had died before 1548, leaving a son, Richard Barnard. Joanne married Christopher Peyton, whom she bore six children.[15]

The senior Thomas Mildmay, "yeoman and merchaunte," died January 22, 1551. His will,[16] written three years earlier, directed that his body should be buried in the parish church at Chelmsford, to which he gave 3s. 4d. "in dischardge of my conscience for tithes and oblacions negligently forgotten." He left a further bequest "for the salarye of an honest priest for to singe for my soule and all Christen soules in the peroche church of Chelmsforde by the space of oon hole yere next and immediatly after my decease, if it may stand by the orders hereafter to be taken, or otherwise to be distributed emongest the poore by the discrecion of myne executours." His doubts regarding the effect of the dissolution of the chantries must have been shared by many mid-century testators. Thomas left his smaller house, Mayes, to his widow, and Guy Harlings to Thomas II, his oldest surviving son. Other tenements, possibly among those which he had purchased from the King in 1536 for £ 79 6s. 8d.,[17] were bequeathed to his sons William

---

[14] The article on Sir Walter Mildmay in the *DNB* is in error in referring to Thomas I as the auditor of Augmentations.

[15] St. John Mildmay, *Memoir,* p. 14 and *passim*; Sir Walter Mildmay's will, Prerogative Court of Canterbury, 51 Leicester, Somerset House, London.

[16] ERO MSS, D/ABW 25/92.

[17] *LP,* XIX, Pt. I, No. 610 (116); St. John Mildmay, *Memoir,* p. 14.

6

and John. As executors Thomas named his wife Agnes and his sons Thomas, Walter, and William.

Although no verifying documents remain, we may assume that Walter Mildmay attended grammar school in Chelmsford. About 1538 he proceeded to Cambridge, where he matriculated fellow-commoner of Christ's College, Lady Margaret Beaufort's new foundation.[18]

The University of Mildmay's time was much quieter than it had been in the 1520's, the great decade of Cambridge reforming zeal. Robert Barnes, whose sermons had set Cambridge aflame, had been silenced in 1526 and was ultimately to be executed. Hugh Latimer, memorable for his sermons of 1529 at St. Edward's Church, had been charged with heresy but finally had submitted to Convocation and was rewarded with the bishopric of Worcester. Thomas Bilney, whom Foxe called "the first framer of that university in the knowledge of Christ,"[19] had been burned in 1531 at Norwich, before a large crowd, after preaching Lutheran doctrines despite his earlier forced recantation. No longer were Protestant views aired at the White Horse Tavern.

Reform, however, continued, manifesting itself more in the curriculum than in sermons. The study of canon law was abolished, divinity lectures were based on "the true sense" of the Scriptures, not on scholastic commentators, and students were encouraged to study Melanchthon as well as Aristotle.[20] Many of Mildmay's later ideas about religion and education must have sprung from seeds planted during his years at Christ's.

Mildmay must also have examined the impressive buildings rising during his years. The supremely beautiful new chapel of King's College was first used in 1536, following the collapse of the old chapel after a

---

[18] C. H. and T. Cooper, *Athenae Cantabrigienses,* II, 51–55; John and J. A. Venn, *Alumni Cantabrigienses,* Pt. I, Vol. III, p. 188. The date cannot be established exactly because the University matriculation records begin only in 1544, and the College admission books not until 1622. I am indebted to Miss Heather E. Peek, keeper of the University Archives, and Dr. A. L. Peck, librarian of Christ's College, for information about the records in their care.

[19] John Foxe, *Acts and Monuments,* ed. S. R. Cattley and George Townsend, IV, 651.

[20] J. B. Mullinger, *The University of Cambridge,* I, 631.

vesper service.[21] The first court of St. John's College, founded like Christ's by Lady Margaret, finally stood complete after a series of delays.[22] Great St. Mary's, the University church, had been almost completely demolished and rebuilt between 1478 and 1519, and the tower remained unfinished in 1540. But while new edifices arose others fell into decay, for the houses of friars, so important in medieval Cambridge, were surrendered to the Crown in 1538. It is tempting to suppose that the young Mildmay witnessed the dissolution of the Dominican house, on whose site he was to erect Emmanuel College, and of the Franciscan friary, where later rose Sidney Sussex, another Puritan foundation.

We do not know what Mildmay studied at Cambridge or how long he remained. He left without a degree and was certainly in London by 1540. It may be that some of the volumes which he later gave to Emmanuel College are those he had used as a student. A number of these are treatises on mathematics: a commentary on Euclid, a volume of Dürer on geometry, and Tunstall's *De arte supputandi,* which Mildmay ornamented with Latin and Greek mottos as well as mathematical calculations. Written on a flyleaf is a list of popular classics—Arrian, Euripides, Sophocles, Isocrates, Aristotle—together with an unusual group of mathematical subjects.[23] Was Mildmay already aiming at governmental service in the revenue courts and carefully learning mathematics, a subject not commonly taught in the universities?

While Walter Mildmay studied at Cambridge his older brother Thomas was making his way to a position of some prominence in the government. As early as January, 1535, he was one of the auditors in the office of First Fruits and Tenths, newly established to deal with the revenues resulting from the statute of 1534 annexing clerical taxation to the Crown, and he helped compile the survey of ecclesiastical

[21] H. C. Porter, *Reformation and Reaction in Tudor Cambridge,* p. 17.

[22] Robert Willis and J. W. Clark, *Architectural History of the University of Cambridge,* II, 239–242.

[23] The volume, EC Lib. MSS, 4.2.28, is headed "Cantabrige, Walterus Mildmaius me possidet," which would seem to indicate that it was used by Mildmay at Christ's, but it also, inexplicably, bears the date 1555 written in two places.

8

revenues known as the *Valor Ecclesiasticus*.[24] He was to profit from his early involvement in ecclesiastical revenue administration, a branch of the government which grew rapidly as the King asserted his headship of the Church.

After the parliamentary act of 1536 decreeing the dissolution of the lesser monasteries, commissioners were named to oversee their actual surrender. From July, 1536, to February, 1537, Thomas was busy valuing the lands and goods of suppressed houses in Norfolk and Suffolk.[25] He also helped draw inventories of monasteries and nunneries in Hertfordshire, Northamptonshire, London, Middlesex, Cambridgeshire, and Huntingdonshire.[26] In April, 1537, he was named one of the ten auditors of the Court of Augmentations, which had been established to handle the monastic revenues, with an annual salary of twenty pounds and fees.[27] A month later he was given the reversion of the auditorship of the Duchy of Cornwall,[28] and in October he was granted monastic lands in Ashfield and Badwell, Suffolk.[29] It may be that Walter Mildmay helped take over some of these properties, for he was probably the writer of a letter addressed "to my brother, Mr. Thomas Mildmay," which describes the buildings of the friary at Badwell and estimates the amount of lead remaining on the roofs.[30]

From the profits of governmental office Thomas Mildmay was able to purchase, on July 23, 1540, the manor of Moulsham, just across the River Can from Chelmsford. Moulsham, with its thirteen hundred acres and two hundred tenants, had belonged to the Abbey of Westminster since the eleventh century; Thomas paid the Court of Augmentations £ 622 5s. 8d. for it. By his time the manor house was badly decayed, so he ordered it pulled down and in 1542 erected a new man-

---

[24] *LP*, VII, No. 149 (42, 55). The *Valor Ecclesiasticus* was published in six volumes by the Record Commissioners, 1810–1834. See W. C. Richardson, *Tudor Chamber Administration, 1485–1547*, pp. 334–336; Philip Hughes, *The Reformation in England*, I, 283.

[25] *LP*, XII, Pt. I, Nos. 455, 510.

[26] *Ibid.*, XII, Pt. I, No. 571; XIII, Pt. I, Nos. 404, 405; XIII, Pt. II, No. 1203.

[27] *Ibid.*, XIII, Pt. I, p. 573.

[28] *Ibid.*, XII, Pt. I, No. 1330 (13). He had succeeded to the post by 1553 (see HMC, *Fifth Report*, p. 307).

[29] *LP*, XIII, Pt. I, p. 587.

[30] *Ibid.*, Pt. II, No. 1213; undated [?1538].

sion which "was then accounted the greatest esquire's building within the said county of Essex," as a survey of 1591 reported.[31] It was a house fit to receive a sovereign, as indeed it did in 1579 when Queen Elizabeth visited for four days.[32]

By 1540 a prosperous and prominent Thomas Mildmay was able to help launch his younger brother Walter on a career destined to eclipse his own.

[31] Quoted in Philip Morant, *The History and Antiquities of the County of Essex,* II, 2–3. See also J. H. Round, "The Mildmays and their Chelmsford Estates," *Transactions of the Essex Archaeological Society,* new ser., XV (1921), 9.

[32] John Nichols, *The Progresses and Public Processions of Queen Elizabeth,* II, *sub anno* 1579, pp. 111–112. The house was demolished in the eighteenth century, and a new mansion in the classical style was built by Benjamin Mildmay, nineteenth Baron Fitzwalter.

## 2. UNDER TWO KINGS, 1540–1551

IN 1540 WALTER MILDMAY joined his brother Thomas in the Augmentations office. There is no record of his appointment, for he doubtless began as a clerk, and patents were not made for such inferior positions. But a memorandum of June 9, 1540, relating to the purchase of monastic lands near Bury, is signed "per me Wa. Mildmay" and is in Walter's hand. It reveals that he was serving in the office of John Eyer, one of the seventeen receivers of the Court of Augmentations.[1]

Two years later Mildmay sought a more important position as auditor of the revenues from lands formerly held by Edward Stafford, Duke of Buckingham, who had been arrested on dubious charges of treason and executed in 1521. Mildmay had the support of his brother and probably of Anthony Denny, keeper of the Palace of Westminster and one of Henry's favorite councillors,[2] but in the end he was not successful. The office, with its salary of £ 10 a year, was granted to William Notte.[3]

But Walter's rise was not long delayed. In May, 1543, he and Francis Southwell, another Augmentations official, were appointed to the new post of auditors of the King's military and naval works and of all moneys advanced in prest.[4] Prests were very commonly used as a means of providing funds for such governmental officers as military

[1] *LP,* XV, No. 763.

[2] *Ibid.,* XVII, App. 17; SP 1/244, fol. 19. The latter document, a letter from Walter to Thomas Mildmay, is undated but was probably written shortly after August 31, 1542.

[3] *LP,* XVII, No. 881 (30).

[4] *Ibid.,* XVIII, Pt. I, No. 623 (58). It is difficult to be certain exactly what the meaning of the document is; see W. C. Richardson, *History of the Court of Augmentations, 1536–1554,* pp. 144–150. Mildmay's salary in this post was £ 40 a year.

treasurers and ambassadors; their advantage was that the official received the money in advance and accounted for its expenditure later,
instead of producing bills before payment could be made. The system,
necessary as it was, was obviously vulnerable to abuse; the creation of a
unified system of audit seems to have worked a marked improvement in
the efficiency of the revenue administration.

The first duties of Mildmay and Southwell related to the rather
pointless war with France which Henry had begun in alliance with
Charles V. Only a small English contingent saw battle in 1543, but
during the next year Henry sent off a large army and in July followed it
himself, although he had become so corpulent that he had to be carried
in a litter. During the campaign Mildmay and Southwell disbursed
funds as need arose in France, serving under Sir Richard Rich, who
had resigned as Chancellor of the Court of Augmentations to become
treasurer of the war.[5] English troops were able to capture Boulogne,
but naval affairs went badly: the *Mary Rose*, with her four hundred
men, was lost, even the *Great Harry* was at one point in difficulty, and
the French actually succeeded in rowing their galleys up the Solent.
Charles made peace in September, 1545; Henry, insistent on retaining
Boulogne, did not conclude a treaty with France until the following
June.

Mildmay's part in these operations can be discerned dimly from the
financial records. A list of wages to be paid at Calais for the week
beginning November 6, 1544, includes a payment to Mildmay of 56s.[6]
By the following January he had returned to England, for on the fifth
he and Anthony Rous, master of the Jewel House, were paid £ 16
12s. 8d. for "carriage of one load of the King's Majesty's treasures
and books of the wars" from Calais to London, for waiting at Calais
ten days to take the account of the water bailiff for transportation of
the army, and for "perfecting the remembrances of the estates of the
furniture and victuals" used by Henry at Calais.[7] In February Southwell
and Mildmay compiled the accounts of the sheriff of Norfolk, Sir
Francis Lovell, who had furnished 399 horses and 114 carters for the

---

[5] *LP*, XIX, Pt. I, No. 134; W. C. Richardson, *Tudor Chamber Administration, 1485–1547*, p. 329.

[6] Add. MS 5753, fol. 8, calendared in *LP*, XIX, Pt. II, No. 524.

[7] Add. MS 5753, fol. 123, calendared in *LP*, XX, Pt. I, No. 19.

war at a cost of just over £ 656.[8] Two months later Thomas Chamberlain, writing from Antwerp to Sir William Paget, the Principal Secretary, asked for acquittance of his "last year's account with young
Myldemaide."[9] Finally, on April 7, 1546, the Council ordered William
Cavendish, treasurer of the King's Chamber, to pay Mildmay the
money remaining due for his services in Boulogne.[10]

Meanwhile Walter continued his work in Augmentations, examining a number of accounts relating to monastic lands.[11] In June, 1545,
he and his brother Thomas were granted jointly the auditor's position
which Thomas had previously held alone.[12] The brothers were responsible for the counties of Norfolk, Suffolk, Cambridge, Huntingdon, Essex, Hertford, Middlesex, and London, and were to share the
salary of £ 20 a year supplemented by the usual fees and diets. Further
promotion followed rapidly: in December, 1545, Walter was appointed one of the three chief officers of the Court of General Surveyors.[13] The General Surveyors had been charged with the administration of Crown estates and castles since the reign of Henry VII, and
their function as the King's principal auditors had been confirmed by
statute in 1542. The Court thus became one of the several specialized
revenue bureaus which rose following the erection of Augmentations.
Its work was not new to Mildmay; he had probably handled matters
pertaining to the General Surveyors as well as Augmentations since
1540. A book of fees compiled sometime in 1545 lists him as one of
the twenty-four auditors of General Surveyors, along with Thomas
Mildmay and Southwell.[14] In September, 1546, he became also auditor

[8] *LP*, XX, Pt. I, No. 134.

[9] *Ibid.*, XX, Pt. I, No. 550.

[10] *Ibid.*, XXI, Pt. I, No. 561.

[11] For instances of his activities see *LP,* XIX, Pt. II, App. 11 (ii); XX, Pt.
II, No. 481; XXI, Pt. I, Nos. 1032, 1120, 1151, 1157, 1168, 1249 (2), 1351,
1401. In 1549 Mildmay, Sir Richard Sackville, and Sir Thomas Moyle spent
two weeks at Sheen and Sion House and were rewarded by an additional payment of £ 81 17s. 2d. (E 315/258/67; Richardson, *Augmentations,* p. 338 n. 35).

[12] E 315/236/192–193, calendared in *LP,* XXI, Pt. I, No. 1538. On the duties
of the auditors see Richardson, *Augmentations,* pp. 54–57.

[13] Richardson, *Chamber,* p. 366.

[14] *LP,* XX, Pt. II, App. 13. In this office Mildmay was succeeded by his son
Anthony (Robert Somerville, *History of the Duchy of Lancaster,* I, 437).

of the Duchy of Lancaster, responsible for lands north of the Trent.[15]

In 1545 Mildmay sat in Parliament for the first time. He probably owed his seat for Lostwithiel to his brother Thomas, who as receiver-general of the Duchy of Cornwall had considerable influence in that Cornish borough. In the Parliament of 1547 Mildmay sat for Lewes, probably under the patronage of Thomas, Lord Seymour, a brother of Henry VIII's third Queen. Mildmay's ownership of lands at Danbury and Apethorpe no doubt explains his return as a burgess for Maldon, Essex, in Edward VI's Parliament of 1553 and for Peterborough in Mary's Parliament called later the same year. He was conspicuously absent from Mary's later Parliaments, perhaps because he had been too staunch a defender of Protestantism in 1553, but he reappeared as one of the Knights of the Shire for Northampton in all the Elizabethan Parliaments to meet before his death.[16] His genius at parliamentary affairs may have been discernible as early as Edward's reign, although we have no detailed knowledge of his activities before the 1570's.

Walter Mildmay was admitted to Gray's Inn, one of the Inns of Court, in 1546.[17] It is unlikely that he actually took time to study law at this stage in his career; he must already have learned a good deal in his governmental posts, and his admission may have been merely an acknowledgment of his stature.

As the multiplicity of Mildmay's positions indicates, English financial administration had become unnecessarily complex. Henry VII's chamber system and Thomas Cromwell's specialized revenue courts had been instituted in an attempt to cut through the red tape and bureaucracy of the outmoded Exchequer, but they in turn had grown wasteful, particularly in their useless duplication of local officials. By 1546 reform and simplification were badly needed.

The first steps were taken in the spring of that year. A commission,

[15] *LP,* XXI, Pt. II, No. 199 (12). He owed the appointment to Secretary Paget's favor.

[16] *Return of Members of Parliament,* I, *passim.* Mildmay's name appears on a list of those who "stood for the true religion" in 1553 (MS Bodley e Museo 17), but as not all the men named were unyielding Protestants the meaning of the list is doubtful.

[17] Joseph Foster, *The Register of Admissions of Gray's Inn, 1521–1889,* col. 18.

including such men as Lord Chancellor Thomas Wriothesley, Bishop Stephen Gardiner, Secretaries Sir William Paget and Sir William Petre, and Sir William Paulet, master of the Household and president of the Council, was appointed on June 30 to examine the state of the revenues in the various courts and to expedite the payment of debts owed the King. Mildmay was ordered to attend upon the commissioners, and any order given by him in their name was to have full validity. It is likely that he did most of the work, for he had actual experience of the operation of the courts and he was probably the only member not over-burdened with other duties.[18]

Mildmay spent May and June surveying Crown revenues. Debtors were summoned to appear before him, either in person or by deputy, and a record was made of their explanations and of decisions reached in each case. Although some debts were as large as £ 188, most were under £ 20, and some were as small as one pound. In the main they consisted of arrears of rents payable to Augmentations.[19]

The principal work of the commission, however, was not to drive in debts which had already become delinquent, but rather to suggest how the financial machinery might operate more efficiently in the future. The commissioners ultimately decided that this aim could be accomplished by merging the Courts of General Surveyors and Augmentations into a reconstituted court of "Augmentations and Revenues." As Crown lands accumulated by Henry VII and Henry VIII had accounted before the General Surveyors and the former monastic lands before the Augmentations, the amalgamation of the courts meant that virtually all royal lands except the Duchy of Lancaster, by tradition a separate unit, came under the jurisdiction of a single office.

The patent establishing the new court is dated January 1, 1547, and is of considerable interest.[20] It complains that hitherto the duties of the

[18] *LP*, XXI, Pt. I, No. 1166 (71). Although the patent is dated June 30, the commissioners are said to have been at work since April 1, and the patent gave full force to what they had already done. See Richardson, *Augmentations*, pp. 111–159.

[19] *LP*, XXI, Pt. I, No. 1280 (1).

[20] C 66/790, mm. 15–28, inadequately summarized in *LP*, XXI, Pt. II, No. 771 (1). See also Richardson, *Chamber*, pp. 330–333, 366–368, and G. R. Elton, *The Tudor Revolution in Government*, pp. 223–230.

officers in the various courts had not been clearly defined, "so that suche ambyguyties and doubtes have rysen amongest our officers of the saide courtes for lacke of good rules and orders to theym prescribed that they coulde not by any meanes knowe directlie howe to order the same accordinge to our expectation and their duties." Revenues have thus been "very moche and greatlye disorderyd" to the King's great detriment and loss. In the old Augmentations and General Surveyors, particularly, there were "a great nombre of superfluous officers and ministers, wherby hathe ensued not onely a greate and inordinate charge, . . . but also a greate confusion and mysorder."

Therefore the two courts were to "ceasse and absolutelye be . . . extinguished and no longer to contynewe and endure." In their place the new Court of the Augmentations and Revenues of the King's Crown was established, "forever to endure." Sir Edward North, Chancellor of the former Court of Augmentations, was named first officer of the new court, while Walter Mildmay and Sir Thomas Moyle, the former heads of General Surveyors, were given life appointments as general surveyors of the new foundation and together constituted its second officer. North was to be paid £ 300 a year, Mildmay and Moyle £ 200 each.[21] Other officers were to be a treasurer, two masters of woods, a clerk, ten auditors, two auditors of prests, and eleven receivers. Although the bureau perhaps remained larger than necessary, a significant reduction in staff had been effected; over two-thirds of the local officials of General Surveyors were eliminated, as were most of the auditors.[22]

It was perhaps to be expected that the new court would experience some difficulty in establishing its authority. The case of John Hanby, one of the displaced auditors, may be cited as an example: on December 12, 1546, North and Mildmay wrote to inform him of the changes and to order him to deliver the books of revenues previously in his

[21] *LP,* XXI, Pt. II, Nos. 647 (37), 774. As late as 1568 Mildmay was still receiving £ 200 a year as compensation for his office as general surveyor, although the Court of Augmentations was finally abolished in 1554 and its business transferred to the Exchequer. See Lans. MS 171, fol. 344, and Elton, *Tudor Revolution,* p. 250.

[22] The former Court of Augmentations had seventeen auditors, General Surveyors twenty-four.

charge.[23] He failed to comply, and on January 26 North, Mildmay, and Moyle were obliged to write again, peremptorily ordering Hanby to present a certificate by February 20 so that the revenues might be received properly on March 25, the Feast of the Annunciation.[24] Presumably he finally obeyed.

Although little evidence concerning Mildmay's personal life during his early years in governmental service survives, we do know that he was married on May 25, 1546, to Mary Walsingham.[25] She was the youngest of the five daughters of William Walsingham, a London attorney, and his wife, the former Joyce Denny, a sister of Sir Anthony Denny whose favor Mildmay had invoked in 1542. Mary's brother, Francis, was to become the great Elizabethan Secretary and one of Mildmay's closest friends. Mary was six years younger than her husband; she has been described by a recent writer as "a stiff, stern woman and a hard and rigid Puritan,"[26] while according to the kinder judgment of one of her daughters-in-law she was "a virtuous woman and dutiful to her husband, in all chastitie, obedience, love and feare towards him, as ever I did know anie."[27] The only surviving portrait, painted in 1574 when she was forty-six years old, makes both descriptions credible.[28]

King Henry VIII, physically an old man although only fifty-five, died in the early hours of January 28, 1547, to be succeeded by his only son, the nine-year-old Edward. The coronation took place February 20, and when the boy King held his first investiture two days later Walter Mildmay was among those knighted.[29] It was an extraordinary honor for a civil servant of relatively humble birth, less than thirty years old.

---

[23] *LP,* XXI, Pt. II, No. 534. On Hanby's later career see Richardson, *Augmentations,* p. 442.

[24] *LP,* XXI, Pt. II, No. 749.

[25] H. A. St. John Mildmay, *A Brief Memoir of the Mildmay Family,* p. 58, where the year is misprinted 1646.

[26] *Ibid.*

[27] MS diary of Grace Mildmay in the Northampton Public Library, quoted in Rachel Weigall, "An Elizabethan Gentlewoman," *Quarterly Review,* CCXV (1911), 124.

[28] The portrait (Plate 3) is at Emmanuel College, Cambridge.

[29] C. H. and T. Cooper, *Athenae Cantabrigienses,* II, 51.

With the new King came new duties, some of them routine but some of sweeping significance, for governmental officials. Sir Walter Mildmay found himself busy examining the accounts of the mint, making an inventory of the late King's possessions, and assisting in the dissolution of the chantries.

Mint accounts were supposed to be taken annually, but through oversight the records of John Browne, keeper of the coinage in the Tower, had not been examined regularly during Henry VIII's reign. Mildmay, Sir Ralph Sadler, Sir Edmund Peckham, and Sir William Sharington were commissioned on July 21, 1547, to perform an audit, cooperating with William Dunche, auditor of the mint. The accounts examined cover the periods from July 1, 1542, to March 31, 1543, when 541 pounds of gold and 22,053 pounds of silver were coined, and from September 29, 1543, to March 31, 1544, when the coinage amounted to only 213 pounds of gold and 2,408 of silver.[30] The commissioners' report does not mention the debasement of the coinage, a problem which Mildmay would soon have to face.

In September, 1547, a commission composed of Sir William Paulet (now Lord St. John), Lord Russell, the Earl of Warwick, and Mildmay was ordered to compile an inventory of the household goods left by the late King. Any two of the commissioners were empowered to complete the survey; Paulet and Mildmay actually did the work.[31] Their amazingly complete list[32] includes possessions at the Tower, Greenwich, Hampton Court, Oatlands, Nonesuch, Windsor, Woodstock, the More, Richmond, New Hall, Nottingham, St. John's, and Bedington as well as in numerous chambers at Westminster: "the guarderobe, the secreate guarderobe, the Kinges owne Juelhous in the olde gallorye, the studye at the nether ende of the long gallorye, the chairehous [throne room], the glasse hous, the studie next th'olde

---

[30] The commission is calendared in *CPR, Edw. VI*, I, 116; the report is Harl. MS 698, fol. 35, calendared in *LP*, XIX, Pt. I, No. 267. Sharington, master of the mint at Bristol, was attainted in 1549 for buying Somerset church plate which had been declared superfluous and for converting it into base shillings contrary to an explicit order of the Council.

[31] *LP*, XVII, No. 267; *CPR, Edw. VI*, I, 138–139.

[32] The first part of the inventory is Add. MS 46, 348, the second, Harl. MSS 1419A and 1419B. Part II is calendared in *LP*, XXI, Pt. I, No. 754.

beddchambre, the olde juell hous, [and] the newe lybrarie." Each item is fully described. The entry under "crymsen clothe of golde," for instance, begins "eleven peces of crymsen clothe of golde, playne, wrought with borders, as well with the Kinges armes as allso with roses and portecullices" and goes on to list the length of each piece.[33] "Canapies, traverses, counterpoyntes, windowe curteyns, fustians, pillowes, sheetes, vanes, targettes, closett stuffe," altar frontals, vestments, carpets, even the late King's shoes and gloves are elaborately itemized. Included in the interesting list of musical instruments are two double virginals, "a litle paire of virginalles single, twoo faire paire of newe longe virginalles made harpe fasshion of cipres with keies of iverie," basses, recorders, flutes, crumhorns, bagpipes, "a litle Venice lute," and "sondrie bookes and scrolles of songes and ballattes."[34]

A memorandum added to the inventory in 1549 records that many of the goods at Westminster were in the custody of Protector Somerset, Edward VI's uncle,

. . . untill the tyme of his trowble, being in Octobre, anno tercio Regis E. VI[ti], at which tyme the keys were delyvered to the Kinges most honorable Counsaill and by their commaundement the doores sealed untill the said xij[th] day of Novembre, at which tyme by their appoyntment Sir William Herbert, knight of th'ordre, M[r] of the Kinges horses, Sir Edward Northe, knighte, one of the Kinges Pryvie Counsaill, & Sir Walter Myldmay, knight, entered into the same howses and there toke a perfect survey and vyewe of all suche thinges as they founde there remaynynge, and the same stuffe by lyke ordre of the Counsaill they delyvered in chardge to t'handes of James Rufforthe to the Kinges use.

The commissioners duly noted items listed in the 1547 inventory which were missing after Somerset's fall.[35]

Mildmay's most significant employment during Edward VI's reign was as commissioner for the sale of chantry lands and the continuation of grammar schools formerly staffed by chantry priests. Some few of the chantries—endowments for the support of priests to sing masses

---

[33] Harl. MS 1419A, fol. 5[r].
[34] *Ibid.,* fols. 204–205.
[35] *Ibid.,* fol. 118[v].

for the souls of the dead—had been dissolved by private action during the last years of Henry VIII's reign, and an act of Parliament in 1545 had authorized the King to appropriate the revenues of the dissolved establishments.[36] It is doubtful that any chantries were actually surrendered to the Crown under the 1545 act, and its authority expired with Henry's death. But the government was still determined to acquire the revenues, and in 1547 Edward's first Parliament passed its famous act under which 2,374 chantries were dissolved.[37]

The preambles to these statutes, expressing as they do Parliament's justification for the actions taken, are of great interest. Henry's act says merely that the governors of the chantries do not commonly apply the endowments in accordance with the founders' intentions, and that the revenues may therefore be better used to help offset the unusual expenses of the King's wars with Scotland and France, as well as the heavy cost of maintaining the King in befitting state. There is no hint of theological objection to chantries; that comes only in the act of 1547, which asserts

. . . that a great part of superstition and errors in Christian religion hath been brought into the minds and estimation of men by reason of the ignorance of their very true and perfect salvation through the death of Jesus Christ, and by devising and phantasing vain opinions of Purgatory and masses satisfactory to be done for them which be departed, the which doctrine and vain opinion by nothing more is maintained and upholden than by the abuse of . . . chantries.[38]

Chantries encouraged superstitious belief in the efficacy of prayers for the dead, which seemingly diminished the importance of the faith and good works of the living.

Dissolution of the chantries meant more, however, than the cessation of masses for the dead, since chantry priests commonly taught in schools supported by chantry endowments. Indeed Henry VIII's act had been so broadly phrased as to endanger the continued existence of

[36] 37 Henry VIII, c. 4.

[37] J. R. Tanner, *Tudor Constitutional Documents*, pp. 103–107. On the dissolution see Richardson, *Augmentations*, pp. 170–177.

[38] 1 Edward VI, c. 14, printed in Henry Gee and W. J. Hardy, *Documents Illustrative of English Church History*, pp. 328–357; extracts in Tanner, *Documents*, pp. 103–104.

the universities of Oxford and Cambridge, together with such schools as Eton and Winchester. It was never the aim of the government to interfere with these establishments of higher learning, and they are specifically exempted from the act of 1547, along with cathedral churches or colleges "where a bishop's see is." Edward's act refers also to the "erecting of grammar schools to the education of youth in virtue and godliness, the further augmenting of the universities, and better provision for the poor and needy" as appropriate uses of the former chantry endowments.

Since a complete survey of properties and local needs was necessary before the changes could be effected, the act provided for commissions of local gentlemen and governmental officials to list the endowments and to recommend allowances for the maintenance of schoolmasters, endowment of vicarages, support of additional clergy in populous places, maintenance of sea walls and banks, relief of poor persons, and pensions to the former chantry priests. These commissioners reported to Mildmay and Robert Keilway, the surveyor of the Court of Wards, who were to make final decisions and who were empowered to sell chantry lands to the value of £ 5,000 a year "for the relief of the Kinges Majestes charges and expences, which do dayly growe and encrease."[39] The work was finished with uncommon speed, Mildmay and Keilway presenting complete accounts July 20, 1548.[40]

[39] The Council authorized Mildmay and Keilway to sell lands and fix pensions April 17, 1548 (APC, 1547–50, pp. 184–186), and their patent was dated ten days later(CPR, Edw. VI, II, 57–58). On June 20 they were further commissioned to assign chantry lands for schools, preachers, and other purposes (ibid., I, 417–418). A list of the local commissioners, county by county, is in ibid., II, 135–137. Keilway, an able administrator, is chiefly remembered as the author of legal reports first printed in 1602.

[40] These certificates are in the PRO, E 319/1, files 1–25 and rolls 1–14. None has been printed, although the reports of the commissioners who surveyed some of the chantry lands in 1545 can be read in print. See especially William Page, ed., The Certificates of the Commissioners Appointed To Survey the Chantries, Guilds, Hospitals, etc., in the County of York. The orders taken by Mildmay and Keilway concerning schools in Yorkshire are listed in ibid., XCII, vii–x; those for Cornwall are summarized in A. L. Rowse, Tudor Cornwall, pp. 260–261. Rowse says that Mildmay and Keilway were "sent down as commissioners," but their reports make it clear that they merely received and acted upon the

Several historians have criticized the actions taken by Mildmay and Keilway and have deplored the severe damage to the educational system wreaked by the government's greed. A. F. Leach, writing in 1896 with the avowed aim of demolishing Edward VI's reputation as a founder of grammar schools, admitted that Mildmay's sympathies "were likely to be with the encouragement of learning and the maintenance of Grammar Schools. Still, an official charged with getting in money at a time when the State was avoiding bankruptcy by depreciating the currency, was only too likely to take an 'official view'." Keilway he called "a mere lawyer and official, not likely to care much to save Grammar Schools." The commissioners "had a unique opportunity of reorganizing the whole educational system of a nation from top to bottom, without cost to the nation," but they threw it away.[41] Philip Hughes has echoed this gloomy view.[42]

More recently, however, there has been a reaction against this analysis. The chantry priests, it is argued, did little teaching and were ill equipped for what they did; with the dissolution of the chantries "only the shell" of the old system was cracked and cast aside. A modernized system could then be erected by the Crown and gentry out of the profits of ecclesiastical land.[43] In his magistral study of *Philanthropy in England, 1480–1660,* Professor Jordan has written, "it would be our judgment that the spoliation of the monasteries and the expropriations of the chantry endowments benefited rather than harmed the slender educational resources surviving from the Middle Ages."[44]

Reading the reports of Mildmay and Keilway, one is impressed with the number of foundations which are continued, and with the generosity of the pensions for the displaced priests, rather than with the number of establishments stricken down. There seems to be some

---

recommendations of local commissioners. They could not have visited all the involved localities, in every county, between June 20 and July 20, 1548.

[41] A. F. Leach, *English Schools at the Reformation, 1546–1548,* pp. 14, 122.

[42] Philip Hughes, *The Reformation in England,* II, 150–156.

[43] Joan Simon, "A. F. Leach on the Reformation," *British Journal of Educational Studies,* III (1955), 128–143, and IV (1955), 32–48, and "The Reformation and English Education," *Past & Present,* XI (1957), 48–65.

[44] W. K. Jordan, *Philanthropy in England, 1480–1660,* pp. 285–286. See also A. L. Rowse, *The England of Elizabeth,* pp. 489–503.

variation by county: Essex, York, and Stafford, for instance, fared unusually well; Kent, Hertford, Cambridge, and the Welsh shires badly. Probably a good deal depended on the condition of the schools before the dissolution and the attitude of the local investigators. But it can hardly be maintained that, in any county, the commissioners abolished many flourishing foundations.

The greatest damage came not in the dissolution of schools but through the system whereby the institutions were awarded fixed monetary payments rather than the varying income from lands. Had the economy remained stable there would have been no problem, but as the inflation of the sixteenth and seventeenth centuries continued schoolmasters found it impossible to live on the £ 8 or £ 10 which had been adequate in 1548. The final result may be seen in the instance of Birmingham, where the town was able to buy back the lands which had produced £ 21 in 1547. By the end of the nineteenth century they were bringing in more than £ 30,000.[45] But Mildmay could scarcely have foreseen this change; concerned as he was to be with keeping the economy on an even keel, he would have deplored it.

Though there was no great national outcry at the loss of the chantries, at least one local incident occurred. In 1548 the inhabitants of Seamer, a Yorkshire village near Scarborough, rioted, lighting a beacon and

[45] Hughes, *Reformation,* II, 156. Mrs. Simon tries, rather unconvincingly, to minimize the effect of the change from endowments to fixed stipends ("A. F. Leach," *British Journal,* IV, 46–47). Leach admits (*English Schools,* p. 77) that the pensions to former chantry clergy "seem to have been very fairly paid." Priests who had received incomes up to £ 6 13s. 4d. were given £ 5 a year, those with incomes between £ 6 13s. 4d. and £ 10 were given £ 6, and those who had received between £ 10 and £ 20 were paid £ 6 13s. 4d. This was a more generous settlement than that given the clergy displaced in the dissolution of the monasteries. Mildmay's concern that the pensions should be honestly paid can be seen in a letter which he sent to John Arscot, a surveyor of the Duchy, on January 15, 1549. He wrote,

Whereas labor is made for a pencion for one Nycholas Bradshawe, one of the cannons in the colleage of Newark in Leycestre, forasmuche as in your certificatt no mencion is made of hym, I requyre yow furthewith to repaire hither to sende your deputye to entre the same in your book or otherwise to make answere therein as your knowleage dothe serve.

Arscot replied that Bradshaw's name had been properly entered (Harl. MS 284).

collecting a company said to number three thousand. They dragged Matthew White, a commissioner for the sale of chantry land, a servant of Mildmay's named Berry, and three other men from their beds, carried them to the woods, and murdered them. The insurrection was promptly quelled and its leaders executed; it is of significance only in showing that some localities, at least, protested the loss of their endowments and the accompanying economic changes. There is no reason to think that the men of Seamer were concerned with the loss of educational facilities.[46]

An account of Mildmay's activities in refounding the grammar school at Chelmsford may be appended as a suitable epilogue to the story of his work with the chantry commissioners. According to the 1548 survey there had been two schoolmasters in Chelmsford, paid out of the revenues of Mountney's chantry. Mildmay and Keilway found the school "very mete and necessarie to continue," and they ordered its maintenance. In 1551 the school was refounded at the request of Walter and Thomas Mildmay, Sir William Petre, and Sir Henry Tyrell. They were named governors of the foundation, which was given lands to the value of £ 22 1s. 10d. annually, the former endowments of chantries in Great Baddow, Ulting, and East Tilbury. The grant did not provide for a school building, but Thomas Mildmay made available a dissolved friary in Moulsham with two acres of gardens and orchards. He seems to have acted as the school's chief financial agent; his descendants and Sir Walter's served on the board of governors for generations.[47] Walter Mildmay clearly possessed an abiding concern for the English educational system, and he did what he could, both as a governmental official and as a private benefactor, to strengthen it.

Increased prestige and wealth naturally accompanied Mildmay's growing prominence in the government. In 1547 he was first named a justice of the peace for Essex, an acknowledgment of his status, and he

---

[46] Page (ed.), *Certificates*, XCI, xvi. The chantry survey lists two chapels and a chantry priest at Seamer but makes no mention of a school there (*ibid.,* XCII, 515–516).

[47] J. H. Johnson, "Chelmsford Grammar School," *Essex Review*, LIV (1945), 45–51; *CPR, Edw. VI*, IV, 116. On Petre's connection with the school see F. G. Emmison, *Tudor Secretary: Sir William Petre at Court and Home*, p. 94.

acquired the manors of Seynclers and Herons in Danbury.[48] The next year he bought additional lands in Essex for £ 1,213.[49] In 1550 he was rewarded for services in the Court of Augmentations by the King's grant of the manors of Bisley, Gloucestershire, and Benham Valence, Berkshire, worth together more than £ 56 a year.[50] There is no indication that he resided on any of these estates. But in April, 1551, he restored Bisley and Benham Valence to the Crown and was granted instead the manor of Apethorpe in Northamptonshire with its splendid manor house and £ 147 worth of adjoining lands in Apethorpe, Wadenhoo, Wood Newton, Tansor, and Yarwell.[51] Two years later, upon the surrender of an annuity of two hundred marks, he acquired the manor of Yarwell, Northamptonshire, the neighboring manors of Woodston and Farcet in Huntingdonshire, and further lands in Cornwall and Essex valued at £ 103. In 1562 he added the manor of Stanground, Huntingdonshire.[52]

Apethorpe was to remain Sir Walter's country seat until his death and the home of his descendants until the twentieth century. It is a pleasant area where the Willow Brook winds through low-lying meadows on its way to join the River Nene near Fotheringhay. The manor was originally part of Rockingham Forest; it remained Crown demesne until 1231, later forming part of the dower of Queen Eleanor of Provence. In the fifteenth century it came into the hands of Guy Wolston, sheriff of Northampton and holder of several Crown offices; the oldest parts of the present house probably date from his time. It

[48] *CPR, Edw. VI,* I, 210; Westm. MSS, 1, XII, 13.

[49] This purchase included the house and site of Bicknare Priory and the manors of Bicknare, Canon Barnes, and Norton. See Westm. MSS, 1, XII, 13. Mildmay purchased the land from Henry Polstead, an agent of Thomas Cromwell who had enriched himself at the time of the dissolution of the monasteries.

[50] *CPR, Edw. VI,* III, 177.

[51] Add. MS 4484, fol. 14^r, a copy of the letters patent; *CPR, Edw. VI,* IV, 92, 101–102. Mildmay was also given the manor of Beckley, Oxon, which he in turn granted to Sir John Williams (*ibid.,* IV, 85).

[52] Add. MS 4484, fol. 14^v; *CPR, Edw. VI,* V, 255; *CPR, Eliz.,* II, 261; Westm. MSS, 1, XII, 6, 13, and 15; Westm. MSS, 2, II, 5. In 1571 Mildmay bought some additional land in Rockingham Forest for £ 30 (SP 12/80/16; Cot. MS Vespasian F. IV, fols. 71–72), and in 1576 he purchased lands near Stanground from Sir Christopher Hatton for £ 887 (Westm. MSS, 2, III, 1D and 5J).

later belonged to Thomas Empson, the son of Henry VII's ill-fated Chancellor of the Duchy, and to Princess Elizabeth, although she never resided there.[53]

The house, about 240 by 120 feet in size, is built around two court-yards which are separated by the hall range. This central core is still much as it was in Mildmay's time. On the exterior its principal features are the entrance porch and the canted bay window, both projecting into the eastern or principal courtyard. Inside, the great hall has an early Elizabethan fireplace and roof, both doubtless added by Mildmay, who probably also built the small, two-storied bay windows at the corners of the hall range. In the adjoining portion of the north range the gateway with its attractive oriel window and polygonal stair turret dates from about 1500. Most of the present interiors are Jacobean or later, but a splendid chimneypiece erected by Mildmay in 1562 sur-vives. The stone fireplace surround has pilasters with sunken panels and roundels; the overmantel bears Mildmay's motto, *virtute non vi,* and a moralistic inscription framed by scrolly ornament and flanked by two rows of decorated Ionic pilasters.

After Mildmay's death the mansion passed to his older son, An-thony, whose elaborate tomb dominates the parish church, and then to Anthony's son-in-law, Sir Francis Fane, the first Earl of Westmorland. Fane remodeled much of the interior and added the parapet and finials to the hall range. Apethorpe remained in the hands of Mildmay's descendants until 1904; the house still stands but is now used as a school.[54]

Although Mildmay spent several months each summer at Apethorpe, governmental duties naturally required his presence in London most of the year. He owned a home in Hackney, a suburb made fashionable by Thomas Cromwell's erection of a mansion there, and about 1545 he acquired a house at Smithfield from Sir Richard Rich, who had turned the buildings of St. Bartholomew's Priory into dwellings for

[53] *Victoria History of the Counties of England, Northampton,* II, ed. R. M. Serjeantson and W. R. D. Adkins, pp. 542–550; article (signed *T.*) on Ape-thorpe in *Country Life,* XXV (1909), 414–423, 450–459.

[54] Nikolaus Pevsner, *The Buildings of England: Northamptonshire,* pp. 76–80. One of Mildmay's inscriptions from Apethorpe is now in the library of Emmanuel College, Cambridge.

governmental officials.[55] Mildmay must have found his proximity to Rich, Petre, and Sir Roger Manwood useful professionally, although probably less pleasant than the company of William Cecil, William Fitzwilliam, and Christopher Hatton, his Northamptonshire neighbors.

[55] Rowse, *The England of Elizabeth,* pp. 200–201 (where Rich is erroneously called Sir Robert); Emmison, *Petre,* p. 84.

## 3. FINANCIAL CRISIS AND REFORM
### 1551–1553

BY 1551 THE ENGLISH GOVERNMENT found itself in the grip of the worst financial crisis of the sixteenth century. Henry VII's considerable hoard had long since disappeared, followed by most of the property acquired in the dissolution of the monasteries and chantries. Some of these resources had been dissipated in Henry VIII's wars with France and Scotland; others had provided luxury for the King and wealth for his favorites; still others were absorbed by the increasing cost of governing in a time of rising prices. The Crown's capital had been largely spent, and normal annual income fell far short of annual expenses. Nor was the government of John Dudley, Duke of Northumberland, popular enough to count on much in the way of parliamentary taxation, especially in peace time.

In this desperate situation the government tried a number of devices. A start was made by calling in debts owed the King, estimated by Edward VI in his journal as amounting to £ 100,000.[1] In February, 1551, the Chancellor of Augmentations was ordered to bring before the Council a list of all debts pending in that court, and similar directives were probably sent to the chief officers of the other financial departments. A year later, in January, 1552, a powerful commission was set up to call in, or at least examine and renew, all obligations owed the King or his father. Its members were Thomas Goodrich, Bishop of Ely and Lord Chancellor; John Russell, the Earl of Bedford, Lord Privy Seal; Sir John Gate, Vice-Chamberlain; Sir William Petre, Principal

---

[1] F. C. Dietz, *English Government Finance, 1485–1558,* p. 192. W. C. Richardson observes that Mildmay sat on no fewer than thirty-five special commissions, most of them concerned with the revenues, during the period from 1547 to 1554 (*History of the Court of Augmentations, 1536–1554,* p. 183 n. 49).

Secretary; Sir Robert Bowes, Master of the Rolls; and Sir Walter Mild-may.[2] They met with some success, collecting nearly £ 17,000 by Michaelmas, but this amount was vastly insufficient and other revenues had to be found. Something could be obtained from the sale of such chantry land as remained, and in July and November Mildmay and others were commissioned to sell any lands they deemed necessary, so long as each transaction amounted to less than £ 1,000.[3]

Meanwhile the government had been unable to resist the temptation to debase the coinage, the easiest and worst financial expedient of the age. For centuries before 1543 English silver coinage had been kept to a high standard, eleven ounces two pennyweight of silver to eighteen pennyweight of alloy. In 1543 Henry VIII had reduced the fineness to ten ounces of silver alloyed with two ounces of copper, not without some justification, since most European coinages had been debased and fine English coins were being hoarded abroad. This debasement proved so profitable that Henry carried it further, and by 1545 the mint was issuing coin which was half copper, the little blushing shillings of a contemporary satirical couplet. The standard of fineness was improved slightly in 1549, but each coin was made lighter and in consequence contained no more fine silver than its predecessors.[4] The nadir was reached in April, 1551, when the Council ordered the minting of coin composed of three parts silver to nine parts alloy. Profits of £ 160,000 on the issue were anticipated.

This last orgy was intended as a prelude to currency reform, which also was resolved on in April; the base money was to produce profits "by which the debt of the realm might be paid, the country defended from any sudden attempt, and the coin amended."[5] In the end not all

[2] *CPR, Edw. VI*, IV, 144. They were further ordered on May 29 to accept the certificates of those owed money by the King in partial payment of debts due the Crown (*APC, 1552–54*, p. 64).

[3] *CPR, Edw. VI*, IV, 354 (July 13) and 390–391 (November 18). A further commission of March 15, 1553 (*ibid.*, V, 184), to last until it is revoked, specifies that all sales of Crown land must be approved by Mildmay or Sir Richard Sackville.

[4] C. W. C. Oman, "The Tudors and the Currency, 1526–1560," *Transactions of the Royal Historical Society*, new ser., IX (1895), 167–188; A. E. Feavear-year, *The Pound Sterling*, pp. 43–59.

[5] Journal of Edward VI, quoted in Dietz, *Finance, 1485–1558*, p. 194.

the base money was struck, for the Council, possibly conscience-stricken, ordered an end of the issue in July, after profits of £ 114,500 had been realized.

Actual reform was begun May 6, when the Council decreed that on July 9 the shilling would be called down to 9*d*. This would bring its face value closer to its intrinsic worth. On May 23 Mildmay and Sir Edmund Peckham, treasurer of the mint, were ordered to send the Council "a perfaict certificat in writing of the proportion artycles and th'other thinges requisite for the standerd of ix ounces fyne that was in the time of the Kinges Majestie deceassed."[6] It is likely that their report, now lost, recommended a return to the standard in use before 1543, a proportion finer than that stipulated by the Council. In August the value of the shilling was again called down, this time to 6*d*., so that the base coins passed for half their old face value, or approximately their true worth.[7] With base money thus devalued the Council could proceed with a new issue of finer coins. These began to appear in September minted eleven ounces and one pennyweight of fine silver to nineteen pennyweight of alloy, a standard probably approved by Mildmay and Peckham and nearly that of medieval silver coin. The new coins, however, remained light: shillings were coined sixty to the pound, whereas only forty-five of the old shillings had been minted from a pound of bullion.[8]

Individuals who found the value of their coins halved obviously bore the brunt of the devaluation, for the government did not offer to exchange base coins for good ones: it could not have afforded such generosity. Nor was the currency even tidied up by calling in the base coins for reminting at the new standard. The confusion created by the varying values of coins in circulation was not to be ended before the great Elizabethan recoinage of 1560.[9] Northumberland no doubt hoped to profit from the chaotic situation by paying the government's debts

[6] *APC, 1552–54*, p. 57.

[7] J. A. Froude, *History of England from the Fall of Wolsey to the Defeat of the Spanish Armada,* V, 346–352.

[8] Oman, "The Tudors and the Currency," *Transactions,* n.s., IX, 183.

[9] Contemporary concern for further reform may be seen in the treatise on the coinage written in 1553 by John Pryse (New College, Oxford, MS 317, iii; printed by W. A. J. Archbold in "A Manuscript Treatise on the Coinage by

with the issue of base coin while demanding silver of the new standard in settlement of obligations due the Crown. Concessions were made only in the case of certain financial officials who had suffered from the effect of the devaluation on the money in their care; on November 24, 1552, Mildmay, Gate, Bowes, and Sir Richard Cotton were commissioned to examine the suits presented by royal treasurers, bailiffs, customs collectors, and the like, and to make appropriate adjustments.[10] The whole scheme is typical of Northumberland: shrewd but unjust. Mildmay very likely had little to do with it except in recommending a high standard for future coinage. His operation of the mint under Elizabeth was to reveal his reverence for fine coin.[11]

All these measures—calling in debts, selling land, debasing the coin —were mere palliatives. They failed to strike at the root of the financial problem, which grew increasingly serious. By the early summer months of 1552 the treasuries were often actually empty. A reduction of the fleet, ordered in May, could effect only small savings.[12] In August the government was reduced to suspending all payments, for the specious reason that "his Highness is presently in progress and resolved not to be troubled with payments until his return." The urgency of the situation may be judged by Northumberland's reluctant decision, taken in September, to disband the mercenary army which he had

---

John Pryse, 1553," *EHR*, XIII [1898], 709–710). Pryse points out the evils created by (1) coin of debased standard, (2) coin of fine standard but light in weight, and (3) "lack of equivalence in the coin current, forasmuch as one testoon [shilling] is better than another, the new fine coin better than the base universally, and yet all at one estimate in the market, which inequality is cause of much robbing of the treasure of the realm, while the best money is ever picked, and carried over[seas], and the worst only left us."

[10] *CPR, Edw. VI*, IV, 278. V, 184–185. Petre, treasurer of the Court of First Fruits and Tenths, was discharged of the £ 3,844 lost in his court by the devaluation (*ibid.*, V, 200; March 28, 1553). See also *CPR, P&M*, I, 196 (March 10, 1554), for a commission to consider the losses of Peckham, treasurer of the mint.

[11] In December, 1551, Mildmay was ordered to oversee the signing of an indenture by the mint officers at York (*APC, 1550–52*, p. 444). For details of his other work with the mint see *APC, 1552–54*, pp. 84, 88; *APC, 1554–56*, pp. 210, 302.

[12] *APC, 1552–54*, p. 46.

gathered the previous year to insure the security of his regime. But for the financial crisis his plan to rule through Lady Jane Grey might have had some chance of success.[13]

In this crisis Northumberland and the Council decided to appoint a commission "for the survey and examinacion of the state of all his Majesties Courtes of Revenue,"[14] especially "suche latter courtes as have bene erected for the revenues in the tyme of [the King's] father."[15] The nine commissioners named in March, 1552, were men of considerable dignity and power: Lord Darcy, Lord Chamberlain; Thomas Thirlby, Bishop of Norwich; Sir Richard Cotton, Comptroller of the Household; Sir John Gate, Vice-Chamberlain; Sir Robert Bowes, Master of the Rolls; Sir William Petre, Chancellor of the Court of First Fruits and Tenths; Sir Thomas Wrothe, a gentleman of the privy chamber and a favorite of the King; John Gosnolde, solicitor of Augmentations; and Mildmay. For some reason Wrothe, Petre, and Gosnolde did not actually serve, or at least did not sign the commission's report. As Elton has noted, the absence of Petre and Gosnolde reduced the number of financial experts on the commission to one: Mildmay.[16] Possibly it was felt that more impartial judgments might be rendered by a group of outsiders, with Mildmay to guide them through the tangles of financial procedure and documentation. Sir Walter seems to have acted as a sort of executive secretary to the commission, if

[13] Dietz, *Finance, 1485–1558*, pp. 196–197.

[14] Harl. MS 7383, fol. 1.

[15] *CPR, Edw. VI*, IV, 353.

[16] G. R. Elton, *The Tudor Revolution in Government*, p. 230. The work of the commission is discussed at length by Elton, pp. 230–251. The intention of Northumberland and Edward VI seems to have been to make most of the members of this commission members of the Council with continuing responsibility for financial matters; a memorandum of 1553 lists forty councillors, of whom eight, including Mildmay, Cotton, Wrothe, Gosnolde, and Bishops Thirlby and Nicholas Ridley, "be now called into commission," that is, to membership in the Council. The document continues to establish committees within the overlarge Council: Darcy, Thirlby, Wrothe, Bowes, Cotton, Gosnolde, and Mildmay are to "look to the state of all the [revenue] courts . . . [and] see the revenues answered . . . [and] consider with what superfluous charges they be burdened, and thereof shall make a certificate which they shall deliver." Quoted in Gilbert Burnet, *History of the Reformation*, V, 117–120. See also Richardson, *Augmentations*, pp. 197–213.

indeed he did not do all the work, for a letter sent by the Council on September 22 ordered him "to finishe and bring hither the bookes of the survey of the Courtes as sone as he may conveniently finish the same."[17] But the survey was too complex for rapid completion; the report of the commissioners was not presented until December 10.[18]

It is in three sections. The first, with its list of certainties, or fixed annual income, and casualties, or revenues of varying yearly amount, was perhaps of greatest interest to the Council, although of less abiding significance than the portions which follow. Here the report proceeds court by court, setting out the revenues received in each and the salaries and other expenses met from these receipts. Augmentations accounts for the largest sum by far—more than the other courts combined—and most of its income was certain, coming from properties actually in its possession. Augmentations was also credited with more than £ 12,000 in reversion, due the Crown when its present recipients died. The Exchequer continued to receive the ancient revenues, most of which were treated as casualties; the Duchy of Lancaster collected the income and the incidents from its lands; the Court of First Fruits and Tenths was responsible for its tax on the clergy, formerly paid to the Papacy; the Court of Wards listed nearly £ 32,000 of casual revenue from wards' lands and fines, but no fixed income. The account of payments made by the treasurer of the Chamber is possibly the most interesting portion of the first section, for it is not concerned with the salaries of officials but rather with such items as £ 16 for "the children of the Kinges chapple, for their breakfastes," £ 23 6s. 8d. to "players of interludes," £ 388 9s. 2d. for "huntes," including fees for the keepers and meat for the hounds, and £ 1,350 6s. 8d. for the King's musicians.[19]

The commissioners put the total annual revenue at £ 271,913, but

[17] APC, 1552–54, p. 128.

[18] The original report does not survive, although three membranes at the PRO (E 163/12/19) may have been part of it. A contemporary copy is preserved in the BM (Harl. MS 7383), as is what I take to be an eighteenth-century copy (Add. MS 30,198) purchased from the Marquis of Lansdowne in 1876. Harl. MS 7383 bears no signatures; Add. MS 30,198 has copies of the signatures of Darcy, Cotton, Bowes, Gate, Thirlby, and Mildmay.

[19] Harl. MS 7383, fols. 29r–33v.

after the payment of salaries, fees, and pensions only £ 36,514 remained. The surplus was uncomfortably small, and even that amount was not clear, for from it had to be met the charges of the Great Wardrobe, the Admiralty, the Ordnance, Ireland, Calais, the King's household, his private purse, and his New Year's gifts. The annual loss on Calais alone exceeded £ 5,000. It was obvious that the revenues would not support inefficient management or extravagant spending.

Recommendations for increasing revenues and decreasing expenditures form the second section of the report. They are arranged court by court and are surprisingly detailed. Mildmay and the other commissioners began with thirty-one recommendations for improving the operation of the Exchequer, mainly through stricter procedures. The men dealt with the other courts more briefly, perhaps because the operations of these courts, which had been designed by Cromwell, stood in less need of modernization. Still there was much to criticize: pensions granted by collusion, unwarranted numbers of musicians and falconers, salaries for keepers of abandoned castles and of deerless parks.

The third section suggests over-all reforms which might produce economies. Some of the proposed changes are sweeping.

The commissioners began with an account of the salaries, allowances, and other charges borne by the financial courts. The cost of collecting the Crown's revenues, they found, amounted to £ 18,128. This included a number of fees and allowances increased without warrant; if the King wished to continue the existing organization of the revenue courts he might at least cancel increases amounting to £ 3,713. If he eliminated superfluous offices also, he might save an additional £ 2,716. Thus annual economies of £ 6,429 could be realized by appropriate reforms within the structure of specialized courts.

But Mildmay and his colleagues were not satisfied with reform of so limited a nature. It had become apparent in their survey that the functions of the courts overlapped and that unnecessarily large numbers of officials were employed when each bureau had its own auditors and local agents. If the King were willing to reduce the number of courts, the commissioners believed further substantial savings possible. They recommended as one possible scheme the retention of a revitalized Exchequer, to which would be annexed the Courts of First Fruits and

Wards, and the creation of a new Court of the King's Revenue to perform the functions previously in the hands of Augmentations and the Duchy. Such an arrangement would be logical and convenient, since virtually all Crown land would fall within the survey of the new court, while other revenues would be received in the Exchequer. Elimination of superfluous offices in the new Exchequer and its merged courts would save £ 5,228 annually; similar economies in the new court would amount to £ 4,393.

The commissioners envisaged also the possibility of greater reform. "If his Highnes pleasure be to have all his revenues aunswered in one courte as in the tyme of diverse his Majesties progenitours hathe ben used," they wrote, then all revenues, of whatever sort and from whatever source, might be received in the Exchequer. It would obviously be necessary to create certain new positions in the Exchequer and to increase the salaries of some officials to correspond to their enlarged responsibilities, but even so this scheme would produce a saving of £ 10,242, of which about a third could come immediately and the remainder in time, as posts fell vacant.

The most comprehensive scheme of reorganization, then, held out the greatest promise of economy. Substantially more than half of the cost of revenue collection as it stood in 1552 might be saved, although admittedly many economies would not be immediately effective.[20]

---

[20] It is possible that the third section was never presented to the Council. One copy of the report in the BM (Add. MS 30,198) does not include this section, and in the other (Harl. MS 7383) a reference to it made in the introductory certificate has been crossed out. The three membranes at the PRO (E 163/12/19) constitute this section; it seems likely that they were detached from the report given the Council and thus not lost with the remainder of the original document. If this hypothesis is correct it is difficult to understand why the commissioners were loath to present their recommendations. Possibly they felt that drastic measures were not likely to find approval, especially in the hectic transition from Edward's reign to Mary's; possibly they feared the political repercussions of abolishing offices held by men prominent in the government; possibly they realized that their economies were unrealistic, since no allowance was made for increased salaries in a time of rising prices and since the number of officials retained would probably have proved insufficient for the volume of work to be handled.

Certain of the commissioners' recommendations were speedily given effect. Edward's second and last Parliament, which sat throughout March, 1553, passed two important statutes designed to remedy at least some of the defects noted in the report. Mildmay held one of the seats for the borough of Maldon, Essex; we have no account of his activities, but it seems likely that he helped push the measures through Commons.

The first piece of legislation, "an act for the true answering of the King's Majesty's revenues,"[21] was designed primarily to make operative the recommendation that all receivers, bailiffs, treasurers, and similar officers be required to post bond for the true payment of moneys in their charge. It appointed specific dates for the payment of all revenues —Easter receipts by June 20 and Michaelmas receipts by January 20— and set out severe penalties for officers who failed to appear for such accountings. Various detailed provisions were included: sheriffs, for instance, might be fined if they neglected their responsibilities concerning the King's revenues, and penalties might be invoked against revenue agents found to profit unduly. Bishops were exempted from making bond for the payment of the clerical tenth, which they collected, but this exemption was cancelled by another statute which required that "all patentees of collectorships of tenths be bound for their collection."[22]

---

[21] 7 Edward VI, c. 1. The bill was introduced into Lords on the first day of business, March 7, 1553, and was passed by the Upper House on March 18, seven peers dissenting. It was given its first reading in Commons on the same day, the eighteenth; the defective Commons' journals do not mention its third reading and passage.

[22] 7 Edward VI, c. 4. Mildmay seems to have enforced these statutes strictly during his years as Chancellor of the Exchequer. In 1572 Valentyne Browne, a military treasurer at Berwick, wrote Mildmay complaining that he had been ordered to appear and put in sureties for the true execution of his office, although he had no certain revenues or charges and thought the statute was not meant to apply to treasurers for wars. By May, 1573, he was admitting that he would have to post bond but was seeking additional time in which to raise it (SP 46/29/105, 133). A similar letter of April, 1572, from John Hales, receiver of the Hanaper, states that since Hales had held the office before the statute was passed he thought himself exempt, a view in which Mildmay almost certainly did not concur (SP 46/29/109).

In addition Parliament passed an act "for the dissolving, uniting, or annexing of certain courts lately erected by the King that dead is," granting Edward VI during his lifetime broad powers of dissolving or uniting existing revenue courts or erecting new bureaus.[23] Under this authority the Council doubtless hoped to effect some simplification of the financial machinery. The statute also clears away legal doubts which had arisen in connection with the merging of General Surveyors into the reconstituted Augmentations in 1547. There seems to have been considerable discussion of the bill in Commons, and the *Journal* records a speech by Bowes, Master of the Rolls, probably explaining the recommendations of the commission and urging passage of the measure. It was given final assent only after the addition of a proviso assuring revenue officers that no reorganization would deprive them of the fees or annuities they enjoyed as of March 27.[24]

Other steps were taken on the Council's own authority. In December, 1552, Mildmay and other commissioners were appointed to inquire into the disposition of bell metal and roofing lead from the dissolved religious houses.[25] Mildmay was also ordered to examine the accounts of those who had received money or victual from the King and of those who had purchased or exchanged lands without paying the proper fees.[26] "Forasmuch as the King's majesty had need presently of a mass of money," the Council had ordered as early as February, 1551, that superfluous church plate be confiscated and "employed unto his Highness' use";[27] the first commissioners were sent out in the spring of 1552, and in February, 1553, Mildmay and others were named to collect certificates relating to the plate, jewels, and furniture of the churches in the various shires. They were to allow parish churches to

---

[23] 7 Edward VI, c. 2.

[24] The bill was passed by the Lords on March 20; by Commons, with the proviso, on the thirtieth. The further concern of this Parliament with finance may be noted in its revival of a statute of Edward IV making it a felony to carry gold or silver coin or bullion out of the realm, as well as in its passage of a revenue bill authorizing collection of a subsidy and two tenths and fifteenths.

[25] *CPR, Edw. VI*, IV, 391.

[26] *Ibid.*, pp. 391–393, 397–398.

[27] Dietz, *Finance, 1485–1558*, p. 193.

retain but one chalice, and cathedrals not more than two, and they were to remove unnecessary vestments and furniture, leaving only surplices and an honest wooden communion table in place of an altar.[28] A letter from Robert Kyrkham of Peterborough suggests that Mildmay was particularly active in this work: Kyrkham relates that certain men of Peterborough had been summoned to appear before Mildmay and Sir Richard Cotton concerning "a certyne crose of sylver the wyche the[y] sold by the consent of the hole towne for the reparyng of ther bryg and also of ther church, as they can declare to yow." Mildmay appended a note to Cotton, asking him "to take such procedure with thes men as you do with the rest of that nature, wherin I do the rather trowble you, for that they be my neighbors and frendes."[29]

Although Parliament had authorized the reorganization of the revenue courts, the Council was unable to effect any changes before Edward's death in July, 1553, and the statutory powers died with him. But Mary's government—which, contrary to a common view, retained a great many of Edward's officers—soon addressed itself to the problem. In the final arrangement the Courts of Augmentations and First Fruits were dissolved and their business transferred to the Exchequer, which had Augmentations procedures somewhat uneasily imposed upon it. The Duchy and Wards were allowed to continue as separate courts, the former "because all the tennantes of the same hold theyre landes by meane tenure, except it be in the County of Lancaster, and have bene since th'ereccion of the same court allwayes ordered by the same in all theyre causes,"[30] the latter perhaps because Mary wished to raise her Catholic favorite, Sir Francis Englefield, from Chancellor of the Duchy to the profitable post of Master of the Wards.

A complex series of orders was necessary to bring about the change. In October, 1553, Sir Richard Sackville, Chancellor of Augmentations, surrendered his patent, and a commission was named to receive his

[28] *CPR, Edw. VI,* IV, 392–393.

[29] Stowe MS 141, fol. 71. Stowe MS 141, fol. 72, may concern a similar affair: it is a vague letter from Sir Edmund Peckham to Mildmay, dated June 20, 1553, asking Mildmay's favor for Peckham's neighbors.

[30] Cot. MS Titus B. IV, fols. 129–131, a paper headed "An answer to certen articles propounded for diminishing the charges & the safe answering the revenew of the Crowne."

seals, manage the affairs of the court, and eliminate superfluous offices as they fell vacant.[31] The commissioners, a powerful, expert group, included Sir William Paulet (recently created Marquis of Winchester), Sir Richard Rochester, Sir Robert Southwell, Englefield, Moyle, and Mildmay. By December 4 Parliament had passed an act giving to Mary the powers of dealing with the revenue courts which had been granted to Edward; on January 23 letters patent were issued for the dissolution of Augmentations and First Fruits, and on the following day further patents transferred their operations to the Exchequer.[32]

But for the accident of the King's death these Marian reforms would have been credited to Edward's government. The final arrangement lacks the logic of the commissioners' plan for two clearly differentiated bureaus, the Exchequer and a land revenue office, and it stops far short of their proposal for the union of all financial organs. It was nevertheless an acceptable compromise, probably the best attainable at the time. It was destined to endure without significant alteration until the Civil War.[33]

[31] *CPR, P&M,* I, 300.

[32] For a fuller account of the change-over see Elton, *Tudor Revolution,* pp. 238–251; Richardson, *Augmentations,* pp. 246–270.

[33] The Court of Wards ceased to function in 1645 and was abolished by statute (12 Charles II, c. 24) in 1660; revenues of the Duchy of Lancaster were transferred to the Exchequer in 1686.

## 4. MARIAN SERVICES, 1553–1558

THROUGHOUT Mary's half decade as Queen, Mildmay continued his work in financial administration. It may surprise those who think of him as a stern Puritan, the founder of a reforming college, to realize that he did not join Walsingham and the hundreds of other Marian exiles who fled to the continent to escape the Queen's counter-reformation. He chose rather, as Fuller said, to practice the precept *bene vixit qui bene latuit*—he lives well who conceals well.[1] Although a convinced Protestant, he was, like Winchester, of willow, not oak, and could bend with the wind until it once again blew his way. Indeed amazingly few governmental changes accompanied the religious revolution; Mary's Council included as many of Edward VI's councillors— a dozen—as of her own adherents, and at lower levels the continuity of the civil service was greater still.

There are no clear indications that Mildmay's religious position was at all suspect. He was included in the Queen's general pardon, his release being dated November 8, 1553, and he was sufficiently trusted to serve with Paget, Petre, Peckham, and Sir Thomas Pope on a commission of May, 1554, to receive the fines levied on those who had joined Northumberland's plot to place Lady Jane Grey on the throne.[2] It is said that Mildmay, at his own cost, brought 140 horsemen to Mary's aid during Wyatt's rebellion.[3] One of Mildmay's servants,

[1] Thomas Fuller, *The History of the Worthies of England,* I, 356.

[2] *CPR, P&M,* I, 412, 194–195.

[3] The only source for this statement is the not entirely reliable panegyric written by Henry Roberts after Mildmay's death, *Fames Trumpet Sounding,* which includes the stanza:

> His valour showne in person brave and stoute,
> Ile not omit when Prince his ayde did neede.
> Seaven score odde men on horseback in a route

Thomas Penny, did run afoul of the government; in 1557 he was convicted of writing and circulating "a leude seditiouse booke," and was
committed to the Fleet.[4] It would be interesting to know just what he
had written—probably an anti-Spanish tract—and whether Mildmay
secretly approved the contents.

Mildmay's principal financial services under Mary were connected
with English affairs on the continent. As early in the new reign as
May, 1554, he was among those commissioned to examine the accounts
of the marshal of Calais for food and other supplies provided in 1551
and 1552.[5] It has been suggested that Mildmay and Sir John Mason,
Mary's treasurer of the Chamber and ambassador to Charles V, en-
croached on the activities which would normally have been performed
by Sir Thomas Gresham, the English agent in the Netherlands, who
was out of favor with Lord Treasurer Winchester.[6] This view is
attractive but is supported by little evidence other than that which links
Mildmay to the ill-fated siege of Calais in 1558.

England's involvement in the war which led to the loss of Calais had
begun in 1557, when Philip visited Mary for the sole purpose of impelling her into his conflict with France and the Papacy. All the circumstances militated against effective English action: there was little
money, since Parliament had voted Mary but one small grant, and that
two years before; the Queen was ill and vacillating; her subjects felt
no enthusiasm for a war not really their own; English garrisons and

---

All furnisht well to doe some noble deede,
At his owne cost, they forward did proceede
Against *Sir Wyat* to defende her right,
For which desert she dubt him then a Knight.

The last assertion is certainly incorrect; Mildmay had been knighted by Edward
VI in 1547.

[4] *APC, 1556–58*, p. 62. The Council later ordered Penny transferred to New-
gate prison, to be dealt with by the mayor and recorder of London, who were
proceeding against several other men similarly charged (*ibid.*, p. 76). The
London officials seemingly did not act in an expeditious manner; the Council
had to write again on August 7 asking them what they had done (*ibid.*, pp.
144–145). Penny was probably freed in September, 1557 (*ibid.*, p. 170).

[5] *CPR, P&M*, I, 302.

[6] J. W. Burgon, *The Life and Times of Sir Thomas Gresham*, I, 118.

fortifications at Calais and Guisnes had been allowed to decay for want of funds; the English navy proved to be unseaworthy. Still England declared war in June, and in July she sent a force of seven thousand men to Philip's assistance. It was for a time successful, but the French soon recovered, drove Philip's army back, and began to reconnoiter the walls of Calais, a stronghold they had been watching covetously for a decade.

In July, 1557, Sir Thomas Cornwallis urged that the defenses of Calais be greatly strengthened, although the cost would be considerable. Little was done, for Mary's Council was confident that no serious campaigning could take place before the following spring. French troops took advantage of the English complacency. On December 22 a note sent to England contained warnings that danger might be near; by the twenty-seventh it was known that Henri de Lorraine, the Duke of Guise, was approaching Calais with a large army. Mary ordered reinforcements to be raised, but on December 31 she countermanded the commission, apparently convinced that the alarm was false. Unfortunately it was not; on New Year's Day the French began the siege.[7]

By January 2, 1558, the Earl of Rutland was feverishly collecting troops. Parliament had been summoned for the twentieth, and it was hoped that funds would be forthcoming. And on the ninth Mildmay was chosen to oversee the finances of the expedition: Mary, persuaded by "the good opynyon wee have of your fidelitie, wysdom and redye good will to serve us wherinsoever it shall please us to employ you," appointed him "treasourer of soche sommes of money as ar orderid to be disbursed for our present service beyonde the seas."[8]

Mildmay's instructions, dated January 11, are worth reading at length.

First, the said Sir Walter shall withe as muche dilligence as he maye receave of our treasorer and comptroller of our mynte in the Towre or of th'one of them by vertue of our warraunte[9] addressed unto them for that purpose the some of five thousand poundes of our good silver money of the newe coynage. And shall further receave suche other somes of money by

[7] J. A. Froude, *History of England from the Fall of Wolsey to the Defeat of the Spanish Armada*, VI, 490–496.

[8] SP 11/12/14.

[9] *APC, 1556–58*, p. 241; warrant dated January 16, 1558.

t'handes of any other person as shalbe appointed to him from tyme to tyme. And when he shall have receaved the same money our pleasure is he shall with all the spede he can transporte himselfe withe our said treasour unto the towne of Dunkirk in Flaunders, taking his waye thether either along the seas or partelie by land and the rest by sea as he shall understand may be best and surest for our treasour and him.

Being savely arived at Dunkirk aforesaid, he shall issue and paie owte the said treasour in prest unto suche noblemen, gentlemen, and other captaynes as shall come thether owte of this our realme with nomber of men to be taken unto them, as by waye of prest for suche nomber as eche of them shall bringe with them for th'expenses of the said men untill th'arrivall of our lieutenant.

And we will that he shall after the arrivall thether of our right trustie and right welbeloved cosen and counsaillour the Earle of Pembroke, whom we have appointed our lieutenaunte, . . . make paymente to any person or persones of all suche somes of money as shalbe appointid and limited in any warraunte or warrauntes to be signed withe t'hande of our said lieutenaunte, whoes warraunte or warrauntes with th'acquitaunce of the partie receaving the money shalbe his sufficient dischardge for the same . . . .

And here we will that he shall take good head [heed] that we be not doble charged for anie thinge to any man, considering that some men have alreadie receaved conducte money heare, and some othere also at Dover, wherein he shall give his best dilligence to understand what hathe ben done.

Mildmay was further instructed to remain at Dunkirk or to remove to any other place ordered by Sir William Herbert, Earl of Pembroke. He was allowed 26s. 8d. a day for his own diets, four clerks at 2s. daily, and twenty men at 8d. each, all allowances to be counted from January 9, "and also suche somes as he shall desburse and paie for cariage, transportawns, chestes, and all other necessaries."[10]

The body of men which Mildmay was instructed to pay could not help the defenders of Calais, who had been forced to surrender January 7. News of the disaster stirred Mary's government to greater action: proclamations were sent out, calling on the counties to raise their musters, and by the tenth thirty thousand men had made their way to Dover. But just when the Queen ordered their crossing to Dunkirk a great gale blew up, destroying or damaging many of the

---

[10] SP 69/12/717, pp. 385–389, calendared in *CSP, For., 1553–58*, pp. 358–359.

ships and disorganizing the rest. Mary, despondent, ordered the troops sent home.

Meanwhile Lord Grey, with a garrison of eleven hundred men, was attempting the defense of Guisnes, the last fortress in the continental Pale, but without reinforcements he could do nothing. Guise's men opened fire on the seventeenth, Grey was wounded, and the three days' bombardment brought no alternative to surrender. The last English foothold on continental soil was gone; Calais, "the brightest jewel in the English crown" though a costly and useless possession, was irrevocably lost.[11]

Unfortunately we know little of Mildmay's actual role in the sordid affair. Possibly he crossed briefly to Dunkirk; more likely he spent most of January in Dover, trying to prevent financial tangles and needless expenditures. At such moments of crisis and confusion funds were bound to leak away—even the considerably more efficient government of Elizabeth found it so—and Mildmay's restraining hand was badly needed.

By February the post-mortem financial examination had begun. On the twenty-sixth Mildmay was named to a commission instructed to receive the accounts of Sir Thomas Cornwallis, the former treasurer of Calais, for the period since October, 1556,[12] and in April he helped examine George Stonehouse and Anthony Weldon, who had been surveyors and masters of the victual for the army at Calais and had likewise not made account since 1556.[13] Necessary as such accounting was, it could restore neither territory nor money.

Whatever experience Mildmay acquired in military finance was supplemented by his other governmental activities, particularly those relating to foreign trade. In December, 1557, the Council was concerned with the exchange rates; it noted that gold and silver bullion and plate were exported, counterfeit money was brought into the realm, usury was practiced, and the customs were greatly decayed, all because of "subtle practices used . . . by native and foreign merchants."

[11] Froude, *History of England,* VI, 504–507.
[12] *CPR, P&M,* IV, 73–74.
[13] *Ibid.,* IV, 11.

Mildmay and other commissioners, including the Solicitor General and the governor of the Merchant Adventurers, were therefore to inquire into foreign trade and into exchange transactions, as well as evasion of customs duties, since the beginning of the reign.[14] If the commissioners completed a formal report it is not now known to survive. The troubles at Calais doubtless diverted their attention, and they may not have had opportunity to return to the survey before Mary's death in November.

Mildmay worked also with a number of minor commissions. He examined the accounts of the mint, including the Spanish funds received through Gresham in 1556 and the profits from conversion of base moneys into small coins.[15] He helped collect debts still owed for the purchase of monastic lands.[16] He audited the records of Sir Richard Cecil, yeoman of the King's Wardrobe who had died a few months before Edward VI, and gave an acquittance to Cecil's son William, a rising figure in the government.[17] He sat on the Commission of Sewers, which was charged with the regulation of draining in fenny East Anglia.[18] He examined the accounts of Richard Wilbraham, master of the Jewel House, concerning sums lent the Crown during the Calais crisis.[19] His general position in the government may be deduced from a memorandum sent by de Feria, the Spanish ambassador, to Philip in 1558. It names six men as responsible for English finance: Paget, Thirlby, Englefield, Sir John Baker, Sir Edward Waldegrave, and Mildmay.[20] As the junior member of this council of finance Mildmay was free for assignment to any particularly trying financial problem. Busy with a thousand details, he was always learning, preparing himself for the day when he would have to shoulder heavier responsibilities.

Although Mildmay acquired the bulk of his lands before Mary's accession, he was able to increase his holdings through two Marian

---

[14] *Ibid.*, IV, 71; comm. dated December 2, 1557.

[15] *Ibid.*, III, 23.

[16] *Ibid.*, I, 332; comm. dated December 24, 1553.

[17] *CPR, Edw. VI*, V, 185 (April 8, 1553); *CPR, P&M*, I, 503 (July 24, 1554).

[18] *CPR, P&M*, II, 109; comm. dated January 26, 1555.

[19] *Ibid.*, IV, 14; comm. dated May 11, 1558.

[20] *CSP, Spn., 1554–58*, p. 369.

grants. In 1557 he was given the reversion of the bailiwick of Sule-
fermes and Shortwood, parts of Rockingham Forest adjoining his lands
at Apethorpe, with the rights of appointing a woodward and of gathering wood and hay.[21] A year later, in consideration of the surrender of
some land in Northamptonshire and the payment of £ 745, he received
the manor of Queen Camel in Somerset, valued with its appurtenances
at £ 67 a year.[22] Mildmay never lived on this estate, which was named
for Eleanor, Queen of Edward I, an earlier owner; at his death he
bequeathed it to his son Anthony.

Some correspondence between Sir Philip Hoby and Sir William
Cecil provides an unusual glimpse of Mildmay's private life during
these years. In November, 1557, Hoby, who was Master of the Ordnance and who frequently served as an English diplomatist on the
continent, wrote Cecil: "I pray you, take your nagge, and come to
Byssham, bycause I would fayne talke with you; but above all other
things, I praie you faile not to be there this Christmas, . . . to make
mery there with a company of our friends. . . . And I praie you exhort
our frend Mr. Mildmay and his wiffe likewise to be there, that the company may be complete."[23] Cecil replied that he could not come because
his wife had to stay home with their fifteen-month-old daughter, for
whom Mildmay had stood as godfather. But Hoby would not accept
the refusal:

You knowe how longe it is sithens I did enjoie you, and if you now deprive
me and this good assemblie of your company at that tyme, I must thinke it
so great a synne as cannot be either forgotten now, or forgyven herafter;
and in your so doing, you shall be th'occasions why I shall not have here
him whom I so moche desire, and to whom I am so moche bound, namely
Mr. Mildmay and my Lady his wife.[24]

In the end Cecil did spend Christmas with Hoby, although Lady
Cecil stayed behind. We do not know whether the Mildmay family

---

[21] *CPR, P&M*, III, 304–305.

[22] *Ibid.*, IV, 377. In 1586 he acquired additional lands at Queen Camel and
Charlton Musgrove (Westm. MSS, 2, XV, 1, C4).

[23] Quoted in Burgon, *Gresham*, I, 225–226.

[24] *Ibid.*, pp. 226–227; cf. F. G. Emmison, *Tudor Secretary: Sir William Petre
at Court and Home*, p. 206.

joined the party at Bisham. By the time of Hoby's invitation two sons had been born to Walter and Mary Mildmay: Anthony, about nine years old in 1557, and Humphrey, some seven years younger.[25] The thought of the Mildmays, the Hobys, Cecil, and their friends celebrating the last Marian Christmas together is attractive. One hopes their holiday was joyous.

[25] The exact birth dates of Mildmay's children are not known. The age of his sons is deduced from the fact that in 1562 Anthony matriculated at Peterhouse, Cambridge, where Humphrey followed him in 1569. Probably at least one and perhaps all of Mildmay's three daughters—Winifred, Martha, and Christian— had been born by 1557.

## 5. MILDMAY, THE EXCHEQUER, AND THE MINT
## 1559–1570

MARY DIED on November 7, 1558, shortly followed not only by Cardinal Pole, her principal advisor, but also by Sir John Baker, her Chancellor of the Exchequer. One of Elizabeth's first duties as Queen was therefore the appointment of a new Chancellor. On December 23 Sir William Paulet, the Marquis of Winchester, wrote Sir William Cecil, the new Principal Secretary, "Now John Baker is departed this lif (whom God pardon), I pray you remember Sir Walter Mildmay for that office, who is as [ably fitted] for it as any that I kno."[1] The Queen concurring, Mildmay's patent was issued on February 5,[2] and Sir Walter entered upon the most important phase of his public career. All of his earlier services, indeed, may be viewed as preparation for his work in Elizabethan government.

The principal Exchequer officers whom Mildmay joined in 1559 were Winchester, the Lord Treasurer, who had already worked with Mildmay on a number of commissions and who knew his qualifications

---

[1] SP 12/1/42. The bracketed words are doubtful, as the manuscript is nearly illegible.

[2] C 66/941, m. 11, calendared in *CPR, Eliz.,* I, 57. The original letters patent, with the seal still attached, are in the Westm. MSS, 1, I, 16. There has been considerable confusion about the date of Mildmay's appointment. The article on his life in the *DNB* says that he became Chancellor only after the death of Sir Richard Sackville in 1566. Several writers have followed this entry in making Sackville Chancellor from 1559 to 1566; see, e.g., F. C. Dietz, *English Public Finance, 1558–1641,* p. 2, and G. R. Elton, *The Tudor Revolution in Government,* p. 257 n. 1. Perhaps the confusion arose from Sackville's position as Chancellor of Augmentations before the union of the revenue courts in 1554, or more probably because he was Under-Treasurer from 1559 to 1566. Mildmay's appointment as Under-Treasurer is dated January 17, 1567 (Westm. MSS, 2, XV, 2, A6).

well, and Sir Richard Sackville, a distant relative of the Queen, who was Under-Treasurer from 1559 to 1566. After Sackville's death Mildmay united the post of Under-Treasurer with the Chancellorship; when Winchester died in 1572 at the great age of eighty-seven, Cecil—by then Lord Burghley—became Treasurer. The surviving Exchequer papers suggest that Winchester, Sackville, and Mildmay shared the work of running the Exchequer fairly evenly, Winchester making the more important decisions and Mildmay handling routine affairs. After Sackville's death, and with Winchester handicapped by advancing years, Mildmay increasingly assumed responsibility. Later, he and Burghley corresponded extensively about Exchequer matters and probably joined in all major decisions; Burghley's multifarious duties, however, kept him from exercising much more than supervisory influence, and Mildmay seems to have been the effective head of the department.[3] To Mildmay, together with Thomas Cromwell, Chancellor of the Exchequer from 1533 to 1540, belongs the credit for transforming the Chancellorship into an office of real importance.

The organization of the Exchequer determined, to some extent, the duties of its officers. For centuries there had been two principal divisions: the Receipt, or Lower Exchequer, which received and disbursed moneys and kept records in the form of pells and tallies, and the Account, or Upper Exchequer, which was responsible for auditing, for compiling such accounts as the Pipe Roll, and for driving in delinquent payments. In addition the Exchequer Court sat during the four legal terms to try cases involving disputed financial obligations. The Lord Treasurer was responsible for all these operations, but over the years other officers had evolved to assist him in the several departments. The former Treasurer's clerk in the Receipt had developed into the Under-Treasurer, the head of the Lower Exchequer,[4] while the Upper Ex-

---

[3] These judgments are based on the memoranda of the Exchequer office, 1559–1589, SP 46/27–35, nine volumes of papers collected by Henry Fanshaw, Queen's Remembrancer until 1568, and his nephew Thomas Fanshaw, Remembrancer 1568–1601. The office of Queen's Remembrancer remained in the Fanshaw family for five generations. Cf. W. C. Richardson, *History of the Court of Augmentations, 1536–1554*, pp. 436–474.

[4] J. L. Kirby, "The Rise of the Under-Treasurer of the Exchequer," *EHR*, LXXII (1957), 666–677.

chequer was dominated by the Chancellor of the Exchequer, once a deputy of the Lord Chancellor but since the thirteenth century an independent officer.[5] When Mildmay in 1566 combined the offices of Chancellor of the Exchequer and Under-Treasurer, he became the principal officer in both divisions, subject only to the direction of the Lord Treasurer and, of course, to the will of the Queen and Council.

*The Practice of the Exchequer Court,* a treatise written in 1572 by Thomas Fanshaw, helps clarify the officers' functions.[6] As Queen's Remembrancer, Fanshaw was Mildmay's principal clerk or routine administrator for more than twenty years; he had ample opportunity to observe the department at work.

The Treasurer alone, Fanshaw wrote, or the Treasurer and the Under-Treasurer by his direction, "doe survey and order all the Receipt, and all the officers & matters thereof, and of the Treasory, and doe direct paymentes and staies of paymentes by their discretion, and doe examine all receiptes commyng in & exitus going out of the Receipt, but can suffer noe peny to goe out but by Privy Seale from the Prince, or by decree or writt from the Court."[7]

The Under-Treasurer's other duties were numerous.

He in King Henry the VII[th] his tyme (as I have heard saie), the report of the remayne of the treasure in the Receipt being brought then to the King at the end of every terme, did chest the same upp and did content every chest what somme & sorte of money was in yt, intitling the same B. or C. as in the course it fell out, and carryed it to the Kinges Treasure in

---

[5] M. S. Giuseppi, *Guide to the Manuscripts Preserved in the Public Record Office,* I, 72.

[6] Fanshaw's treatise was not printed until 1658. (The copy of this edition in the BM [E. 1928] was the gift of George III.) The printed title page says that the work was composed at the request of Thomas Sackville, Lord Buckhurst, who became Treasurer after Burghley's death. The manuscripts of the treatise, however, bear the date 1572 and include a list of officeholders as of October 9 of that year, so it seems clear that the work was originally written for Burghley's instruction (see Conyers Read, *Lord Burghley and Queen Elizabeth,* p. 83). The work may have been revised for Buckhurst in 1599. The best manuscript is perhaps that preserved among the Caesar papers, Lans. MS 171, fols. 408–434.

[7] Lans. MS 171, fol. 413[v].

the Tower, and entered the same in the Kinges booke he kept in his deske, leving ever in the Receipt sufficient money to pay ordinary fees & sommes of money yt was charged with betwene that & the next terme, and herupon I think the Vice-Treasurer was first made to see this done both of trust, and for the ease of the Lord Treasurer, as being too base a thing for his Lordship to be troubled with, and yet meete to be done by some manner of trust and great secrecie.

He being Chauncellor also of the Court in the late Lord Treasurers [Winchester's] tyme and absence, and before the uniting of the said courtes of Augmentacions & First Fruites & Tenthes, did order & commaund all thinges as the Lord Treasurer in the Court of the Exchequer and in the Receipt, saving that as was done *per consideracionem baronum* upon plees, informacions, judgmentes.

As Chancellor, Mildmay was charged specifically with supervision of First Fruits and Tenths. As Under-Treasurer he handled matters involving customs duties and smuggling, he appointed the steward, cook, and butler, and he was responsible for the provision of the Star Chamber.[8]

The Chancellor, Fanshaw added, "hath in Court the upper place of the bench above the Lord Treasurer." Another Elizabethan account notes that

. . . Thomas Cromwell being Chauncellor & the Kings Secretary & after Lord Privy Seale did take place uppon the first bench *ex dextra domini Thesaurarii*; but Sir John Baker being the next Chauncellor & after Under-Treasorer also did alwayes sit uppon the second bench where the Under-Treasurer now doth. And Sir Walter Mildmay next Chauncellor after him did take place & sitt where the Lord Crumwell did, but by what authority or reason the Chauncellor hath sitten in these severall places it appeareth not in writing found.[9]

Probably Cromwell usurped the upper place and Mildmay found it expedient to follow his example.

Offices were provided for Mildmay, at least after 1566, in St. Stephen's, the building occupied by the Exchequer of Receipt and de-

[8] *Ibid.*, fols. 413ᵛ–414ʳ.
[9] E 369/118, fols. 12ᵛ–13, quoted in Elton, *Tudor Revolution*, pp. 113–114.

scribed by Mildmay's son-in-law, William Fitzwilliam, as lying "beside the Star Chamber stair." Mildmay also had "the help of some other rooms," probably at the Upper Exchequer.[10]

His emoluments were considerable. As Chancellor his salary was only £ 26 13s. 4d., but he was also entitled to £ 12 17s. 4d. annually for livery, and he probably received much more in fees and gifts from suitors. When he became Under-Treasurer he obtained an additional £ 174 6s. 8d. His allowances were increased in July, 1559, because since the annexation of Augmentations, First Fruits, and General Surveyors the Chancellor was "greatlie charged with business and attendaunce bothe in terme and out of the terme muche more than the Chancellors of the Exchequire were accustomed"; he was granted £ 100 in diets and £ 40 for attendance in the vacations.[11] This increased allowance continued only until 1566; in the following years Mildmay received only £ 40 in diets, presumably because his salaries as both Chancellor and Under-Treasurer were deemed ample. Throughout all these years Mildmay continued to collect a £ 200 annuity for his former post in the Augmentations. He thus received annual payments in excess of £ 500, and perhaps as much again in fees, during his three decades at the Exchequer. He was one of the most highly paid Elizabethan officials and had ample opportunity to amass the wealth with which he later endowed Emmanuel College and other educational and charitable institutions.[12]

During the opening months of Elizabeth's reign Mildmay's name appears on a number of commissions to examine particular aspects of government finance. In December, 1558, he was asked to survey the records of the treasurer of the Chamber and to determine the order in which creditors should be paid.[13] He was ordered "to understande what

---

[10] G. R. Elton, "The Elizabethan Exchequer: War in the Receipt," in *Elizabethan Government and Society,* ed. S. T. Bindoff, J. Hurstfield, and C. H. Williams, p. 245, quoting Fitzwilliam to Robert Peter, December 2, 1577, E 407/74, and Vincent Skinner to Sir William Cecil, July 7, 1559, SP 12/271/177.

[11] Lans. MS 168, fol. 174, quoted in Elton, *Tudor Revolution,* p. 257.

[12] The figures in this paragraph are based on contemporary lists of fees in Lans. MS 171, fols. 344r and 241v.

[13] *APC, 1558-70,* p. 27.

landes have been graunted from the Crown in the late Queenes tyme,"[14] to take the accounts of Richard Wilbraham, master of the Jewel House,[15] and to examine the records of Sir Thomas Gresham's activities at Antwerp during Mary's reign.[16]

The new year brought further duties, many of them still involving the confirmation of Marian accounts. In February Mildmay was to determine what sums the lieutenant of the Tower had received since the death of Henry VIII, to allow his expenses for entertainment and imprisonment, to receive his arrears, and to give him acquittance.[17] In September he helped oversee the transfer of robes and cloth from Sir Edward Waldegrave, master of the Great Wardrobe under Mary, to John Fortescue, Elizabeth's appointee.[18] Two months later Mildmay was surveying the jewels, plate, and other goods in Winchester's keeping, comparing them with the lists of Henry VIII's possessions, which he had earlier helped compile.[19] In 1561 he was again dealing with Gresham's affairs, especially with the £ 32,000 which Gresham had borrowed from merchants in Antwerp during Mary's reign; Gresham was eager to have his accounts approved and wrote Cecil on August 7, "most humblie desiring you to have in your remembrance the passing of myne accompt, and that it maye please you to write to Sir Walter Myldmaie to be at Enfilde, agaynst the Queenes Majesties coming thither (as my trust is in God and you), considering the great charge and burden that lies upon me."[20] Mildmay received also the accounts of Roger Alford, who had been collector of the debts owed to the Crown by clergymen at the beginning of Elizabeth's reign,[21] and of Thomas Hobbes, a yeoman of the wardrobe under Mary.[22]

[14] *Ibid.*, p. 28.
[15] *CPR, Eliz.*, I, 50.
[16] *Ibid.*, p. 51.
[17] *Ibid.*, p. 67.
[18] *Ibid.*, p. 118.
[19] *Ibid.*, p. 443.
[20] Quoted in J. W. Burgon, *The Life and Times of Sir Thomas Gresham*, I, 393–394. Commissions to examine Gresham's accounts are dated June 30, 1561; October 17, 1561; April 22, 1562; May 15, 1563 (*CPR, Eliz.*, II, 36, 112, 237, 623).
[21] *CPR, Eliz.*, II, 60; comm. dated March 1, 1561.
[22] *Ibid.*, II, 170; comm. dated May 12, 1561.

Other activities represented new approaches to traditional problems. Elizabeth's first Parliament had complained about smuggling; in an attempt to reduce it Mildmay and other officials examined the ports, rivers, and creeks at Great Yarmouth and King's Lynn.[23] Mildmay was authorized to compound for the order of knighthood with persons listed in the sheriffs' returns as having more than forty pounds a year;[24] he was, in consultation with Winchester, Sackville, and other specified officers, empowered to sell such Crown lands as might be necessary to raise ready money;[25] he, Winchester, and Sackville were commissioned to handle leases of lands within the survey of the Exchequer.[26] In 1561 a sort of financial council was created to determine what revenues might be expected in the Exchequer, Wards, and Duchy, and to list the still-outstanding obligations from Mary's reign. This committee, composed of Mildmay, Winchester, Pembroke, Cecil, Sackville, Sir Nicholas Bacon, and Henry Fitzalan, Earl of Arundel, was to continue its work during the Queen's pleasure and to send reports to Elizabeth from time to time.[27] A year later Mildmay was ordered to oversee the restoration of decayed castles and forts in Northumberland, Cumberland, Westmorland, and County Durham, so that the defenses of the northern borders might be strengthened,[28] and to examine leases of Crown lands in Wales, which were said to have fallen into disorder through the neglect of Marian officials.[29] In 1564 he was also asked to inquire into the subtle practices of merchants who had imported commodities since 1550. The Council thought that their manipulations were responsible for an unfavorable balance of trade and for nonpayment of customs duties.[30]

[23] *Ibid.*, I, 31–32; n.d. [1559].

[24] *Ibid.*, I, 118; comm. dated March 28, 1559.

[25] *Ibid.*, I, 119. This commission, dated June 28, 1559, was to continue during the Queen's pleasure.

[26] *Ibid.*, I, 444–445. The commission, dated November 14, 1559, was renewed in 1566 (*ibid.*, III, 493–494).

[27] *Ibid.*, II, 92–93; comm. dated June 19, 1561.

[28] *Ibid.*, II, 274–276. The commission, dated July 8, 1562, was renewed in 1565 (*ibid.*, III, 213–215).

[29] *Ibid.*, II, 278–279; comm. dated August 1, 1562.

[30] *Ibid.*, III, 31–32, 125. Between 1561 and 1563 Mildmay was also involved in arbitrating a dispute between the inhabitants of Yaxley, Huntingdonshire,

Taxing though these duties were, by far the heaviest charge laid on Mildmay in these years was the regulation of the mint. The variety and baseness of the coinage was the greatest immediate financial problem facing Elizabeth's government. After the reforms of 1551 Northumberland had not called in the vast amount of base money in circulation, and Mary had never found opportunity to clear the monetary chaos. Good coins had indeed been minted under Edward and Mary, but most of them were hoarded or exported, and the circulating medium included coins of at least four different standards.[31]

Elizabeth was gravely concerned, and in 1559 she herself drafted a memorandum on prices and coinage.[32] Her proposals were in the main unworkable; it is fortunate that the Council sought more expert advice by creating a powerful committee to examine the whole state of the mint and coinage. Lord North, a Privy Councillor and former Chancellor of Augmentations; Sir Thomas Parry, treasurer of the Household; Sir William Cecil; Sir Ambrose Cave, Chancellor of the Duchy of Lancaster; Sir Edmund Peckham, master of the mint; and Mildmay were ordered to determine which officers of the mint should be continued in service and what regulations should be ordained, to ascertain what standards of coinage, both in weight and fineness, should be kept, to inquire how much base coin had been issued and how much of it was still in circulation, and to advise how the base money might be reduced to a single fine standard with as small a loss to the Queen and her subjects as possible.[33] They were to prepare a written report, but it is not

---

and the dean and chapter of Peterborough concerning a market held in the village (Dean Piers Book, fols. 376, 380, 389; W. T. Mellows and Daphne H. Gifford, *Elizabethan Peterborough*, pp. 26–31). In 1565 Mildmay helped take the musters of horses and geldings in Northamptonshire (Add. MS 25,079, fols. 16–17). In 1562 he was a justice of the peace of Northamptonshire and Middlesex, and in 1567 he was Lord Lieutenant of Huntingdonshire (*CPR, Eliz.*, II, 440; Westm. MSS, 2, XV, 2, D7).

[31] C. W. C. Oman, "The Tudors and the Currency, 1526–1560," *Transactions of the Royal Historical Society,* new ser., IX (1895), 184–185; A. E. Feavearyear, *The Pound Sterling,* p. 71.

[32] J. A. Froude, *History of England from the Fall of Wolsey to the Defeat of the Spanish Armada: The Reign of Elizabeth,* I, 456.

[33] *CPR, Eliz.,* I, 66–67.

known to exist, and since the register of the Privy Council for this period has been lost one cannot be sure that it was ever presented.

Plans for the recoinage were well in hand by the summer of 1560, when it was agreed that the ancient standard of eleven ounces two pennyweight of silver to eighteen pennyweight of alloy should be restored. The Council next wished to determine the approximate proportion of the various base moneys in circulation. This investigation they shrewdly managed in August, when government agents visited the London butchers' shops and examined the contents of their tills under the pretext of settling a wager that the morning's receipts were larger than those taken during the afternoon.[34] The first official action came in a proclamation of September 27, which stated that the Crown, determined to restore monetary stability, had already begun a new coinage of fine money. Base coins in circulation were called down to values roughly equivalent to their true worth: most of the sixpences in circulation, the shillings devalued under Edward, were to pass at $4\frac{1}{2}d$., while the worst sixpences, those issued by Northumberland in 1550, were called down to $2\frac{1}{4}d$. Other denominations were similarly affected.

A second proclamation, of September 29, tried to convince the people that the devaluation was for their ultimate good, and to sweeten the blow it offered an advance of $3d$. on each pound of devalued money brought in for recoinage. The mint was ordered to return good coin for bad within twenty days, and officials were sent out to mark the base coins by stamping a portcullis in front of the King's head on coins in the $4\frac{1}{2}d$. class and a greyhound behind it on those worth $2\frac{1}{4}d$.[35]

Mildmay was active in overseeing the actual work of recoining. On October 29 he was commissioned, in company with Winchester, Parry, Cecil, and Sackville, "to repayre to [the] myntes and to see and survey the proceding and rate therof and direct the same, as well for the refyning of all our base monyes as for the coynadg of new and for the good and spedy satisfaction of all maner people resortyng thyther for eschang of monyes." At least two of the commissioners were to visit

---

[34] The butchers were selected because they sold to people of all social classes; each was given a quart of wine for his cooperation (Froude, *History of England*, pp. 456–457).

[35] Sir John Craig, *The Mint*, pp. 118–119.

the mint each week.[36] Considering Winchester's age and Cecil's duties at court it is reasonably certain that Mildmay, Sackville, and possibly Parry performed the bulk of the work.

Recoinage on so large a scale necessitated new facilities and additional workers. The mint, which was housed between the inner and outer walls of the Tower, was doubled in size by the erection of new buildings, called the "upper mint," and a firm of German moneyers was employed to assist in refining the base metal. The Germans were almost immediately struck by metal poisoning, and although they followed the mint workers' advice of drinking milk from human skulls many of them died. Nevertheless both the nether and upper mints were operating at full capacity by February, 1561.[37]

Meanwhile a number of problems beset Mildmay and his colleagues. The Earl of Sussex, Lord Deputy of Ireland, complained that base coins were being transported into Ireland, where speculators hoped to pass them at their face values. On December 12, 1560, Mildmay, Winchester, and Sackville wrote Cecil, "We have agreed with all diligence to geve ordre and strayt chardg to the serchers and others of trust in the portes towardes that realme, to use such travaille and circumspection therin as we trust that inconvenience shalbe stayed, praying you so to advertise my Lord that he may use the like diligence on th'other side."[38] This Sussex did: in a proclamation of January 24 he prohibited the importation of base coin and ordered the immediate arrest of anyone attempting to tender coins marked with a portcullis, since they must have been brought in since the devaluation in England.[39] The Ex-

---

[36] SP 12/14/33.

[37] Conyers Read, "Profits on the Recoinage of 1560–1," *Economic History Review,* VI (1936), 188. The first trial of the pyx for the new coin was held May 18; as this test of the fineness of the metal was conducted quarterly, the large-scale recoinage probably began in mid-February. See Craig, *The Mint,* p. 121. The German workers obtained a warrant from the Council "to take off the heads upon London Bridge"—heads of traitors who had been hanged— "and make cuppes thereof, whereof they dranke and founde some reliefe, though the mooste of them dyed" (quoted in Robert Carrier, *The Vanished City,* p. 38).

[38] SP 12/14/59.

[39] *Acts of the Privy Council in Ireland* (HMC, *Fifteenth Report,* Appendix, Part III), p. 114.

chequer officials agreed that a revaluation of Irish coins should be deferred "until theis matiers of moneyes here be further executed and you [Cecil] advertised of the Quenes Majesties pleasure therein."[40] In fact the base money remained current in Ireland until the last of April, when the Irish recoinage was begun.[41]

On January 7, 1561, Winchester, Sackville, and Mildmay again wrote Cecil about mint affairs. They agreed to send £1,000 in new money to Wales "when our myntes be fullie going," but noted that there were other outstanding charges, especially Gresham's continental obligations, which could not be met "but by borrowing and other wise as your self hath written." They assured Cecil that the German refiners would obtain their own lead from Flanders, and reminded him that it should enter England duty free; they listed decayed buildings in England whose roofs might also yield the metal. Wood, too, was needed, and the Exchequer officers confirmed that "if ye canne not be served at St. Jones [John's] wood ye shalbe furnished at Wimbleton according to your desire."[42]

A list of mint officers and employees, detailing their duties and fees, had been issued under the Great Seal in December. We do not know if Mildmay helped prepare it, but in June he and Cecil were still corresponding about the subject. "For myn opinion," Mildmay wrote, "I think that aftre the brunt of this recoynage be over diverse of thoes offices will be found superfluous and of thoes that shall contynew the fees allso may veary well be diminished," although not until the retirement of the incumbents. Mildmay objected to a proposal that certain mint salaries be paid out of the Exchequer, since the payment "was wont to be of the revenues of the mynt."[43]

By September, 1561, the recoinage was virtually complete. The mints had issued about £758,102 in new coin and had paid out about £666,267 for the base money brought in. Thus the gross profit was approximately £92,000. Expenses seem to have exceeded £50,000, so

---

[40] SP 12/14/59.

[41] Proclamation by Sir William Fitzwilliam and the Council, March 24, 1561 (*APC, Ireland,* p. 119).

[42] SP 12/16/3.

[43] SP 12/17/29.

that the net profit was between £ 40,000 and £ 45,000.[44] The government certainly prospered through an operation in which ordinary subjects lost substantial amounts of money.[45] Profit, however, was not one of the principal aims, and the Queen and Council had probably not anticipated so favorable an outcome.[46]

The great undertaking was brought to a ceremonial conclusion with the striking of a medal "Bene Constituta Re Nummaria." Even if the subjects had borne the cost of the recoinage, most of them appeared grateful at the prospect of a sound, stable currency. A few years later the recorder of Warwick praised Elizabeth for bringing "the restoration of God's true religion, the speedy change of wars into peace, of dearth and famine into plenty, of an huge mass of dross and counterfeit money into fine gold and silver."[47]

It is not easy to assign credit for the success of the recoinage. Sir Thomas Gresham has commonly been praised for conceiving the scheme, Cecil for seeing that it was carried out.[48] Certainly Gresham

[44] The text figures are taken from Read, "Profits on the Recoinage," *Economic History Review*, VI, 186–193. One more frequently sees figures based on Lans. MS 4, fols. 213–214, which is possibly Cecil's memorandum on the recoinage. These figures are cited in Oman, "The Tudors and the Currency," *Transactions*, n.s., IX, 186; Froude, *History of England*, p. 470; Feavearyear, *The Pound Sterling*, p. 77; and Craig, *The Mint*, p. 122. Read, however, has shown that the Lans. MS figures are not entirely reliable and has constructed others from the more direct evidence of the mint accounts. I suspect that Read's estimate of £ 45,000 as the net profit is too high; for example, it apparently fails to take account of the cost of erecting and equipping the upper mint.

[45] Craig (*The Mint*, p. 123) calculates that "people at large lost nearly two-thirds of the amounts for which the coin had been originally issued."

[46] Conyers Read (*Mr. Secretary Cecil and Queen Elizabeth*, pp. 196–197) says that the government probably anticipated making a substantial profit, partly because it fixed the values at which debased coins were accepted a little below their intrinsic worth. Raymond de Roover has calculated that the coins accepted at $4\frac{1}{2}d$. were actually worth $5\frac{1}{2}d$. and those taken at $2\frac{1}{4}d$. were worth $2\frac{3}{4}d$. (*Gresham on Foreign Exchange*, p. 65). But these figures do not allow for wear or deliberate clipping of the coins, or for the cost of refining and recoining. I have seen no convincing evidence that the government aimed at anything more than breaking even.

[47] Quoted in J. Hurstfield, *Elizabeth I and the Unity of England*, pp. 84–85.

[48] F. R. Salter (*Sir Thomas Gresham*, p. 87) thinks that the recoinage was

was concerned; a few days after Elizabeth's accession he had written her a long letter concluding that, if she wished "to restore this your realm in such estate as heretofore it hath been, first, your Highness hath none other ways, but when time and opportunity serveth, to bring your base money into fine of 11 ounce fine, and so gold after the rate."[49] Clearly the recoinage could not have been accomplished without Cecil's active support. But other men were as deeply involved: Winchester, Mildmay, Peckham, Sackville, Parry, and Ambrose Cave. Indeed Peckham and Mildmay, since they had been advisors in the recoinage of 1551, should have known more about the mint and the coinage than either Gresham or Cecil. In point of fact the recoinage was advocated by diverse people—merchants, governmental officials, even the Queen herself—and it was carried through by no single administrator but rather by a group of the government's financial officers. It is doubtful that any was more active, conscientious, and experienced than Mildmay.[50]

---

due largely to Gresham's suggestion; Read (*Cecil*, p. 194) writes that "Gresham furnished the initial impulse and Cecil . . . provided the ways and means."

[49] Quoted in Read, *Cecil*, p. 194. Note that Gresham recommended a standard slightly less fine than that actually adopted.

[50] Mildmay evidently spent considerable time studying financial problems related to the coinage. Among his books at Emmanuel College is the *Tractatus commerciorum et usurarum* by Carolus Molinaeus (Charles Dumoulin), a work dealing with foreign exchange, trade, and coinage. Mildmay inscribed it with his name and the year 1560; he must have obtained it to increase his knowledge of the effect of coinage on trade. He procured also a copy of the manuscript "Booke To Understand the Exchaunge" (F[M]P 86). In "Gresham, Mildmay, and the Memorandum for the Understanding of the Exchange" (*Notes and Queries*, CCVI [1961], 403–405) I suggested that Mildmay was the author of the memorandum, which Raymond de Roover had attributed to Gresham (*Gresham*, pp. 15–18). But Mary Dewar argues convincingly, in an article as yet unpublished, that the book was written by Sir Thomas Smith in May, 1554. In any case Mildmay's ownership of a copy attests to his serious study of economics. He similarly obtained copies (Westm. MSS, 4, XX, 2) of several earlier memoranda on the Exchequer; these are printed in Sybil Jack and R. S. Schofield, "Four Early Tudor Financial Memoranda," *Bulletin of the Institute of Historical Research*, XXXVI (1963), 189–206.

The years following the recoinage found Mildmay still occupied with the Exchequer and the exchange. In April, 1562, the Queen wrote Winchester, Sackville, and Mildmay of her concern for the safety of treasure in the Receipt. Tellers had been in the habit of carrying money to their homes for storage, and under Mary several had misappropriated funds and had died in debt to the Crown. To prevent recurrence of such abuses the Queen ordered her Exchequer officers to consider whether older but more secure methods of operation might be put into effect again. She further required them to send her notice of vacant positions in the department, so that she might appoint men who "have long served us in our household" but who are "unprovided of lyvinges."[51] The suggestion that the Receipt could be better regulated through the revival of its ancient machinery prefigures the extended controversy which developed later in the reign between the clerk of the pells and the writer of the tallies; it may be that Robert Hare, a protégé of Winchester who had been appointed clerk of the pells in 1560, had already begun his campaign for the restoration of his ancient perquisites.[52]

In 1563 the exchange rate fell, primarily because of an embargo on trade with the Netherlands, and the Queen appointed a commission composed of Winchester, Mildmay, Sir Francis Knollys, and Sir William Cordell to study the problem. Their report, presented in February, 1564, is one of the most significant economic documents of the sixteenth century.[53] It considers "not only howe much a pound of Englishe moneye is worthe of Flemyshe moneye, but also howe the sleightes and cunninges of the usage of the exchange hath byne and may be to the great losse and hinderance of the comone wealthe of England, and howe the same maye be remediede, met withall, and turnede to the benefyte of this realme of Englande." Although the assumption that the bankers were able to rule the exchange rather than being controlled

[51] SP 12/22/59.

[52] See Elton, "The Elizabethan Exchequer," in *Elizabethan Government*, ed. Bindoff *et al.*, pp. 213–222.

[53] Harl. MS 660, fols. 107–118; extracts are printed in R. H. Tawney and Eileen Power, *Tudor Economic Documents*, III, 346–359; discussed in De Roover, *Gresham*, pp. 184–193.

themselves by market conditions was incorrect, the report's other observations were acute.

To remedy the ills resulting from unfavorable exchange rates the commissioners emphasized the importance of increasing English exports and restricting imports. Since trade with the Low Countries had been suspended, they suggested that a mart for English cloths be established in Emden, a city in East Friesland,[54] and they urged customs reforms, to discourage smuggling.[55] They recommended also two novel measures: the creation of an international fund or bank to stabilize exchange rates and the acceptance of French and Imperial coins as legal tender in England. Although neither of these proposals gained approval, the first at least was extraordinarily farsighted.

Trade with Antwerp was resumed later in 1564 and the exchange soon recovered without such drastic action. But the commissioners' report, despite its immediate lack of application, remained the theoretical basis of governmental policy and a vital force in economic thought. Once again it is not easy to apportion the credit, but Winchester's age makes it unlikely that he did the principal work, and Knollys and Cordell lacked experience in finance. Insofar as the treatise was the product of a single hand, Mildmay was probably its author.[56]

In 1568 a new embargo was placed on trade with the Netherlands, but the Queen's grant of exemptions soon threatened its effectiveness. Mildmay explained the situation in a paper presented to the Queen and the Council December 8, 1570.[57]

---

[54] Among the Fitzwilliam of Milton Papers is a treatise on trade between England and East Friesland written in 1564 (F[M]P 249). It suggests that increased trade between the two countries would be profitable to both and that it would weaken Philip II and the Catholics. Although the treatise is not addressed to Mildmay it may have been sent him with the hope that he would favor trade with Friesland.

[55] De Roover says that "what all this discussion about the reform of the customs has to do with the exchange is far from clear" (*Gresham,* p. 191). But surely imports would be reduced, or at least better regulated, if smuggling could be stopped, and regulation of imports was one of the commissioners' chief concerns.

[56] This view is tentatively advanced by De Roover (*Gresham,* p. 193 n. 50).

[57] Four MSS survive. Mildmay's own text was apparently F(M)P 171; it is

Two yeres before this or thereabouts the Duke of Alva, Governor of the Lowe Countreys for the King of Spayne, upon a suddeyne did arrest not only the persons of the English marchantes but also their shipps and goods & therewith also prohibited any more traffique betweene England & thoes countreyes: which doing of his gave occasion to her Majestie to do the like here to the subjectes of thoes places, likewise restreyning traffique betweene them and us. And for that purpose [she] gave commission to certeyne of her Privy Councell to see the same well observed and to punish th'offenders, which they did accordingly.

This restreynt of trade was sought to be broken by certeyne of the Quenes servantes that, being offered by some covetuouse men great sommes of mony, did procure lycence from her Majestie to dispence with them and their factors for the bringing from the Low Countreyes certeyne wares, the restreynt notwithstanding.

Whereupon informacion being given to her Majestie that the granting of such lycences during the restreynt was very hurtfull to her Majestie and the realme, it pleased her to send to me, being one of the commissioners, that I should consider of the case and wryte unto her myn opinyon.

Mildmay thought the granting of such licenses was against honor, policy, and justice. In typically methodical fashion he elaborated each point. English merchants had reluctantly agreed to direct their trade to Hamburg rather than Antwerp only on condition that all commerce with the Netherlands cease. This agreement could not, in honor, be broken. Further, irregular trade through licenses was "utterly against the politie of this present tyme," since one object of the embargo had been to show "how this realme might fynde sufficient traffique without [the Netherlands], and had not so much neede of them as by their continuall injuryes they seemed to thinke, and thereby to bring them to more reasonable condicions" whenever her Majesty might wish to negotiate for a general revival of trade. Finally, since the commissioners had severely punished merchants who violated the embargo, condoning its breach through the licenses seemed manifestly unjust. "There appeareth no reason in justice why, to serve any lycencer, other subjects should be punished."

---

fuller than the other copies: Sloane MS 326, fols. 30–32; Harl. MS 6265, fols. 83–84; and Add. MS 37,021, fols. 100–102.

One copy of the memorandum speaks specifically of hops, noting

... the great disceate that maie bee used in the carriage of hoppes, which ar packed in greate sackes not easelie to bee searched, under cooller wheareof ar like to bee conveied silke, spice, and such other wares; and hoppes also ar not a merchandies of such necessitie, but it weare better for the realme to forbeare them presentlie, then by benefitinge the Lowe Coontrie so much to hurte so greatelie the bennifite of the state.[58]

Unfortunately the paper does not state whether the Queen accepted Mildmay's reasoning. The embargo remained in effect until 1573; satisfactory treaties with the Netherlands were negotiated in 1574 and 1575.

Amidst these cares of state Mildmay found time for pleasant social gatherings. In September, 1562, Richard Bertie and his wife, the widow of the Duke of Suffolk, did some hunting with Mildmay at Apethorpe.[59] Their talk was perhaps of religious reform, for the Berties had been Marian exiles and shared their host's Puritan outlook. The next year, on December 10, Cecil gave a dinner at Windsor Castle for Mildmay and a number of other governmental officials who had fled from the plague in London. Roger Ascham, the Queen's tutor, was also present, happy to be "in the companie of so manie wise and good men togither, as hardly than could have beene piked out againe, out of all England beside." Conversation drifted to education as Cecil remarked that some boys had run away from Eton, in the valley below the castle, for fear of beating. The Secretary deplored excessive corporal punishment, which he said drove boys to hate learning before they comprehended its meaning. Petre, more severe, thought "that the rodde onelie was the sworde that must keepe the schole in obedience and the scholer in good order." Mildmay, unfortunately, "said verie litle," but Ascham spoke at length, suggesting that children should be allured to learning by love rather than the rod, and Sackville, who himself had been flogged at school, urged him to write a book elaborating his views. Thus was born Ascham's famous treatise *The Scholemaster*.[60]

Mildmay found time also to care for his family. In 1562 he sent his

---

[58] F(M)P 171, fol. 1ᵛ.
[59] Evelyn Read, *My Lady Suffolk,* p. 153.
[60] Roger Ascham, *The Scholemaster,* ed. Edward Arber, pp. 17–19.

older son, Anthony, to Peterhouse, Cambridge, where he delivered a highly successful oration during the Queen's visit of 1564.[61] Humphrey followed his brother at Peterhouse in 1569. Provisions were made too for Mildmay's daughters. Christian, the youngest, remained at home with Lady Mildmay, but about 1565 Martha was married to William Brounker, and in 1569 Winifred wed William Fitzwilliam, scion of another prominent Northamptonshire family.

On July 7, 1566, Mildmay's services to Elizabeth's government were capped by his appointment to the Privy Council. A copy of the oath which he swore at St. James's happens to survive. It emphasizes the importance and secrecy of the Council's work.

Ye shall as far forth as your cunning and discretion sufficeth truely, justlye, and uprightlye counsaile and advise the Queenes Highnese in all matters which you shall be made privey, or called unto to be commoned, treated, and demeaned in the Queenes Counsaile, or by you as the Queens Counsaillor, and generally in all thinges that may be to the Queenes honor and behuffe and to the good of her, not leavinge or eschewinge soe to doe for affection, love, mode, dowbt, or dreade of any person or persons; and you shall keepe secret the Queenes Counsaile and all that shall be commoned by way of counsaile in the same, without that you shall common it, publish it, or discover it by word, wrytinge, or in any wise to any person out of the same Counsaile, or to any of the same Counsaile if it touch him or if he be partye therto. And that you shall receive noe gift, mede, nor good, nor promise of goods of any person for promotinge, favouring, declaringe, lettinge, of hinderinge of any matter or thinge to be treated or done in the said Counsaile. Ye shall alsoe with all your might and power helpe and strengthen the Queenes said Counsaile in all that shall be thought unto the same Counsaile for the universall good of the Queene or her realmes, and to the peace, rest, and tranquilities of the same, and withstand any person or persons, of what estate or degree that they be of, that would any way attempt or attend unto the contrarye, and generally [you] shall observe, keepe, and doe all that a good and trew Counsaill[or] ought to doe unto his Soveraigne and Leige Lady, soe help you G[od and] the contents of this Booke.[62]

[61] John and J. A. Venn, *Alumni Cantabrigienses,* Pt. I, Vol. III, p. 187.
[62] Add. MS 34,216, fol. 1. The bracketed words are supplied where the edge of the MS has been torn. Mildmay's oath is somewhat longer and more elab-

As Mildmay moved between the Exchequer office, the Council table, his home at Great St. Bartholomew's, his house in Hackney, and his country estate at Apethorpe, he may well have felt the glow of satisfaction as well as the press of business and family life. No longer a young man seeking wealth and position, he had made his place in the world.

orately worded than an oath of 1570 printed in *Tudor Constitutional Documents* by J. R. Tanner (p. 225).

## 6. MILDMAY AND MARY, QUEEN OF SCOTS
### 1567–1570

As ONE OF Elizabeth's Privy Councillors, Mildmay became involved in the maze of problems centering around Mary Stuart, the beautiful but ill-fated Queen of Scots. Indeed most of his surviving papers for the years between 1567 and 1570 deal with aspects of Elizabeth's policy towards the Scottish Queen.

Although the English had been concerned at Mary's marriage to Francis II and the Guise rule in Scotland, tensions relaxed as the 1560 Treaty of Edinburgh ended French influence. Elizabeth was displeased when Mary, widowed at eighteen, returned to Scotland and wed Henry Stuart, Lord Darnley, who had some claim to the English throne, but the Scottish problem did not assume truly alarming proportions until February 10, 1567, when the murder of Darnley shocked the Scots and the English alike. It is now generally accepted that James Hepburn, the Earl of Bothwell, on whom Mary's impulsive affections had fallen, was the murderer, while Mary herself may have had full knowledge of the crime;[1] but Bothwell tried to shield himself by spreading the rumor that the Protestants, who had disliked Darnley, were responsible.

One of the chief Protestant lords, James Stuart, the Earl of Moray, was Mary's half brother, and was ultimately to become the Regent for Mary's infant son, James. In 1567, however, Moray's position was far from secure; he wrote Cecil in March asking for a passport, so that he might weather the storm in a safe foreign port. By April 16 he was in London, where he conferred with the Queen and Cecil, and at the end of the month he left for the continent.[2]

[1] See Maurice Lee, Jr., *James Stewart, Earl of Moray*, p. 198.
[2] Conyers Read, *Mr. Secretary Cecil and Queen Elizabeth*, pp. 376–377.

Meanwhile affairs in Scotland deteriorated rapidly. Bothwell's farcical trial resulted in the expected acquittal, and on May 15 he and Mary were wed in Protestant rites at Holyrood House. Mary thus lost, for the time being at least, the support of the continental Catholics; vastly more important, she forfeited the loyalty of the Scottish lords, who had already planned revolt and who were now galvanized into action. Although Mary and Bothwell attempted to gather an army they met with little success, and Mary's position was so weak that she was forced to capitulate to the lords on June 15, when it was obvious that they would gain the victory at Carberry Hill. Bothwell escaped; Mary was taken in captivity to Edinburgh, where she was greeted with cries of "Burn the whore! Burn the muderess of her husband!"[3] Two days later she was transferred to the fortress of Loch Leven.

The English government naturally hoped to influence the outcome of the Scottish rebellion. As early as April 23 the Council had discussed the situation, and although it took no action it kept abreast of events. After Mary's surrender Elizabeth decided to send Sir Nicholas Throgmorton as an envoy to Scotland; remembering her own kinship with Mary, and distressed at the idea of revolt against a crowned queen, Elizabeth hoped that Throgmorton could persuade the lords to free Mary. Cecil was unenthusiastic about the prospect of Mary's liberation, perhaps because he realized how unlikely the Scots were to accept it; Mildmay doubtless shared his misgivings. Elizabeth and her Councillors agreed, however, that Darnley's murderer should be punished and that James should be preserved from danger. Indeed Cecil hoped that the English might obtain custody of the prince.[4]

Throgmorton left London July 1, spending some time with Mildmay at Apethorpe on his way to the border. His reception in Scotland was discouraging; the lords were not disposed to accept his advice and had no intention of freeing Mary or handing James over to the English.

Surviving correspondence makes it clear that Cecil, Mildmay, and Throgmorton kept in touch throughout the summer. Indeed we are fortunate that Mildmay spent July and August in the country, as was his custom. Had he remained in London he and Cecil would doubtless

---

[3] T. F. Henderson, *Mary Queen of Scots*, II, 469.
[4] Read, *Cecil*, pp. 379–381.

have conferred personally, and we should have no record of their talks.

Mildmay's earliest letter in this series is dated July 20. In it he thanked Cecil for sending news of Throgmorton's mission, "for thowgh Sir Nicholas Throkmorton passed by me, yet his tarying was so short, and the company such by chaunce, as my talke was small with him: so as, thowgh summarilie, yet I did not so particularlie understand the cause of his legation as now I doe by this your gentle advertisement." He hoped for good success in Scottish matters but was not optimistic:

I promise you to my understanding, they remayne yet in dowbteful termes, speciallie if a man considre the practises of the Frenche and the natur of the Scotts, which heretofore have been mervaylously carried by them.

Therefore in my pore opinion, it behoveth us to be the more carefull, and by no meanes to suffre the French to have that auctoritie or credyt emongest them which they seek: for if they have, you see well inowgh how nire our trowble is. If thees lords in Scotland agree, the case is the bettre; if not, that good end which is to be desired I feare will not follow.

Ending on a more personal note, Mildmay expressed his regret that Cecil was unable to spend the summer at Burghley House, his Northamptonshire estate, only a few miles from Apethorpe.

I wisshe, as you doe, that ye were here to visite your owne thinges for a while. And thowgh theis Scottish matiers will scaresly suffre you, yet me thinketh it shall goe hard but ones er sommer passe ye may performe your desire, which I pray you in any wise doe. In the meane tyme, if occasion serve here that may concerne you or yours, that litle I can doe shalbe readye. . . . Your sonne and I entend to mete sometymes, thowgh we cannot have you. Surelie you have cause to be glad of him, for he is veary honest and well liked emongest his neighbours.[5]

Mildmay wrote Cecil again on August 4. By this time Mary had abdicated, to Elizabeth's disgust and distress, and James had been crowned King at Stirling. Moray was offered the title of Regent and control of the government; late in July he was again in England, explaining to Elizabeth that he had formerly favored Mary's restoration but that her obstinate passion for Bothwell had rendered this course impossible.

---

[5] SP 12/43/27; contemporary copy in the BM, Add. MS 4126, fols. 106–107. Mildmay presumably referred to Thomas Cecil, the Secretary's eldest son.

Unmoved, the Queen decided to recall Throgmorton, who had accomplished nothing, and threatened Moray and the Scottish lords with her wrath if they did not free her cousin.

Moray, on his way to Edinburgh, spent a night with Mildmay, who formed a high opinion of his ability. Mildmay wrote Cecil:

> If the government rest onely in the Erle of Murray, it will be well, as I thinke, for stablishing of religion and contynuance of amytie here: for otherwise, as you know, emongest many are many affections. His lordship, passing homwards, was content to come so ferre owte of his way as to lye with me on Friday night last. I found him veary wise and well affected to the mayntenance of good frendship between thes twoo realmes, remembring to me veary thankefully benefyts receyved. . . . Dowbtefull me thought he was to receave his prepared auctoritie; but, when he cometh home, it is like inowgh that, for avoyding of confusion, he will be drawen to it, thowgh veary hardelye.

Mildmay's comment on Mary's fall has a typical moralizing tone: "a mervaylous tregedy, if a man repete it from the begynning, shewing the issue of such as lyve not in the feare of God."[6]

On the same day Mildmay wrote Throgmorton a long and interesting letter, lamenting Elizabeth's stubborn support of Mary. It is worth quoting at length:

> Sir, the oftener ye wright the more is your travayle, but the more am I beholding to you, that doeth vouchesauffe to bestowe so moche payne uppon him that cannot requyte it. Your last lettres of the last of July delivered to my handes this day conteyne suche particular and certaine declaration of the state of Scotland at this present as it is easie to judge whoes partie is greatest and most like to holde, and therfore I cannot but mervayle what respect moveth us here to stryke against the streame and to trowble ourselfes with unnecessary quarrelles. For even as you wright, I have been advertised from the court that thes proceadinges have been and yet are so displeasaunt, as by no meanes they canne be digested. And yet how litle that is for our policie, you that are there seeth better than I. Sory I am that you are so straytelie injoyned to deale otherwise than I perceave your selfe thinketh to good purpose. Nevertheles I hope that uppon your playne and direct advertisment some bettre consideration will be had, which I wisshe lest their follow repentaunce, not easy to be cured.

[6] SP 12/43/36; contemporary copy in the BM, Add. MS 4126, fols. 164–165.

Mildmay again voiced his respect for Moray,

. . . a gentleman in myn opinion veary wise, zealous in religion, and well affected to the mayntenaunce of th'amitie. Dowbtefull I found hym to take uppon him any singular governement, in respect of daungers that might follow to hymself, but surely if he doe not accept the place, I shall remayne in small hope to see thoes two endes which you note in my first lettres take that effect which you and I desire, that is, propagation of Goddes true religion and perpetuall amitie betwene thes twoo countries. Emongest many governors are many affections, and thoes breede easilie confusion. And therfore I was so bold in talke to advise hym not to be hastie in refusall, seing that he might doe God such acceptable service and thes twoo realmes so moch good. And if you be of myn opinion, because your acquaintaunce is more with hym, ye shall doe well to comforte him therin. He hath been moche sowght on in Fraunce, and well received here, but yet not without greate wordes and greate misliking of thoes proceadinges; but he hath been so used to them, as it semeth he wayeth them as they be.

Mildmay hoped that Elizabeth had sent Throgmorton new and more realistic instructions.

I dowbte not but er this ye have receaved commission and instructions of other forme, for when voluntarye actions fayle, yet unwilling folkes are fayne oftentymes to make vertue of necessitie. And so I hope your hard begynnyng shall bring forth a good ending. It will not be long aftre th'arrivall of th'Erle of Murray but the full issue of this matier will be seene, for me thinketh till Bodwell be put downe, as they terme it, the tempest is not over.[7]

Elizabeth ordered Throgmorton home in a dispatch of August 6. On the fifteenth an unhappy Mildmay wrote Cecil, "I am sory he shold reatorne before ye saw what shold become of this new intended governement." Mildmay's Protestant orientation made it impossible for him to share the Queen's concern for Mary, but he felt that Moray as Regent would preserve "religion" and Anglo-Scottish friendship; "and I never looke for the latter to hold long, except the first be surelie stablisshed."[8]

By the eighteenth Mildmay had received letters from Robert Dudley,

[7] SP 70/93/1213.
[8] SP 12/43/50.

71

Earl of Leicester, confirming Throgmorton's recall, and from Throgmorton himself. He wrote Throgmorton again, this time expressing fear that the French would fill the vacuum created by Throgmorton's departure.

I dowbte that when ye are goon, the French shall have more scope to work that they seeke. And I am the more afrayde of it, bicause in a late lettre from Mr. Secretary I understand the Queen's Majestie contyneweth in offence against the procedinges in Scotland, and that more openly than some there thinke politiquely, as he termeth it. So as if they be desperate of favor here, ye may be sure they will seeke supportation where they may fynd it. But of thes we shall talk more lardgely when we mete.

Throgmorton had promised to visit Apethorpe on his return journey; Mildmay asked him to "wright me twoo lynes, whan ye will arrive, bicause I will not be from home, for I have appointed the next week a litle progresse to be mery with my neighbors, yet not so farre from home but I will be allwaies ready for you." He sent his commendations to Moray, "in whoes handes, I am sure you thinke as I doe, it is metest for all respectes that the government shold rest. . . . God send you sauffe to reatorne," he concluded, "and send you no blame, thowgh it semeth you loke for small thankes."[9]

For some months we hear no more of Mildmay's concern for Scottish affairs. Throughout August Cecil's position as Moray's advocate at London remained strained, partly because—as the Spanish ambassador observed—Mildmay and the other Councillors on whom he relied for support were away from court.[10] Moray accepted the Regency on August 22, with the reluctance which Mildmay had anticipated, and by November Elizabeth had become reconciled to his government.[11] Throughout the winter the Scottish problem appeared to have solved itself.

Nevertheless the Council ordered a precautionary examination of border fortifications, lest Anglo-Scottish violence break out. The Earl of Bedford, Sadler, and Mildmay compiled the report, which was sub-

[9] SP 59/14/1239.
[10] Read, *Cecil*, p. 387.
[11] Lee, *Moray*, p. 213.

mitted on February 3, 1568.[12] It began by listing fortresses and castles, describing the condition of each, and recommending appropriate action. Berwick, the principal English fortification, was "somwhat in decaye," and its repair was put in hand. Some castles— Wark, Etal, and Harbottle—were to be repaired; others were to be abandoned. Bamborough, for instance, was "much in decay, [and] a place not veary apt for service, for it is xii myles away from Scotlande." The commissioners agreed to make further inquiry about the nature of the decay at Norham Castle and about possible revenues which might be available for restoring the structure.

More general recommendations were also included. The commissioners thought that tenants in the borders should have freedom from feudal fines, since they had to maintain their enclosures and tenements and were liable for military service. No lands within twenty miles of the boundary should be let to strangers not resident there, the commissioners decided, and no Scotsman should be allowed to inhabit a farm within two miles of an English fort. Border residents should be prevented from selling horses to Scots. A joint commission of English and Scots was suggested as a means of dividing "batable ground" between the two realms. Finally, the commissioners expressed their concern for religion and education in the marches; they recommended increased salaries for curates in such places as Alnwick and Bamborough and the establishment of a free school at Berwick, to which the Queen might give the eight pounds annual income she received from chantry rents in the town.

Stronger defenses were soon needed, for in May the smouldering Scottish problem burst into fresh flame. On the second Mary escaped from Loch Leven and fled west to the territory of her principal supporters, the Hamiltons, with whose aid she raised an army of some six thousand. She hoped that Moray would be sufficiently cowed to consent to a bloodless restoration, but when he refused she ordered her troops to challenge his control of Glasgow. Although outnumbered, the Regent's men were more experienced, and on May 13 they were able to rout Mary's army at the village of Langside. Mary herself es-

12 SP 59/14/1569.

caped and after three days of panic made her way across the border into England, trusting in Elizabeth's favor and hoping for her active support.

Elizabeth's quandary is well known. She could ill afford to support a Catholic claimant to her own throne, a ruler discredited and defeated in her homeland; but she could not utterly abandon her own cousin or appear to sanction the violent overthrow of a crowned queen. The example touched her too nearly. Elizabeth herself strongly favored Mary and still hoped for her restoration. Cecil, more skeptical and realistic, proposed that Mary be kept in close confinement while the charges against her were investigated.[13]

On June 20 the Council met to consider the situation. Mildmay was present; indeed the attendance included virtually all the Councillors except Knollys, who had been dispatched to Carlisle to guard Mary. The Council decided that Mary should be moved farther from the border—to Nottingham, Fotheringhay, or Tutbury—and that Elizabeth could not aid Mary, see her personally, or allow her to depart before the issue between her and the Scots was examined and tried. If Mary were really guilty of complicity in Darnley's murder nothing could be done for her, and she would have to remain under surveillance lest she foment rebellion.[14]

By mid-July the chief Councillors, and probably the Queen too, had read copies of the so-called Casket Letters, which Moray had sent to England in the hands of his secretary, John Wood. The vexed question of the authenticity of the letters need not concern us here: the English, although eager to see substantiating evidence, thought them damning. Cecil and his fellow Councillors were thus more desirous than ever of a thorough investigation, which they believed could only reveal Mary's guilt; ultimately Mary and Moray acquiesced. On August 10 Cecil was writing, "I think the Duke of Norfolk, my Lord of Sussex, and Sir Walter Mildmay shall be commissioners to treat in the North between the Queen of Scots and her subjects."[15] Cecil would doubtless have liked Mildmay to serve, for Mildmay probably shared the Secretary's views more fully than did Thomas Radcliffe, Earl of Sussex, or Thomas

---

[13] Read, *Cecil*, p. 399.
[15] Read, *Cecil*, p. 407.

[14] *CSP, Scot.*, II, No. 708.

Howard, Duke of Norfolk. But in the end Elizabeth sent Sir Ralph Sadler instead. She perhaps thought Sadler more sympathetic to Mary than was Mildmay; certainly Sadler was more experienced in Scottish affairs.

The commissioners, in any case, began their work at York on October 4. A week later Moray produced the famous casket, and the properly horrified commissioners sent a detailed account of its contents to Elizabeth. By November 3 she had decided to recall the investigation to London, so that the entire Council might examine the evidence; perhaps, too, she suspected that Norfolk, already dreaming of marriage with the Queen of Scots, had become entirely too friendly to her cause.[16]

At a meeting of the Council in late October it was agreed that if the commissioners for Mary and Moray did appear in London the Councillors not already present should be specially summoned: Norfolk, Winchester, Petre, Arundel, Mildmay, and several other peers.[17] For some reason the conference at Westminster did not get under way before November 25. At its second session Moray, who appeared personally, produced the "eik," or addition to his earlier statement, formally charging his sister with murder. Mildmay was not one of the English commissioners, but he had an opportunity to discuss the situation and examine Mary's statements at a meeting of the Council held at Hampton Court December 12.[18] Moray produced the casket and the evidence to substantiate its authenticity, and they were studied by the Council on the fourteenth and fifteenth.

On December 16 the Councillors received Mary's representatives, who argued that she should be allowed to appear and defend herself.[19] This arrangement the Council could not permit—it would be improper for Elizabeth to receive a suspected murderer and adulteress—but Mary was asked to send someone authorized to answer the charges, or to answer them herself before an English delegation which might be sent to her. Mary declined; Moray pressed for a decision; Elizabeth refused

---

[16] The best account of the York-Westminster Conference is found in Lee, *Moray,* pp. 235–252.

[17] Read, *Cecil,* p. 411.

[18] *CSP, Scot.,* II, No. 918.

[19] *Ibid.,* No. 925.

to condemn Mary unheard. The matter was finally ended, although hardly settled, on January 10, when Cecil announced the Queen's Janus-like conclusions: nothing said thus far had impaired Moray's honor or position, but nothing had persuaded Elizabeth to think badly of Mary. It was "perhaps the most absurd judicial opinion ever left upon record,"[20] although it is not easy to discern a politically expedient alternative. Moray's friendship was bolstered by a £ 5,000 English loan, and Mary was sent to the Earl of Shrewsbury's safekeeping at Tutbury. Once again the incendiary Scottish affair had been damped down.

The year 1569 did not, however, prove a calm one. On the contrary, it brought the first crisis of Elizabeth's reign, the greatest the realm faced until the Spanish Armada.

Difficulties began in February, when a group of the more conservative noblemen attempted to contrive Cecil's overthrow. Led by Norfolk, who now strongly favored Mary and who cherished hopes of marrying her, the peers—probably Leicester, Northampton, Arundel, Pembroke, and possibly Winchester—resented Cecil's domination of English foreign policy and his strong Protestant leanings, which had been manifested through his support of the rebels in France and in the Low Countries as well as through his opposition to the Scottish Queen. Details of the peers' activities are vague, but, according to one account, Leicester told Elizabeth that Cecil's policies placed the realm in grave danger and urged her to insist that the Secretary justify his decisions. The Queen, to her credit, would have none of it (Cecil's policies, after all, were her policies); she reiterated her confidence in her chief minister, and the affair blew over.[21]

Unfortunately no account of Mildmay's role in this plot survives. He was certainly one of Cecil's principal advocates, although Mildmay's views may not have counted for much with the noblemen: perhaps their underlying grievance against Cecil was his acquisition of power unsupported by title or ancestry, and they doubtless also resented Mildmay's more modest rise. Still Mildmay was probably Cecil's

[20] P. F. Tytler, *History of Scotland*, VII, 217.
[21] Read, *Cecil*, pp. 441–454, is perhaps the best account of the plot.

closest friend on the Council; he could be relied on to uphold Cecil's position and to perform the routine work required to put Cecil's policies into effect. Indeed we catch a glimpse of the two men acting together at exactly the time of the plot. On February 21 they conferred with an envoy sent from the Netherlands to negotiate for the resumption of friendly relations after the English seizure of Genoese gold destined for the Low Countries, late in 1568, and the retaliatory seizure of English goods in the Netherlands by the Dutch. On the same day Cecil and Mildmay informed the Queen and the Council of the negotiations. On February 22—Ash Wednesday, the day of Leicester's angry speech to the Queen—Cecil drafted a reply to the Dutch, which was read to the Councillors present and accepted by the Queen the following day. "And her Majesty . . . commanded Sir Walter Mildmay to impart it to the Lord Keeper, the Lord Treasurer, and the Lord Steward, being absent, who did the 25th of February and reported their several allowances."[22]

With the Queen's support for Cecil manifest, the conservative noblemen were forced to raise their sights, to aim at undermining the entire government. This they attempted in November.

Their discontent lay covered during the seemingly quiet summer. Mildmay probably spent most of the time at Apethorpe with his family. His older son, Anthony, had passed several months in Paris with Sir Henry Norris, the English ambassador, but Mildmay called him home in March.[23] Two years earlier Anthony, although "more willinge to travile to get experience of the world than to marry so soone," had wed Grace Sharington, the fifteen-year-old daughter of Sir Henry Sharington of Lacock Abbey in Wiltshire. According to Grace's own account "his father told him, yf he did not marry me, he should never bring any other woman into his house, upon which importunitie of his father he was content and entered into communication what joynter he would make me, and what allowance he would give for our mainte-

---

[22] Cot. MS Galba C. III, fol. 189, quoted in Read, *Cecil*, p. 444. It is perhaps indicative of the intimacy between Cecil and Mildmay that Cecil in this reply refers to the other Councillors by title or full surname but calls Mildmay only "Mr. M." The envoy's statement and Cecil's answer are calendared in *CSP, For., 1569–71*, Nos. 129, 136.

[23] *CSP, For., 1569–71*, No. 185 (March 22).

nance in his owne tyme; his father promising with tears to give him all that he had."[24] Grace and Anthony no doubt summered at Apethorpe with Anthony's parents, his younger brother Humphrey, who was preparing to enter Peterhouse in the autumn, and his younger sisters.[25]

August at Apethorpe must have been a busy time of preparation for the marriage of Sir Walter's daughter Winifred to William Fitzwilliam, son of Sir William Fitzwilliam of Milton, one of the ablest Tudor administrators in Ireland and, like Mildmay, a great Northamptonshire landowner. Mildmay mentioned plans for the wedding as well as matters of state in a letter to Cecil of September 8. His epistolary style appears here at its best:

> Sir, I most hartelie thanke you, that in the heape of the carefull busines wherwith you are daylie pressed, you wold vowchsaufe to visite me, so farre absent, with your lettres. Gladder I wold have been to have seene you here at your owne, emongest your frendes, as heretofore I have doon, but because that will not be, and untill leasoure may bettre serve you, I will take the use of your sonne, my good neighbor and frend, whom I assure you

[24] MS diary of Grace Mildmay in the Northampton Public Library, quoted in Rachel Weigall, "An Elizabethan Gentlewoman," *Quarterly Review,* CCXV (1911), 122. There were later serious difficulties over Grace's inheritance. Her father had willed his lands to his three daughters in equal parts, with the provision that "everie of them sholde be eche others heire, if any of them should dye without issue." This clause should have come into effect when the oldest sister, who had married Sir Ralph Sadler's son, died childless; but John Talbot, husband of the second sister, "alleadged that Sir Henrie Sharington by will made the daie before he died had graunted in revertion after his wiffe, the most parte of all his landes to the said John Talbot and his wiffe, and to hir heires, for one thousand yeares, without any rent; by that meanes leaving nothing to my sonnes wiffe but one mannour, and that not altogeather without controversie." Mildmay had to bring suit to recover Grace's estates. See his memorandum, SP 12/151/8.

[25] In April, 1570, Mildmay wrote a brief "Memorial" for his son Anthony. Published by the Rev. Arundell St. John Mildmay in 1893 from a MS at Apethorpe, it is reminiscent of Polonius's proverbs: "Speak well of all. Speak ill of none. . . . Let thy house the poor but not the vagabond relieve. Consider thy revenue and frame thy charge thereafter. . . . Grieve not thy tenants with exactions. . . . Love God. Fear Him. Learn to live and die." A copy is in the BM, shelfmark 1882. c. 2 (164).

I cannot make so moche of as he doeth deserve towardes me; but to my powre he shall fynd my good will aunswerable to his curtesie.

Apparently Cecil had asked Mildmay if the Northamptonshire gentry were discussing the proposed match between Mary and Norfolk, news of which seemed to spread the more rapidly because it was secret. Mildmay answered:

It is veary true that moche hath been spoken here in the countrye towch- ing the matier ye wright of, and as men are diversly affected, so the same is diverslie received. I have had litle understanding of certaintie save this from you, with whom I joyne and agree, with all my hart, that nothing be don without the Queens Majesties good contentacion and safety, and the pres- ervation of the cause of religion, uppon which twoo principall pillers, as you know, the hole state of our commonwealth is fownded, and which neglected, we canne looke for nothing but ruine and desolation. But whie thus to you? And yet I could not but expresse thus muche of myn owne disposition, which I am sure is knowen to you well inough. God, I trust, will conduct all to the best, and for his glorie. To him I doe commend you and my good Lady, with a remembraunce of good will and old frendship from me and my wiffe to you both.

And if you and my Lady could be here with a wisshe, we woulde be glad to have you on Monday next, at which day, God willing, the mariage shalbe ended betwene my dawghter and yong Mr. Fitzwilliams. Whereat wilbe present many of your frendes in this countrie, to whom I will not fayle to deliver your commendations, according to your desire.

And so I leave to trowble you, ending with my hartie thankes for the Frenche newes ye sent me.[26]

Mildmay probably returned to London soon after the wedding. On October 1 Moray, who was effectively pacifying the borders, wrote to his "verie loving and assuerit freend" Mildmay from Kelso. The Regent had sent Robert Pitcairn, the commendator of Dunfermline, to explain to Elizabeth and the Council the dangers which would result from any plan to restore Mary. "I will not weare yow . . . with the repeticion of anything quhilk [which] I have committit to his suf- ficiency," Moray wrote, with characteristic Scots spelling; "bot trusting

[26] SP 12/58/22.

yat ye will heare and credit him in that quhilk he sall speik on my behalf as myself, I commit yow in the protection of God."[27]

By the time Dunfermline arrived his instructions must have been of
little relevance, for Elizabeth grew more wary of Mary and Norfolk
late in September. Norfolk, who had offended the Queen with his
marriage plans, gave further offense by leaving London without her
consent. He was sent to the Tower early in October, and Arundel,
Pembroke, Throgmorton, and Lumley were arrested and interrogated.
Leicester, who still sympathized with Norfolk and disliked Cecil's
policies, abjectly begged pardon and escaped with a severe censure.[28]

The suspicious activities of Norfolk and his supporters caused the
Council to reconsider its policies regarding Mary. A memorandum of
Mildmay's views, presented before the Privy Council October 26 at
Windsor, has survived.[29] His position is typically moderate and well
considered; he weighs the arguments on each side, refutes some of
them, and finally draws his tentative conclusions, subject to modifica-
tion if other Councillors advance telling criticism.

Mildmay's paper attempts to decide "whether it be less perilous to
the Queen's Majesty and the realm to retain the Queen of Scots in England, or to return her home into Scotland." He lists first the dangers
which will be encountered if she is kept in England:

Her unquiet and aspiring mind, never ceasing to practice with the
Queen's subjects. Her late practice of marriage between the Duke of Norfolk and her, without the Queen's knowledge. The faction of the Papists,
and other ambitious folks being ready and fit instruments for her to work
upon. The commiseration that ever followeth such as be in misery, though
their deserts be never so great. Her cunning and sugred entertainments of
all men that come to her, whereby she gets both credit and intelligence. Her
practice with the French and Spanish ambassadors, being more near to her in
England than if she were in Scotland; and their continual solicitation of
the Queen for her delivery, the denial whereof may breed war. The danger

---

[27] Westm. MSS, 2, XII, 1, D13. See Lee, *Moray*, p. 264.

[28] Read, *Cecil*, pp. 450–453.

[29] Printed in E. and G. Goldsmid, eds., *A Collection of Eighteen Rare and
Curious Historical Tracts and Pamphlets*, XV, 3–10, and in Gilbert Burnet,
*History of the Reformation of the Church of England*, Part II, Book III, No.
12, pp. 369–372. I have not been able to trace the original.

of her escaping out of guard, whereof it is like enough she will give the attempt. So as remaining here, she hath time and opportunity to practice and nourish factions, by which she may work confederacy, and therefore may follow sedition and tumult, which may bring peril to the state. Finally, it is said that the Queen's Majesty, of her own disposition, hath no mind to retain her, but is much unquieted therewith, which is a thing greatly to be weighed.

Should the Council favor Mary's return to Scotland, Mildmay urges a number of cautionary measures. Mary should be delivered safely into Moray's keeping. She should agree not to meddle in government or religion, and she should give hostages to insure that she would abide by her promises. The "auld alliance" between Scotland and France should never be renewed but should be replaced by a perpetual league with England. Finally, "the faults whereof she hath been accused, and her declining and delaying to answer the accusation," should be "published to the world, the better to discourage her factious party, both here and in Scotland."

Mildmay feared, however, that such precautions would be insufficient. He was doubtful whether Mary should be allowed to enter Scotland at her liberty or should be delivered to the Regent under guard; "for if she be delivered in guard, that came hither free and at liberty, how will that stand with the Queen's honour, and with the requests of the French and Spanish kings, that have continually solicited her free delivery, either into Scotland or France; or if she die in guard, either violently or naturally, her Majesty shall hardly escape slander." If, on the other hand, Mary were given her liberty, Mildmay foresaw new dangers:

The suppressing of the present government in Scotland, now depending upon the Queen's Majesty, and the advancing of the contrary faction depending upon the French. The alteration of religion in Scotland. The renewing of the league offensive and defensive between France and Scotland, that hath so much troubled England. The renewing of her pretended claim to the crown of this realm. The likelyhood of war to ensue between France, Scotland, and us. . . . The supportation that she is like to have of the French and Spanish kings. . . . The likelyhood she will revoke the Earl Bothwell, now her husband, though unlawful, as is said, a man of most evil and cruel affection to this realm and to his own countrymen: or, if she should marry

81

another that were alike enemy, the perils must needs be great on either side.

Some of these threats, Mildmay admitted, might be guarded against by making Mary sign a treaty and give hostages. Still, she might later maintain that no document signed in England was binding, "for she will alleage the same to be done in a forreign country, being restrained of liberty." Wherever she is kept in Scotland she is likely to escape; "the country being, as it is, greatly divided, and of nature marvellously factious, she is the more like to bring it to pass." Although Moray's alliance with England seemed firm enough, he might capitulate to Mary, or he might suffer defeat or assassination, "the like whereof is said hath been attempted against him." Did Mildmay actually realize that the Hamilton faction was plotting to kill Moray, or suspect that within six months they would succeed? Yet the Regent was essential to the English cause. "The case is very tickle and dangerous to hang upon so small a thread as the life of one man, by whom it appeareth the whole at this present is contained." Hostages could not insure safety, for Mary "will make little conscience of the hostages if she may prevail, and the punishing of the hostages will be a small satisfaction to the Queen's Majesty for the troubles that may ensue."

Mildmay concluded that Mary should be continued in English custody: "more safe it is for the Queen to keep the bridle in her own hand, to restrain the Scottish Queen, than in returning her home to commit that trust to others, which by death, composition, or abusing of one person may be disappointed." It had been suggested that Elizabeth herself would never be quiet so long as Mary remained in England. "That is a matter greatly to be weighed, for it were better to adventure all, than her Majesty should inwardly conceive anything to the danger of her health." But Mildmay hoped that the perils of retaining Mary might be made plain to Elizabeth and, overoptimistically, that the English Queen might "be induced easily to change her opinion, and thereby may follow . . . her Majesty's great satisfaction and quietness."

If the Council and the Queen agreed that Mary should be retained, Mildmay felt that several precautions were necessary. She should be brought closer to London, so that the government might know about her actions more easily. She should be delivered to the custody of men "most sound in religion and most void of practice." The number of her retainers should be halved, to reduce expense and to give Mary fewer channels for intelligence. All letters, messages, and visitors, except those approved by her guardians, should be forbidden her. Lastly, England should attempt to gain the support of continental rulers through propaganda, by showing "the occasion of this streight guard upon her to be her late practice with the Duke of Norfolk, which hath given the Queen cause to doubt, further assuring them that she shall be used honourably, but kept safe from troubling the Queen's Majesty or this state."

While the Council anxiously balanced Mildmay's thoughtful recommendations against the Queen's more emotional sympathies, several of the Northern noblemen plotted rebellion and the forced release of the Scottish Queen. This, the famous Rising of the North, may be considered a larger-scale sequel to the earlier intrigues against Cecil within the Council. It was led by Thomas Percy, Earl of Northumberland, and Charles Neville, Earl of Westmorland. Both had long opposed the new religion and the new nobility which dominated the government, keeping them from membership in the Privy Council. They had been persuaded by the Spanish ambassador to endorse the Norfolk marriage plan, and they counted on the support of hundreds of ordinary subjects in the North, still Catholic at heart.[30]

The activities of the two earls had aroused suspicion as early as September, 1569, when the Privy Council ordered the Earl of Sussex, president of the Council of the North and the government's principal representative there, to be on guard against seditious speeches and unlawful actions. Sussex, who was a friend of Norfolk's and perhaps sympathetic to the earls, replied that there was no need for concern. But rumors continued to reach London, and late in October the Queen ordered Northumberland and Westmorland to court, where they could be watched. The earls refused to appear; their followers celebrated mass in Durham Cathedral, dramatically treading the Prayer Book underfoot. On November 13 Sussex finally proclaimed Northumberland and Westmorland rebels and began action against them.

In an attempt to insure the loyalty of local officials, the government

[30] One of the best accounts of the rising is found in Read, *Cecil*, pp. 455–468.

on November 18 required justices of the peace and certain other prominent gentlemen to subscribe to the Oath of Uniformity, promising to observe the Act of Uniformity, to attend their parish churches regularly, and to receive the Sacrament from time to time. Mildmay was among the Northamptonshire signatories.[31] Two days later he and Sir Robert Tirwhit were named lieutenants-general for Huntingdonshire, to prepare the county's resistance against the rebels; similar commissions were sent out for the other shires.[32]

It soon became apparent that Sussex was unable to raise adequate forces in the North itself, so the Council dispatched Lord Admiral Clinton with an army from Lincolnshire and the Earl of Warwick with Warwickshire troops. Hunsdon, Bedford, and Sadler were also sent north to aid Sussex and report on his performance.

Mildmay scribbled a long letter to Sadler November 30. He was "veary glad, by your lettres of the 26th, to understand of your sauffe arrivall at Yorke, the rather as that fynding the passage stopped, you were driven to take another way." Since Sadler had doubts that the Council would support him adequately, Mildmay assured him that the forces would "be in better strangth shortlie. . . . Of the army prepared from hence for your assistance under the Erle of Warwik and my Lord Admirall I am sure you here. They goe forwardes with all spede possible. . . . Order is geven for your help in munition, and for money there is presentlie sent you 2000[11]." As a final word of comfort, Mildmay wrote that "the Queens Majestie liked well of your spedy repayre to York, and reposeth in singuler trust in you for the furtheraunce of hir issue there, wherof every man here is most assured."[33]

Mildmay and Cecil both sent their sons north to join the army. Cecil's weak older son, Thomas, commanded three hundred horses under Sussex; Anthony Mildmay served under Clinton. The Admiral acknowledged Anthony's arrival on December 1 in a letter directed "hast, hast, post hast, with all dyligence" to Sir Walter. With a military man's disregard of the niceties of spelling and grammar, he wrote:

Good Mr. Myldmay, I do most hartely thank you for the trust you have comyttyd to me of your sone, who this day aryvyed here with me in good

[31] SP 12/59/22.
[32] HMC, *Cal. Salisbury MSS*, I, No. 1409.
[33] Add. MS 33,593, fol. 39.

helth. Sir, you myght a sent hym to som other parsinage of beter abylety to have shoyd him more plentifulli then I am, bot seurly no man can be gladar of his friend then I am of his company, nor can be better welcom to none then to me, and think myself more bownd to yow that doth declare so moch favor to me as to trust me with your sone, and will se hym fornyshed with all thinges that is mete for him in this sarvys. My Lord of Leyster hath very ernestly wrytyn to me to have specyall regard to hym and to se hym ussyd in all thinges as I best may, which I hope I shall obsarve with as good a wyll as any man may doo.

Clinton, like Sadler, complained of the army's weakness: he had experienced great difficulty in gathering harquebusiers, and those he could recruit were "very unexpert and unredy"; he also found few "and bot wekly horsid" cavalrymen.[34]

Mildmay wrote Sadler again December 17 to inform him that "hir Majestie hath resolved to send six thowsand poundes more to be delivered to your handes, part wherof is to be paid in grosse to Mr. Carew by my Lord Admiralles order and yors for that company, and the rest to be with you for my Lord of Sussex band."[35]

The rebellion in fact did not amount to as much as the Council had feared. Rebel forces melted away as Sussex took the offensive. The two earls fled into Scotland on December 21. Hunsdon put down the last flicker of resistance in February, defeating Leonard Dacre in the only major engagement of the campaign.

The government's leaders next concentrated on finding rebels to be punished. Here Clinton and Warwick came into violent conflict with Sussex: they took affairs into their own hands, flouting Sussex's superior authority by pardoning rebels and plundering at will. Sadler and Hunsdon, as impartial observers, sided with Sussex. Hunsdon, in a letter to Cecil, grieved that the Queen was persuaded to think worst of those who served her best.[36] Sadler poured out his woe to Mildmay on January 9, 1570. He had "not sene in my lif any nobleman" act with more "diligent care and travaile then [Sussex] doth. . . . Surely he is one of the most paynefull [painstaking] men, and in my judgement so sufficient to execute this office as I know not many lyk him in England."

[34] SP 12/60/9.
[35] Add. MS 33,593, fol. 63.
[36] Read, *Cecil*, p. 463.

If his work were misconstrued it was therefore the more tragic. "Howbeit, as I am sure he shall not be condempned before he be hard, so shall you fynde him well able to answer to all his doinges here in such part as I trust it shall well appere that no fault can be justly imputid unto him."[37] Cecil agreed with this view, and he and Mildmay probably did what they could to raise Sussex's stock with the Queen and the other Councillors.[38]

Sadler added that Mildmay could "do us greate pleasure here to helpe us with money, for it hath not been our lucke to have any good porcion of that which hath bin sent hither. . . . I assure you 6000[11] will not discharge that which is due here at this present, wherof I trust my lordes you and others of the Councell will have such consideracion as the portaunce of the mater doth requyre."

Cecil favored harsh action against the rebels, hoping to make examples of them and to improve the government's finances through confiscations. Some five hundred of the poorer sort were executed; wealthier men lost their lands or were allowed to compound for them. With such legal action added to the Southern army's illicit plunder the Northern shires, always poor, were pushed to the verge of destitution and starvation.

On November 15, two days before the twelfth anniversary of her accession, Elizabeth acknowledged the rebellion's collapse by revoking her extraordinary commissions to lieutenants-general. Her grateful letter to Mildmay and Tirwhit explains:

Wheras upon the attempt of the late rebellion in a part of the Northe we did cheise and ordeyn youe of speciall trust by our lettres patentes to be our Lieutenauntes Generall in our county of Huntingdon, to exercise the same during our pleasur; forasmoch as by the goodnes of Almighty God through the faithfull and chardgeable service of our good subjectes in all degres, not only the said rebellion was spedely supressed, but the rest of our realm was stayd and now so contynueth in quiet order and good peax, wherin your care hath ben very good and thankfull: we have determined to ceasse the sayd commissione through our realm. And therfore we do also signifie to youe by thies presentes that we are pleased to relieve youe of the burden and chardg of the sayd office, and by thies presentes do dischardge

[37] Add. MS 33,593, fols. 105–106.
[38] Read, *Cecil,* p. 462.

you of the same commission, therwith also giving you our harty thankes for your care and paynes taken and chardgeably susteyned therin. And do requier youe to contynue in all maner good assistence to our ordinary officers, as namely our Shireif and the Justices of Peax in the same countye for the contynuance of good peace amongst our good subjectes, and to avoyde all ryottes and disorders against the common peax of the same, and specially to provide that the sowers of seditious rumoure may be diligently seen unto and sharply punishid.[39]

Peaceful though England might be, new disorders had broken out in Scotland, involving the Council in a reassessment of its policies and Mildmay in an embassy to Mary, Queen of Scots.

[39] Westm. MSS, 2, XII, 1, D7.

# 7. NEGOTIATIONS WITH MARY
## 1570–1571

O N JANUARY 23, 1570, the Earl of Moray was assassinated at Stirling. As Regent he had succeeded in controlling Scotland and placating Elizabeth; with his death the whole Scottish question was reopened. The English government was faced with awkward alternatives: should it give formal recognition to Mary's son, James, thereby risking the intervention of France and Spain, or should it attempt to restore Mary to her throne in the face of Scottish opposition and in spite of her religion?

To show England's strength and to punish the Scots for their cooperation in the Northern rising, the Council and the Queen agreed to send Sussex on an expedition into the border country, where he burned strongholds of Marian support as far north as Jedburgh and Kelso. On the more fundamental question, however, the Council was divided. Leicester and Arundel, with the sympathy of the greater noblemen and the Queen, favored Mary's restoration on suitable terms; Cecil, Bacon, and probably also Mildmay, Bedford, Sadler, and Sussex argued that the King's party must be strengthened and that it would be disastrous to free Mary.[1]

On April 29 the Queen herself sat with the Council to debate Scottish policy. Since the Council register covering this period is lost, we do not know whether Mildmay took part in these deliberations. On May 24, when the register resumes, we find him attending the Council session at Hampton Court. He was present on May 29, when there

---

[1] Accounts of the Council's discussions are not so full as one would wish, but this explanation of its position seems the most probable. See Conyers Read, *Lord Burghley and Queen Elizabeth*, pp. 18–22.

must have been worried consultation about the Papal bull, excommunicating Elizabeth and absolving subjects from allegiance to her, which had been nailed to the Bishop of London's door four days earlier. It has been suggested that the bull was the impelling factor in the negotiations with Mary,[2] but the reverse seems to be correct; Elizabeth wrote in a letter of June 6 that the "new indirect course taken here and practiced on the Scottish Queen's behalf to abuse us" had moved her "not to proceede either in such sort or with such speed to her advantage as before we were inclined."[3] In any case the Council was not stampeded into action, but continued to discuss the situation throughout the summer. Mildmay was among the six or seven Councillors who attended regularly in June, although he was absent during July, August, and the first half of September.[4] He probably spent the months at Apethorpe.

By September Elizabeth and her Councillors had decided to negotiate with Mary, to see if she would meet the conditions they thought necessary for her restoration. On September 1 the Bishop of Ross, Mary's representative, had audiences with Elizabeth and Cecil. Shortly thereafter the Bishop heard that the Queen had named Cecil and Mildmay as her agents in the discussions, and that Mildmay had been ordered to court.[5] By the seventeenth he was at Reading, attending a Council meeting and receiving instructions. He did not relish his assignment: "God be our guide," Cecil wrote, "for neither of us like the message."[6]

News of the impending embassy spread. On September 16 Thomas Randolph wrote Sussex that the only Scots who had so far received word were Matthew Stuart, Earl of Lennox, the new Regent, and James Douglas, Earl of Morton, a leader of the King's party.[7] The Queen herself wrote her ambassador in France on September 25, hoping that

---

[2] Read, *Burghley*, p. 24.

[3] Sloane MS 3199, fol. 51ᵛ.

[4] *APC, 1558–70, passim.*

[5] *CSP, Scot.*, III, No. 437.

[6] Read, *Burghley*, p. 27. Cecil feigned illness but soon recovered when the Queen decided to send Knollys in his place; cf. La Mothe Fénelon, *Correspondance Diplomatique*, ed. Alexandre Teulet, III, 310–311.

[7] *CSP, Scot.*, III, No. 464.

news of the negotiations would please the French court.[8] On the same day she sent word to the Earl of Shrewsbury, Mary's keeper, requiring him to give Cecil and Mildmay his assistance.[9] The Queen also wrote Sussex, who had remained in Scotland, officially notifying him of the embassy and ordering him to prevent, if he could, the assembly of a Scottish Parliament which might take action against Mary. He was also to secure an extension of the truce between her party and the King's.[10]

Although masses of papers relating to the negotiations survive, the story of the embassy has never been written in detail. Cecil's most recent biographer seems to assume that its failure was a foregone conclusion, that even Elizabeth did not expect it to succeed but thought it might for a time soothe the Catholics in Paris, Madrid, and Rome. He supports this view by noting that both Cecil and Mildmay were of the party which had opposed Mary's restoration.[11] Other writers, including most of Mary's biographers, have glossed over the discussions, probably because in the end they proved fruitless and did not alter Mary's position.[12] One who reads the instructions and letters of the negotiators, however, finds it hard to believe that the embassy was not a serious attempt to settle the Marian problem. Mere play acting would not have required so much paper and ink.

Elizabeth's instructions to Cecil and Mildmay were issued September 17. In them she emphasized the "motions . . . made to us by our good brother the Frenche Kinge, & by his mother the Queene, and by other princes to here & understand what offres and condicions the Queene of Scottes . . . will make to us for recoverie of our favour, & for assurance of better amitie to be made & contynued betwixt us & our countryes." She mentioned also Mary's "sondry lettres and messages to us," offering "in generalitie to assent & accorde unto anie condicions

[8] *Ibid.,* No. 485.
[9] HMC, *Cal. Salisbury MSS,* I, No. 1521.
[10] *CSP, Scot.,* III, No. 509 (October 7).
[11] Read, *Burghley,* p. 26.
[12] See, e.g., J. B. Black, *The Reign of Elizabeth,* second ed., pp. 146–147; T. F. Henderson, *Mary Queen of Scots,* II, 537; Samuel Cowan, *Mary Queen of Scots,* II, 70–72; N. Brysson Morrison, *Mary Queen of Scots,* pp. 259–260. Philip Hughes refers briefly to the negotiations as a "sham" and as "disingenuous" (*The Reformation in England,* III, xv, 277).

that wee should require reasonably of her." The conciliatory phrases were perhaps designed more for the French court than the envoys:

Wee having alwayes a naturall disposition to have lyved in suche love, amitie & accorde with the said Queene as was mete for us, specially shee being soe nere to us in bloode & neighbourhoode, and to that ende having passed over at [divers] tymes, otherwise then other princes have done in like cases, su[ch re]venge as wee might by manie wayes have taken for her unkind injurious devises, attemptes & faites: yet nowe of mere compass[ion for her] sondry calamities, and hoping that Almighty God will by her adversities induce her to reforme her usages towardes us according to her promises, . . . wee doe sende yow two, being of our Privie Councell and persons of singuler truste for your fidelities towards us, to repair to the said Scottish Queene to understand from [her]selfe and by her owne mouthe in what sorte shee meaneth . . .

The envoys, if they found Mary sincere in her desire for a settlement, should seek her approval of the articles in the draft treaty. They were to "enlarge [their] speaches to her by waye of intreatie to move her to consent to the same, or to the substaunce therof, as shall seme . . . best for our service."

Elizabeth was also concerned that Mary should come to suitable terms with James's party in Scotland. Although she had not entered into detailed discussions with members of the King's faction, perhaps because she realized that they were not likely to accept Mary's restoration even if it were on terms suitable to England, Elizabeth "annexed certeyne other articles by way of memorialls, suche as not having had any speciall conference with the Kinges partie to that ende, we have thought it metest in our oppinion for their suretie." Cecil and Mildmay were to discuss these "withowte making any full conclusion with [Mary] therin." Should representatives of James's party arrive while the envoys remained with Mary, Elizabeth was "pleased you shall motion unto her suche thinges as they shall requier, soe as you shall thinke them agreable to reason and not againste our honnor." If Mary peremptorily refused to accept any material part of the treaty, the ambassadors were to return without delay.[13]

[13] Add. MS 34,216, fol. 4. The edge of the MS is damaged; missing words are supplied in brackets. Another copy is Cot. MS Caligula C. II, fol. 424, calendared in *CSP, Scot.,* III, No. 497.

The proposed treaty contained twelve articles. The most important called on Mary to renounce any claim to the English throne so long as Elizabeth or her issue lived, to stand aloof from any alliance directed against England, to deliver into Elizabeth's hands the Earl of Northumberland and all other rebels in Scottish custody, and to prosecute the murderers of Darnley and Moray. She was not to undertake marriage negotiations, or receive intelligence from England, without Elizabeth's consent. "For the more suretie of the person of the young King against his enemies that murdered his father, . . . and also in consideration that he shall be one hostage for the Queen his moder," the treaty provided that James should be brought into England and reside there, under the government of appropriate Scottish lords, during Elizabeth's pleasure. He was to be restored to the Scottish throne on Mary's death, or earlier if she chose to abdicate in his favor.

For further assurance that the terms of the treaty would be observed, Elizabeth asked Mary to give six hostages—three earls and three other lords of Parliament—who would remain in England for three years after Mary's return to Scotland. Elizabeth also sought control of certain castles on the Scottish border and in Ireland. Should Mary aid in any plot to depose Elizabeth, she would thereby forfeit all rights of succession to the English throne. Finally, Elizabeth required that the treaty be confirmed by a Scottish Parliament.[14]

Cecil and Mildmay were armed with a series of "reasons to move the Queene of Scottes" to accept the treaty; these were to "be used as cause shalbe gyven by her manner of aunsweres." The ambassadors were first to remind Mary of her wrongdoing: she had "pretend[ed] title to the crowne of England, and attempt[ed] by sondry wayes to attaine to the same"; she had refused to confirm her renunciation of the Scottish throne "althoughe she was bounde therto bothe in honor and by her greate seale"; "she did allure the L. Darnley, the Queen's kynnesman

---

[14] A number of copies of these articles exist. Add. MS 34,216, fols. 5–6, is a copy of the instructions and articles given to Cecil and Mildmay. Sloane MS 3199, fols. 47–51, contains the articles and Mary's answers to them. Three copies are held at Hatfield (see HMC, *Cal. Salisbury MSS*, I, No. 1524). Cot. MS Caligula C. II, fol. 42 (calendared in *CSP, Scot.*, III, No. 494), is a draft, corrected in Cecil's hand, of additional articles relating to the settlement of Scottish lands and offices.

and naturall subjecte, to come into Scotland, and did marry with him againste the Queen's will"; "she did secretly kepe and mainteyne fugityves owte of England, to practise with them against the Queen's Majestie"; she had continued scheming against Elizabeth even while her guest in England; she "procured" the rebellion of Westmorland and Northumberland; she "practised secretlie aboute a mariage withowte the Queen's consent."

Despite these wrongs, Elizabeth had treated Mary with every consideration. Mildmay and Cecil were to point out that Elizabeth had saved Mary's life at Loch Leven, had refrained from charging her publicly with the murder of her husband, and had "taken noe avenge upon her person here in England, as manie worldly princes would have done," instead treating her honorably and maintaining her courtly household. Further, Elizabeth had refused to lend full support to James or to recognize his title to the throne, thus keeping open the possibility of Mary's restoration.[15] These arguments, although one-sided, were in the main true enough. Indeed they expressed the precise reasons for some Councillors' irritation with Elizabeth.

Mildmay and Cecil left Reading September 26.[16] They should have reached Chatsworth, where Mary was living in Shrewsbury's custody, after several days' ride, but heavy rains and floods delayed them. "We could not," they wrote the Queen, "before this day, being Sonday [October 1], well come to theis howse, the wayes being soe harde to passe with anie speede."

They spoke with Mary almost immediately after their arrival.

And being come hether aboute three of the clocke, . . . after some pawse used by ourselves, we repaired to the Queene of Scottes, being in her privy chamber where she was under her clothe of estate. And at our entry she came towardes us, and after our reverence done and your Majestes lettres

[15] Add. MS 34,216, fol. 7. Another copy of these arguments is Cot. MS Caligula C. II, fol. 452; they are calendared in *CSP, Scot.*, III, No. 498.

[16] Read, *Burghley*, p. 27. Guerau de Spes, the Spanish ambassador, gives September 27 in a dispatch to Philip (*CSP, Spn., 1568–79*, No. 220), but Fénelon says in a letter of the twenty-ninth that the ambassadors left the previous Tuesday, which would have been September 26 (*Correspondance*, III, 319).

delyvered to her, she saied that ther could be nothinge on the earthe more welcome to her then to have anie persons sent from your Majestie her gude sister, after that shee hath bene soe longe here in your realme withowte anie comfort, and also to receive lettres from your Majestie, which she had not nowe of longe tyme done.

When Mary opened Elizabeth's letters, however, "she chaunged her countenaunce as seeming to be muche trowbled therewith." Weeping, she said that "she was . . . muche greeved to perceive that her good will & minde to please your Majestie was not soe understand, and nothing more greeved her then to be noted by your Majestie with the cryme of ingratitude."

Cecil and Mildmay proceeded to explain the reason for their coming. Mary was not pleased; seizing the opportunity for a dramatic scene,

. . . she then lifted upp her speache somewhat higher, and said that she never did offende your Majestie in anie speache wherof she would be reported by anie that ever was in her companie, and for her thought she referred herselfe to the indulgence of Allmightie God, and wished that her harte & thoughtes mighte lye open to your Majestie, with sondry other vehement speaches to that purpose. Wherupon we were bold to replye, and sayed that thoughe God had not ordered that the hartes of creatures should be opened to expresse the inward thoughtes, yett the actes & deedes of creatures did allwayes discover and lay open the hartes, and therof we were sure that your Majestie had good proofes by manie sondry her former actes to thinke that she had dealt unkindlye, yea injuriouslye with your Majestie and evill recompenced for your kindnes. And therfore wee thought her best waye was to persiste in that she had heretofore soe often tymes and nowe to us declared, that she would doe anie thinge to make satisfaccion for the same to your Majestie, which yow woulde no wise seeke but with condiccions reasonable, favourable and honorable, and the cause of the delaye hetherto to treate hereof hath onely proceeded of herselfe, and such as have avowed their evill doinges under her authoritie.

At this Mary again changed her countenance and said that she "woulde in anie thinge to be requiered doe her uttermost to make amends." She especially hoped that she might talk with Elizabeth personally, but Cecil and Mildmay explained that this was unlikely, since "princes be lyke mountaynes that hardely can meete; . . . they lacke therin the commoditie which pryvate persons doe enjoye." At this the interview ended.[17]

Next morning the commissioners and Shrewsbury met with Mary and her chief advisor, the Bishop of Ross, in a private gallery. They had hoped to enter into detailed discussions of the draft treaty, but Mary again protested the charges against her and the interview "was somewhate clowdye by her often weepinge." Cecil and Mildmay described the scene for Elizabeth.

She said she could not but contynue her greife that [she] conseaved by your Majestes lettres, and before she could enter into anie communicacion of anie other matter, she desyered us to heare what [she] coulde saye in her defence, and also whate wee could charge her with, so as she mighte answere. Wherunto we tolde her that we had noe meaning to charge her with anie thinge, except by her defence of [her]selfe she woulde occasion us so to doee. And in the ende she assent[ed] and entred into greate earnest attestacions of her conscience & howe muche she desyered your Majestes favour, & howe voyde shee was of [any] evill thought, and then we begonne to charge her with all maner of [things] conteyned in our instruccions, beginning att her pretence made to prejudice your Highnes title, and soe with all thinges unkyndly done in Scotland, [and] perilous thinges here in England. To all which she laboured to make particuler aunswers, but we found her most trowbled and amazed with that we charged her to have had intelligence with your Majestes rebels, wherin she would not denye but she understood diverse thinges from [them], but they never had comforte from her; [when we said] that she did not well concealing of thinges uttered to her, she saied, when [she] made so earnest sute at Bolton to come to your presence, she ment then to have shewed your Majestie some thinges that she otherwise could not doe. In the debate of theis matters, she often tymes fell into weepinges & sorrowfull speaches, and soe wee contynued by her owne occasions and repeticions of her defences untill xij of the clocke, soe as we left of[f] withowte entering into the articles of our instructions.

Finally on Monday afternoon Cecil and Mildmay discussed the articles with Mary. She proved surprisingly cooperative.

. . . she made answere very readilie and willinglie to the more parte in nombre, and of all others she most earnestlie assented and with speaches

[17] Add. MS 34,216, fol. 7ᵛ.

to appearaunce from her harte, yelded to the articles that provide the penalltyes to be deprived of anie title she can have to this crowne, and that your Majestie shall sett up her sonne yf she attempte anie thinge prejudiciall to your crowne.

She asked for a copy of the articles and said that, after she had studied them, she would make her answers in writing. Cecil and Mildmay thought that she depended heavily upon the advice of the Bishop of Ross, who was "very ready . . . to move her to assent." His position seems to have been that any concession was justified so long as it brought Mary closer to regaining her throne.

While these negotiations were going forward the weather remained foul. "This morning," Cecil and Mildmay wrote, "we have seen winter entred into thes freakishe mountaynes, having a large snowe fallen rounde aboute us, soe as yf the weather followe as it hath begonne we shall wishe ourselves awaye."[18]

Three days elapsed before the envoys wrote their second report, which they sent to Elizabeth October 5. They found Mary less willing to assent to the articles than she had seemed at first; she told Mildmay and Cecil that "upon the reading and further wayenge of them she founde moe difficulties for her then she before conceaved." When they met with her,

. . . she shewed us sondry dowbtes that she newlie conceaved, wherof some she sayed appeared to her very harde to be kepte, som perilous for her to assent to, thoughe she ment never so sincerlye, and in some other partes, she desyered to have some wordes only chaunged or mitigated. And after some newe conference & debating with her & the B. of Rosse, by whose advice she openlie appeareth to us to be most directed in theis causes, she was by us better resolved in manie pointes and so induced to forbeare sondry of her alteracions. But as to the rest that shall upon the reading appeare to your Majestie upon collacion of both to differ from ours, we could not by anie perswacions move either her or the Busshoppe to forbeare the chaunge in them.

The envoys told Mary that they had no power to yield to her alterations, but they did finally agree to submit them to Elizabeth's judgment.

Most of Mary's objections were to the wording of the articles, not

18 *Ibid.*, fols. 7ᵛ–8ᵛ.

to their real substance.[19] For instance, she complained about a reference to "her sonnes tyme" because it implied recognition of James's kingship, and in a clause relating to her claim to the English throne she insisted that only Elizabeth's "leeful issue," not "any issue to come of her body," should have precedence. A few matters were more serious. Mary demanded insertion of a section pledging Elizabeth not to allow any act of Parliament to prejudice the rights of the Stuarts. She would not agree to repatriate Northumberland and the other rebels who had fled into Scotland unless Elizabeth promised to grant them clemency, for "the Queen of Scotts cannot think that it may stand with her honor to delyver those who are cumming for refuge within her country as it were to entre them to the place of execution." Mary conceded that Darnley's death should be avenged; concerning Moray's assassination "she was content the murder should be punished, but she would not covenaunte to prosecute it in like sorte as she would doe for her late husband."

Mary accepted more willingly than might have been expected the idea that her son should spend his minority under Elizabeth's care, but she did ask for several concessions. At first she thought that six years in England should suffice, but in the end Elizabeth's envoys "broughte her to xv yeres as in th'article, which is one full yere after he shall accomplish the yeres of consent." Mary insisted that she should have the right to name "one . . . to be aboute her sonne, . . . as well to shewe her love towardes him, as for that . . . he mighte be otherwise induced by sinister meanes to hate her or mislike her." She asked also for the privilege of visiting James once or twice a year; "her first request was to have the tymes oftener, and when wee sawe we coulde not prevaile therein, wee thoughte this privately to ourselves to be the worste, that for once in a yere or seldomer, the Prince being broughte to the castles of Norham or Warke being situat upon Tweede, she mighte be permitted to passe onely over the ryver & see her sonne in one of theis castles withowte comming anie further into this realme." Finally she asked Elizabeth to make some yearly contribution to the expense of maintaining James's household in England.

[19] Sloane MS 3199, fols. 47–51; Add. MS 34,216, fols. 12–13; printed in Alexandre Labanoff, ed., *Lettres, Instructions et Mémoires de Marie Stuart*, III, 90–105. Cf. HMC, *Cal. Salisbury MSS*, I, No. 1530.

As to the assurances that the treaty would not be broken, Mary was willing to yield to most of Elizabeth's demands. She did seek to have the number of hostages reduced and to obtain the exemption of certain "officers suche as could not be spared" in Scotland.

Mary and the envoys discussed the arrangements to be made within Scotland for her restoration, should she and Elizabeth come to terms. Cecil realized that nothing could be finally determined without the concurrence of the King's party, but he had prepared a program which seemed reasonable to the English Queen and Council. He advocated the summoning of a Scottish Parliament to declare that, although Mary's abdication in favor of her son had been valid, nevertheless she should resume the throne until he grew old enough to rule and she chose to give him power.[20] At the mention of her abdication Mary flew into another histrionic tantrum.

[When we said] that her sonne should kepe a Parliament, and therby render [the] crowne to her, she fell into a greate passion of weepinge, and would not suffer us to reade anie furdre, but vehementlie sayed that rather then . . . consent to anie thinge that should mean her dimission to have bene good, or that her sonne should be a[ccepted] as a King, . . . she would remitt herselfe to your Majesties mercy and remaine prisoner here during her life.

And yet to quiett her, we sayed that yf she would better consider of the articles she should finde that therby was not meante that anie thing should be uttered in her person to make the dimission good, but in the person of her sonne, whome she also seethe to have raigned by force or colour of that dimission. But no suche reason would satisfie her in that pointe, the Busshoppe in her presence alleadging that yf the Prince be not Kinge indeede, as they doo not take him, then a Parliament holden by him is to noe purpose, and if he were Kinge, as his partie woulde have him, then in lawe he saied no act don by him to dispossesse himselfe of the crowne in his minoritie coulde serve to anie purpose, wherunto thoughe we did not appeare to them to assent, yet we are in some dowbt howe with good reason to impugne it.

Mary also disliked other provisions, but the envoys thought that she could be brought to yield on many points: "yt semeth that she will accorde for your Majesties sake to pardon all whome you will, & gyve

[20] Cot. MS Caligula C. II, fol. 40, calendared in *CSP, Scot.,* III, No. 493; HMC, *Cal. Salisbury MSS,* I, No. 1525.

suretie to all for the tyme comminge, and assent to the observacion of the lawes for religion and suche other thinges as shalbe thoughte reasonable, soe as they will obey her as good subjectes." Cecil and Mildmay wrote that they would continue to discuss these matters while awaiting Elizabeth's reaction to the amended articles;[21] in fact Cecil, finding further negotiations not very useful and suffering from the gout, slipped away for a few days to take the waters at Buxton.[22]

Elizabeth's answer was not long delayed. By October 13 she had consulted the Councillors remaining at court and dispatched a long letter to her envoys.[23] Her attitude had obviously hardened as the negotiations at Chatsworth had progressed. Perhaps she was aware that Mary and the Bishop of Ross were in continued correspondence with Norfolk;[24] perhaps she found the Council dominated by Bacon and other strong opponents of Mary's restoration. Or perhaps she was moved by a treatise sent into England by the leaders of the King's party.[25] Undated but certainly of this period, it is a bitter denunciation of Mary as a murderer and an evil sovereign. Morton and his followers adduced examples from the history of France, Spain, Naples, Denmark, Lacedaemonia, and Scotland itself to prove "first, that the nobilitie of Scotland has power to correct thair kingis; secondlie, that a part may als wele do it as the haill [whole]; and thirdlie, how dangerous a thing it is that the subjectis qua [who] have anys schene [once shown] thame selfis contraries to the iniquitie of there wicked princes ever credit thame agane or becum subject to thair governament."[26]

In any case Elizabeth refused to allow most of Mary's alterations in the treaty. Although angered by Mary's implication that Elizabeth might bear an unlawful child—Mary, she wrote, "may peradventure measure other folkes dispositions by her [own] accions, which we

[21] Add. MS 34,216, fols. 9–10.

[22] Read, *Burghley*, p. 28.

[23] Add. MS 34,216, fols. 13–15; Cot. MS Caligula C. II, fol. 59, calendared in *CSP, Scot.*, III, No. 523. Fénelon (*Correspondance*, III, 329) says that Elizabeth assembled her Council immediately ("tout incontinent") on receipt of Mary's articles, and dispatched her answer the following morning.

[24] See *CSP, Scot.*, III, Nos. 520–521.

[25] Sloane MS 3199, fols. 52–57.

[26] *Ibid.*, fol. 54ᵛ.

truste in God shalbe alwayes farre from us"—Elizabeth did agree that only her children "by anie lawfull husbande" should have a claim to the throne. She instructed her envoys to press Mary for Northumberland's surrender and, "rather then the conclusion of this treatie should for that cause be broken off," she agreed that she would never allow him to be executed, although she refused to give a fuller pardon. Regarding Mary's desire to name one of her son's companions, Elizabeth did "not much disallowe therof, soe it be therwith provided that he be such a one [as] we shall have no cause to mislike of, for otherwise the Queen of Scots mighte make choise of some suche as should be a practiser here and [a] meanes to disturbe the quiett of bothe the realmes." She refused to promise Mary the right to visit her son, but she suggested that if Mary behaved well it might be granted subsequently. She saw no reason why James's expenses should be greater in England than in Scotland or why she should help meet them. She rejected Mary's suggestion that certain noblemen and officeholders should not be chosen as hostages, "considering that the persons by her excepted are the chiefest that wee are to make choise & accompt of for the suertie and observacion of this treatie." Finally, she insisted on obtaining castles along the border and in Ireland.

Elizabeth's general position was that she saw no reason to alter the original articles in any significant way, and she hoped that Mary would immediately accept or reject them as they stood. She wrote Cecil and Mildmay:

We thinke it veary necessarie that uppon your nexte conference to be had with the sayd Queen after the receipt of theis our lettres yow doe earnestly press her to growe to some conclusion, either by yeldinge unto the reasonable condicions that are offered unto her, or by plaine refusall of the same, to th'intent that uppon her resolution in one sorte or other wee maye revoke you from thence withowte anie further protracte of tyme, which we woulde be very lothe should be by her delatorie aunswers spent in vaine, your service being more requisite here for our necessarie affayres then it can be there in suche an unlikelyhoode of anie reasonable conclusion.[27]

Unfortunately Cecil and Mildmay did not write a description of their subsequent conferences with Mary. Since they were soon to return to

[27] Add. MS 34,216, fol. 15.

court, they doubtless waited to give the Queen and the Council a personal account. Cecil did make a memorandum of "the second answer of the Queen of Scots to the notes sent from the court, upon the first articles,"[28] and on the same day, October 16, Mary herself wrote Elizabeth expressing her satisfaction at the successful conclusion of the negotiations. She had been greatly honored, she said, that Elizabeth had sent two of her most agreeable and trustworthy Councillors as envoys; she had opened her heart to them, although she still hoped for a personal meeting with Elizabeth in which she might disclose its deepest secrets.[29] Apparently she gave her tentative consent to all of Elizabeth's demands before Cecil and Mildmay left. By October 25 they were back at Windsor, their mission accomplished.[30] Elizabeth told the French ambassador she was well pleased with the results of the embassy and eager to proceed with the treaty.[31]

No final settlement, however, could be made until representatives of the King's party had been consulted. It had been obvious all along that they were opposed to Mary's restoration and to any policy which would weaken the position of the Protestants in Scotland.[32] Attempts were made to mollify them: on October 18 Sussex sent Richard Wrothe to Lennox, the Regent, with an explanation of the conference and an assurance that no treaty would be signed until Scottish commissioners had conferred with Elizabeth.[33] But James's party continued to regard the prospect of Mary's restoration with horror. Morton, for instance, thought that it would endanger both realms: it was "a course quhilk . . . can nevir be suir for her Majesteis self, and so the pathway to our destruction."[34] Lennox did send an envoy to talk with Sussex,

28 HMC, *Cal. Salisbury MSS*, I, No. 1527.

29 Labanoff, *Lettres*, pp. 106–109. Mary, as usual, wrote in French.

30 De Spes says that they had been at Chatsworth longer than had been anticipated (*CSP, Spn., 1568–79*, No. 221). Cf. Read, *Burghley*, p. 29. I have found no evidence to corroborate Read's statement that Cecil and Mildmay left Chatsworth October 15; it seems too early.

31 Fénelon, *Correspondance*, III, 362.

32 Cf. Thomas Randolph to Sussex, October 16, *CSP, Scot.*, III, No. 531.

33 *CSP, Scot.*, III, No. 532.

34 *Ibid.*, No. 540. See also Sussex to Cecil, October 27, in *ibid.*, No. 545.

but he showed no inclination to name commissioners, and as early as October 26 Elizabeth was complaining about his dilatory and uncertain policy.[35]

Finally, early in December, the Abbot of Dunfermline appeared at the English court. He was not authorized to negotiate, but was to prepare for the coming of Scottish commissioners, whose dispatch the Queen urged him to hasten.[36] Next arrived a delegation from Mary and her followers still in Scotland, armed with instructions to press for Mary's proposed alterations in the treaty but ultimately to accept anything which held promise of her liberation.[37] Cecil, Mildmay, Sussex, Bacon, and Leicester were named as a committee of the Council to deal with them.[38]

By January, 1571, Cecil, who had been receiving vehement objections from the Scottish Protestants with nearly every mail from Edinburgh, had decided that the treaty held small hope of success. Unwilling to alienate the King's party, England's only support in Scotland, he now argued strongly against Mary's restoration and even drew up a five-page "note of resons remembred in Counsell to move the Queen's Majesty not to restore the Queen of Scottes."[39] It rang the changes on the familiar arguments, emphasizing particularly that if Mary were freed Elizabeth would appear to condone the "heinous crime" of Darnley's murder. Cecil's politic suggestion was that the negotiations be drawn out until Mary refused to accede to some demand, after which it might be put abroad that her stubbornness had caused their collapse.

Unfortunately there is no record of Mildmay's views, but probably they did not differ considerably from Cecil's.[40]

Late in February representatives of the Scottish Protestants, led by

[35] *Ibid.*, No. 543.
[36] *Ibid.*, No. 577.
[37] *Ibid.*, No. 587.
[38] Read, *Burghley,* p. 35.
[39] Cot. MS Caligula C. II, fols. 93–98, calendared in *CSP, Scot.,* III, No. 632. Cf. Read, *Burghley,* p. 35. Cecil continued to write similar memoranda (*CSP, Scot.,* III, Nos. 634, 643).
[40] As Chancellor of the Exchequer he did order the customs officers to deliver some furniture and other articles sent to Mary from Paris "without any further stay or serche" (Add. MS 24,459, fol. 175).

Morton, reached London. They presented Mildmay, Cecil, newly ennobled as Lord Burghley, and Elizabeth's other commissioners with a long treatise justifying James's title to the Scottish throne and presenting historical arguments to support the legality of Mary's abdication.[41] Although they entered into discussions readily enough, they maintained that they had no authority to negotiate with Mary and Elizabeth; only commissioners named by a Scottish Parliament could do so. Cecil prepared another memorandum, suggesting that Morton and his colleagues be allowed to return home and that Mary's supporters be told "that the commissioners for the King have been dealt with by all good means to induce them to receive the Queen home, . . . and that they peremptorily said they cannot condescend thereto, [for] they . . . have no authority to bring the King's estate into question [and] they allege many things to prove the Queen's demission good, and the King's coronation lawful."[42] He realized that no Scottish Parliament would accept Mary's restoration—that the treaty was lost—and he hoped that some means of pacifying and uniting Scotland under the leadership of James's party might be found. On March 23 Elizabeth granted Morton license to return to Scotland, hold a Parliament, and send fresh commissioners at the end of May.[43] But by May Mary had been implicated in the Ridolfi plot to unseat Elizabeth. It precluded any possibility of her liberation; indeed, it provided a convenient excuse for dropping the treaty altogether.

Mildmay and Cecil thus found their endeavors fruitless, or nearly so: the discussions at least placated the French for a time, until Elizabeth's flirtations with the royal dukes came to serve that purpose. The entire episode could easily be dismissed as nothing but insincere talk and procrastination; the Spanish ambassador held that opinion from the beginning.[44] But such a view is almost certainly incorrect. Cecil and Mildmay were not the sort to dissemble. They must have regarded the proposed treaty as an honest attempt to dispose of the Marian problem by placing her at the head of a unified Scotland, bound to England

[41] Cot. MS Caligula C. II, fols. 520–531, calendared in *CSP, Scot.*, III, No. 640.

[42] *CSP, Scot.*, III, No. 658 (March 15, 1571).

[43] *Ibid.*, No. 672.

[44] De Spes to Philip, October 5, 1570, *CSP, Spn., 1568–79*, No. 220.

and to Protestantism by suitable guarantees. But for the plots of Mary's followers and the factiousness of the Scottish noblemen the attempt might have succeeded. As it was, Mary's party in Scotland dwindled and finally surrendered Edinburgh Castle, its last stronghold, in 1573. The Queen of Scots herself remained in England, a continuing threat to Elizabeth's rule.

## 8. COUNCIL, EXCHEQUER, AND MINT
### 1571–1579

ALTHOUGH MARY'S ACTIVITIES continued to concern Elizabeth's Councillors, other matters occupied the center of Mildmay's public life after his embassy. He became involved in the Council's discussions of foreign policy, especially regarding Elizabeth's proposed French marriage, as well as in problems of administration at the Exchequer and the mint.

The Queen was impelled into negotiations with France partly by the Ridolfi plot. Fearful of the union between Mary's partisans in England and Hispano-Papal opposition abroad, she sought foreign support. An alliance with France offered the greatest hope of success, and the proposed marriage between Elizabeth and the Duke d'Anjou, brother of the French King Charles IX, seemed the best way of cementing the accord.

The French had hinted at the marriage as early as 1568, but Elizabeth did not evince much interest before 1571. In that year, however, she ordered Sir Francis Walsingham, Mildmay's brother-in-law and the resident ambassador in Paris, to undertake serious negotiations.[1]

Walsingham's letters to Mildmay are filled with financial complaints, not news of the marriage. He returned to France, after a brief stay in England, on New Year's Day, 1571.[2] On January 2 he wrote from Boulogne, "If my charges contynue as they beginne, wherof there is no small hope to the contrary, except there be some extraordinary consideration had of me by your good meanes in my transporta-

[1] On the negotiations see Conyers Read, *Lord Burghley and Queen Elizabeth*, pp. 51–65, and J. B. Black, *The Reign of Elizabeth*, seconded., pp. 147–155.
[2] *CSP, For., 1569–71*, No. 1492.

tion, my alloweance will not suffice to beare halfe my charges."[3] He reached Paris just as the anticipated entry of the King and his new bride had raised prices, and although he did not live in what he thought fitting estate the expense of maintaining his house and horses reached seven pounds a day.[4]

Walsingham was finally received by Charles "with great curtesie and favour, as alsoe by his mother and bretheren. I leave to you," he wrote Mildmay, "to gesse the cause of this kindnes"—desire for the marriage? He believed that Charles could be brought to favor the Protestants; there had been some doubt of his sincerity,

... yet surelie, Sir, they that knowe him throughlie are of opinion that if the matters prove to newe troubles he will incline to those of the Religion. This oration, Sir, wherof I send you a coppie procurred and delivered unto him by the ambassador of the princes of Germany hath put him in some good courage, wheras before by the faction of the Guisses he was put in great feare of the Catholiques as well forraine as at home.[5]

The negotiations thus began well enough. Thomas Sackville, Lord Buckhurst, spent February and March in Paris helping Walsingham; he found Catherine de' Medici, the Queen Mother, well disposed towards Elizabeth.[6] The chief obstacle was the matter of religion. Elizabeth did not feel that Anjou could be allowed Catholic priests and masses in England, although she would not require his immediate adherence to the English Church. Catherine thought the restrictions "very hard." "This knotty piece of religion is the only matter of difficulty," Walsingham wrote Burghley on April 28, adding that he

[3] Stowe MS 147, fol. 233r.

[4] *Ibid.*, fol. 244v. The entry was delayed until March "by reason of the new Queenes sicknes, who is now in way of recovery" (Walsingham to Mildmay, February 8, in *ibid.*, fol. 255r, and Harl. MS 260, fol. 13v). On March 11 Walsingham was again complaining that his allowance was inadequate by £ 10 a week (*CSP, For., 1569–71*, No. 1607).

[5] Stowe MS 147, fol. 245r.

[6] *CSP, For., 1569–71*, No. 1614. Buckhurst was assisted by Guido Cavalcanti, a Florentine merchant who enjoyed dabbling in diplomacy. See F. J. Levy, "A Semi-Professional Diplomat: Guido Cavalcanti and the Marriage Negotiations of 1571," *Bulletin of the Institute of Historical Research*, XXXV (1962), 211–220.

thought the French attitude proceeded more from regard to honor than conscience.[7] Walsingham told Anjou—rather insincerely, considering his Protestant views—that the English Communion was much like the Roman Mass, and he intimated that Anjou might have services in French if he wished. The ambassador even asked Burghley to send him a copy of the Prayer Book translated into French.[8]

Discussions continued as the French sent D'Archant, captain of Anjou's guard, to England in July and De Foix, one of Catherine's councillors, in August. Walsingham wrote that the Cardinal of Lorraine, a member of the Guise family, had so alienated Anjou from the Protestant cause that even toleration for the Duke's religion could not effect a compromise.[9] The King, angered at this turn of events, stormed that Anjou should have disclosed his objections earlier or learned to swallow them, and both Anjou and Catherine wept.[10] Talks dragged on until January, 1572, but there was no real hope for the match. Walsingham could only suggest, not very enthusiastically, that Elizabeth consider Anjou's younger brother, the Duke d'Alençon, whose religious scruples were less pressing.[11]

Although Burghley, subordinating religion to policy, had hoped that the Anjou marriage might succeed,[12] Mildmay was decidedly opposed to any religious concession. On September 3, 1571, just as De Foix returned to France, Mildmay wrote Burghley, "The French, as I heare, are departed with that aunswere your L. wrote me of. I am glad of it, for yelding in that point of religion will offend God and surely perill her Majestie. But God, that hath put that cunstancy in hir, will no dowbte preserve hir from all perill."[13] Although Mildmay was glad that the negotiations had failed, he feared that their breakdown might cloud his brother-in-law's position; in November he wrote Burghley, "I nede not to desire your L. favor to my brother Walsingham, knowing suf-

[7] CSP, For., 1569–71, Nos. 1675–77.

[8] Ibid., No. 1729.

[9] Ibid., No. 1883.

[10] Ibid., No. 1886.

[11] Ibid., No. 2067. Cf. Read, Burghley, p. 64.

[12] Read, Burghley, pp. 52–53.

[13] SP 12/81/4. Mildmay wrote from Apethorpe and lamented Burghley's inability to visit Northamptonshire.

ficiently that you are his onely refuge . . . I pray you contynew his good
L. as you have alwaies been."[14]

As the prospect of the Anjou match receded, the English concentrated on obtaining a defensive league with France. This was ultimately
accomplished, thanks to the skilled diplomacy of Sir Thomas Smith and
Sir Henry Killigrew, in April, 1572. The Treaty of Blois, which confirmed the alliance, redounded more to the benefit of England than
France, since by it the French abandoned their support of Mary Stuart.

It was fortunate that these negotiations were completed before August, when the massacre of St. Bartholomew's Day shocked the English.
Within France the massacre reopened the festering religious sore as the
Catholics attempted, unsuccessfully, to subdue the Huguenots at La
Rochelle. Elizabeth refused to consider the profferred match with
Alençon, which both Charles IX and Burghley regarded favorably, so
long as the oppression of the French Protestants continued; but when
peace was concluded in 1573 on terms favorable to the Huguenots discussions for the marriage were revived. Elizabeth was never enthusi-
astic about Alençon—he was pockmarked and she was very sensitive
to masculine beauty—but she regarded protracted negotiations as a useful tool of diplomacy, and at the beginning she may have entertained
serious consideration of the union. Leicester and Burghley certainly did.

The Alençon affair was discussed at a meeting of the Privy Council
January 6, 1574. Mildmay delivered a lengthy address, for which both
his brief notes and the full text are preserved among the Fitzwilliam of
Milton Papers.[15] He thought Alençon much too young for the Queen,
since her age was twice his. Nor was the Duke's nationality favorable:
as a Frenchman he was "proude, insolent, lascivious, inconstant, [and]
unfaithfull," and his mother's Italian blood rendered him "faulse,
subtile, irreligious, voide of vertue, full of vice." He was also a Papist
—ignorant of the true God—and a professed enemy of all Protestants.
Clearly the marriage would prove dangerous, both to the Queen and
her realm.

Among the dangers to Elizabeth, Mildmay foresaw "greefe of
minde, miscontentation, [and] shortening of hir time"; the realm, he

[14] SP 12/83/8.
[15] F(M)P 111, fols. 1–7.

feared, might "coom to be annexed to the French crowne [and] governed by a viceroie," and factions would grow "by the Papistes havinge a Prince of theire owne religion." He dismissed the idea that the French could be bound by oaths and promises; these would not hold against the "dissimulacion, fraude, falshoode, perjurie, violence, [and] cavillinge interpretacions" manifest in the French dealings with the Huguenots.

Some Councillors had suggested that Alençon offered the last hope for Elizabeth's marriage. Mildmay thought it very strange that there was "no other prince Protestant in the worlde, . . . nor anie other verteous & religious within the realme nor without that hir Majestie can vouchsafe to hear of." But if it were to be this marriage or none, Mildmay wrote,

I saie in my simple opinion rather none then this, accompanied with so mennie daungers to hir Majestie and the realme, which stande not uppon a doughtfull contingent but ar most like to followe. . . . I [had] rather abide Godes good leisure and trust uppon his provision in time than in seeking to prevent a mischeefe to coom hereafter bringe uppon oure heades a mischeefe present. . . .

Besides if with a politicke and worldlie eye wee seeke a mach for oure soveraine with a Papist Prince, thearebie haserding the cause of religion not onelie heare but in all Europe, let us bee assured that God will confounde all oure devises: Hee hath sett us a rule that wee shoulde not doo evill that good maie coom of it. The matter of religion is such as maie admitt in Godes sight no mixture nor qualifinge tollerance. And than wheareas wee bee afraide to faule into the handes of men wee shall faule into the handes of God, which is most terrible and inevitable, for there is no wisedoom nor counsell against Him.[16]

Mildmay concluded that an absolute breach of the negotiations was most desirable. If the Queen thought that foreign relations would profit from temporizing—how well he knew her dilatory proclivities! —she might keep diplomatic channels open by saying that she would consider the proposal more favorably whenever the French proved themselves well disposed to the Protestants.[17]

This temporizing policy was adopted. Throughout the next decade

[16] *Ibid.*, fol. 4ᵛ.
[17] *Ibid.*, fol. 5ʳ.

Elizabeth blew alternately hot and cold about the match, with Mildmay administering further cold douches whenever her enthusiasm waxed too warm.

Although Mildmay had sat for Northamptonshire in all of Elizabeth's Parliaments, the session of 1572 is the first in which he took a leading part. The Queen had summoned Parliament reluctantly, yielding to the pressure for legislation against Mary built up by the Ridolfi conspiracy. The session began unusually late—May 8—and Commons spent the month fulminating against the Queen of Scots, demanding first her execution and then, when it became clear that Elizabeth would not go so far, her exclusion from the succession and Norfolk's death. To this last request Elizabeth finally bowed, and on June 2 England's sole duke went to the block. He apparently bore Mildmay no ill will despite Mildmay's aid in drawing up the charges against him; shortly before his execution he gave Mildmay two elaborate goblets and a number of gold spoons trimmed with pearls.[18]

The House next considered a long bill against Mary, passed by the Lords and sent down on June 5. It began with a preamble setting out the history of Mary's intrigues, pronounced her unworthy of any title to the crown, said that if she took part in any further conspiracy she should be judged a traitor and punished accordingly, and made it treason for any to give her aid, comfort, or support, or to attempt to restore Papal authority in England. Since the bill was complex, and since the Queen desired as much speed and as little debate as possible, it was committed to "certain of the ripest wits within the House," as an anonymous parliamentary diarist put it—eight members, led by Sadler and Mildmay. They were to "have conference upon every point in the bill; and after, upon the reading of it by articles, they should utter their opinion . . . and so leave it to the House to judge upon. This resolution," the diarist added, "eased the House of much labour, and saved the expense of much time."[19]

Thomas Cromwell's diary records that thirteen Members, Mildmay

[18] C. H. and T. Cooper, *Athenae Cantabrigienses*, II, 53.
[19] Quoted in Sir John Neale, *Elizabeth I and her Parliaments, 1559–1581*, pp. 285–286.

among them, spoke to the bill before the House on Saturday, June 7.[20] Mildmay wanted its words to "be tryed like drammes of gold" with attention to their effect "in our lawe, not [in] the civell lawe or in logique." After due consideration the bill passed unanimously, with a proviso specifically denying any implication that Mary had previously possessed a valid claim to the English throne. But the medicine was too strong for Elizabeth: she did not reject the bill, but neither did she allow it to become law, having recourse instead to the old formula "la roigne se avisera." She would think on it. Meanwhile she prorogued the Parliament until November 1, then postponed a second session indefinitely. The meeting of 1572 had provided a vent for the boiling anti-Marian sentiment, but it otherwise accomplished less than did any other Elizabethan Parliament.

Mildmay and Burghley, sharing responsibilities in the Privy Council since 1566, began their association at the Exchequer in 1572, when Burghley was named Lord Treasurer. He succeeded Winchester, who had died in March, only three years short of his ninetieth birthday. Burghley's appointment took place on July 15, although he must have known of it earlier, perhaps in April when he was made a Knight of the Garter. He relinquished the post of Principal Secretary to Sir Thomas Smith, but continued to exercise supervision over every aspect of the government.[21]

Mildmay must have been appreciative of Burghley's help, for he had become increasingly weighed down as Winchester aged. Indeed virtually the only surviving criticism of his work at the Exchequer dates from April, 1572, during the interval between Winchester's death and Burghley's appointment: Lord Hunsdon, who was involved in a dispute over fishing rights at Berwick, wrote, "I could never have the matter harde thurely [heard thoroughly], but now a pece and then a pece, so at every hearing your Mr. Myldmay was so occupyd with other

[20] Crom. d., fol. 55ᵛ.

[21] Read, *Burghley*, pp. 80–82. La Mothe Fénelon, the French ambassador, says that Leicester was offered the Treasury but refused it (*ibid.*, p. 80). Burghley's earliest surviving memorandum as Lord Treasurer is dated July 26; perhaps for the novelty of it, he signed it "W. Burghley, Thes: Angl." (SP 46/29/156).

men as eythar he hard lyttell of the matter, or els wold heare but of suche thynges as made agenst my farmars."[22] Poor Mildmay! One sympathizes with his rather pained answer, which assures Hunsdon that the "proceadinge in the matter hath byn lawfull, indyfferent, comely in respecte of every person who was touched therein, and answerable in any place" and warns him that the Exchequer will continue to find against him whenever he is in the wrong.[23]

Few changes at the Exchequer can be ascribed to Burghley. In the main he, like Mildmay, accepted the financial machinery as he found it but tried to make it function more efficiently. Shortly after his appointment he and Mildmay drew up new and more stringent rules for the tellers, who had indulged in some irregular practices during Winchester's dotage.[24] Burghley did not disapprove of farming the customs, as Winchester had; but he did see that the farmers paid well for their privileges, and he tried to eliminate smuggling. He allowed merchants and farmers who were liable for purveyance—the supply of victuals for the court—to compound for specific quantities at fixed prices.[25] He invested much energy in attempting to reduce the expenses of the royal household, persuading the Queen to drop interlude players from the payroll and to reduce the number of sackbuts in her musical establishment even though he could not dissuade her from employing additional violinists and flutists. He was able to hold expenses to £40,000 but, as Dietz says, he had to abolish breakfast to do it.[26] He greatly reduced also the number of pensions and annuities granted to the Queen's servants.

Such measures obviated the need for parliamentary taxation for several years. The Parliament of 1571 had granted a subsidy and two tenths and fifteenths, which yielded about £100,000 in 1572 and

[22] SP 46/29/119.
[23] SP 46/29/121.
[24] E 36/266/80; cf. G. R. Elton, "The Elizabethan Exchequer: War in the Receipt," in *Elizabethan Government and Society: Essays Presented to Sir John Neale*, ed. S. T. Bindoff, J. Hurstfield, and C. H. Williams, pp. 234–235. Mildmay worked hard to make the Exchequer function effectively: in February, 1575, for instance, he wrote admonishing the auditors "to make diligent expedition in taking of the Customers accomptes for the last yere" (SP 46/30/386).
[25] Read, *Burghley*, p. 84.
[26] F. C. Dietz, *English Public Finance, 1558–1641*, pp. 32–35.

£ 74,000 in 1573.[27] The money was sorely needed: in 1570 the Queen had been reduced to seeking loans under the privy seal, and in May, 1571, she wrote Mildmay, one of the collectors for Huntingdonshire, explaining that the Easter revenues were insufficient for the discharge of the loans and asking lenders to wait until Michaelmas.[28] By the end of 1572, however, the Exchequer had a comfortable surplus of £ 140,000,[29] and no further taxes were required until 1576. Mildmay's concern for such matters is attested by the presence among his personal papers of forty-three volumes of Exchequer accounts covering the years between 1576 and 1589.[30]

The Exchequer memoranda in the Public Record Office, together with a few letters preserved elsewhere, throw light on a myriad details of Mildmay's work. He personally supervised the grant of lands given to Sir Christopher Hatton, one of the Queen's favorite courtiers and captain of her bodyguard; and, when the title to some of them proved uncertain, he arranged an exchange.[31] He ordered payment of "exhibitions" of fifty marks a year to the four daughters of the Earl of Northumberland, who was handed over by the Scots and executed in 1572, and to the wife and three daughters of the Earl of Westmorland, who had lost his estates and gone into exile after his attainder.[32] He ordered that proceedings against Norfolk's heirs for recovery of the Duke's debts to the Queen be delayed until he ascertained Elizabeth's pleasure.[33] He, Sir Thomas Smith, and Sir William Cordell compiled a book of rules for foreign merchants trading at Norwich; it lists customs on imported cloths and orders civil disputes to be settled by the mayor and aldermen, religious quarrels by the bishop.[34] He, with the assistance of Burghley and Sadler, drew up a list of the Queen's jewels and plate in

[27] F. C. Dietz, *The Exchequer in Elizabeth's Reign*, pp. 80–89.

[28] Westm. MSS, 2, XII, 1, D5. The Queen had also borrowed £ 6,200 from the London merchants, which Gresham wrote was to be repaid in November, 1571 (SP 12/83/20).

[29] Dietz, *Finance, 1558–1641*, pp. 47–48.

[30] Westm. MSS, 4, XIX, 1–17; 4, XX, 1–21; 4, XXII. Similar accounts are in the BM (Add. MS 34,215) and the PRO (SP 12/125/75 and SP 12/137/13).

[31] Westm. MSS, 2, XII, 1, D3.

[32] Add. MS 24,459, fol. 176.

[33] SP 46/30/65 (second numbering series).

[34] SP 12/77/58.

154 folios, enumerating everything from the crown itself to "basons & fountaines" and "boyling pottes of silver."[35] He, Leicester, and Burghley negotiated a new lease of the customs farm on wine, a bargain he regarded as "good for hir Magestie, and . . . the best I yet here of."[36]

Among the most interesting items in Mildmay's correspondence are those relating to ecclesiastical affairs. In many of these his concern for the welfare of the Church and the clergy, even at the expense of governmental revenue, is notable. As early as 1568, for instance, he ordered that the Vicar of Wendover, Buckinghamshire, should no longer be required to pay the Queen a yearly annuity of 60 s., since his living was too poor to support him decently.[37] In 1570, he and Cecil agreed that the widow of Bishop Oglethorpe of Carlisle, who had been the only Marian bishop willing to assist at Elizabeth's coronation, should enjoy the Bishop's castle and lands during the vacancy of the see.[38]

Several letters written to Mildmay by Edmund Grindal, while he was Archbishop of York, survive. They include personal comments which make it evident that the two men were acquainted and that Grindal thought Mildmay well disposed towards the Church. Grindal first complained about a lease of lands pertaining to a prebend which had been improperly granted by John Story to a Papist "in Queene Maries tyme, when all thinges was lawfull to men of his qualities"; Grindal sought to have it given instead to a good Protestant.[39] Two years later he was expressing concern for the Vicar of Kirkburton, who on several occasions had been unjustly troubled in the Exchequer Court on charges that his glebe lands were "concealed," that is, had changed hands without proper notice or payment to the government.[40]

---

[35] Stowe MS 555. The list, made in 1574, was intended partly as a check on earlier inventories, such as the one compiled in 1559 by a commission which had included Mildmay. Each folio of Stowe MS 555 is signed by Mildmay, Burghley, and Sadler, a bit of seemingly unnecessary routine.

[36] SP 46/29/75; cf. SP 46/29/49 and SP 12/83/15.

[37] SP 46/28/89.

[38] SP 46/28/207. Mildmay was also lenient in collecting the arrears due from the Bishop's lands; see Stowe MS 150, fol. 7.

[39] SP 46/29/36.

[40] SP 46/29/143.

Grindal's most revealing letter pertains to the priest of Workington, Cumberland, who was deprived by the provincial commissioners for ecclesiastical causes on a charge of simony—he had bought his living from the patron—but who had brought suit at the Exchequer for reinstatement. Grindal had no doubt of the man's guilt, and wrote,

I have procured a good preacher to be instituted and inducted in the said benefice, beinge but seaven myles distante from the place where I was borne, but he is disturbed by the patrone aforesaid, who more estemeth the gaine he receiveth of his lease then the edifyinge of Gods people. I have written also herein to my L. Threasorer, but his businesses are infinite, and therfore I truste he will recommende the cawse unto you. We all assure our selfe that nowe under you two, religion and learninge shall fynde patronnie in the Exchequer, where in tymes paste they have not moch been considered of.[41]

Other bishops also sought Mildmay's aid. John Scory of Hereford wrote of certain parish churches in his diocese, especially that at Bromyard, which "time out of mind" had been served by several priests with the rectorial tithes divided into two or three parts. Some "young men" had been attempting to have these rectories dissolved as colleges under the terms of the chantries act, but Mildmay and the Council agreed that they should continue.[42] Edwin Sandys, who followed Grindal at York, similarly complained of attempts to take land from Southwell Minster:

This churche was erected by Kinge Henry and therefore not to be solde any parte of yt by Kinge Edwarde. These men that nowe make this troble bought of him, who had no right to sell, and so that purchasse is voyde. This thinge was called into question in Queen Marys tyme and by lawe overthrowne, as the Master of the Rolls can testify. At my last being at London I sued to hir Majestie for statutes for this churche, that the same mighte be well ordered and established forever, which her Highnes of hir gratious favor towardes this churche willinglie granted me, but nothing can stay theis covetous cormorantes which seke ther gayne by other mens losses and gredely pray upon the poore patrimony of the Churche.[43]

[41] SP 46/29/235.
[42] SP 46/29/127, 190, 195, 239.
[43] SP 46/33/301; October 15, 1585.

William Chaderton of Chester, one of the poorest bishoprics, wrote Mildmay seeking leniency in the collection of his debts to the Crown; if he were made to pay his predecessor's arrears he would have to "breake up my house, and go sojorne somewhere for a long tyme, not being able to beare them."[44] Mildmay's reply was doubtless sympathetic. Gilbert Berkeley, Bishop of Bath and Wells, expressed a general feeling when he wrote Burghley, "I [have] receaved a lettre from your Lordshippe and Sir Walter Mildmay . . . wherein I perceave the greate good love that her Majestie beareth unto her cleargie for theire greate peace and quietness."[45] Perhaps the Queen's ministers deserved the praise more than the Sovereign herself.

The ecclesiastical suit about which we know most involved John Robson, curate of Auckland St. Andrew in County Durham, and Christopher Pickering, farmer of the Deanery of Auckland. Bernard Gilpin, the "Apostle of the North" and one of the saintliest figures in the Tudor Church, wrote Mildmay on October 10, 1581, asking favor for Robson. Pickering, he said, "goeth about unjustlie (if I say not cruelly) to take away a good portion of his lyvinge, and to beggar him, havinge tormented him in the lawe thre yeares togither, firste at Yorcke and after at London." Gilpin knew Robson well, for Robson had been "broughte up in my house of a younge scholer, and after certaine yeares spent at th'universitie, was hired to the parishe of Duntonn in Buckinghamshire." He was brought to Auckland by "Bishop Pilkington of blessid memorye"; he came because he was born there, although it was not so good a living as his previous parish. He had been especially conscientious in teaching the children. "May it please your honour therfor, for Christes sake, and for the love you bear to his Gospell," Gilpin ended, "to be so gratious unto him, that he may by your honors godlye meane, beinge a worthie patron of the poore destitute ministers, . . . be defendid in his just cause."[46]

Richard Barnes, Bishop of Durham, wrote four days later echoing Gilpin's sentiments. He thought Robson "a very godlie and zealous minister." Of Pickering he commented:

---

[44] SP 46/34/90; October 11, 1586.
[45] SP 46/31/446; May 3, 1579.
[46] SP 46/32/157. On Gilpin see the article in the *DNB*.

The Deanery (as I am crediblie informed) is worth yearlie unto the farmer £ 400, and I assure your lordship he neither releiveth the poor therof, kepeth anie hospitality, procureth the quarter sermons, nor repaireth the chauncell, but (as it semeth) of a mynd too insatiable coveteth part of the poor curates living, who deserveth much more then at anie time he hath had, both in respect of the greatnes of the chardge and of his painfulnes therin.[47]

The final decision speaks well for the Queen's ministers. The Exchequer Court heard the case with unusual speed, rendering a decree in Robson's favor on April 27. "He shall quyetly from hencefurth enjoy the tithes, oblations, fees, and profittes in constansie . . . He shalbe dismissed with his costes, which shalbe assessed by the Court upon a bill therof."[48] Gilpin and Bishop Barnes had not interceded in vain.

The universities, too, occasionally appealed to Mildmay. In 1573 four masters of Cambridge colleges—John Whitgift of Trinity, Thomas Ithell of Jesus, Thomas Aldrich of Corpus, and John May of Queens'—wrote concerning a suit instituted by Sir Robert Chester, who was trying to gain title to certain meadows and commons in St. Ives. This act, if successful, would harm the residents of the town, and "the severall colledges whereof we are maisters, haveinge land in the same towne, are herewith lykewyse to susteine greate detryment." Whitgift and his colleagues offered to show evidence of their rights; they must have experienced little difficulty in enlisting Mildmay's support.[49]

Affairs at the mint also demanded Mildmay's attention, for although the great recoinage had been successfully completed, the mint was very far from running smoothly during the 1560's and 1570's.

In 1567 the goldsmiths complained to Winchester, Cecil, and Mildmay. Their petition made six requests: that Richard Rogers, the assay master of the Goldsmiths' Company who had been acting as assayer at the mint, be released and serve only the company; that the treasurer of the mint receive gold and silver bullion whenever it is presented;

[47] SP 46/32/159. Barnes also wrote Burghley (SP 46/32/161), as did Robson himself (SP 46/32/173).
[48] E 123/8, fol. 53ᵛ.
[49] SP 46/29/247.

that such bullion be paid for within fourteen days; that the treasurer be bound by greater sureties; that the assay master not be allowed to buy and sell gold and silver himself; and that the treasurer "indifferentlie mingle the journeys of money that be made and so paid out," that is, run together the lots of coin so as to reduce the possibility of profit or loss in unusually good or bad journeys.[50] The mint commissioners examined the treasurer, Sir Thomas Stanley, who was willing to yield on most points, and they made their own answers to the goldsmiths, subject to confirmation by the Queen and Council. The Queen's final orders commanded compliance with every particular of the petition.[51]

Stanley, however, did not obey, and the goldsmiths brought further charges in 1568. He sometimes failed to pay for bullion until forty days after its receipt, so that the goldsmiths, not knowing when they would receive payment, had to send their apprentices to wait on him daily. He had been absent from London for five weeks or more, leaving outstanding debts uncollectable "to our greate losse and damage." He manipulated weights "by false sleight of hande at the ballance." Indeed there was so much complaint on this particular that the wardens of the Goldsmiths' Company attempted to examine his weights,

. . . at whose comminge to the Tower Mr. Stanley faynid great busynes in the meltinge house till the wardens were gone, and then came up, tooke downe his ballance[s] presentilie and sent them to mendinge, and said to suche as taried there, he must go home in hast to send awaie a cart of stuffe. But his hast was to the Goldsmithes Halle to conferre with the sizer of his weightes, then founde untrulie sized, as the wardens can witnes, so that by former conference with the same syzer this faulte in the weights might be better coverid.

The goldsmiths concluded:

By theise and suche other his dealinges we have just occasion to suspect that he, not havinge the feare of God before his eies, nor yet due consideration of the place he occupieth, but rather inordynatelie sekinge hys owne unlawfull gaynes with manifest contempt of so honorable orders as aforeseid, and with as light regarde of his former promises made to so honorable

50 SP 12/42/50.
51 SP 12/42/51.

personages [Winchester and Mildmay], will so deale in this his place of so greate credyt, that by the least, the goldsmithes and merchantes repayringe to the seid mynte shall susteigne some greate losses.[52]

Stanley admitted the substantial truth of some of the charges, but maintained that they were exaggerated. Although he had not always been able to make payment within fourteen days, he had paid as soon as possible; he thought that no one had had to wait so long as forty days; when he left London he had had the permission of the Council, and there was only £139 outstanding. He denied the irregularities in weight rather too vehemently for his own credit, crying that these claims were "faulslye & sklanderouslye wrytten," and sought to know who accused him of working for his own gain so that they might "receave reproche and smarte." In fact he was so angry that he drew up a table of "mysdemenor of certayne goldsmithes towardes Thomas Stanley," including charges that Richard Martin, who had complained of Stanley's weights, had faulty scales himself, and that the servant sent daily by William Dixon to await payment—although none was due him—had been found trying to pick the lock on a storehouse door. One of Stanley's requests seems to confirm the story about his balances: he asked that the weights at the Goldsmiths' Hall and at the mint be tried against the Queen's standard, for he believed that "a recent change" had rendered those in the Tower too light.[53]

Complaints continued. The next petition directed to Mildmay and Burghley is undated but cannot be before, or much after, February, 1571.[54] The goldsmiths reported that Stanley, after the commissioners' admonition, did for a time make prompt payment for bullion, whereupon the goldsmiths brought "great masses of silver and gold" to be coined. But the treasurer again declined from his orders, and "it was apparentlie seen that [he] had paid his old debtes with bullyon of new brought in." He remained "indebted in sondrie great somes of money to your poore supplyantes, whereof they cannot get payment in any wise, and the mynt brought agayne (as before) to suche discredite as

[52] SP 12/46/26.

[53] *Ibid.*

[54] SP 12/77/21. The address to Burghley places it after February 25, 1571, when Cecil was ennobled; the references to Stanley would be inappropriate much later.

nowe in manner there is no bullyon at all brought thither, although there be verie much readie daylie to be brought . . . if any good order might be there observed."

These persistent troubles, coupled with the inordinately high cost of operating the mint, led to a thorough revision of its management. Since 1544 the government had run the mint directly, appointing all its officers and paying them fixed salaries. This method resulted in extravagance and inefficiency, for the Council had scant time for mint matters and even such skilled commissioners at Winchester, Mildmay, and Burghley were busy elsewhere. It was therefore decided to return the mint to its ancient constitution: operation by a master, who named his subordinates, paid their fees, and was allowed a set sum for the expense of coining each pound of gold or silver, with some check provided by a warden named, like the master, by the Queen.

Stanley rightly feared that one of the objects of the reorganization was his ouster, and in July, 1571, he wrote Burghley begging that the new orders should not interfere with his office.[55] His claims do not seem to have been seriously considered, but several others did negotiate for the farm of the mint. The principal difficulty arose over setting the fees which would be paid the master. In the end, on April 19, 1572, John Lonison was named master, without salary and with the beggarly allowances of 1$s$. 6$d$. a pound for gold and 8$d$. for silver.[56] Richard Martin, who had been in the mint since 1559 and who was an important figure in the City, was made warden. Many of the subordinate posts were marked for abolition, with the result that mint salaries were gradually reduced from a peak of £ 2,000 during the period of direct management to something like £ 350 by 1587.[57]

Lonison seems to have been so eager to secure the mastership that he contracted to produce coin at fees which did not cover his expenses. Shortly after Lonison's appointment Martin made the first of a series

[55] *CSP, Dom., 1547–80*, p. 416.

[56] *Ibid.*, p. 440; Sir John Craig, *The Mint*, pp. 123–124.

[57] It is interesting to note that the reorganization, which was worked out primarily by Burghley, coincides almost exactly with his appointment as Lord Treasurer. He may have had in mind a thoroughgoing overhaul of the financial machinery, since he and Mildmay tightened up the operation of the Exchequer soon after the reform in the mint.

of protests that the master was turning out coins below standard in fineness and weight.[58] Considering Lonison's paltry allowance he could do little else. His fees for silver were raised by 1*d.* a pound in April, 1574,[59] but the increase did not meet the need and Lonison was not even able to pay his moneyers regularly. They complained to Burghley and Mildmay, probably in November, 1574, that they had received no wages for August, September, and October, and that they were at their wits' end, especially since their pay was reckoned by the pound coined in a period when the amount of coinage was falling.[60] In another petition of about the same date the moneyers also protested that Lonison had withdrawn the allowance for waste in coining gold which they had previously enjoyed, and that they had sustained great loss because the mint was producing mainly "small moneyes," coins of small denomination which required more work for each pound coined than did larger ones.[61]

In the next phase of these troubles Mildmay was deeply involved, as a staggering number of his papers testify. Lonison now attempted to make ends meet by subtle manipulation of the procedures for melting metal before coining. In order to obviate remelting when inevitable small variations in fineness were discovered, mint regulations had long allowed alloyed silver for coinage to pass the assay if it were not more than two pennyweight in the pound above or below the standard (eleven ounces two pennyweight silver to eighteen pennyweight copper). This permissible variation was called the master's "remedy." Lonison now took advantage of it, intentionally producing metal a pennyweight or two below the standard and pocketing the profit. The watchful Martin protested, seeking power to oversee the melting so that he could prevent any willful variation from the standard; and Mildmay was obliged to make a thorough study of mint regulations and procedures in order to advise the Council what action to take.

A series of eleven "questions propounded conserning mint causes," with answers, probably represents Mildmay's first attack on the prob-

[58] *CSP, Dom., 1547–80,* p. 547; n.d. [?1572].
[59] Craig, *The Mint,* p. 125.
[60] SP 12/99/44.
[61] SP 12/99/43. The waste in melting gold was about 2*s.* or 3*s.* in the pound (Craig, *The Mint,* p. 127).

lem.[62] It may date from the last months of 1574. The fundamental question, for Mildmay at least, was whether money could lawfully be made less fine than the standard. His answer was unequivocal: "The master woorker hath in the . . . indenture plainelie undertaken to make the moonie of this standerd." The remedy is "alowed for accidentall variation in the assaie, and not for anie wilfull action in alteration of the standerd." Remedies are necessary because "the silver is molten and cast into manie smaule ingottes, and after those ingottes cut into manie smale peeces and coyned within the coyninge press, which gather siltes and dust; and th'alloie and silver molten cannot so equallie be conmixt as everie vi d. maie alwaies houlde the verie just part of his alaie, & hit the verie standerd." To the query "whether ought the warden to see the rates of the pottes of bullion put to meltinge and to knowe the qualitie of th'allaie put to the moonnies," Mildmay answers, "yea, the warden ought to doo & of necessitie must doo all thease, for in the . . . indenture hee is charged to kepe a meltinge booke declaringe the finenes and quantitie of all manner of bullion put to meltinge; but unles the warden bee privie to the whole allaie . . . he can never make certaine & true entre . . . of the finenes." "Whi, then you pretende the warden such an officer for the Queene as that hee shall oversee the moonnies at all times," someone may protest; but Mildmay replies, "Yea, in the 27 article of the indenture it is so especiallie apointed, videlicet, to take heade and oversee the monnies at all times."

These answers seem to have been the raw material from which Mildmay wrote a more formal memorandum. Preserved at Northampton, it is headed "Notes touching the standerd of sterlinge silver: collected by Sʳ W. M. for his owne remembrance, 14 Januarij 1574" (1575).[63] Mildmay again emphasized that the master must not intentionally fall from the standard:

The subject that bringeth to the mintt a pounde weight of silver . . . delivereth the same to the mint master, to the ende that hee shoulde put the same silver to the fier, and of that deliver back againe to the subject a pounde weight of sterlinge moonneies made of the same silver, withoute that the master shoulde ad or deminish anie thinge of the finnes from the silver so deliverid unto him.

[62] F(M)P 82, fols. 1–4.
[63] F(M)P 90.

And if the silver brought by the subject bee not of the [standard fineness], then hee aloweth to the master so much in valeue as shall make up the same silver to bee of the full finenes . . . , for the conyage of which pounde weight into sterlinge moonnies, and for all charges theareunto incidentt, the subject dooth paie to the Queens Majesties use to t'handes of the warden xviij d. . . .

Mildmay cited "divers auncient statutes," records, a Star Chamber decree, and the Red Book of the Exchequer to prove that the subject should receive coin as fine as the bullion he brought to the mint. "If the mint master take anie thinge from the xj oz. ij d. weight of fine silver which the subject delivereth him and put theareof but xj oz. fine silver to the fier, or anie thinge les then the saide xj oz. ij d. weight fine silver, & theareof maketh moonnies, he dooth breake the standerd and all the auncient lawes, statutes, and presidentes."

The master may object that any procedure in melting is lawful so long as the silver passes the assay. But Mildmay has an answer to this too.

Silver maie shewe better at the pot assaie then it was put to meltinge. And if the mint master will saie that though hee put but xj oz. fine silver and xx d. weight of copper into the fier in the pounde weight, yeat the same at the pott assaie after the meltinge dooth and maie often arise to bee above xj oz. fine (as for example xj oz. j d. weight fine silver, so that there lacketh but j d. weight of the full standerd, which is the halfe remedie alowed to him in his bargaine): that is but a question in tearmes of fine silver, which is a substance, and finenes in silver, which is a matter of computation subtill (a thinge fitt to bee judge[d] of by woorkemen). But sure it is that the master putteth no parte of the saide ij d. weight of fine silver into the pott which the subject delivered him.

This Mildmay thought dishonest.

He also considered the master's fees and concluded that they should be raised, so that Lonison would no longer need to take advantage of the remedy. Subjects were paying 18*d.* for each pound of bullion coined at the mint, of which the master took 8*d.* and the Queen 10*d.* Mildmay recommended that the master's allowance be raised by 6*d.*, which he calculated as the amount the master could profit from the remedy; he proposed that the Queen bear half the increase and the subject half, so that if his proposal were adopted the subject would pay 1s. 9d., of which the master would receive 14d. and the Queen 7d. Even at this rate the Crown's profit should not be less than £ 1,400 a year.[64]

On March 17 the mint commissioners met. They issued ten articles, which in the main followed Mildmay's proposals.[65] It was agreed that silver put to melt should be of the full standard and that the warden should be privy to the melting. The remedies would still be allowed in case of legitimate variation, but "no scope bee left to the master or officers to seeke advauntage by the saide remedies." The commissioners agreed that the master's allowance was insufficient and suggested (more liberally than Mildmay) that the Queen forego all her seigniorage, so that the master might receive 18d. for each pound coined without increasing the charge to the subject.

The next day Lord Keeper Bacon jotted down his views about the mint. "I thinke it vearie good," he wrote, "that such orders weare taken as neither the warden nor the master might receave any gaine or proffitt . . . other then the particular feese that maie bee speciallie alowed to them . . . , and thearefore I coulde bee content theire feese weare the greater." But he did think that the cost of coinage was unnecessarily high; he had heard that the Flemish mint operated more economically. He apparently did not accept the proposal that the Queen should raise Lonison's fees at her own expense.

In any case the commissioners' report was not immediately adopted. Lonison's fees were not increased, and it looked as if he would lose the advantage of the remedy without compensation. He therefore began canvassing the Council against Martin, presenting it with a paper which attempted to prove that the wardens had never meddled in the melting.[66] The Council presumably was convinced, for on June 5 it ordered Martin to forego control of the melting unless a commission of goldsmiths and merchants should determine that the warden had

[64] In studying fees Mildmay prepared a table of allowances under Henry VI, Henry VII, and Henry VIII, headed "Wal. Myldemaye with his owne hande coppied out," which is part of F(M)P 82.

[65] F(M)P 85. There is also a copy of the articles in F(M)P 82.

[66] HMC, *Eighth Report* (1881), App. I, p. 65, calendar of a copy preserved among the papers of Sir Isaac Newton, a later master and warden.

customarily been privy to the rating of the pot. To phrase the question in this form was to stack the cards against Martin, as was shortly demonstrated by affidavits taken to prove that his predecessor had not overseen the melting. The Council also ordered Martin to deliver the articles in which he "pretended" that Lonison was gaining £ 500 annually from the profits of his office, so that Lonison could reply; Lonison, not waiting for them, sent the Council a tract calling Martin's charges slanderous.[67]

Mildmay, perhaps already at Apethorpe for the summer, had not attended this session, and he was doubtless horrified at the way in which Lonison had gone to the Council behind his back.[68] He continued to press his policies, however, and on June 15 he formulated another set of "notes touchinge the controversie in the myntt."[69] These notes, perhaps the basis of Mildmay's argument in the Council, are better organized than his earlier memoranda but add nothing substantial to them. The paper does not include the recommendation for increased fees, although Mildmay may have discussed this informally. It was certainly an essential feature of his program. Probably of about this same date is "a breviate of thinges in the mintt woorthy of present consideration & reformation" written in Mildmay's own hand.[70] Here he reiterates that the Queen should be willing to give up at least part of her profit: "it is a smaule recompence to hir Majestie, when the master hath so disorderlie taken 3d. to himself, to gett hir other 3d. of th'impoverishinge of hir coine to hir & hir people."

The Council's mill ground exceeding slow. Nothing had been done by December, 1576, when Martin again complained against Lonison.[71] Action still did not follow immediately, but finally, on January 26, 1578, the Council adopted a compromise which probably satisfied no one fully.[72] Subjects were still to bring bullion of the full standard—11 ounces 2 pennyweight silver to 18 pennyweight copper—for coining, or to make good any deficiency. But silver put to melting was to be one

---

[67] *Ibid.*

[68] The Councillors present had been Bacon, Burghley, Sussex, Leicester, and Smith (*ibid.*).

[69] F(M)P 89.      [70] F(M)P 91.

[71] *CSP, Dom., 1547–80*, p. 533.

[72] F(M)P 88; cf. *CSP, Dom., 1547–80*, p. 582.

pennyweight less fine—11 ounces 1 pennyweight silver to 19 penny-weight copper. The Queen was to have the profit from this debasement, which was calculated at 3*d.* a pound. Lonison's fee was raised from 8*d.* to 15*d.* a pound, and it was agreed that the warden could supervise every phase of his operation. This arrangement accords well with Mildmay's original recommendation that the Queen and her subjects share the expense of raising the master's fees. The principal difference is that Mildmay would have preserved the standard but charged the subjects more for having their bullion coined; the Council's award hit subjects indirectly, through coins debased a pennyweight from the former standard. Mildmay's recommendation was perhaps politically inexpedient but sounder economically; the Council's solution contributed to the continuing inflation of the age.

Even with his fees nearly doubled Lonison continued to be argumentative. In December, 1578, the Council ordered Mildmay to examine the standard of gold coinage in hope of abolishing clipping and "other unlawful diminishinge of the same." He reported on January 24 that the lawful weight of gold coins could not be determined because of a dispute over the standard weights at the mint. Lonison was possibly as guilty of tampering with the scales as Stanley had been in 1568; in any case he had refused to accept the verdict of a commission of twenty-one goldsmiths and merchants who examined the weights in 1575. Nothing therefore had been accomplished: "in [this] suspence," Mildmay wrote the Council, the matter "remayned ever sithence without any resolution." He had again tried to compose the differences between the master and the commissioners, but without success. He could only suggest that a new commission be asked to try once more.[73] Members of the 1575 commission were obviously angry with Lonison. One of them, Andrew Palmer, wrote Burghley and Walsingham, "I cannot be induced for any thinge that I have harde to dislike of our verdict . . . , neither will Mr. Lonyson be brought by me to like thereof. Yf he wold, our agrement were made in that matter alredy. In al th'exceptions that hitherto I have harde Mr. Lonyson make there is nothinge which was not by us before remembred and considered."[74] Mildmay must

[73] SP 12/129/19.
[74] SP 12/129/21; January 27, 1579.

have felt relief when, in August, 1581, Lonison retired and Martin took on the mastership in addition to his post as warden.[75] Although the arrangement was not ideal, since there was no one to check on Martin, the mint thenceforward ran more calmly.

One final mint matter may be mentioned in conclusion. In January, 1576, Christopher Bumstead petitioned the Council for authority to erect a mint at York for the issuance of "small moneyes"—pennies, halfpennies, and farthings—containing but half the fine silver of the sterling coins.[76] Bumstead alleged that small coins were very necessary but in short supply,

... by whant [want] wheareof the subjectes ar greatelie endamaged, as that in the North partes theie ar driven to exchaunge oure good moonnies for base Scotish monnies, beinge but copper, and in the West partes theie ar driven to breake the pennie into 2 partes: & in thease partes both vinteners, grocers, chaundelars, tiplers and other retailours doo coine in theire houses severall tokens of lead & doe cause them to go in steade of pence, haulf pence, and farthinges.

Coins of the full standard would be too small to handle conveniently, but with the addition of copper they could be made of manageable size.

Mildmay undertook to answer all of Bumstead's arguments, so that the Councillors, not so experienced as he in financial matters, might not be too easily impressed with Bumstead's specious reasoning.[77] Mildmay granted that there was "sum lack of smaule moonneies" but thought the use of foreign money or broken pennies "sum rare chaunce rather then anie common use." Lead tokens did indeed circulate, but they were not legal tender and no one could be compelled to accept them. Although more small coins were desirable, Mildmay could not tolerate those of debased value; he had too recently struggled through the recoinage. "No one will denie," he wrote, "but that it was famous to all other coontries about us and exceding greate honoure to hir Majestie and all hir noble counselloures to have restored all the coine of this realme from dros to the auncientt standert both of silver and goulde, which if ye graunte to bee true the consequence of the con-

---

[75] Craig, *The Mint*, p. 126.
[76] F(M)P 84, fol. 2.
[77] *Ibid.*, fols. 3–4.

trarie will easelie appeare." One can almost see Mildmay's hackles rising as he concludes:

It seemeth . . . that by your over earnest desire of sum privat proffit you neither sawe that it is Godes coorse [curse] when the goulde or silver of anie nation is torned into dros, nor what blemish it might be to the former fame & honor which hir Majestie and hir noble counsellors have yeat in all forreine coontries for restoringe fine moonies in this hir Highnes kingdom . . . Surelie smale cause hath the common wealth to thanke you for youre paines, but verie great cause as well to deeme youre opinion woorthie to bee indited of grosnes (as your self hath theareof trulie confessed) as also to condeme of your devises as utterlie unjust and unprofitable.

A fifteen-page treatise which Bumstead sent Mildmay did nothing to change his opinion.[78] Indeed Mildmay proceeded to scribble, for his own guidance, a little tract explaining why debased coinage led to inflated prices. Its brief argument ran: "Yf the standard bee brought to a more fines it is the richer and so treasure; being treasure the more among men estemed; being estemed so much the better kept; and so consequentlie the dearelier bought, as a greate deale of wares for a litell moonnie." Mildmay concluded that "the finer the standarde bee, the cheaper all manner of necessaries."[79] New debased coins could only bring new economic dislocations.

A month after Bumstead's naive request, while the controversy between Martin and Lonison was at its height, the parliamentary session of 1576 commenced. With Burghley now in the Lords, Mildmay became the chief spokesman for the Crown and Council in the Commons. Beneath his guiding hand the session proved one of the most peaceful of Elizabeth's reign.[80]

---

[78] F(M)P 87.  [79] F(M)P 92.

[80] In 1575 Mildmay was also burdened with the custody of two sons of Gerald Fitzgerald, the slippery eleventh Earl of Kildare, who was suspected of disloyalty to the English government in Ireland. After nearly a year with Mildmay the boys, who became in turn the twelfth and thirteenth Earls, were released to their mother, the daughter of Sir Anthony Browne, in January, 1576 (Westm. MSS, 2, XII, 1, A5).

## 9. THE PARLIAMENT OF 1576

"A ROMANCE BETWEEN the Queen and her faithful Commons," Sir John Neale has called the parliamentary session of 1576.[1] In creating the "magical atmosphere of this curious session"[2] Mildmay's skill was of great importance.

The Chancellor of the Exchequer, now about fifty-six, was at the height of his powers. He had been in Commons since 1545; in all of Elizabeth's Parliaments he had sat as a Knight of the Shire for his home county, Northampton. Until 1572, so far as our evidence allows us to know, he had played the good backbencher, listening and acquiring experience. In the session of 1572 he had done valuable work in committee, especially in considering the bills against Mary, Queen of Scots, but he was not noted for speeches from the floor. Four years later he emerged as the government's principal spokesman in the Commons, an orator of thoughtful eloquence and a political manager of great patience and finesse.

The session began February 8. Since the Parliament had been elected in 1572 and was meeting on prorogation, there was no formal opening ceremony. Supply was the principal business of the session—no parliamentary taxation had been voted since 1571—and Mildmay probably stood by with his carefully prepared oration, ready to explain why the Queen had summoned her Knights and Burgesses and what her requirements were.

Before he could read it there was trouble. Hardly had Speaker Robert Bell called the House to order when Peter Wentworth, a Puritan hothead, was up with a fiery motion about free speech. Liberty of de-

---

[1] Sir John Neale, *Elizabeth I and her Parliaments, 1559–1581,* p. 354.
[2] *Ibid.*

bate, he thought, had been dangerously infringed in the sessions of 1571 and 1572, especially when the Queen had blocked bills against Mary. She had also told Members that they should not deal in any matter of religion: "God, even the mightie God, was shote [shut] out of the doores." In rejecting the bill against Mary "her Majestie had commytted greate faultes in being so careless of her owne and our safety," he continued; "it was a dangerous thing for her Majestie to abuse her moste loveing subjectes of the Lower House, and to oppose herselfe against her nobilitie."[3]

Wentworth had more to say, but by this time the House saw the trend of his discourse and would have none of it. "For unreverend and undutiful words uttered by him in this House, of our Sovereign Lady the Queen's Majesty," as the Commons' journal runs, he was sequestered, examined by a committee including Mildmay and all other Privy-Councillor Members, and ultimately committed to the Tower, there to languish until the end of the session.[4]

After this stormy beginning the Commons more than ever needed Mildmay's calm guidance. By Friday, February 10, the floor had been cleared for his address on supply. This speech, one of his greatest, is so well organized and compellingly worded that contemporaries, with justification, regarded it as a model oration.[5]

He began, not by stating his subject outright, but by reminding the House of three things: "first, how the Queene found the realme; next, how shee hath restored and conserved it; and thirdly, how we stand now." His historical disquisition showed clearly what he thought of Mary's rule.

No man can be ignorant that our most gracious Quene at her entry found this noble realme, by reason of the evill government preceding, miserably overwhelmed with Popery, dangerously afflicted with warr, and greviously oppressed with debt. The burden of which three cannot be remembred without greife.

[3] Crom. d., fol. 116ᵛ. The remarkable parliamentary diaries of Thomas Cromwell, an otherwise obscure Member for Bodmin, are invaluable in reconstructing events in the Commons from 1572 to 1585. Although Professor Neale has used them extensively, they have further riches to yield and deserve publication.

[4] *CJ*, I, 104; Neale, *Parliaments, 1559–1581*, pp. 325–330.

[5] Cf. Neale, *Parliaments, 1559–1581*, p. 346.

Specially if wee call to mynde how this kingdome, being utterly delivered from the usurped tyranny of Rome, and that many yeres together, was nevertheles by the iniquity of the later tyme brought back agayne under the former captivity to the greate thraldome both of body and soule of all the people of this land.

A wretched tyme and wretched ministers, to bring to passe so wicked and wretched an act. To strengthen this bondage of Rome, wee saw how that there was brought hither a strange nation [Spain], to presse our necke agayne into the yoke. . . . From them and by their occasion came the warr that wee entred into with Fraunce and Scotland, not upon any quarrel of our owne, but to helpe them forward to their great advantage and our greate losse and shame.

The memory of Calais must still have rankled.

How different was Elizabeth's rule! Well knowing the Puritan temper of the House, Mildmay emphasized the religious reform.

The realme being thus miserablie oppressed with Popery, with warr, and with debt, the Queen our most gracious Sovereigne hath thus restored and conserved it. She hath delivered us from the tyrannous yoke of Rome, and restored agayne the most holy Religion of the Gospell, not slaking any tyme therein, but even at the first doing that which was for the honor of God, to the inspeakable joy of all her good subjectes. But adventuring thereby the malice of the mighty princes of the world her neighbours, being enemyes of our religion, whereby did appeare how much she preferred the glory of our God before her owne quietnes. This done, she made peace with Fraunce and Scotland, th'one a mighty nation, th'other though not so potent, yet in respect of their neirnes and of their habitacion with us upon one continent more dangerous. . . .

And that is brought to passe the rather for that her Majesty by two notable jorneys with her forces, th'one to Lithe, and th'other to Edenburgh Castle, hath both quieted that realme and taken away all occasions of hostility that might arrise against this countrey also: by the first delivering Scotland from the French, which had so greate a footing there as without ayde from hence they must needes in short tyme have tyrannized over that countrey to their perpetuall servitude, and to the perill also of this countrey being so neire them, and they so ill neighbours to dwell by; and by the second, ending and trewly putting out the fyre of the civill warre amongst them to the preservation of their young King and the perpetuall quietnes of that realm.

Although these expeditions to Scotland had done much good, they had been expensive. So had the repression of the Rising of the North. Nevertheless, the Queen had "most carefully and providently delivered [the] kingdome from a greate and weighty debt wherewith it hath byn long burthened, a debt begon foure yeres at the least before the death of King Henry the VIII[th] and not cleired untill within theis two yeres." She had thus raised the realm's credit abroad and abolished interest payments, "a cancre able to eate upp, not only private men and their patrimonyes, as by daily experience is too much seene, but also princes and their estates."

All these godly, provident, and wise acts, Mildmay concluded, had brought these effects:

That wee be in peace and all our neighbours in warr.
That wee bee in quietnes at home and safe inough from trowbles abroad.
That wee live in wealth and in all prosperity.
And that which is the greatest, wee enjoy the freedome of our consciences delivered from the bondage of Rome, wherewith we were so lately pressed.
And thus we stand now.

After so glowing a preamble Mildmay approached the question of finance. He was at some pains to explain why, if all stood so well, the Queen needed money. The theory that taxes should be voted only in time of emergency was wearing thin, but it had not become completely eroded and any request for funds required justification. Mildmay gave it:

But for all this, as wise maryners in calme weather do then most diligently prepare their tackle and provide to withstand a tempest that may happen, even so in this our blessed tyme of peace that wee enjoy by the goodnes of God, through the ministry of her Majestie, wee ought in tyme to make provision to prevent any storme that may arrise either here or abroad, and neither to be too careless nor negligent, but to thinke that the tayle of thoes stormes which are so bitter and so boystrous in other countryes may reach us also before they be ended. Specially if wee do not forgett the hatred that is borne us by the adversaryes of our Religion, both for our profession and for that also this realme is a mercifull sanctuary for such poore Christians as fly hither for succor.

It was essential that the Queen "be sufficiently furnished of treasure to

put in order and maynteyne her forces by land and sea, to answer anything that shalbe attempted against her and us."

Some might wonder how the subsidy of 1572 had been spent. Although Mildmay made it clear that the Queen was not to render an
account of her expenditures, he set out the main items: clearing the
debt, suppressing the Northern Rebellion, quieting Scotland, and
maintaining order in Ireland. These expenses had been met only because the Queen drew upon her own revenues, respecting the realm
more than her personal gain and "lyving as you see in most temperate
manner, without excesse either in building or other superfluous thinges
of pleasure." She had refused to debase the coin, to sell Crown lands,
or to borrow on interest—ruinous expedients used by her father, her
brother, and her sister. But her standing expenses were heavy, and
because of inflation their cost increased daily, as "every man [may]
judge by the experience he hath of his private expences." Elizabeth
could not continue to meet them without parliamentary aid.

Mildmay concluded eloquently:

To draw to an end, for avoyding of your trowble, I trust theis few things
may suffice, to remember us how her Majestie found the realme, how she
hath restored and preserved it, and how the present state is now. And therewith also may serve as reasons sufficient to perswade us to deale in this
necessary cause, as her Majestie, being the head of the commonwealth, be
not unfurnished of that which shalbe sufficient to maineteyne both her and
us against the privy or open malice of enemyes. Wherein lett us so proceed,
as her Majestie may fynde how much wee thinke ourselves bound to God,
that hath given us so gracious a Quene to reigne over us, and shew thereby
also such gratuity towards her as she may performe the course of her government *cum alacritate*.[6]

The Chancellor of the Exchequer had done his work well; the Commons' love of their Queen was roused. A committee on supply was
ordered to meet the same afternoon, doubtless under his guidance. It
recommended the usual grant of a subsidy and two tenths and

---

[6] Sloane MS 326, fols. 1–8. Another copy of the speech is Harl. MS 6265,
fols. 77–78; Cot. MS Titus C. VIII, fol. 11, is a fragmentary report of it. Cf.
*CJ*, I, 104; Neale, *Parliaments, 1559–1581*, pp. 346–348. The speech was, surprisingly, not reported by Cromwell.

fifteenths. The supply bill cleared the House rapidly, being given its third reading February 23.[7] It also passed easily in the Lords.[8]

There is some evidence that Mildmay, in preparation for his address, had spent considerable effort marshalling his ammunition. Among his papers there survives "a summary collection of all such subsidies, dismes, fifteenes, releifes, contributions, taxes, guifts, graunts, benevolences, & payments (by what name soever they have beene called) as have been exacted & levied of the subjects of this realme of England since the conquest therof by the Normans."[9] Its thirty pages are carefully written, with authorities cited by page and line in the margin. Although Mildmay probably did not compile the list himself, it must have been drawn up for his use. When he discussed taxes he knew whereof he spoke.

With the subsidy safely passed, other issues came to the floor of the Commons. Chief among them was religion. Puritan clamor for further reform in the Church had already become a standard feature of Elizabeth's Parliaments, and it could generally be counted on to open a serious rift between Commons and the Queen. In 1576, however, even the religious issue was transmuted, largely through Mildmay's alchemy, into romance.

Religion was first debated on Wednesday, February 29, two days after the passage of the subsidy bill.[10] Tristram Pistor, a conscientious but artless Puritan who had spoken for reform of the Prayer Book in the 1571 session, broached the subject, declaring "with greate zeale" (according to the diarist Thomas Cromwell) "the greate prejudice [that] grewe to the realme by the unlearnednesse of the ministerie, abuse of excommunication, want of disciplin, dispensations and tollerations for not residancy, and such like."[11] His suggestion that a petition calling for reform be submitted to the Queen was enthusiastically supported, and the Speaker appointed a committee including

[7] *CJ*, I, 104–107.

[8] The bill was introduced February 27, was given its three readings on three successive days, and was passed March 1 without being referred to a committee (*LJ*, I, 737–739).

[9] Add. MS 34,216, fols. 60–90. Mildmay once owned this volume of MSS.

[10] *CJ*, I, 109.

[11] Crom. d., fol. 124$^v$.

all Privy-Councillor Members to draft the supplication. Pistor, Robert Snagge, Edward Lewkenor, and John Audley—Presbyterian zealots—were also named to the committee; Mildmay, although he desired a learned ministry as much as any, must have labored to tone down their demands and phrases.

Be that as it may, the petition was duly prepared. It lamented the lack of true discipline in the Church, the number of ministers "who are not only altogether unfurnished of such gifts as are by the word of God necessary and inseparably required . . . , but also are infamous in their lives and conversations," and the consequent lack of preaching. Blasphemy, licentiousness, heresy, atheism, even the spread of Papistry were natural and all too common results. The Queen was entreated either to allow Parliament to provide remedy through legislation or to take action through some other means.[12]

After the petition was read in Commons on March 2 and approved, it was presented to the Queen by a group of Privy Councillors including Burghley and some other Lords. Elizabeth, who had been angered when earlier Parliaments attempted to legislate on religious matters without her consent, was gratified that Commons had learned at last that religion was part of her prerogative, a matter for petition rather than statute. She was not ignorant of abuses in the Church and had in fact already taken steps to deal with them. Legislation would not be required.

It was Mildmay who, on March 9, relayed the Queen's answer to the House, cloaking it in his own phraseology. Although Elizabeth had already initiated reform,

. . . yeat she aloweth well that hir subjectes . . . have in such sort and dis-create manner both opened theire greefes and remitted them to bee re-formed by hir Majesty. . . .

And consideringe that reformation hereof is to bee principallie sought in the clargie, and namelie in the bishops & ordinaries, hir Majesty did in the beginning of hir Convocation confer with sum of the principals of them, and such as she thought weare best disposed to reforme thease errors in the Church, from whome if she shall not finde sum direct dealinges for the

[12] What was probably Mildmay's own copy of the petition is preserved as F(M)P 162. Cf. Neale, *Parliaments, 1559–1581,* pp. 350–351.

reformation, then she will by hir supream auctoritie, with advice of hir counsell, direct them hirself to amende, wheareof hir Majesty doughteth not but hir people shall see that hir Majesty will yeouse [use] that auctoritie which she hath to the increase of t'honor of God, and to the reformation of th'abuses in the Church.[13]

The Queen thought well of Commons' proceedings, they of hers. The journal records that Mildmay's "message and report was most thankfully and joyfully received by the whole House with one accord."[14] And so a matter which previously had divided Queen from Commons now united their hearts and affections.

In three relatively minor matters Mildmay acted as liaison between the Commons and the Lords, explaining the position of the Lower House to a committee of the Upper.

His first such employment came as a result of the bill for reforming excess in apparel. This bill had been the first introduced into the Lords. The Queen and Burghley, distressed by the extravagances in dress affected by subjects of middling and lowly station, sought authority to regulate apparel. Mildmay has left us an account of the proceedings in this matter.[15] The effect of the bill, he wrote, "was that the Quenes Majestie from tyme to tyme might by her proclamacion appoint what kynde of apparrell every degeree of persons within the realme should weare, not exceeding for the punishment of the offendor the penalty lymitted in the bill."

The bill passed the Lords February 16, not, apparently, without some difficulty: the original measure was rewritten in a committee headed by Sussex and Leicester.[16] Commons gave the revised bill its first reading February 29, the day of Pistor's motion on religion; but real discussion was deferred until March 10, when opposition became apparent. The bill was handed to a committee which again included all the Privy Councillors in the House and which was doubtless dominated by Mildmay. "The committees," he wrote, "after deliberate consideracion of every part of the bill, at the last agreed to attend upon

---

[13] F(M)P 181. Another copy is Add. MS 33,271, fol. 13.
[14] *CJ*, I, 113.
[15] Sloane MS 326, fols. 15–18.
[16] *LJ*, I, 729–733.

the Lords to conferr with such of them as should be appoynted by the Upper Hous, and so did."

Mildmay acted as spokesman for the Commons,[17] informing the Lords

... that the bill for reformacion of excesse in apparrell that came from their Lordshipps, being upon the second reading much impugned in the Common House, and rather likely to quaile then to proceed in that sort, they thought yt convenyent, both in respect of the matter and in respect of their Lordships that passed the bill, to attend upon them to open such thinges as moved the misliking of the same. Wherein they ment not to trowble them with all that had byn objected, but only with some few thinges such as they could remember and such as they tooke to be of most weight.

Some, he said, misliked the whole bill utterly, grounding themselves specially upon this reason, that where the subjectes of the land have not byn heretofore bound to anything, but unto such as should be certeynly established by authority of Parliament, this act proceeding, a proclamacion from the Prince should take the force of law, which might prove a dangerous precedent in tyme to come. . . .

Some other, . . . not thinking the matter to be so dangerous, becawse the proclamacion is circumscribed within certeyne lymittes, and the penalty sett downe expressly in the act, did nevertheles object against the bill as yt was penned.

They complained of a provision making the proclamations effective throughout the realm immediately after a single publication in one place: generally proclamations had been read at numerous places in every shire, and subjects were given time "to reforme themselves." They thought the penalties too severe, since the bill called for a fine of £ 10 a day plus forfeiture of the offending garment. Henry VIII's Statute of Apparel had prescribed a fine of only ten groats (3s. 4d.). They objected to the "comberous and quarrellous" manner of execution, which would allow "any officer, were he never so inferior, to arrest any man whom he thought to offende, and to take from his back the garment"; only justices of the peace should have such authority. Finally, they thought that seven years, as specified in the Lords' bill, was too long a trial period for such experimental legislation.

[17] The MS account, perhaps out of modesty, does not name Mildmay, but Neale (*Parliaments, 1559–1581*, p. 354) infers, no doubt correctly, that he was the speaker.

To theis objections, answere was made by one of the Lords, after consultacion amongest themselves, in effect thus.

To the first, that they agreed with the Common House in opinyon, thinking the same worthy of reformacion, as a fault happening by the negligence of the drawers of the bill, fore except the proclamacion were published at the least in every county, and a tyme also of warning to such as might offend, they thought yt no reason that any man should be bound.

To the second, that yf the penalty were not greater then in that act of King Henry, the terror would be so small that the mischief would not be reformed.

To the third, that without such a exeqution as was expressed in the bill they dowbted there would follow little good of this act.

To the fowerth, that they tooke the tyme of vij yeres to be little ynough for a tryall what this law would worke.

Nevertheles, they could like very well that the Comon Howse should reforme or alter anything in the bill, as they saw cawse, so as the substance were reteyned.

After the conference the committee did draw a new bill remedying the defects of the Lords' version. It was passed and sent to the Lords March 13. "But of this came nothing," Mildmay's account concludes, "for the Lords, misliking the smallnes of the penalty, the manner of the exeqution, and certeyne other thinges in the new bill, gave yt only one reading, and that session of Parliament ending within two dayes after, the matter proceeded no further." Actually the Lords, according to their Journal, read it twice, on March 13 and 14, but since the fourteenth was the last day of business it was never passed.[18]

Similar difficulties arose over the bill concerning justices of the forests, which the Lords sent down March 8. Again we are fortunate to have Mildmay's running account.[19] The bill, he wrote,

. . . did conteyne an inlargement of the justices of the forestes authority, the effect whereof was that they should not be driven to keepe their justice seates in every forest, which the bill affyrmed was over chargable for men of their calling, and a great delay of justice, butt might by authority of this act send for the swanimote books, and open them, and proceed to the punish-

[18] LJ, I, 749–750.
[19] Sloane MS 326, fols. 9–14, and Harl. MS 6265, fols. 78–80. Cf. Neale, Parliaments, 1559–1581, pp. 355–356.

ment of the offenders as they should see cawse, according to the lawes, usages, customes, and ordinaunces of the forests.

Commons immediately disliked the bill, fearing that it would infringe upon the liberties of the subjects. It was sent to committee and finally to a conference with representatives of the peers, Mildmay again acting as spokesman. He told the Lords that many criticisms had been hurled against the bill, but—how typical of his genius for systematic organization!—he thought four points of prime importance. The measure was unnecessary, chargeable, dangerous, and obscure: unnecessary, because the justices already had authority to act through deputies and did not have to travel through the forests themselves; chargeable to the subjects, because, if the bill were passed, justices might summon offenders to appear anywhere, not necessarily in their home county; dangerous, because "the tryall [may not] be very indifferent, which taken out of the county may be dowbted"; obscure, because the act allowed justices to enforce the customs of the forests, which were "knowne only to the officers and ministers of the forrestes and are so farr from the common knowledge of other men, as few or none that are learned in the lawes of the realme have any understanding in them."

The Earl of Sussex, whom Mildmay acknowledged as a wise Councillor and an experienced man in forest affairs (he was a justice of the forests himself), replied for the Lords.

To the first, confessing that by authority of Parliament the justices of the forestes might appoynt their deputyes, [he] said nevertheles that thoes also could not holde their sittings without greate charge, and their doinges should not be obeyed nor esteemed as the act & proceedinge of the justices themselves, and therefore thought this law necessary.

To the second, third, and fowerth, he said that there was no meaning by the Lords that passed the bill to bring upon the subjectes any of thoes incownveniences that were noted by the Comon House: howsoever the bill might be penned contrary to their intentions, and yett he thought that the wordes were misconceyved, and drawne to a harder sense then there was cawse. Nevertheles, he said, the Lords could be well content that the Comon Howse should reforme such things in the bill, touching thoes poyntes, as they should fynde convenient.

The committee reported back to the House, and the Speaker moved Members to appoint some to amend the bill. "But the whole Howse, a very few excepted, said they would heare no more of it," Mildmay recorded, "and so yt stayed without any further proceeding becawse it appeared the Comon Howse did not thinke their objections sufficiently answered by the Lords." Again his efforts had been largely wasted, although he had prevented any outbreak of ill will between the two Houses.

A third Lords' bill did lead to several acrimonious scenes. It was the measure to restore in blood John Stourton, ninth Baron Stourton, whose father had been hanged for murder in Mary's reign "and thereby his blod corrupted," as Mildmay's long account of the affair has it.[20] Stourton had apparently approached the Queen and found her favorable to his suit; she had signed a bill which he may well have drawn up himself. The Lords, taking the Queen's signature to be a sufficient recommendation, passed the bill without incident.

Not so the Commons, who raised two objections. Mildmay tells us that some Members thought Stourton "not . . . worthy of so much favor," and some others thought that the bill did not sufficiently guarantee the title to land which subjects had bought from Stourton's father and other ancestors. The Commons were touchy about the question of titles because the Lords had just rejected a bill saving subjects generally from errors which might be discovered in their forebears' land transactions. The House ordered the bill committed.

Mildmay and his fellow committeemen met on Monday afternoon, March 12, just after the rewriting of the Lords' apparel bill. They decided to add to Stourton's bill a proviso, "the speciall poynt whereof was to barr the Lord Sturton that he should not take advantage of any error that might happen to be in any fyne, recovery or other conveyance passed by his father or other his auncestors, but he should be in that respect as though his blood were not restored, in which state he cann bring noe wrytt of error." They also attached a similar rider to the bill for restitution in blood of one Anthony Mayney, a gentleman of Kent.

---

[20] Copies of this account are Sloane MS 326, fols. 33–40; Harl. MS 6265, fols. 84–86; and F(M)P 152.

1. Apethorpe, northwest corner of the eastern quadrangle.

2. Apethorpe, Mildmay's mantelpiece.

AN° DINI .1574.
Ætatis suæ. 46

Lady Mildmay
Wife to Sir Walter

By kind permission of the Master and Fellows of Emmanuel College, Cambridge .

3. Portrait of Lady Mildmay, 1574, at Emmanuel College.

4. Portrait of Sir Walter Mildmay, 1574, at Emmanuel College.

poſſit et valeat poſſint et valeant perpetuis

5. Portrait of Queen Elizabeth I, from the Emmanuel College
charter in the College Library.

6. Portrait of Ralph Symons, at Emmanuel College.

7. Portrait of Sir Anthony Mildmay by Nicholas Hilliard.

MORS NOBIS LVCRVM.

HIC IACET GVALTERVS MILDMAY MILES, ET MARIA VXOR EIVS,
IPSE OBIIT VLTIMO DIE MAII 1589.
IPSA DECIMO SEXTO MARTII 1576.
RELIQVERVNT DVOS FILIOS, ET TRES FILIAS.
FVNDAVIT COLLEGIVM EMANVELIS CANTABRIGIA.
MORITVR CANCELLARIVS, ET SVBTHESAVRARIVS SCACCARII,
ET REGIAE MAIESTATI A CONSILIIS.

8. Tomb of Sir Walter Mildmay, Church of St. Bartholomew the Great, London.

So far everything had proceeded smoothly enough. But Lord Stourton, hearing that his case was being discussed, appeared at the committee chamber and asked to be heard. When the committee granted his request, his counsel labored to show that the saving clause in the bill was sufficient, "but being answered to all that he said, he could not much reply but seemed to be satisfyed."

His demeanor was deceptive. Stourton immediately returned to the Lords and persuaded them to send Commons a message urging passage of the original measure without alteration or addition.

Now began the growth of bad feeling between the two Houses. "The Comon Howse," Mildmay wrote, "tooke this manner of dealing to be very strange, not having heretofore received any such message from the Lords tending to prescribe them what they should do in the accions of that Councell, and therefore notwithstanding this message meant to proceed as they had begonne." The next day, March 13, Stourton procured another "earnest message" from the Lords, asking Commons to name a committee which could explain the reasons why they had dealt "so hardly" with the bill.

We may now follow the matter in the *Commons Journal*. The Lords' message, it records, "was not well liked of, but thought perilous and prejudicial to the liberties of this House; whereupon it was resolved by this House that no such reason shall be rendered, nor any of this House to be appointed unto any such committee."[21] When the Lords reiterated their demand in another message the same afternoon, the Commons, obviously in a huff, resolved that they "will (if they see cause, and think meet) pray conference therein with their Lordships themselves: and else not."[22] They did, however, reach what they hoped was an end of the matter by passing the bill with the proviso attached.

Now, with different bills passed by the two Houses, conference was appropriate, and the Commons sent Mildmay and some others to talk with the Lords. They were badly treated, as Mildmay's account reveals. When the Lords appeared, "after a greate pawse," Burghley complained of the Commons' procedure,

. . . specially for that they had passed the bill with a proviso annexed notwithstanding their sundry messages sent to them in [Stourton's] favor, and

[21] *CJ*, I, 114.    [22] *Ibid.*

lastly one message to have conference with them for resolucion of such dowbts as were moved, wherein they tooke themselves greatly touched in honor and thought that the Comon Howse did not use that reverence towards them as they ought to do.

The Lords objected to the proviso because the Queen herself had signed the original bill and because the judges in the Upper House deemed the addition unnecessary. Burghley demanded to know "what reasons did leade them to proceed in this ordre," but the committee-men replied that they were not authorized to make any statement without consulting the House.

Their report of Burghley's chiding moved Commons to many arguments and vehement speeches. They thought their liberties threatened in three points: "one, that they might not alter or add to any bill signed by the Queen; another, that any conference should be looked for, the bill remayning with them, except themselves saw cawse to require yt; and the third, to yeild a reason why they passed the bill in that sort." They resolved to return a defense of their action to the Lords.

Mildmay was again their spokesman. It is hard to picture him and Burghley on opposing sides, and he was manifestly trying to oil the troubled waters when he said that the Commons

. . . were very sorry that their Lordshipps had conceyved such an opinion of the Howse, as though they had forgotten their duety to them, praying their Lordshipps to thinke that the Netherhowse did not want consideracion to thinke of the superiority of their estates, in respect of their honorable calling, which they did acknowledge with all humblenes, protesting that they would yeild reverence as farr as the same were not prejudiciall to the libertyes of their Howse, which yt behoved them to leave to their posterity in the same freedom they received them.

The Commons' procedure in Stourton's case, Mildmay continued, was not "in any wise unduetifull or unsemely," for they had given the bill speedy consideration and had committed it, not with a "disposition to overthrowe the bill, butt to further yt both in respect of her Majesties signature and that yt came passed from their Lordships." They thought that they could not have granted the Lords a conference so long as the bill remained under consideration in their House without breach of their liberties. The Queen's signature they took to be "only a recommendation of the cawse," and they thought they might without offense add a proviso if they saw fit. "Greate and sufficient reasons" had moved them to do so, but they refused to "yeild an accompt of their doinges and of thinges passed in their Howse, which they could not in any wise agree unto, being so prejudiciall to their libertyes."

This conciliatory speech ended, the Lords again pressed for the reasons why Commons had added the proviso, only to meet again with polite but firm refusal.

When the committee reported to the Commons, the House was "much satisfyed, seing that so greate a storme was so well callmed, and the libertyes of the Howse preserved." The bill, however, did not pass, for the Lords would not stomach the proviso and the Commons refused to retract it.

Trouble between the Houses there had been, even in this happiest of Parliaments. But it did not touch the Queen. Indeed she and Mildmay had yet another love trick in store for the willing Commons.

On March 12, two days before the session was scheduled to close, Elizabeth pardoned Peter Wentworth and agreed to restore him to the House. She was, Christopher Hatton told the Commons, convinced that his warm words had proceeded from overabundant zeal, not from malice.[23] Mildmay immediately saw the opportunity to praise the Queen and moralize about parliamentary privilege, but—doubtless wanting time to polish an oration—he did not speak to the matter until the last day, March 14. His words provided a fitting close to the activities of the Lower House.[24]

The Wentworth episode, Mildmay began, offered occasion to consider three things: "her Majesties good & clement nature, her respect to us, and our duetyes towards her." Since Elizabeth had governed so quietly, so justly, and so providently, Wentworth's fault in criticizing her was grievous. Lesser princes would not have forgiven it easily. But Elizabeth, moved by:

[23] Cf. Neale, *Parliaments, 1559–1581,* pp. 330–332.
[24] Three copies of the speech exist: Sloane MS 326, fols. 40–43; Harl. MS 6265, fol. 86; and F(M)P 60.

... the favor that she had conceyved towards us, proceeding from just tryall of our duetifull affeccions towards her, had so qualified her displeasure as she was contented for our sakes to pardon the whole, and that so freely as we would not at any tyme thinke of yt agayne (for thoes were her words), a marvellous grace towards us and never on our partes to be forgotten.

So much was prelude to Mildmay's sober comments on freedom of speech. Commons should learn from Wentworth's example how to behave thereafter:

And not under the pretence of liberty to forgett our bounden duety to so gracious a Queen. Trew yt is, that nothing can be well concluded in any councell but where there is allowed in debating of the cawses brought in deliberation, liberty and freedome of speech. Otherwise, if in consultacions men be eyther interrupted, or terrifyed, so as they cannot, or dare not, speake their opinions freely: like as that councell cannott be reputed but for a servill councell, even so all the proceedings therein shalbe rather to satisfy the will of a few then to determyne that which shalbe just & reasonable.

But herein we may not forgett to putt a difference betweene liberty of speech and lycencious speech: for by th'one men deliver their opinions freely, but with this caution, that all be spoken pertinently, modestly, reverently, and discretly. Th'other, contrary wise, utterreth all impertinently, rashly, arrogantly, and irreverently, without respect of person, tyme, or place. And though freedom of speech hath alwayes byn used in this Great Councell of the Parliament and is a thing most necessary to be preserved amongst us, yett the same was never, nor ought to be, extended so farr as though a man in this Howse may speake what and of whom he lyst. The contrary whereof, both in our owne dayes and in the dayes of our predecessors, by the punishment of such inconsiderate and disorderly speakers hath appeared.

And so to returne, lett this serve us for an example to beware that we offend not in the like hereafter, lest that in forgetting our duetyes so farr we may give just cawse to our most gracious sovereigne to thinke that this her clemency hath given occasion of further bouldnes, and thereby so much grieve and provoke her, as contrary to her most gracious and milde disposition, she be constreyned to change her naturall clemency into necessary & just severity.

This disregard, Mildmay trusted, would never spring from the wise and dutiful men who composed the House.

When Mildmay's lecture was ended, Wentworth was brought to the bar of the House, where the Speaker declared to him the greatness of the Queen's mercy and he humbly acknowledged his fault and craved pardon. "To the greate contentment of all that were present" he was restored to his place.

It is difficult to see how Mildmay managed so many activities on the last day of the session. At eight o'clock in the morning of Wednesday, March 14, he had conferred with the Lords, hearing Burghley's angry speech on the Stourton affair.[25] Later in the morning he had returned with his answer. It was probably afternoon before he was able to deliver his speech about Wentworth. Still later the Commons were called to the Parliament chamber, where the Queen and her Lords were ready for the ceremonies which would bring the session to its end.

Speaker Bell, addressing the Queen on behalf of the Lower House, echoed Mildmay's subsidy address in praising "the great blessing we had received under her Majesty . . . : the restoring of religion, the delivery from foreign tyrannical jurisdiction, our quiet and peace."[26] The Lord Keeper would normally have responded for the Queen immediately, bills would have been accepted or vetoed, and Parliament would have been dissolved or prorogued. But it had grown late. Perhaps the Queen sensed the weariness of Mildmay and the other Members; perhaps, moved by the warmth of her subjects' love, she wanted time to compose a fitting reply. The Parliament was ordered to meet again the next afternoon.

At this last gathering the romance came full circle. First Bacon addressed the Houses. "Her Majesties pleasure," he said, "was that he should say . . . that her Majestie most hartely wished that all those royall vertues recyted by the Speaker were so present in her as might best serve to the advauncement of Gods glory, the profitt of the commonwealth, & increase of the love of her most loving subjectes."[27] Because of her favor toward the Parliament, he concluded, she had decided to prorogue, not dissolve, it. The Members could look forward to another session, which the Queen ultimately called five years later.

[25] Neale, *Parliaments, 1559–1581*, p. 357.
[26] Quoted in *ibid.*, p. 360.
[27] Crom. d., fol. 113r.

Elizabeth was not content, however, to voice her sentiments through Bacon's lips. She spoke herself, delivering a curiously convoluted yet eloquent oration.

After some prologue she came to the blessings of her reign, which had been eulogized by Mildmay and Bell. It was not often, she said, that a prince could please his people. "No, no, my Lords. How great my fortune is in this respect, I were ingrate if I should not acknowledge. And as for those rare and special benefits which many years have followed and accompanied me with happy reign, I attribute them to God alone, the Prince of rule, and account myself no better than his handmaid." Dangers would threaten the realm—how soon, perhaps none realized—but with God's grace and her subjects' support she would win through. "And thus, as one that yieldeth you more thanks (both for your zeal unto myself and service in this Parliament) than my tongue can utter, I recommend you unto the assured guard and best keeping of the Almighty, who will preserve you safe, I trust, in all felicity."[28]

As the Commons and the Queen parted each had occasion to rejoice. The Queen had received her subsidy. The Commons had been promised religious reform and had seen Wentworth liberated. Each was assured of the other's affections.[29]

Some eighty years later James Harrington, explaining the rise of the House of Commons, was to write of Elizabeth as Queen Parthenia, "who converting her reign thro the perpetual Lovetricks that past between her and her People into a kind of Romance, wholly neglected the Nobility."[30] Who can say that without Mildmay's wisdom and eloquence the romance would so have flourished?

[28] Quoted in Neale, *Parliaments, 1559–1581*, pp. 365, 367. Cromwell could hear "scant one word of xx$^{ti}$, no one perfect sentence" of the oration (Crom. d., fol. 135$^r$).

[29] It may be worth adding that one of the bills to pass the Parliament was an act against diminishing and impairing coins, which was probably desired by Burghley and Mildmay as insurance against clipping and against such debasement as that suggested by Christopher Bumstead. The bill was probably drawn up by Burghley—it was introduced in the Lords—but Mildmay discussed it with a Commons' committee and helped smooth its passage. Cf. *LJ*, I, 729–731, and *CJ*, I, 105–107.

[30] James Harrington, *Oceana*, p. 69. The *Oceana* was first published in 1656.

## 10. RELIGION AND DIPLOMACY, 1576–1581

PARLIAMENT WAS NOT to reconvene until 1581, when Mildmay would again help manage the Commons. During the five years between sessions, however, he found little leisure, as governmental problems in religion, diplomacy, and finance required his attention.

Hardly had the session of 1576 ended when a dispute arose between the Queen and her second Archbishop of Canterbury, Edmund Grindal. Although a conscientious reformer, Grindal had little gift for administration or political compromise. It is rather surprising that Elizabeth agreed to his appointment, since his views were considerably more radical than her own; but after Matthew Parker's death it was difficult to find a cleric whose stand coincided with the Queen's, and Burghley recommended Grindal highly. Perhaps he hoped that Elizabeth might be persuaded to countenance such moderate changes as would appease at least some of the Puritans.

Mildmay and Grindal may have known each other since their days at Cambridge, for they were about the same age and had probably been at Christ's together. Grindal had remained at Cambridge, as a fellow of Pembroke College, for several years after he graduated bachelor of arts in 1538. Later he was chaplain to Bishop Ridley and a Marian exile. On Elizabeth's accession he was named Bishop of London and, concurrently, master of Pembroke; he was translated to York in 1570 and to Canterbury on Parker's death in 1575.

In 1563 Grindal and Mildmay had been in contact again, for Grindal, as Bishop of London, wished to take roofing lead from the derelict monastic Church of St. Bartholomew for use in repairing St. Paul's Cathedral after a fire. Mildmay, one of the principal householders in St. Bartholomew's parish, had to be consulted; apparently he objected. John Strype, whose life of Grindal provides our only information about this episode, concludes that the lead and building stones were utilized by private persons rather than by the Bishop.[1] It is unfortunate that we do not know more of the affair. At least it did not lead to bad feelings; we have already seen Grindal, while Archbishop of York, asking the favor of the Chancellor of the Exchequer and praising Mildmay's concern for the maintenance of true religion.

Grindal's relations with the Queen were less pleasant. He was doubtless one of the bishops to whom Elizabeth had referred the reformation of abuses in the Church, as she had told the Commons in 1576. His efforts would have been pleasing enough to Pistor and the parliamentary Puritans, for his great aim was the increase of a learned and preaching ministry. This he hoped to achieve partly through the use of "prophesyings," poorly named meetings of clergy in various localities for the purpose of study and religious instruction. Prophesyings had, in fact, been tried under Parker, but since he was unsympathetic they had not spread. After 1575, however, Grindal nursed them; they flourished.

Unfortunately for the reformers, the Queen was violently opposed. She had never cared much for preaching—she preferred the safer homilies, from which the offending phrases could be excised before the laity were exposed—and she feared the prophesyings as opportunities for the spread of dissenting Presbyterian notions.

The progress of the quarrel may be followed in a memorandum preserved among the Fitzwilliam Papers and probably written by Mildmay himself.[2] It explains "the occasion wheareuppon the displeasure grewe from the Queen's Majesty to the Archbishop of Caunterburye" thus:

> The Queen's Majesty being infoarmed that by the exercises of religion which weare used in divers countries [counties] theare weare like greate tumultes and rebellions to growe, for that at those assemblies greate disorders happened amonge the common people, she sent for the Archbisshop of Caunterburye, advertisinge him theareof & willinge him to enquire of

[1] John Strype, *The History of the Life and Acts of Edmund Grindal*, p. 63. The *DNB*, under *Grindal*, says categorically that Mildmay frustrated Grindal's plan, but this seems to be an oversimplification of Strype's vaguer statement.

[2] F(M)P 70.c.

the troth of the matter, saiinge that if it weare so she would discharge them all generallie. Wheareuppon the Archbisshop sent presentlie to all the bisshops thorowgut [*sic*] Inglande in whose dioses those exercises weare to understande by them the troth of the reporte so made to hir Majesty.

Grindal found that the Bishops of London, Bath, Lichfield, Gloucester, Lincoln, Chichester, Exeter, and St. David's thought the exercises good and wished their continuation, while the Archbishop of York and the Bishops of Ely, Hereford, and Winchester disapproved.[3]

With thease advertisementes the Bisshop retoorned to the Queen againe, but in the meane time hir Majesty was so moved against those exercises that downe she woulde have them, and willed the Bisshop by his owne authoritie to proceede against them theareafter. Wheareunto hee, repliing that his authoritie woulde not strech so far by law, for that everye bisshop at the entrance into his office & oth takinge had the proper and onelie powre himself within his dioses over all such causes, with all humblenes refusid the execution of hir commaundement in that sorte.

Since the Queen would not listen to his defense of the prophesyings, Grindal was reduced to writing her a long letter, "the most extraordinary communication ever made to the Queen by any of her subjects."[4] A copy survives among Mildmay's papers, suggesting that he studied it closely.[5] The letter begins:

It may please [you] to be advertised that the speaches which it pleased yow to deliver unto me when I attended laste on your Highnes, concerning abridginge the nomber of preachers and the utter suppression of all learned exercises and conferences amonge the ministers of the Churche, allowed by there bishopps and ordinaries, have excedingly dismayed and discomforted me. Not so much for that the saide speaches sounded verye hardlye againste myne owne person, being but one perticuler man, and not much to be

[3] The letters of these bishops are included in a group of Tudor and Stuart ecclesiastical papers acquired by Lambeth Palace Library in October, 1963. As the papers are not yet catalogued, it is impossible to give specific references. Copies of the letters, made by the Rev. G. Harbin, are in the BM, Add. MS 29,546, fols. 40–56.

[4] Philip Hughes, *The Reformation in England,* III, 184.

[5] F(M)P 54. The letter is printed in Strype, *Grindal,* App., pp. 74–85; its date is December 20, 1576.

accompted of; but moste of all for that the same might . . . tende to the publicke harme of Godes Churche.

He had never intended to offend the Queen, unless in the cause of God and his Church, but he could not serve her properly by dissembling or by keeping silence.

Preaching, he concluded, was instituted by Christ and supported by tradition. "I cannot marvail enough," he wrote, "how this strange opinion should once enter your mind, that it should be good for the Church to have few preachers." Laymen must be instructed and admonished, and the effect of homilies is "nothing comparable" to that of sermons. But since so many clergymen are unlearned they cannot be brought to preach without such exercises as the prophesyings. These meetings do not spread false doctrine, as the Queen alleged, because they are held only under the supervision of the diocesan bishops, who will not condone incorrect interpretations of the Scriptures. Indeed the regulations were strict: only clergymen licensed by the bishop were allowed to address the prophesyings; no laymen were permitted to speak; no discussion of any matter of state or no criticism of any individual was tolerated.

Grindal concluded,

I am very well assured both by reasons and arguments taken out of the Holy Scriptures, and by experience (the most certain seal of sure knowledge), that the said exercises, for the interpretation and exposition of the Scriptures, and for exhortation and comfort drawn out of the same, are both profitable to encrease knowledge among the ministers, and tendeth to the edifying of the hearers.

He gladly offered his resignation, but he could not in good conscience suppress the exercises. He reminded the Queen, finally, that although she was a mighty princess,

He that dwelleth in Heaven is mightier. . . . Wherefore I do beseech you, Madam, *in visceribus Christi*, when you deal in these religious causes, set the majesty of God before your eyes, laying all earthly majesty aside; determine with yourself to obey his voice, and with all humility say unto Him, . . . "Not mine, but thy will be done."

Elizabeth's heart, rather understandably, was not softened. Indeed

—to revert to Mildmay's account—"hir indignation [was] so kindled against [the Archbishop] as that deprived she woulde have him from his see, utterlie refusinge his resignation which hee willinglie offered."[6] In June, 1577, she ordered him sequestered and stripped of authority for six months. Her ire continued, and in November, when the sequestration was about to expire, she determined on further action. Grindal was ordered to appear at the Star Chamber November 30, "theare to have confessed himself faultie for refusinge to doo his commandement in this matter before his deprivation: but as God would have it, being visited with the stone, his apparaunce failed."

Lord Keeper Bacon dismissed the Councillors, telling them that the Queen would not proceed against any man who was unable to appear and defend himself. He added:

Though theie knewe not wheareuppon this grevous and heavie disgrace should proceede from hir Majesti to the Bisshop, yeat was it manifest to the Lords theare present how hee was accused of greate and waightie causes neither in secrett nor by anie privat person, but by magistrates, judges, and of good caulinge, & bisshops, and that both by letters and messages, as heareafter should be manifested to them, so as that theie woulde both marveile at the heinous matters so committed by him, and also not disalowe nor mislike of hir Majestes proceedinge against the same.[7]

Mildmay seems to have objected to Bacon's strong words, and indeed to the whole idea of a hearing in the Star Chamber. "Neither any commission [has been] graunted from hir Majesty to the Lords of the Counsell for th'examinacion of the cause and the proceedinge hearein," he told the Councillors, "[nor] the cort had anie thinge to doo with such causes." He wondered whether Grindal, when he did appear, would confess his error or "stifflie maintain his dooinges"; if the latter, "he desired them to consider what might theareuppon followe, the people addicted to the matter as theie weare."[8]

The Council at length agreed that Mildmay and Sadler should go to Grindal and "perswade him if it might bee to confes himself faultie." This was probably the occasion on which Burghley sent the Archbishop a private note urging him to yield, "to allow of the Queen's proceeding" and to crave pardon. He suggested "that his Grace may say, that

[6] F(M)P 70.c.    [7] F(M)P 70.a.    [8] F(M)P 70.c.

he is very sorry that he hath in this sort offended her Majesty, as he is charged. And that he requireth her Majesty to pardon him; and not to interpret his doing to have been with any meaning to offend her Majesty." If Grindal could set out such an answer in writing, Burghley would consider it and suggest emendations.[9]

Burghley's letter had no effect. Mildmay and Sadler found Grindal

. . . so settled in his opinion as before hee woulde yealde himself guiltie hee woulde bee torne in peeces with horses, for his conscience did assure him that [the exercises] weare necessarie and he was able to prove it by Scripture and by exsample of other reformed churches, that theie weare so needefull amonge the people as hee was fullie perswaded never to find mercie at Godes hande if hee should confes the contrarie.[10]

Mildmay returned to the Council with a letter from Grindal, who again defended the prophesyings: it might be possible for the Queen or some other bishop to suppress them with a clear conscience, but he could not. He did not think that the Queen had dealt harshly with him, for she might easily "have used greater and sharper severity," but he did grieve at the loss of her favor. If it could be restored, he would be humble, dutiful, and obedient—except, presumably, in the matter of the exercises.[11]

In the end the case was never heard in the Star Chamber, and Grindal was never deprived. Sir Francis Knollys probably expressed the attitude of the whole Council when he wrote that "if the Archbishop of Canterbury shall be deprived, then up starts the pride and practice of the Papists, and down declines the comfort and strength of her Majesty's safety."[12] It was unwise to manifest the discord in the Church and impolitic to antagonize the Puritans unnecessarily. And so, as Mildmay's account concludes, "from that daie forward hee remained in his house as prisoner, continuing in his opinion." He was to die in 1583 without having regained favor.[13]

[9] Strype, *Grindal*, pp. 234–235.

[10] F(M)P 70.c.

[11] Cot. MS Cleopatra F. 2, printed in Strype, *Grindal*, pp. 236–237.

[12] Printed in Strype, *Grindal*, p. 238.

[13] Strype thinks that Grindal's sequestration was removed in 1582 (*ibid.*, p. 271), but there is no definite evidence of such an act. By 1582 he was blind and ill, and his resignation had been discussed for several months before his death.

Mildmay must have suffered some pangs of conscience over the prophesyings. He desired the increase of a godly and learned ministry, but he eventually concluded that the exercises were not the proper path toward it. In a memorandum dated January 22, 1578, he considered the prophesyings in his usual outline form. Her Majesty, he wrote, was willing to allow anything that might tend to the advancement of true religion, but the exercises "rise by privat authoritie, in sum places by the bishop, in sum without his alowance: a thing not sufferable that any shall sett up anie thinges in the Church without publick authoritie, nether hath the bishop such powre." To illustrate, he recalled that after Mary's death "the new praiers [were] necessarie to all in Inglish, and yeat not used before it was alowed by Parliament." Prophesyings could not be necessary, for they had not been used under Henry VIII, or indeed held in any part of the Christian Church for many centuries. It was no matter of conscience to disallow them, for they are "not commanded by express wordes in the Scriptures" and are "not of the nature of preaching and administration of the Sacramentes, which without perill of conscience cannot be omitted." Their restoration would bring grave dangers: "perill of contention and confusion; daunger that the bishop under the pretence of conscience should hearebie geve occasion to the enemies to slaunder the profession; to set the Queens conscience in dissenting from the Archbishop; to condemne the conscience of all other bisshops which have yelded to the suppressing of the exercises."[14] Mildmay anticipated Richard Hooker in calling the prophesyings *adiaphora*—things indifferent, not necessary to salvation—which are not to be used without authority. Although he might sympathize with the Archbishop, Mildmay would in such matters support the Queen.[15]

[14] F(M)P 70.b.

[15] Probably of this period is a Puritan tract (F[M]P 58) which Mildmay endorsed "A forme for reformation of religion which Mr. Josefe gave me." It ends: "The exercises of the Church are preaching, prophesing, prayer, admynistration of Sacramentes." Mildmay had earlier, in 1573, been involved in proceedings against Edward Deryng, a learned but extreme Puritan. On examination before the Privy Council Deryng complained about the Prayer Book, especially the Psalms and Canticles: if the *Te Deum* remains, why not *Ave Maria* also? See F(M)P 59; Conyers Read, *Lord Burghley and Queen Elizabeth*, pp. 113–115.

153

While Mildmay worried over Grindal's position troubles arose in Scotland again. Elizabeth and her Council had not been much concerned with Scottish affairs since 1572, when the Earl of Morton had become Regent, for he saw the advantages of alliance with England and ruled the Scots with a firm hand. Firmness, however, was not necessarily a means of winning the support of the ambitious and disorderly Scottish earls. Factions opposed to Morton grew and allied, and by 1577 his fall seemed imminent. The English government, realizing that the French might exploit the situation, sent Robert Bowes, the treasurer of Berwick, across the border to bolster Morton's position, but to no avail.

As the crisis moved to its climax, Thomas Randolph, an old hand at Scottish diplomacy, and Mildmay's son Anthony were dispatched to Edinburgh. But it was too late. They arrived just as the thirteen-year-old James, tired of being dominated by Morton and now influenced by the Regent's enemies, dismissed Morton and announced his intention of ruling directly.[16]

On March 9, 1578—five days after Morton's fall—both Randolph and Anthony wrote to Mildmay. They were not optimistic: "We see no other aparance but of greate trobles in this coontrie," Randolph's letter began. Morton had suggested conditions on which he would voluntarily surrender control of the government, but they were unacceptable to the earls and strife seemed inevitable.[17] Anthony, more than Randolph, thought the noblemen incorrigible. He wrote his father that the situation

. . . is now altogether withoute hope, for the faction against the Regent is at this present growen so stronge and so wilfull that theie have without anie grave consultation (as it semeth) rashlie and of malice displaced the Regent, by proclemation onelie, whome before by the consent of the whole estates of this realme theie had established. This disorderlie proceedinge in a cause so waightie geveth great occasion to suspect theire evill meauninge toward th'amitie which theie in woordes at this instant profes to hir Majesty and Realme; theire inconstansie and desire of change will not (I feare) bee satisifed without altering and removinge all thinges in this coontrie.[18]

As Anthony predicted, further troubles followed rapidly. On March

[16] Cf. Read, *Burghley*, pp. 230–232.
[17] F(M)P 153.          [18] F(M)P 222.

20 he wrote his father that the Scottish Chancellor, "a man of greate understandinge and modestie," had been murdered by Lord Crawford's man, while "at the verie same instant there grewe greate dissention for victualls betweene the castell and towne of Edenboorgh, which in th'ende waxed so furious that four of the towne lost theire lives in the action." Morton had retained control of the castle as surety for his own safety, but his enemies appeared ready to besiege it. Their victory, Anthony thought, would endanger England, for "theie ar all addicted to the Frenche" and "will presentlie as it is thought joine themselves with the French againe to oure great incoomber and distoorbance, the which it is verie expedient for hir Majesty to prevent with all expedition possible."[19]

Randolph, writing Mildmay the same day, viewed the situation with greater maturity and higher hope. He praised Morton's wisdom and patience, which had "greatelie staid the inconveniences like to have issued," and he reported that the Scots had agreed to send Elizabeth an ambassador to explain their position. "I have had manie good daies sence my being heare," he concluded; "I entende upon this litell shewe or token of faier wether to retire myself homeward for feare of greater blastes or more daunger."[20]

Randolph's estimate was the more nearly correct, in the short run at least. Morton remained in the Council and within a month had recovered a dominant position if not unquestioned authority. The Commendator of Dunfermline, who was dispatched to Elizabeth, suggested continued alliance cemented by English pensions. These grants Elizabeth did not immediately see fit to approve. Nevertheless the situation rocked along well enough until September, 1579, when James's French cousin, Esmé Stuart, Seigneur d'Aubigny, landed in Scotland. D'Aubigny, soon created Earl of Lennox, achieved Morton's imprisonment almost immediately and, in June, 1581, his execution. And so another of Anthony Mildmay's gloomy auguries proved true. Scotland was again dominated by the French.[21]

---

[19] *Ibid.*          [20] F(M)P 153.

[21] On October 22, 1580, King James had written one of his several surviving letters to Mildmay, asking him "to heare and credite" Alexander Hume, whom he had sent to England with messages for the Queen and Council (Westm. MSS, 2, XII, 1, D2).

Nor was Scotland the only area threatened. French domination in the embattled Netherlands seemed a distinct possibility as the Duke d'Alençon, who had taken the title Anjou when his older brother succeeded to the throne in 1574, offered his services in helping rid the Low Countries of the hated rule of Don John and the Spanish.

Elizabeth and her Councillors did not at first view the idea of French intervention in the Netherlands with relish. The Queen realized that the Dutch needed assistance, but she was unwilling to provide it directly. She preferred the Protestant aid which John Casimir, Duke of the Palatinate, agreed to give the Estates General early in 1578. Anjou, however, continued to fancy himself as the saviour of the Dutch, and the passing months proved the need for the forces he could command. By June Elizabeth had decided to dispatch a large embassy headed by Walsingham and Henry, Lord Cobham, to ascertain the views of Casimir and the Estates on alliance with Anjou and, if possible, to frighten Don John into capitulation.

One of the members of Walsingham's entourage was his nephew Anthony Mildmay, who had just returned from Scotland. Although he was not one of the more important negotiators, he was entrusted with bearing messages to Casimir and reporting the Duke's reactions. Walsingham hoped that "by the use of his hand and head I may ease my own, tired with the writing of over many letters."[22]

In mid-July Anthony talked with Casimir, who could still muster no enthusiasm for French support. Anjou, he thought, could not be trusted and could not obtain the good will of the Germans fighting in the Netherlands: "obedience cannot exist with distrust," he commented, "and there are too many reasons for distrusting both him and those nearest him, persons corrupt, abandoned to all manner of dissolute living, faithless and lawless."[23] But Casimir feared that it was too late to prevent Anjou's involvement.

Equally gloomy sentiments fill a contemporary memorandum from Mildmay's pen. Sir Walter feared that Anjou would bring the Netherlands into the hands of France, a prospect which he viewed, very modernly, as upsetting the European balance of power. It was "suretie

[22] *CSP, For., 1578–79*, No. 67.
[23] *Ibid.*, No. 96.

to England," he wrote, "to have Fraunce and the Lowe Coontries in the handes of towe [two] princes; the bringing of them to Fraunce will be perill to England," and there will be "greate daunger of all Europe by the greatenes of Fraunce." He was concerned also that the French might interfere with English trade in the Netherlands, "discharginge of the traffick of Inglonde and [levying] impositions at theire wils."[24]

Mildmay's horror of French domination was not entirely justified, for it soon appeared that Anjou's Dutch project was purely personal. In fact his brother the King disapproved of it. Casimir's fears were better grounded. On August 13, 1578, the Estates signed a treaty giving Anjou the title défenseur de la liberté Belgique and a share in the military command. Neither he nor Casimir had much success in the field; their armies were ravaged by the plague, and discipline had broken down. By September Casimir had resolved to disentangle himself before matters became worse. His sojourn had brought him nothing but illness and unfulfilled promises.[25] Only the death of Don John, who succumbed to the plague in October, saved the situation for the time. Casimir withdrew gracefully, rewarded with the Order of the Garter, and Anjou returned to France in triumph.

French influence in both Scotland and the Netherlands had thus increased during 1578, and it is not surprising to find Elizabeth shrewdly reviving talk of a French marriage. She may or may not have been serious—probably not, although her inner thoughts as always remain hidden—but she appreciated the value of keeping the French dangling. When Anjou conveniently made a formal proposal in midsummer, the Council began deliberations without much hope of reaching agreement. Burghley and Sussex favored the match, largely on political grounds, while Leicester, Walsingham, and Mildmay, motivated chiefly by religious considerations, led the opposition.

Mildmay has left us a long memorandum dated August 28, 1578, in which he lists Sussex's arguments for the marriage, refutes each of them, gives Sussex's answers to these objections, and finally comments

[24] F(M)P 111, fol. 13r.
[25] CSP, For., 1578–79, No. 264.

unfavorably on the answers: a veritable debate on paper.[26] Mildmay minces no words. To the suggestion that Elizabeth will gain prestige from a link with the French monarchy he retorts that "aliance with such a house, so defamed thorow the worlde for insolencie and untroth, will prove no honor nor safetie to England." Instead, "this noble realme will bee in servitude and in subjection to the French, and howe intollerable theire governementt is maie appeare in all places wheare theie have been, as latelie in Scotlande, when theire King's eldest sonne was maried to Marie the Queene and heire of Scotlande." The marriage will not be a protection for the French Huguenots; rather it will be "the next waie to overthrowe them," for it will tie Elizabeth's hands. It will also endanger true religion at home: "the Papist subject that is ill affected alreadie will take such corage by that, and the Protestant subject such discorage, as the like trobles ar to bee feared heare that have beene in other coontries. Th'offence beside to God is of all other the greatest, if oure Queene, beinge the patron of the Gospell, shall bee coopled with a Papist."

Sussex's hope that the marriage would frighten Spain into a reasonable peace in the Netherlands Mildmay dubbed "a mervelus unlikeli thing." Of the proposition that Elizabeth and Anjou might simply annex the Low Countries in case of Spanish intransigence he wrote, "Not so easie a matter to conquere such a coontrie, a waie to bringe us into eandles warr and trobles, a thinge voide of justice also." Nor, Mildmay reflected, could the marriage help establish the succession; Elizabeth at forty-six was too old to bear children safely.[27]

Nevertheless the marriage discussions went on, for Elizabeth and Burghley were convinced of their political expediency. In January, 1579, Anjou's agent Jean de Simier, "a most choice courtier, ex-

[26] F(M)P 111, fols. 8–12. Although Mildmay and Sussex frequently disagreed, they remained good friends; after the Earl's death in 1583 Mildmay acted as one of the executors of his will. Inventories which Mildmay helped draw up, together with an account of Sussex's funeral, survive at the ERO (MS D/DP F240).

[27] Mildmay does not seem to have doubted that the Queen could have borne children earlier. Indeed Burghley, in a memorandum of March, 1579, thought her still "very apt for procreation" (Read, *Burghley,* p. 210).

quisitely skilled in love toys, pleasant conceits and court dalliances,"[28] arrived in London with full powers to conclude a treaty. Elizabeth referred him to a carefully balanced committee of Councillors— Burghley and Sussex, Walsingham and Leicester—and it was shortly agreed that Anjou should visit England himself during the summer. Elizabeth, having heard a good deal about his pockmarked visage, refused to proceed further without seeing him.

Simier, in his negotiations, proposed that Anjou be crowned King of England, that he have joint authority with the Queen in giving offices and lands, and that he receive £ 60,000 yearly for his maintenance. Some Councillors felt disposed to accept these conditions, but Mildmay, with greater concern for the realm's finances, protested that Anjou was already wealthy. He had three dukedoms and six earldoms, from which he received £ 90,000, together with the largest allowance ever given a brother of a French King, "which beeinge true he nedeth no supplie of the Queene, speciallie such a one as the Crowne of Englande cannot beare."[29]

But Mildmay was not reconciled to the marriage on any terms. On May 9 he again warned the Council of its dangers. His secretary, probably his son-in-law Fitzwilliam, took his views "in woorde from Sir Walter Mildmaie and afterwarde sett them downe in wrightinge." The Chancellor of the Exchequer was in prime oratorical form:

Tiranye evar governeth by feare; monarchies bee or ought to bee ruled with feare and love together, neither withoute that conmixture can that governement houlde, as for example our state of Englande, whearein beside the reverende feare hir subjectes carrie, hir Majestie hath as much love as anie prince can have, as well appeareth in that she was never denied anie thinge of hir subjectes whatsoever she demaunded. What a thinge weare it then for hir Majestie to go thorowe in this action of Fraunce, thearebie to loose the hole goodwill of hir subjectes hirself thearebie, beinge the strongest prince this daie in Christendoom.

In that as touching religion, it is saide it shall bee no otherwaies with the Duke then with an embassadoure [who might be permitted to practice his

[28] Conyers Read, *Mr. Secretary Walsingham and the Policy of Queen Elizabeth,* II, 8, quoting Camden's *Annales.*

[29] F(M)P 111, fol. 13ᵛ.

Catholic faith]. The difference is verie greate both in consideracion of the place and of the person: for one thinge it is to suffer it privallie in an embassadoure, a private man of himself savinge for the representacion of his place for the presentt; and another thinge to alowe it in a prince, a Kinges sonne and that by mariage shoulde bee our master, and that in coorte, the example wheareof will strech thorowe Englande, and against which in those that will accompanie him theareunto no man dare speake.

If to avoide further mischeefes like to ensue and imminent daungers that otherwaies cannot bee avoided this mariage bee concluded, then feare is the foundacion theareof, the woorst groundewoork in all such causes: for as a reverende feare proceedeth from hartie love and affection, so no true love nor entire affection can issue or springe from oute the fountaine or bouells of constrained or inforced feare. What then is to bee looked for betweene oure soveraine and such hir husbounde but wholie discontent and utter confusion? Miserable thearefore is that remedie accompanied with so manie mischeefes.[30]

During the early days of August, just before Anjou was to arrive, Mildmay and Burghley managed a brief visit to their Northamptonshire estates. On the way they planned to visit the mansion rising at Holdenby for their fellow-courtier Sir Christopher Hatton. Burghley instructed Walsingham to "tell Mr. Vice-Chamberlain that Mr. Chancellor and I, in our way to Northampton, mean to survey his house . . . and, when we have done, to fill our bellies with his meat, and sleep also, as the proverb is, our bellies full, all Monday, at night." On Tuesday they would ride to Northampton, "where after noon we mean to hear the babbling matters of the town for the causes of religion."[31] Northampton was ever a hotbed of Puritanism, and in particular the Council was troubled at reports of nonconformist services held in Peter Wentworth's house.[32] It is not likely that Burghley and Mildmay took stern action, for they sympathized with the Puritans; besides, Wentworth had taken as his second wife the sister of Mildmay's brother-in-law Walsingham. Possibly, as Read suggests, they were able to preach Wentworth the virtues of moderation and outward conformity.[33]

[30] *Ibid.*, fol. 14r.
[31] Quoted in Eric St. John Brooks, *Sir Christopher Hatton*, pp. 157–158.
[32] *APC, 1578–80*, p. 218.
[33] Read, *Burghley*, pp. 215–216.

We hear no more about the babbling religious affairs, but a letter of Burghley's does describe the visit to Holdenby. Burghley had been flattered when Hatton modeled Holdenby on his own new house at Theobalds and was delighted with the result. "No one thing," he wrote Hatton, was "of greater grace than your stately ascent from your hall to your great chamber; and your chambers answerable with largeness and lightsomeness, that truly a Momus could find no fault. I visited all your rooms high and low, and only the contentation of mine eyes made me forget the infirmity of my legs": his debilitating gout.[34]

Anjou arrived at Greenwich on August 17, just a week after Mildmay's visit to Holdenby. No agreement was reached during his two weeks' stay, which was given over to dining and dancing; but Elizabeth appeared to be enchanted by her young suitor, pockmarks or no. Several opponents of the match were sufficiently concerned that they tried vigorously to counteract whatever impression the Duke may have made on the Queen: John Stubbs published his famous diatribe entitled *The Discovery of a Gaping Gulf whereunto England is like to be swallowed by another French Marriage,* and Sir Philip Sidney sent Elizabeth a long letter in the same tenor.[35]

This propaganda had its effect. Despite a proclamation of September 27 officially condemning Stubbs and defending Anjou, opinion turned more and more against the marriage, and when the Privy Council met at Greenwich on October 2 few voices were raised in support of the match.

Mildmay repeated and expanded his arguments against it on the sixth.[36] His speech was a comprehensive analysis of the state of England and of the principal continental powers; he dealt methodically "first of the perills" facing the realm, "next of the remedies, lastly of the marriage itself." The perils confronting England had been greatly exaggerated, he thought, by those who saw the marriage as a panacea for all diplomatic ills. In fact France, although potentially a dangerous enemy, was not very strong—the people were disunited, the

[34] Brooks, *Hatton,* pp. 157–158.
[35] A copy of Stubbs' tract is Add. MS 48,027, fols. 152–195; cf. Read, *Burghley,* p. 217.
[36] Harl. MS 6265, fols. 104–110, is a fair copy of the address; rough notes for a portion of it are in F(M)P 111, fols. 15–17.

treasury empty, the army weak, the navy "farre to slender to take in hande any greate enterprise." There was no need to buy off French opposition through the marriage.

Spain, too, was "not . . . so dreadful to us as it may be pretended." Elizabeth had no other foreign enemy but the Pope, who was "malicious but nowe a poore chapleine, eleven coontries gon from him," with no military power.

England, in contrast, remained united, prosperous, well defended, happily ruled by a Queen careful to maintain justice and true religion. Still certain measures—"remedia," Mildmay called them—might be taken to strengthen the realm. At home, stricter laws were needed to suppress the obstinate Papists, the military establishment required enlargement, and adequate supplies of treasure should be provided, presumably from parliamentary taxation. In the sphere of foreign relations it was most urgent "to contract a firme amitie and league with the King and Realme of Scotland," lest James, now thirteen, marry a French or Spanish Catholic. If necessary England should be willing to give Scotland financial support, so that she might not become dependent upon France. Amity with the French and Spanish should be maintained whenever possible, but England's true allies must be "the kinges and princes of the Relligion."

Turning finally to the marriage itself, Mildmay began by stressing the danger of childbearing at Elizabeth's age, "for like as nothing can be more joyfull to us then to see a braunch of so noble a tree, even so the sorrowe would farre exceed the joye if we should by having that loose her, seing that no child can be so dear to us as her self is." Conversely, if the Queen continued to live after her present temperate manner she might double her years: a better prophecy than Mildmay could know.

But religion was the chief obstacle to the French match. "From his cradle [Anjou] hath been bredd and nourished up in Papistrie." He twice fought the Huguenots. Marriage with him "will prove, as I thinke, offensive to God and the worlde abroad, and dangerous to the realme at home." How could the Queen forbid Catholicism to her subjects while countenancing it in her husband?

Mildmay mentioned also the possibility of Anjou's succession to the French throne. England would then be dominated by France and ruled from Paris; Elizabeth would lack the comfort and company of her husband, as did Mary after Philip's ascension of the Spanish throne. It was true that an attempt might be made to regulate Anjou's position in England by statute, but Mildmay doubted if acts of Parliament could bind foreigners, especially Roman Catholics who felt no need to keep faith with heretics.

Concluding thus that the marriage was neither necessary nor desirable, Mildmay sought pardon for the length of his speech and submitted his arguments to the consideration of the Council. Most Councillors agreed with his position; of the twelve present only Burghley, Sussex, Hunsdon, and Dr. Thomas Wilson, the Principal Secretary, continued to favor the alliance.[37]

All realized, however, that the Queen would follow the dictates of her own heart and mind, and they sent a committee of four to tell her that they reserved judgment until they could learn her desires. Evidently she expected the Council to urge the marriage upon her with one accord, for she was angered at its lack of resolution; and even when, a few days later, virtually the whole body announced themselves willing to support the match if the Queen willed it she remained displeased. In November she declared that she had made up her mind and would hear no more objections. When Simier left for France on the twenty-fourth he carried the signed marriage treaty. But Elizabeth had second thoughts. By January, 1580, even Burghley had concluded that she did not really intend to marry.

The usual arguments pro and con were rehearsed during February in the Council chamber at Westminster, but now the Councillors considered also "the perills ensuing by leavinge of this aliaunce." Chief among these was the danger that Anjou, despairing of Elizabeth, would "seeke the King of Spaines daughter, whearebie his faction shoulde cease in Fraunce, and he shoulde hapelie have the Lowe Countries for his dourie." Spain and France, thus allied, would contrive to dominate Scotland, "would sett up the Queen of Scottes" in England, "would supplant the religion in Europe," and generally would prove an irresistible coalition, especially since the Spanish had just gained control of Portugal following the death of the old Cardinal King.[38]

[37] Harl. MS 6265, fol. 110r.
[38] F(M)P 111, fols. 17–18.

Although we have Mildmay's account of these deliberations, we hear no more of his own views. Indeed there was little point in his reiterating a position he had already made clear. But talk of the marriage was not abandoned; Elizabeth saw a new use for negotiations in her attempt to divide France from Spain, to play off the two great powers on the battlefield of the Netherlands. First Anjou accepted the sovereignty of the Low Countries, offered him by the Estates General in September, 1580. Then came Walsingham's great mission to the French court during the summer of 1581, intended to encourage Anjou without committing the Queen. Finally, in November, Anjou arrived in England for a second courtship. Elizabeth acted her role brilliantly, especially when she exchanged rings and kisses with Anjou on the twenty-second; but she was now motivated only by policy and danced for joy when the Duke finally took his leave in February, 1582, escorted to Antwerp by a large entourage which included Leicester and Anthony Mildmay.[39] Anjou returned to the Dutch wars, but found his position increasingly desperate and Elizabeth increasingly cold and distant. Few mourned his death in 1584. Mildmay, indeed, can only have praised God for the Queen's final deliverance from the temptation of a papistical marriage.

Surviving records pay ample tribute to Mildmay's other activities for the government, particularly in matters financial, during these years. No one enterprise, perhaps, was especially important; it is the number that impresses.

In April, 1577, Mildmay wrote a memorandum on the realm's finances.[40] One wonders if he was trying to convince the Queen and Council that Parliament should be summoned to relieve the Exchequer's want: it had not been dissolved at the end of the 1576 session and was being prorogued almost from month to month. At any rate he began, "Yf we would consider the greate impairing of the revenue with the marvelus increase of charges thene [we] woulde not woonder at the neede of the prince, which dewlie requireth aide of her sub-

[39] On March 10, 1582, Anthony wrote Walsingham to explain that a great storm at Antwerp had delayed his return (*CSP, For., 1581–82*, No. 596).

[40] F(M)P 9. This memorandum includes a note on the ancestry of Philip II and on the methods of electing Holy Roman Emperors.

jects." He listed the increased costs of maintaining the Household, Wardrobe, Admiralty, and Jewel House, as well as the expenses in Ireland and at Berwick. Henry VIII, he wrote, never spent more than £ 15,000 annually for his Household, but "the same costeth hir Majestie £ 45,000, the hole nobilitye hanginge on the coorte, and so nowe alowid begginge theare." Ireland, he noted in an attached paper, "hath cost hir Majestie sithence the beginning of hir raine five hundred thousande poundes, whereas in times past it hath diffraide itself and yealded a yearelie revenue over to the Exchecor."[41] Similar increases for the other departments had eaten up most of the subsidy voted in 1576. The Queen nevertheless was reluctant to call another Parliament so soon, and the government somehow managed until 1581.

In an attempt to improve at least one aspect of finance, Mildmay was commissioned, along with Thomas Fanshaw and Peter Osborne, to consider how the administration of Irish revenues could be rendered more efficient.[42] After conferring with Thomas Snagge, the Attorney General in Ireland, and with Thomas Jenison, the Irish auditor, he composed a report urging certain reforms.[43]

The Council ordered him to study the standard of gold coin, "as well for that the waightes do everywheare disagree, as also by reason of clipping and washing of the saide coyne, whereby their growethe a greate abuse and hinderance unto the subjecte." He was to seek the advice of the warden and master of the mint, the wardens of the Goldsmiths' Company, or any others he saw fit, and was to return his report to the Council.[44]

In addition, the Council regularly asked Mildmay, either alone or in company with other officials, to settle various sorts of quarrels, generally involving financial questions which were too insignificant for examination by the group as a whole.[45]

At the Exchequer, Mildmay was during these years attempting to settle the bitter dispute between Chidiock Wardour, clerk of the pells,

[41] F(M)P 10.

[42] *APC, 1577–78,* pp. 400–401; November 27, 1578.

[43] *CSP, Ire., 1574–85,* p. 164; March 31, 1579.

[44] *APC, 1577–78,* p. 437; December 29, 1578.

[45] Cf., for example, *ibid.,* pp. 390–391; *APC, 1578–80,* pp. 58, 107, 123, 130; *APC, 1580–81,* pp. 123, 230.

and Robert Peter, writer of the tallies. Wardour, an appointee of Winchester, hankered after the fees and prestige which he would gain from a revival of the pells of issue, or journals of disbursements, which had been given up in the later fifteenth century as useless. The really meaningful records in the Lower Exchequer were those kept by Peter, who had close ties with Burghley and who was one of Mildmay's chief aides in running the Receipt. Probably because the clerk of the pells had been able to cajole the senile Winchester, the issue roll did reappear briefly between 1567 and 1569; then it was again dropped, and Wardour began his never-ending endeavor to have it restored permanently.

This "war in the Receipt" produced mountains of paper which, although disclosing fascinating bits of information, soon become repetitive and boring. Certainly Mildmay must have found them so. In 1580 or 1581 he and Roger Manwood, the chief baron, were asked by Burghley to adjudicate the dispute. Their report does not survive, but they apparently decided in favor of the tally writer: Mildmay naturally preferred efficient present administration, which Peter offered, to the useless antiquated practices which Wardour advocated. But the matter was not ended. In 1584 Wardour succeeded in getting a committee to recommend the revival of the pell of issue, and when Burghley did not heed the recommendation Wardour appealed directly to the Queen. Although he was again unsuccessful, the quarrel still hung fire at Mildmay's death in 1589. Indeed the dispute proceeded merrily into the seventeenth century, with new antagonists but no new issues.[46]

More constructively, Mildmay as Chancellor of the Exchequer kept watch over the Queen's rights by examining such grants of land as the one intended for James Blount, sixth Lord Mountjoy, in 1579. In this he found two flaws: since some of the lands fell within the Duchy

[46] A full account of the quarrel may be found in G. R. Elton, "The Elizabethan Exchequer: War in the Receipt," in *Elizabethan Government and Society: Essays Presented to Sir John Neale,* ed. S. T. Bindoff, J. Hurstfield, and C. H. Williams, pp. 213–248. To the references cited by Elton may be added Add. MS 34,215, fols. 72–76, one of Wardour's argumentative petitions to Mildmay.

of Lancaster "yt were requisyte that Mr. Chancellor of the Duchie shold be made aquaynted," and the Attorney General should be consulted about a phrase giving Mountjoy entire authority over the lands in question. "To have autorytie the hole, and hir Majestie no part, is not, as I thinke, in any other graunt, but somwhat to be reserved to the Queenis Majestie," he wrote Burghley. Nevertheless he was well pleased that the Crown should "graciously relieve a good nobleman so greatly distressed;"[47] Mountjoy had dissipated the family fortune in the pursuit of alchemy.

Other men wrote to Mildmay for favor at the Exchequer, either for themselves or for their friends or servants. Their suits were generally of little significance, except of course to the persons involved; but it is interesting to see Walsingham, Sadler, Knollys, Bedford, and Henry Hastings, Earl of Huntingdon, seeking Mildmay's support.[48] More humble folk also made their requests: Elizabeth Methwold wrote for help in recovering the money owed her late husband by William Byrd, not the famous composer but a former customs officer who had been imprisoned in the Fleet for his debts to the Crown,[49] and several gentlemen of Wimborne St. Giles, Dorset, asked "that the Shirif of Poole . . . maie smarte somewhat for his sawcines," since under his direction "the Queenes tithe hathe bine and is to be wronge [wrung] oute as water owte of the flynte."[50]

Another of Mildmay's duties was watching over the Queen's woods in Rockingham Forest, near Apethorpe. Sir Thomas Tresham complained, in April, 1577, of the poor men who gathered wood there; trouble arose because they took green branches, not the dead sticks to which they were entitled, and because of "ye nomber of ye gatherers, which be infinite, and daily do encrease."[51] Later Mildmay corresponded with Toby Houghton, woodward of Northamptonshire and an old friend, ordering him to repair a lodge in Potterspury Park out

---

[47] Harl. MS 6992, fol. 108.
[48] Cf., for example, SP 46/31/289 and SP 46/32/9, 22, 32, 54, 155, 169, and 218.
[49] SP 46/31/326.
[50] SP 46/31/334, 338; January, 1578.
[51] SP 46/31/228.

of forest revenues if possible, or if not by the sale of twelve acres of forest land.[52]

Among Mildmay's surviving letters of this period are a number to Sir Christopher Hatton. They are of interest not only because they reveal the two Councillors at work, but also because of the light they cast on the close relationship between them.

On June 30, 1580, Mildmay wrote that, although he was quite willing to meet with Hatton and Burghley the next morning as they had planned, it was his duty to warn them that "in the very next house to myne here in this towne, one is deade of the plague, and another sick, so as whether yt were convenyent that I should meete with you or no, in respecte of your contynuall accesse to her Majesties presence, I am doubtfull, and referre the same to your consideration. The occasion," he added, "doeth hasten me owte of towne sooner then I had thought," to the purer air of Apethorpe.[53] The epidemic of 1580 struck some outlying areas severely, but London was not hard hit;[54] there is no indication that Mildmay or his family fell ill.

Later in the year the spire of St. Paul's Cathedral—the rickety Gothic predecessor of Wren's masterpiece—was blown down in a storm, and the Council named Mildmay and Hatton to see to its re-erection. Some wag suggested that they set up on the truncated tower the ship in which Drake had just completed his circumnavigation of the world, but in the end the spire returned to dominate the London skyline for another century. The *Golden Hind* was relegated to a shed at Deptford.[55]

When Sir James Dyer, the Chief Justice of Common Pleas, died in March, 1582, Mildmay wrote Hatton immediately "to lett you knowe it, if you have not hard it before." He sent a messenger to tell Hatton "what I woulde desire that it might like you to doo in this matter"— that is, no doubt, whom Mildmay would like to see succeed Dyer.

[52] SP 46/32/60; April, 1580. Apparently the work was still incomplete in 1584.

[53] Add. MS 15,891, fol. 37; printed in Nicholas Harris Nicolas, *Memoirs of the Life and Times of Sir Christopher Hatton*, p. 151.

[54] Charles F. Mullett, *The Bubonic Plague and England*, p. 71.

[55] *APC, 1580–81*, p. 302; Brooks, *Hatton*, pp. 195–196.

Nevertheless the Chancellor deferred to the judgment of Hatton, who could best judge the temper of the Queen and court.[56]

Mildmay's choice seems to have been Christopher Yelverton, the recorder of Northampton and one of the town's Burgesses in Parliament. Someone, however, had tried to poison the Queen's mind against him, probably on account of his Puritan leanings. Mildmay had to write Hatton again in Yelverton's defense:

Sir, upon some thinges conferred of betwene you and me yesterdaye, I did this mornyng speake with Mr. Yelverton, who, at his next repaire to this towne, will attend upon you. In the mean tyme, hee doeth assure me that he is utterly guyltles of any of those matters wherof her Majestie hath ben enformed against hym, and doubteth not fully to satisfie you when it shall like you to here hym, which my request to you is that you will vouchsafe to doo; for it wilbe greevous unto hym that her Highnes should retayne any suche opinion of hym, wherof hee hath geven no just cause. Touching the matter I wroote of to you for hym, I assure you it was altogether without his knowledge or privitie. I remayne of opinion, as I was, that there is nott a fitter man, and these ympediments being removed, I trust her Majestie wilbe his gratious Ladye.[57]

Yelverton, a golden-tongued orator, did not obtain the position in Common Pleas, but he did later become Speaker of the Commons and a justice of the Queen's Bench.

While Mildmay was occupied with these public cares, his private life was saddened by the death of his wife, Mary, on March 16, 1577. We know the date only from the inscription on her tomb at Great St.

[56] Add. MS 15,891, fol. 76; printed in Nicolas, *Hatton*, p. 241. The New Year's gifts which Mildmay and Hatton exchanged with the Queen throw some light on their positions at court. Mildmay gave Elizabeth £ 10 in coin each year, and she gave him a piece of plate—in 1579 a "guilt bole with a cover, of our store"—weighing about 27 ounces. Hatton, in contrast, generally received 400 ounces, but he gave the Queen very elaborate gifts of jewels, bracelets, and necklaces. Burghley, most important of the civil servants who were not favorite courtiers, received 40 ounces. Generally the Queen seems to have reciprocated, giving back plate to the approximate value of the gifts she received. See John Nichols, *The Progresses and Public Processions of Queen Elizabeth*, III, *sub anno* 1578, pp. 100, 111; II, *sub anno* 1603 (but *recte* 1578, 1589), pp. 73, 101.

[57] Add. MS 15,891, fol. 90; printed in Nicolas, *Hatton*, p. 248.

Bartholomew's;[58] none of Sir Walter's surviving papers mentions her illness or funeral.[59] Virtuous, dutiful, chaste, and obedient are the adjectives with which her daughter-in-law Grace described her; she thought that Lady Mildmay had always regarded her husband with mixed love and fear.[60] One may suspect that the marriage was rather cold.

A year after his wife's funeral Mildmay attended a happier event, the marriage of his youngest daughter, Christian, to Charles Barrett, the son of Edward Barrett of Aveley, Essex. They were wed in June, 1578. Mildmay agreed to pay the elder Barrett £ 800 in compensation for some lands which were to form Christian's dower.[61] Charles died a few years after the marriage, leaving Christian with their son and daughter, Edward and Anne. Christian subsequently married Sir John Leveson of Halling, Kent, whom she bore two children, John and Elizabeth.[62] Neither Aveley nor Halling was far distant from London; although no surviving letters prove it, Mildmay may well have eased the care of office and the loneliness of bereavement by spending some time with his grandchildren.

[58] The date on the tomb, which Lady Mildmay shares with her husband, is March 16, 1576 (old style). Cf. John Stow, *Survey of London,* ed. John Strype, Book III, p. 237.

[59] It is possible that Mildmay was away from the Exchequer office for several months during his wife's illness and following her death; no surviving documents were signed or endorsed by him during the unusually long period from March to July. See SP 46/31.

[60] MS diary of Grace Mildmay at the Northampton Public Library, quoted in Rachel Weigall, "An Elizabethan Gentlewoman," *Quarterly Review,* CCXV (1911), 124.

[61] ERO MSS, D/DL 673.

[62] ERO MSS, D/DL 687.

## 11. THE PARLIAMENT OF 1581

THE PARLIAMENT ELECTED in 1572 met for its third and last session, after a series of prorogations, on Monday, January 16, 1581.
Mildmay and Hatton were of course back as the Knights of the Shire
for Northamptonshire, and—as we shall see—they provided the
principal leadership in the Commons. Humphrey Mildmay, Sir
Walter's younger son, had been chosen one of the Burgesses for Peterborough in a by-election following the death of Hugh Fitzwilliam.
Other Members whom we may reckon as closely associated with Mildmay were his brother-in-law, Mr. Secretary Walsingham, who sat for
Surrey; Sir William Fitzwilliam, father of Mildmay's son-in-law,
whose constituency we do not know; William Brounker, Member for
Westbury, Wiltshire, probably to be identified as another of Mildmay's
sons-in-law; and Christopher Yelverton, the recorder of Northampton, for whom Mildmay had attempted to secure a judgeship. Thomas
Cromwell, the diarist, again sat for Bodmin and again is one of our
principal sources for the proceedings in the House.[1]

Two matters chiefly had moved the Queen to recall Parliament: the
threat of the international Catholic "Enterprise" and the need for
parliamentary taxation. The latter had been obvious to Mildmay as

[1] The *Return of Members of Parliament* does not list Sir William Fitzwilliam, but in the *CJ* (I, 121) he is named as a member of one of the committees.
Since he was in Ireland when the Members were originally elected in 1572, it
seems probable that he was chosen in a by-election. The identification of William "Bronker," the spelling given in the *Return,* as the husband of Mildmay's
daughter Martha is speculative, but the surname is not a common one. Henry
Brounker—a brother of William?—was the second Member for Westbury.
Cromwell's diary for this session comprises fols. 96–115 of MS N. 2. 12, Trinity College Library.

early as 1577, when he wrote his memorandum on the costs of government. The former became increasingly manifest as the Irish rebelled in 1579, aroused by a Papal force which was reinforced, partly with Spaniards, in 1580. Even within England a fifth column of Jesuits, among them the devoted and able Edmund Campion and Robert Parsons, was at work, and parliamentary action to strengthen the realm against them seemed essential.

Mildmay, as in 1576, had prepared an elaborate address discussing the dangers facing the state and suggesting means of dealing with them. But—again as in 1576—other matters intruded, and it was several days before he could take the floor. Indeed it was several days before any business could be transacted, because Robert Bell, the Speaker in 1572 and 1576 and chief baron of the Exchequer, had died of jail fever at the Oxford assizes in 1577. In the absence of a presiding officer Sir Francis Knollys informally gathered the Commons and suggested that, following a precedent established in 1566, the Privy-Councillor Members should go to the Upper House and ask the Chancellor and Lords to ascertain the Queen's pleasure. After some objection that this procedure gave undue authority to the Councillors and to the Lords, the Commons agreed to it; Knollys, Walsingham, Mildmay, and Sir James Croft then left for the Upper House.[2] By Wednesday, January 18, the Queen had sent Chancellor Thomas Bromley word to direct the Commons to elect a new Speaker. Again faithful to the precedent set in 1566, they chose the Solicitor General, now John Popham. On Friday the Queen received the Commons and confirmed the election.

The Lower House was thus ready for serious business by Saturday, January 21, and Mildmay probably had planned his speech for that morning. But the Puritan zealot Paul Wentworth had other ideas. Just as his brother Peter had delayed the session of 1576 with fiery talk about free speech, so now Paul moved for a public fast, "to the end that it might please God to blesse us in our actions better then we had beene heretofore,"[3] and for sermons every morning of the session.

---

[2] *CJ*, I, 116, and *LJ*, II, 20; Sir John Neale, *Elizabeth I and her Parliaments, 1559–1581*, pp. 374–375.

[3] Crom. d., fol. 98ᵛ.

The motion sounded innocent enough and was supported by Thomas Wilson, one of the Principal Secretaries, as well as by Cromwell and such "hot gospellers" as Thomas Norton. Indeed it passed easily, even a mild amendment that the fast "be private, everybodie to himselfe," being defeated by fifteen votes. But Elizabeth was greatly displeased: fasts, she thought, were religious matters fit for her own regulation and not for parliamentary motions. So much—and a good deal more —Speaker Popham told the House at its next sitting, after he had been chastized by the Queen. Hatton, who was closer to Elizabeth personally than was any other Member, also spoke, explaining that her objection was not to fasting and sermons, which she liked well (it was expedient to gloss over her reservations about preaching!), but to the overhasty manner in which the Commons had presumed to usurp her prerogative. He thought the House should make humble submission and ask the Queen's pardon.

Mildmay, Croft, and Thomas Seckford, the master of Requests, seconded Hatton, "acknowledging the rash and unadvised error and contempt of this whole House,"[4] and although several of the Puritans clearly remained unrepentant the Commons resolved to render their submission. This Elizabeth, again communicating through Hatton, accepted "very lovingly and graciously" on the following day—the twenty-fifth; with the romance between Queen and Commons again kindled, Mildmay was ready to speak.

His long address is, like his supply speech of 1576, a model oration: sober, logical, tightly constructed, rising to a fine patriotic climax.[5] He thought good to consider the state of the realm, the dangers threatening it, and the provisions necessary to prevent or resist them.

First, England's condition:

That our most gracious Quene, even at her first entry, did loosen us from the yoke of Rome, and did restore unto this realme the most pure and holy Religion of the Gospell, which for a tyme was overshadowed with Popery, is knowne to all the world and fealt of us to our singuler comfortes.

---

[4] *CJ*, I, 119.

[5] Sloane MS 326, fols. 19–29. Another copy is Harl. MS 6265, fols. 81–83; printed in Sir Simonds D'Ewes, *The Journals of All the Parliaments during the Reign of Queen Elizabeth*, pp. 285–288; summarized by Cromwell in diary, fol. 100; cf. Neale, *Parliaments, 1559–1581*, pp. 382–385.

But from hence as from the roote hath sprong that implacable malice of the Pope and his confederates against her, whereby they have and do seeke not only to trowble, but if they could to bring the realme agayne into thraldome.

The rather for that they hold this as a firme and settled opinion, that England is th'only sovereigne monarchie that most doth mainteyne and continue Religion, being the cheife sanctuary for the afflicted members of the church that fly hither from the tyranny of Rome, as men that be in danger of shippwrack do from a raging and tempesteous sea to a calme and quiet haven.

This being so, what hath not the Pope assayed to annoy the Quene and her state, therby as he thinketh to remove this greate obstacle that standeth betweene him and th'overflowing of the world agayne with Popery.

As proof Mildmay cited the Northern Rebellion, the bull excommunicating Elizabeth, and the continuing unrest in Ireland. Although all these conspiracies were undertaken in the name of the Papacy, they were directed and financed by Spain, "for the Pope of himselfe at this present is farr unable to make wars upon any prince of that estate which her Majestie is of, having lost as you know many yeres by the preaching of the Gospell thoes infinite revenues which he was wont to have out of England, Scotland, Germany, Swytzerland, [and] Denmarke."

But despite the Pope and all his friends the Queen had steadfastly resisted all attempts against her:

The Rebellion in the North [was] suppressed without effusion of bloud, wherein her Majestie might say as Caesar did, *Veni, Vidi, Vici,* so expedite and so honorable was the victory that God did give hir by the diligence and valure of thoes noble men that had the conducting thereof; th'enterprise of James Fitzmorrice [in Ireland] defeated and himselfe slayne; the Italians and Spaniards pulled out by the eares at Smirwick in Ireland and cutt in peeces by the notable service of a noble capteyne and valiaunt souldiers.

England, indeed, had been blessed under Elizabeth with a peaceable and happy rule. But dangers faced the realm; there was "but a peece of the storme over, and . . . the greater part of the tempest remayneth behinde and is like to fall upon us," for the Pope, the Spanish, and the Irish could be counted on to renew their "lewd and malicious enterprizes" whenever the English relaxed their vigilance. The Pope, Mildmay noted, was busy "embouldning . . . unduetyfull subjectes to stand fast in their disobedience to her Majestie and her lawes."

To confirme them herein, and to increase their nombres, you see how [he] hath and doth comfort their hollow heartes with absolucons, dispen- sations, reconciliations, and such other thinges of Rome; you see how lately he hath sent hither a sort of hipocrites naming themselves Jesuites, a rable of vagrant fryers newly sprung upp and comyng through the world to trowble the Church of God, whoes principall errand is, by creeping into the howses and familiarityes of men of behaviour and reputacion, not only to corrupt the realme with false doctrine, but also under that pretence to stirr sedition, to the perill of her Majestie and her good subjectes.

How thoes practizes of the Pope have wrought in the disobedient sub- jectes of this land is both evident and lamentable to consider, for such ympression hath th'estimacion of the Popes authority made in them, as not only thoes which from the beginyng have refused to obey, but many, yea very many of those which divers yeres together did yield and conforme themselves in their open accions, sithence the decrees of that unholy Councel of Trent and sithence the publishing and denouncing of that blasphemous bull against her Majestie and sithence thoes secrett absolucons and recon- ciliacions and the swarming hither of Popish preistes and monkish Jesuites, have and do utturly refuse to be of our Church or to report to our preach- inges and prayers. The sequel whereof must needs prove dangerous to the whole state of this Commonwealth.

So much was prologue to Mildmay's proposals for action. He favored new anti-Catholic legislation, since the Queen's "gentle man- ner of dealing with the disobedient contempnours of Religion to wynn them by faire meanes, if yt were possible, hath done no good, but hath bredd in them a more arrogant and contemptuous spirit." They were "dangerous members too much borne with in the entrailes of our Commonwealth."

Mildmay also urged the provision of "forces sufficient to answere any vyolence that may be offered, either here or abrode, for the which you know yt is requisite that her Majestie do make preparation, both by sea and by land." This endeavor would require money, for "theis forces, with their munycion and furniture, can neyther be prepared nor maynteyned to have continuance without provision of treasure sufficient to beare the charge, being as you know termed of old the *Nervus Belli*. This belongeth to us to consider, and that in tyme, that there be noe lacke of the synnews that must hold together the strength of our body." All the money granted in 1576, together with much of the Queen's own revenue, had been expended on the defense of the realm. A new grant was essential, since England's enemies "will spare no cost, nor leave any meane unassayed" in their program of conquest and conversion.

A glowing peroration brought Mildmay's address to an end.

Therefore to conclude, seing the malice of the Pope and his confederates is so notorious unto us, and seing the dangers be so greate, so evident and so imynent, and seing that preparacon to withstand them cannot be made without support of the realme, and seing that our duetyes to God, our Quene and Countrey, and the necessity that hangeth upon our owne safe-gardes, be reasons sufficient to perswade us, lett us thinke upon theis matters as the weight of them deserveth. And so provyde in tyme both by lawes to restreyne and correct the evill affected subject, and by provision of that which shalbe requisite for the mayntenance of forces; as our enemyes, fynd-ing our mynds so willing and our hands so ready to keepe in order our countrey to furnish her Majestie of all that shalbe necessary, may either be discouraged to attempt anything against us, or yf they do, they may fynde such resistance as shall bring confusion to themselves, honour to our most gracious Queen, and safety to us all.

Mildmay's tone toward the Catholics may seem intemperate, but it was effective; he well knew the Puritan mind of the House and the rising hatred of the Jesuits. His handling of the plea for taxation also merits admiration. One notes particularly the skill with which he turns aside the anticipated complaint that, with the rise in prices, men can ill afford a subsidy—the increasing costs experienced by subjects enable them to appreciate personally the government's great expenses. All in all it was, as Sir Simonds D'Ewes wrote some half century later, "a most honourable, grave, wise and honest speech,"[6] and, Thomas Cromwell tells us, "very well liked" by the House.[7] Indeed Thomas Norton rose immediately to declare that, "as he thinketh, none of this

---

[6] D'Ewes, *Journals*, p. 285.

[7] Crom. d., fol. 100ᵛ. The *CJ* (I, 119) agrees that Mildmay spoke "very elo-quently, gravely and wisely."

House can or will mislike of the said motion," and to request that a committee be chosen forthwith to frame the bills Mildmay sought.[8]

The large group appointed by Speaker Popham included all Councillor Members and fifty-seven others. They met first on the afternoon of Mildmay's speech, and frequently throughout the session. From their deliberations finally emerged the subsidy bill and an anti-Catholic act.

Supply, thanks partly to Mildmay's careful preparation of the ground, met with no opposition. A bill for the collection of a subsidy and two tenths and fifteenths was read February 10 and 13 and passed March 1. Neither Cromwell nor the clerk of the House recorded discussion at any stage.

Religious legislation, however, was a complicated and touchy affair. Most of the Commons favored Draconian laws to repress the Catholics, while the Lords tended to be more moderate; the Queen as always was unwilling to persecute subjects for their inward beliefs if they remained outwardly loyal. The result was a complex struggle, almost as difficult for us to follow as it must have been for Mildmay to help mediate.

It began February 7, when the committee introduced a bill "for the obedience to the Queen's Majesty against the see of Rome." Cromwell, who always showed an interest in matters religious, gives a detailed account of its provisions.[9] Among them were penalties for hearing Mass—two hundred marks and a year's imprisonment for the first offense, and for the second the pains of the old Statute of Praemunire: confiscation of all property. Anyone saying Mass was to be adjudged a felon. There were penalties also for failure to attend the services of the established Church, ranging from a fine of £ 20 to praemunire in cases of suspected Papists and from £ 10 to £ 40 for others. Further clauses affected the concealers of such offenders, especially their wives. It was a savage bill, designed to break the Catholics.

After it was read Hatton rose to tell the House that the Lords had a similar measure under consideration and to suggest a conference with them, presumably so that the two Houses might present a solid front

[8] *CJ,* I, 119.
[9] Crom. d., fol. 105.

to the Queen.[10] Mildmay seems to have acted as spokesman for the large Commons' delegation, and on the eighteenth he reported

... that the committees appointed by this House to have conference with the Lords touching the bill of religion have sundry times met together with their Lordships about the same bill; and that the same bill is, by the said committees, in some parts altered, changed, and amended; and in some other parts abridged; and in some others added unto: and so delivered in the same bill as amended, requiring that the same should now be presently read, as for the first reading thereof.[11]

Cromwell says that it "was altered in fewe pointtes save that there is a penaltie of £ 10 layd uppon the wife refusing to come to church and authority given to make search in howses for Jesuites and like offenders."[12] In addition, there were fines for failure to receive Communion twice a year. The bill was harsher than ever.

Days passed; minor business was transacted; but the bill was not put to a second reading. Why, we do not know: Neale speculates that the Councillors were busy trying to gain the Queen's approval for the measure.[13] Then, on February 27, the Lords requested another conference—an unusual step, in that the Commons should have held the initiative, since the bill remained with them. After further meetings a new, third bill was introduced on Saturday, March 4, Knollys rather than Mildmay speaking for the conferees. Cromwell unhelpfully calls it merely "the bill concerning absolvers, persons absolved to Roome, massing priestes, and recusants to come to church." It was immediately read twice and, after considerable discussion, sent to be engrossed.[14] On Monday, the sixth, it passed the Commons, and then breezed through the Lords with no sign of difficulty.

Probably the Commons was not completely satisfied with the bill, for it was a far milder measure than either of the earlier drafts; apparently the Privy Councillors of both Houses modified the measure when they became convinced that the Queen would stomach nothing

---

[10] *CJ*, I, 123; Neale, *Parliaments, 1559–1581*, pp. 386–387.

[11] *CJ*, I, 128.

[12] Crom. d., fol. 107ᵛ.

[13] Neale, *Parliaments, 1559–1581*, p. 388.

[14] Crom. d., fol. 111ʳ; *CJ*, I, 130.

harsher. In its final form the bill condemned as traitors those who withdrew subjects from their natural allegiance or "for that intent" converted them to the Romish religion. The qualifying clause is significant: sedition, not the Catholic faith as such, was the target of the statute. Penalties for hearing Mass and for nonattendance at Church were scaled down, though they would still be crushing for all but the wealthiest subjects, and Catholics were excluded from such influential professions as the law and schoolteaching. It is certain that Mildmay, along with most of his colleagues, would have liked more, but half a loaf was better than none: better a moderate bill which the Queen might digest than a strong one which she would veto. How indebted to her we are for such measure of toleration as existed!

Although this was the principal anti-Catholic bill, there are other religious strands in the parliamentary tapestry which Mildmay was helping weave. Of nearly equal importance was the bill "against seditious words and rumors uttered against the Queen's most excellent Majesty." This measure began in the Lords, where Burghley was doubtless its principal architect; it was first read in the Upper House early in the session, on January 18.[15] Intended to increase the punishments provided by an existing statute erected under the similar if opposite conditions of Mary's reign, it included savage penalties. Cromwell listed them, with the shaky grammar of the note taker, in his diary:

. . . the speaker of sclaunderous wordes against the Queens Majestie should be sett uppon the pillorie, leese his eares, and suffer imprisonment at the Queenes pleasure; if uppon reporte of another, leese one of his eares and a yeares imprisonment, and for the second offence felony; if by writing, printing, etc., felony at the first; and that calculating the Queenes death or concerning the succession, or utter prophecies or will her death, felony.[16]

Felony could, of course, mean death.

The bill came down from the Lords on the last day of January, more than a week before the principal anti-Catholic bill was to emerge from the Commons' committee. At its second reading February 1 the bill was discussed considerably; Norton proposed an addition making

---

[15] *LJ,* II, 22.     [16] Crom. d., fol. 102$^r$.

it seditious rumor, punishable by death, to affirm that the doctrine of the established Church was in any way heretical or schismatical: an attempt to make the bill more clearly an anti-Catholic measure. It was committed to a large group—all the Councillor Members and some three dozen others—where it remained for nearly three weeks. The delay was probably due to the fact that most of the committeemen were busy hammering out the chief anti-Catholic bill. But on February 20 the Lords' bill reappeared "with diverse amendments" and with Norton's addition. It was not considered a new bill but was, after some further discussion, passed on third reading.[17]

The Lords now demanded a conference, to learn why the Commons had altered their measure. Mildmay and a number of his colleagues met with the Lords' committee, but to little avail; the Upper House proceeded to amend the amendments, and on March 11 the bill was once again before the Commons. Cromwell voiced the House's dismay at the Lords' alterations: whereas the Commons had amended the bill so that only speeches "intending the sclaunder and dishonor of the Queenes Majesty" were punishable, the Lords refused to inquire into the intent and had made the bill apply to any words "tending" to her slander. Would pious Puritan sentiments, if they included criticism of the established Church, be comprehended under such a clause? No doubt Norton and the Wentworths were concerned, and very possibly Mildmay too. The Lords had also stricken out one whole amendment and parts of others and had altered "the very substance of the sense" of Norton's addition.

Much discussion, no doubt informed by both sorrow and anger, followed. "It was agreed," Cromwell wrote, "that by this act [of the Lords] we were disabled to deale with the bill, since directly disalowinge of our amendments we could not undoe that which we had donn." After some talk of precedents the Commons concluded that the bill should be returned to the Lords "with a message that we founde it so dealt with as we could not by lawe proceede any farther thereuppon."[18]

The deadlock could hardly be allowed to stand, and Hatton undertook to break it. On March 14 he asked that a new bill be framed—if

[17] *Ibid.,* fol. 108ᵛ.      [18] *Ibid.,* fol. 113ʳ.

the previous one was lost, the House might at least begin afresh—
"to the intent we might shewe ourselves carefull of [the Queen's]
estate." With the end of the session in sight speed was essential; the
new bill was read twice on March 15 and passed by the Commons the
next day. On the seventeenth Mildmay, Hatton, Knollys, Cromwell,
and six others conferred with the Lords about it, and ultimately the
Upper House accepted the bill without significant change.

The new measure represented genuine compromise. The Lords
yielded the most, since the second bill greatly reduced the penalties of
the first. A choice of loss of ears or a fine was introduced, to be "at
the election of the offender"; terms of imprisonment were drastically
scaled down; the saving phrase "with a malicious intent" was included;
the Marian statute was declared repealed, as the Commons had wished.
The Norton addition was, however, now deleted: in this matter the
Lords—and doubtless, as Neale speculates, the Queen too—prevailed.[19] Thus the sedition act, as the measure came to be called, was
made milder by the Commons: an ironic *volte-face* from their position
in the earlier religious bill, although understandable in view of their
fear that the statute might operate against Puritans as well as Papists.

Running parallel to the sedition bill, during its earlier stages at least,
was a Lords' bill against slander of great officers of state, bishops, and
noblemen. Spreaders of such slander, tried and convicted in the Star
Chamber, were to be set upon the pillory and fined and imprisoned at
the discretion of the Court, and "the knower and not revealer" of
slander was to be fined £ 20. At the second reading in Commons, on
February 3, the bill was "impugned for many cawses and at last
commytted" to Mildmay, Hatton, Sir William Fitzwilliam, and some
others. It died in committee, and the Puritans thus remained unham-
pered in their attacks on the prelates.[20]

Attack the prelates the Commons certainly did, in another skirmish
shrewdly handled by Mildmay. On March 3, after four routine bills
had been read, some of the Puritans in the House inquired what had
happened to the petition for religious reform presented to the Queen

[19] Neale, *Parliaments, 1559–1581,* p. 397; *CJ,* I, 135.
[20] Neale, *Parliaments, 1559–1581,* p. 398; Crom. d., fols. 102ʳ, 103ᵛ; *CJ,* I,
121.

in 1576. Elizabeth, it will be recalled, had promised to take action, either through the bishops or on her own authority as Supreme Governor of the Church. But no progress, or at least none visible to Puritan eyes, had been made.

Mildmay, along with Hatton, Walsingham, and Wilson, had apparently anticipated the thrust and had already conferred with some of the bishops. The prelates' answers, however, did not satisfy the House: the Commons resolved, "after sundry motions and arguments," that the four Councillors should "move the Lords of the Clergy" again, this time on behalf of the whole House, "to continue unto her Majesty the prosecution of the purposes of reformation," and also "impart unto their Lordships the earnest desire of this House for redress of such other griefs, contained likewise in the said petitions, as have been touched this day."[21]

Further conference was held, and Mildmay reported the results on March 7. No text of his speech survives, but fortunately the clerk included a fuller than usual summary in his journal.

Mr. Chancellor of the Exchequer declareth that Mr. Vice-Chamberlain, both Secretaries, and himself, have, according to their commission from this House, conferred with some of my Lords the Bishops touching the griefs of this House for some things very requisite to be reformed in the Church; as, the great number of unlearned and unable ministers; the great abuse of excommunication for every matter of small moment; the commutation of penance; and the great multitude of dispensations and pluralities.

Some of the bishops had readily confessed the defects and joined in moving the Queen for reformation. Her answer was that the clergymen to whom she had entrusted the matter after the last session "had not performed the same according to her Highness' commandment; so now her Majesty would eftsoons [again] commit the same unto such others of them as with all convenient speed . . . should see the same accomplished." Mildmay emphasized that failure was due wholly to the "negligence and slackness" of certain bishops, not to any fault in the Queen or the Commons; some bishops, he added, had tried to do something but had accomplished "little or nothing to the purpose."[22]

Mildmay concluded by asking the House to thank the Queen for

[21] *CJ*, I, 127.     [22] *Ibid.*, p. 131.

graciously accepting the petition and agreeing once again to pursue the reforms. There was discussion, then the reading of two routine bills, then more "long speech" about religion. Finally Mildmay, doubtless hoping to make an end of the matter, proposed that the Speaker in his oration at the end of the session "should farther in the name of all the Howse earnestly move her Majestie for the execution" of the reforms.[23] And so the affair was, for the time, settled.

One of the fascinating episodes of this session brought to a climax the parliamentary career of Arthur Hall, Member for Grantham, Lincolnshire. A minor light in literary history as the translator of the first English Homer, Hall was perhaps best described by Sir Francis Knollys: he "had the disease of his father," who was "somewhat inclined to madness."[24] Hall was also, by his own confession, somewhat inclined to "the old Father of Rome," and his conservative views had embroiled him in troubles with the Commons at both of the earlier sessions. In 1572 he had urged mercy for the Duke of Norfolk, a most unpopular sentiment, for which, together with "sundry lewd speeches," both in and out of the House, he was severely chided by the Speaker.[25] Four years later the Commons devoted a great deal of their time to the case of Edward Smalley, one of Hall's servants, who had cut open the cheek of Melchisedech Mallory in a tavern fray incited by Hall. A London jury awarded Mallory £ 100 damages, which his heirs attempted to collect when he died shortly after, though not as a result of, the incident. But Smalley would not pay. The conniving Hall managed to procure Smalley's arrest so that he could complain in the House that parliamentary privilege had been infringed by the incarceration of a Member's servant: his idea was to have Smalley freed in such a manner that he could not subsequently be apprehended for the same offense.

Mildmay had favored the defense of privilege, although he also supported compensation for the Mallorys and spent a good deal of effort working with a committee which ultimately secured payment of the £ 100. This should have been the end of the affair; but several

---

[23] Crom. d., fol. 111ʳ.
[24] Neale, *Parliaments, 1559–1581,* pp. 260–261.
[25] *CJ,* I, 95–96.

Members, seeing through Hall's intrigue, accused him of having dealt "covinously, fraudulently, and cunningly," and the House voted to send Smalley to the Tower on its own authority, as guilty of contempt and abuse of the House. A bill against Hall was also drawn up—it would have excluded him from ever sitting again—but it was finally dropped after Hall submitted and craved pardon.[26]

Again this should have ended the matter, but it did not. Hall proceeded to write *An Account of a Quarrel between Arthur Hall Esq. and Melchisedech Mallerie Gent.*, a bitter tract detailing the events of the dispute from his point of view, and—worse still!—*An Admonition by the Father of F. A. to him being a Burgesse of the Parliament for his better Behaviour therein*, a pamphlet filled with vituperative comments on the House of Commons, its history and procedure. Both had appeared by 1579.[27]

And now we are ready for the parliamentary battle of 1581. It began February 4, when Norton—an old foe of Hall, for obvious religious reasons—angrily informed the House of Hall's blasphemy. His book, Norton said, charged "this House with drunkenness, as accompanied in their counsels with *Bacchus*; and them also with Choler, as those which had never failed to *Anticyra*; and the Proceedings of this House to be *Opera Tenebrarum*," works of darkness. He was followed by Mildmay, who "uttered . . . some speech . . . of the dangerous and lewd contents of the said book." Small wonder that Mildmay, Hatton, and some others were commissioned to examine Hall and his printer and to bring Hall to answer for his statements before the whole House.[28]

Cromwell describes the events of February 6:

This day Mr. Arthur Hall was brought to the barre to answer his offence in publishing, cawsing the booke to be printed, for which he was before apointed to be atached; the cawsing of the booke to be printed he confessed, but he would not by any meanes be induced to confesse that he had offended or given cawse of offence in the doing thereof; only he sayd if he had offended he desired the Howse to be good unto him. He also denied the publishing or having any more of the said bookes then one, and that him-

---

[26] Neale, *Parliaments, 1559–1581*, pp. 333–345, and sources there cited.

[27] A. W. Pollard and G. R. Redgrave, *Short-Title Catalogue of English Books, 1475–1640*, No. 12629.

[28] *CJ*, I, 122.

selfe had also restrained the publishing thereof, but uppon examination of the printer of the booke it fell out that he had xiij of the same, of the which one at the first, six in Michellmas terme was twelvemoneth, and vj in Michelmasse terme last, and that he had also cawsed one to be delivered forth this Parliament tyme.[29]

The committee examined Hall on the ninth—its meeting was put over from the eighth because of a more pressing conference with the Lords over the anti-Catholic bill—and the whole House took up the matter again on the fourteenth. Hatton, who had previously defended Hall, now reported that he had treated the committee disrespectfully and unreasonably; after "long debating what punishment should be inflicted uppon him" it was resolved, "without any one negative voice," that he should be committed to the Tower for six months, or for a longer time if he refused to recant his errors, fined five hundred marks, and expelled from the House.[30] Since he had still not made his submission by the last day of the session, the House agreed on March 18 that Mildmay and the other Councillor Members, or any three of them, should "consider . . . and . . . have the alowance of his said submission during the vacation tyme, without which made in writing to their liking he is ordered not to be delivered after the vj monethes."[31] A fortnight later he yielded, and the Queen remitted the fine and the remainder of the imprisonment. Hall was to live on until 1604 and indeed to procure his re-election in 1584, although he did not take his seat. But his later career is curiously quiet. Perhaps, incorrigible though he was, he had finally learned his lesson.

A number of minor matters round out the story of this session. One bill which came before the Houses, for instance, accounted as aliens those children born in England of foreign parents. This was introduced in the Commons on January 24 and was the next day "much impugned, first as being against equitie, against the lawe [of] nature, an imposition of punishment for the father['s] no offense, and lastly very perilous to all, a thing that might be objected to our children after two or three discents and call every man's inheritance in question." It was

[29] Crom. d., fol. 104.
[30] *Ibid.*, fol. 107$^v$; *CJ*, I, 125; Neale, *Parliaments, 1559–1581*, pp. 407–410.
[31] Crom. d., fol. 114$^v$.

therefore committed to Mildmay, Knollys, Norton, and others, who brought in a new bill providing that children of aliens should be considered subjects so long as they remained within England and in "sole obedience" to the Queen, a phrase perhaps supplied by Norton in hope that it would exclude the Catholics. On third reading, February 7, "diverse great imperfections" were discovered, and the bill was again committed. "Reformed in diverse pointes," it finally passed the Commons February 17; but, as Cromwell noted, it was "not liked of by the Lords," and did not proceed.[32]

Another bill, introduced on January 24, required "it to be made felony to counterfet commissions or other writinges under seales of offices or other courts, or seals of corporations." It was sent on the twenty-sixth to a committee including Mildmay, Hatton, Knollys, and Cromwell. Unfortunately our diarist did not keep an account of the committee sessions; he was perhaps less concerned than was Mildmay, whose work at the Exchequer must have demonstrated the difficulties created by counterfeit instruments and seals. At any rate Mildmay presented the committee's new bill to the House on February 1. It experienced no difficulty until the ninth, when on third reading it was "long disputed of," the Members especially disliking such severe punishment for counterfeiters of documents of municipal corporations. Since the House had already considered eight bills that day, it was put over for further argument, and finally an augmented committee produced a new bill on the sixteenth—an unusual procedure, since the second bill had already been engrossed. The third bill finally passed the Lower House on the twenty-first only to be overthrown by the Lords: again Mildmay's efforts proved futile. Indeed the Lords were peculiarly recalcitrant in this matter, for they also rejected a related bill which would have made the forgery statute of 1563 applicable to "razers [i.e., erasers], adders, subtracters, and alterers of wordes in writings in such degree as if the whole writing had beene forged."[33]

Then the question of improper conduct by sheriffs and juries arose. It was apparently a matter of concern to both Houses, although in the

[32] *Ibid.*, fols. 99$^r$, 99$^v$, 103$^r$, 104$^r$, 108$^r$; Neale, *Parliaments, 1559–1581*, pp. 411–412.

[33] Crom. d., fols. 99$^r$, 100$^v$, 102$^v$, 104$^r$, 106$^v$, 109$^r$, 103$^r$, 107$^r$; *CJ*, I, 120, 121, 124, 127.

end nothing was done. On January 30 the Commons read a bill for the reformation of trials by jury and fees taken by sheriffs. The Lords, however, had already passed a similar measure which was sent down on February 3. On second reading this was committed, and on the twenty-fourth Mildmay brought in "the bill for sheriffs with some amendments and additions, and also a new bill touching the return of jurors." But difficulties were still noted, and the bill was again committed, this time to permanent slumber.

Although the bill was dead, the subject was not. A new bill for "more indifferencie of tryalls by jury" appeared on February 24, the same day as Mildmay's report, and passed its second reading only to be rejected on third reading March 15. Other related attempts proved abortive: there were bills against bribery of officers and against corrupt actions by attorneys and judges, but none survived three readings.[34]

Next we may mention the bill to strengthen the Scottish border. This originated in the Lords. It was read in the Lower House February 25 and committed to all the Privy Councillors in the House and some other Members; they brought in a new bill which passed the House March 8 and was sent up to the Lords by Mildmay and Sadler. The Upper House requested a conference, which was granted on the thirteenth,

. . . uppon which conference the Lords alledged that there was great faulte in us that had made a new bill for the same, rejecting theirs and sending it to them againe without any conference, . . . wherein we alledged that we had donn nothing but we thought we might lawfully doe, and shewed that the like was donn xviij° Eliz. uppon a bill of apparell, and since we might dash a bill we might also make a newe.

After the precedent-quoting and the bitterness, compromise prevailed: on the next-to-last day of the session the Lords sent the Commons' bill back "with the request that certain words might be left out, for that they were superfluous." The Lower House acquiesced, reading the amended bill three times and passing it the same day. It thus became one of the major pieces of public legislation to emerge from the session.[35]

[34] Crom. d., fols. 101$^v$, 103$^r$, 104$^r$, 109$^v$, 106$^r$, 110$^r$, 112$^v$, 113$^v$; *CJ*, I, 129.

[35] Crom. d., fols. 109$^v$, 111$^v$, 113; *CJ*, I, 129, 131–134; *LJ*, II, 52. The Commons also read a bill for provision and regulation of armor and weapons in London, but it did not pass (Crom. d., fol. 102).

Mildmay, finally, spent much time considering the amazingly large number of bills put in for the regulation of the cloth industry. There were measures to redefine the standards for Suffolk and Essex cloths, Devonshire kerseys, Tauntons, Bridgewaters, and several more; all were committed to Mildmay and a few colleagues.[36] The details of their deliberations would interest us little, were they known, but it is important to recollect the fact of such extensive regulation by the government and of such minute consideration by the Parliamentarians.

The session ended March 18, when Elizabeth came to the Lords' chamber to accept or reject its handiwork. Speaker Popham, as he had been directed, reminded the Queen of the "petition made by our House the last session of Parliament for reformation of the unlearned and unfit ministers, for provision against commutation of penance, and against the abuse of excommunication"; she replied, through the Chancellor, that "it needed not any such reiteration: the Howse might have beene satisfied with her answer before made." Although she was probably peeved, she assured the Commons that she would have the bishops deal effectually with the matter and would not hesitate to use her supreme authority over the Church should they fail. She thankfully accepted the subsidy, the anti-Catholic bill, and the sedition measure, questioning, however, the necessity of the last; she pointedly excluded from her thanks "some in the Lower House who forgot themselves"— Wentworth, Norton, and their Puritan choir, no doubt. After she had approved all the bills save a minor one against the sale of adulterated hops, the Parliament was prorogued until April 24, 1582. It did not in fact meet again; the Parliament of 1584 was to be freshly elected. And so the Parliament men chosen in 1572 had at last completed their work.[37]

[36] CJ, I, 122–124; Crom. d., passim. None of these bills found its way to the statute books.

[37] Crom. d., fol. 115; CJ, I, 136–137; F(M)P 148, first section, "A note of the cheife hedes touched by John Popham Esquier, Speaker of the Parliament, in his oracyon before the Queene." Does the survival of this memorandum suggest that Mildmay conferred with Popham about the contents of the speech? The Catholics, incidentally, are said to have offered the Queen 150,000 crowns to veto the bill against them (see A. F. Pollard, History of England from the Accession of Edward VI to the Death of Elizabeth, p. 375).

There are two pendants to the story of this session. The first, appropriately enough, concerns its chief topic, religion. Surviving among Mildmay's papers are a group of "articles concerninge ministers and excommunycatyon, which things were touched in Mr. Speakers oracyon to the Queene after the session ended and delivered by Sir Walter Mildmay to Mr. Secretary Walsingham for him to treat therof with hir Majesty, that they might be enacted at the next Parliament holden whensoever."[38] Unfortunately, this identification is vague, and we possess little corroborating evidence concerning the authorship of the articles. Since they are radically Puritan, one assumes that they proceeded from the Wentworths, Norton, Snagge, Pistor, and probably other minds outside the House. Neale suggests that the articles may originally have been the Puritan platform for legislation in the 1581 Parliament, put over as a program for future change only after it became clear that they could not be passed.[39] Mildmay could hardly have been one of the authors, for articles are included which he certainly would have disliked; but the Puritans, sensing his general sympathy for their cause, may have chosen to approach the Queen through him.

The articles, in any case, propose drastic changes in the organization and government of the Church, changes based largely on the views of the ex-Cambridge Presbyterian Thomas Cartwright. One might think them so radical as to be scarcely deserving of consideration, but Mildmay did pass them to Walsingham, who in turn presented them to the Queen. She promptly sent them to Sandys, who as Archbishop of York was the highest ranking ecclesiastic during Grindal's sequestration, and to five other bishops, Whitgift of Worcester among them. The bishops proceeded to draw up answers, some frankly admitting the desirability of reform, others caustically demolishing the Puritans' arguments.[40]

These articles and answers, however tedious, repay attention, for they focus the position of the opposing ecclesiastical parties. Most of the Puritan requests concern ministers—they embody the standard Presbyterian program for one learned minister in each parish with no

[38] F(M)P 148, second section. A fuller copy of the articles is Add. MS 29,546, fols. 124–125.

[39] Neale, *Parliaments, 1559–1581*, pp. 400–401.

[40] Lans. MS 30, fols. 203–210, one of Burghley's papers, contains both the articles and the bishop's answers.

pluralism, or at least as little as possible, and no nonparochial clergy. The articles seem innocent enough until the bishops' protests appear.

This cannot posseblye be performed without alteracion of the whole state of the Church of England, first because there must be curates and that of necessitie; second because their are other ecclesiastical livinges which require ministers of the worde and sacramentes as well as benefices with cure [of souls], as Deneries, Prebends, Mastershipps and Felowshipps in the Universities, Petty Canons in Cathedrall Churges.

And more generally,

This article is grownded upon a false principle of T.C.[artwright] agaynst ministers havinge no pastorall cure, which neyther he nor any mann ells is able to mayntayne eyther by the worde of God or auncient authoritie, for by *ministerium vagum* the old counsells did always understand suche as were ordeyned *sine patrimonio aut titulo,* that is, not having any staye of lyvinge, as it is manifeste in the Councell of Chalcedon.

The Puritans actually realized that the universities and cathedrals had required numbers of clergymen, but they suggested that such positions might be filled by appropriately qualified laymen. This procedure would violate the statutes of all the Oxford and Cambridge colleges, the bishops pointed out, and would take away the best rewards for learned ministers;

to conclude, it will breede a beggerly and unlearned and contemptible clergie and ministerie. It is the very waie to overthrowe all colleges, cathedrall churches, and places of learninge. It will extinguishe the studye of divinitie, diminishe the nomber of preachers, and breede a great confusion and alteracion in the Church and Commonwelthe. And it is a part of T.C. his platforme.

In all, the bishops found seventeen objections to the proposal.

Some matters the bishops agreed were "very expedient and necessarie and even so provided for by the lawe," as for instance the requirement that anyone seeking ordination should present "suche a testimoniall as is lymyted in the statute of Anno 13⁰ Eliz." The proposition that only masters of arts or licensed preachers be allowed to hold benefices worth £ 20 a year or more was also "to be lyked of," although it might be difficult to enforce.[41]

The articles complain about the use of excommunication as a punishment for temporal offenses and about commutation of penance, and then, in a section concerning dispensations, they return to the ministry and the specific problems of nonresidence and pluralism. No doubt the bishops would have been as happy as the Puritans to see a learned minister in each congregation, but they pointed out that there were about eighteen thousand benefices in England, and the universities could not possibly supply so many clergymen. Was it not better for two parishes to share the services of a learned preacher than for each to have an unqualified minister, or none at all? In one instance the bishops out-Puritan the Puritans: to the statement that nonresident ministers should preach two sermons yearly in each of their parishes the bishops retort, "It is too easie; it is requisite they should preach moe sermons even in their owne persons."

In conclusion the bishops set out "a generall answer to all the articles of excommunication, commutation, and dispensacion":

. . . this alteracion, confusion, and abridgement of exercise of that jurisdiction will shortly decaye the profession of the cannon lawe and civell lawe together, whereby divers nowe are bred upp in learninge in languages and in studye soe that they are inhabled to serve the realme in any forrayne service as well as any one sorte of learned menn in the realme besides.

Not a very convincing argument against the Puritans, one fears: they were concerned for men's souls, not for the provision of civil servants.

It is unfortunate that we do not know exactly what use was made of the episcopal answers. An endorsement on Burghley's copy states that they were "not as yet delivered to any," perhaps an indication that he feared they would only further ruffle the irascible "hot gospellers." If the Puritans did see the answers they were not, apparently, much inter-

---

[41] Perhaps related to this proposal was a bill introduced into the Commons in 1581 to provide that the owners of impropriated tithes in parishes of twenty householders or more should assign to the curate as much of their revenue as necessary to make up a salary of at least £ 19. The bill did not proceed beyond its first reading on March 10 (Crom. d., fol. 112$^r$).

ested; they were too busy framing their *Directory of Church Government* and organizing their regional conferences or *classes* to notice the predictable conservatism of their superiors. Mildmay's position, too, remains somewhat enigmatical. Probably he was sufficiently broadminded to appreciate the good, and to lament the bitterness, on both sides.

Our second postscript concerns the collection of the subsidy voted by the Parliament of 1581. When some of the assessors attempted to disregard traditional immunities and to collect larger sums than usual from schoolmasters a suit was brought in the Exchequer Court, and Mildmay and the barons quickly rendered a decision in favor of the teachers. As Richard Mulcaster put it in his famous *Elementarie,* they paid scant attention to the "to[o] passionat [as]sessors" and construed the statute "as the Parlaments did mean it." Mulcaster continued:

All the teachers in England have great cause to honor the right honorable *Sr. Walter Mildmaie,* knight, Chancellor of Hir Majesties Court of Exchequor and one of Hir Majesties most honorable Privie Counsell, the right honorable *Sr. Roger Manwood,* knight, Lord Chefe Baron of Hir Majesties Court of Exchequor, the right worshipfull master *Robert Sute,* master *John Chlinch,* master *John Sotherton,* esquires and barons of the same Hir Majestes court: the two first, *Sr. Walter* and *Sr. Roger,* great founders to learning both within the universities and in the cuntries about them, the other three esquires great favorers to relligion and learning everiewhere.[42]

It is an appropriate reminder that Mildmay's activities at the Exchequer were not wholly motivated by mercenary considerations, that his interest in good learning and true religion could overrule his concern for governmental revenue.

[42] Richard Mulcaster, *Elementarie,* ed. E. T. Campagnac, p. 290.

## 12. PLOTS AND PERSECUTIONS, 1581-1584

A RMED WITH THE parliamentary legislation of 1581 and increasingly concerned by the activities of the Catholics, the English
government now embarked on a program of ferreting out the Papists
and bringing them to trial. In these political persecutions Mildmay
became deeply involved.

The tragic story begins with the decision of the Jesuits to join the
mission to England undertaken in 1574 by priests from the Catholic
college at Douai. Edmund Campion and Robert Parsons, Englishmen
trained in the Jesuit college at Rome, were chosen and by June, 1580,
had reached England. Mildmay stated the government's view when he
told the Commons that their principal errand was, "by creeping into
the howses and familiarityes of men of behaviour and reputation, not
only to corrupt the realme with false doctrine, but also under that
pretence to stirr sedition."[1] There could be no doubt of the priests'
unusual abilities and devotion to their cause or—to the Council's great
distress—of their effectiveness. For twelve months Campion and Parsons eluded the authorities, touring the realm, preaching, covertly
printing tracts and refutations of governmental propaganda, hearing
confessions, absolving, and reconciling subjects to Rome.[2]

Finally their followers could conceal them no longer; Campion was
seized, together with three Douai priests and various laymen, in July,
1581, only a few months after the close of Parliament, and Parsons
fled to France in mid-August. Action was speedily taken to ascertain
the names of the recusants who had sheltered the pair, and, although

[1] Mildmay's speech in the Commons, January 25, 1581; see Chap. 11.
[2] Cf. Philip Hughes, *The Reformation in England,* III, 306–315; Evelyn
Waugh, *Edmund Campion, passim.*

193

even the rack could not bring Campion to supply full details, the Council soon amassed a list of suspects. Mildmay, who was spending a summer holiday at Apethorpe, helped with this investigation; on August 4 the Council directed him, Sir Henry Darcy, and Sir Edmund Montague to "make their repaire uppon the sodaine unto the house of Mr. Price, in Huntingdonshire," to see if they could find Campion's servant Ralph Emerson or any of Campion's books.[3] Two days later Mildmay was ordered to "send for the Lord Vaux (at whose house Edmunde Campion hath uppon his examination confessed that he hathe ben)," to examine him, and to place him in the custody of some honest gentleman well affected in religion. Mildmay was similarly to apprehend and interrogate Sir Thomas Tresham, who had been reconciled to Rome in 1580—perhaps the Jesuits' greatest triumph—and Sir William Catesby.[4]

After being questioned by Mildmay at Apethorpe, William, Baron Vaux, was sent to Boughton in Montague's keeping and then escorted to London by Montague's son: a painful affair, since Montague and Vaux had long been friends. On the eighteenth Vaux and Tresham were called before Burghley, Leicester, and Sussex. They refused to make any statement concerning their association with Campion and were committed to the Fleet, where Catesby was already in confinement.[5]

Campion himself was tried at Common Law, November 20, interestingly enough not under the new anti-Catholic law but under the old treason statute of Edward III. The government evidently hoped to demonstrate that his crime was stirring sedition, not merely holding the Catholic faith. He was hanged, drawn, and quartered at Tyburn December 1.

In these grizzly proceedings Mildmay seems to have played no part, but he was drawn into the trial of Vaux, Tresham, and Catesby before the Star Chamber November 15. Popham, prosecuting for the Crown, charged them with contempt of court, since they had refused to answer questions and give evidence; Mildmay summed up in his best rhetorical fashion. Clearly the Council felt that the occasion demanded a cannon

---

[3] *APC, 1581–82,* p. 153.     [4] *Ibid.,* p. 155.
[5] Godfrey Anstruther, *Vaux of Harrowden,* pp. 115–120.

blast of propaganda and thought the Chancellor of the Exchequer best able to deliver it.[6]

He began by praising the Queen's maintenance of peace and pure religion for nearly a quarter century, "the like whereof cannot be red so long together in three hundreth yeres before." This was evident, as was the Pope's desire to overturn her peaceable and happy government,

... the rather for that he feeleth dayly that this kingdome of all the monarchies in Christendome doth most shake the dignity of his Triple Crowne. And therefore he hath presumed, by a most ympudent and blaspheamous Bull, to publish even within this cittie a deprivation of our most gracious Queen, acquiting all the subjectes of this realme from any obedience to her, dreaming that (as the supreame monarch of the world) he hath power to putt downe and sett upp kinges and quenes at his pleasure.

After the failure of the bull and the invasion of Ireland, the Pope turned to secret practices to divert the subjects from their dutiful obedience to the Queen, "nourishing closely the sparks of disobedience, that they might burst into flames of open sedityon [when] oportunity should serve." To this end the Jesuits had been sent.

Mildmay spent some time berating them:

... false hipocrites calling themselves Jesuites, abusing the most holy name of Jesus to the inscription of their supersticious secte, and being indeed but a rable of runagate freers, lately cropen into the world and roving about in all countreys to trowble the Church of God and the quiett policie of the countreys where they come. ...

Theis hipocrites authorized by the Pope have presumed to enter into this land, the scope of their dealing here being, by harbouring themselves into the howses of men of reputacion, devoted unto Rome, ... to confirme their myndes ready for any evill that might be enterprized here, thereby to bring her Majestie any perill or trowble they could be able within this realme, as their lewde companions had lately attempted to doe in Ireland, arryving here as yt semeth of purpose at the same tyme to answere the doinges of thoes rebells there.

Growing more specific, Mildmay described the activities of Campion, "one notorious above the rest for ympudency and audacity."

---

[6] Copies of his speech are F(M)P 101; Sloane MS 326, fols. 43–48; and Harl. MS 6265, fols. 86–87. In the last the speech is misdated November 15, 1582.

Campion himself was not of course on trial in the Star Chamber, but he had confessed resorting to the houses of Lord Vaux, Sir Thomas Tresham, and Sir William Catesby, the defendants. Their conduct drew Mildmay's fire:

Notwithstanding [this] confession of Campion, my Lord Vaux, and the other two, being examyned by her Majesties commandement whether Campion was in their howses to their knowledge or privity, have plainely denyed his being there.

Theis men afterwards, being by her Majestes further commandment willed by the Lords of her Privie Councell to testifie the same their denyall of Campion's being at their howses to be trew, first by oath and my Lord Vaux upon his honour and th'other two upon their allegeaunce to her Majestie, have and yett do utterly refuse both.

Mildmay noted in their refusal two points, the first an argument for their guilt.

The other (and that the greater), by this refusall they shew a manifest contempt of her Majestes authority and an utter fayling in their duetyes towards her, that in a matter concerning her Majestie whom they ought to preferr before themselves, and in a civill matter that lyeth within their owne knowledge, and which they may lawfully without danger of life or membre eyther affirme or deny, they do refuse to take an oath ministred unto them on her Majestes behalfe by her expresse commandment, and that not before ordinary commissioners or officers, but before the Lords of her Privy Councell, being the principall and cheife Councell of Estate of the realme.

An example most dangerous to be suffered, and not hitherto attempted by any good subject. For so her Majestes person, her estate, and her realmes might be brought into greate perill if yt were lawfull for men to refuse to declare by oath or upon their allegiaunce thinges that should concerne her so neirely as the practice of theis Jesuites and semynarie preistes doe.

Mildmay concluded by suggesting appropriate punishment: imprisonment until they "do that which hath lawfully byn required of them" and fines, £1,000 for Lord Vaux and 1,000 marks each for Tresham and Catesby. Sir Roger Manwood, Sir Francis Knollys, Lord Norris, and Lord Hunsdon would have liked heavier fines, but Sir James Dyer supported Mildmay's suggestions and in the end they were decreed. Jane Griffin, Ambrose Griffin, and Walter Powdrell, others accused of harboring Campion, also were fined 500 marks each.[7]

Catesby was released from the Fleet by the end of 1582, Vaux and Tresham in the spring of 1583.[8] But Vaux and Tresham were kept under house arrest in London; on October 1, 1583, Tresham wrote both Mildmay and Leicester seeking permission to move to a larger house which he owned in Westminster.[9] The request was denied, but Tresham was given greater freedom so long as he did not leave the parishes of Hoxton and Shoreditch, and Lord Vaux was transferred to a house at Hackney. In 1588, during the threat of the Armada, Vaux was committed to the custody of the Archbishop of Canterbury, Tresham to the Bishop of Lincoln. Tresham was again imprisoned from 1590 to 1593; Vaux, whose mind had weakened during his confinement, was finally allowed to return to Northamptonshire. Perhaps understandably, Tresham and Catesby grew fanatical in their bitterness, if not actually deranged. One is not surprised to find them, along with the young widow of Vaux's son George, leading the Gunpowder Plot in 1605.

Action against supporters of the Jesuits continued during 1582. In May, Stephen Vallenger, a recusant writer of ballads, was indicted in the Star Chamber on charges of publishing seditious libel contrary to the act of 1581, and Mildmay was again called in to underline the government's interest in the case. His oration of the sixteenth is much more concerned with the menace of the Jesuits and the disobedience of anyone who dared to defend them than with Vallenger's offense itself.[10] He dwelled on the grounds of Campion's execution—the Jesuit was arraigned

. . . not for matters or questions of religion, but for horrible treasons, as conspiracy agaynst the Queen's most royall person; the subverting of her

[7] Anstruther, *Vaux*, p. 127.

[8] Add. MS 39,828, fol. 78, is a beautiful fair copy of Tresham's petition to Hatton for release.

[9] *Ibid.*, fols. 91, 92.

[10] Copies of the speech are F(M)P 60; Sloane MS 326, fols. 48–55; Harl. MS 6265, fols. 87–89. On Vallenger (or *Valenger*) see John and J. A. Venn, *Alumni Cantabrigienses*, Pt. I, Vol. IV, p. 293.

whole state and government; the invasion of the realme by strangers; the preparacons of the subjectes of this realme to be ready to take armes to joyne with the Catholique army (as they terme yt); the deposing of our most gracious Quene and the setting up of another.

Campion and his followers had been allowed to defend themselves in every point and had been judged indifferently; "the force of the evidence, grounded upon sondry confessions and testimonies," was such that they were justly found guilty.

These proceedings, Mildmay said, satisfied all men who without malice sought the truth. But, unfortunately, "there be some of so lewde and ill disposition, as they dare by infamous libelle, scattered and disperced abroad both in print and by wryting, most falsely and maliciously [to] slander theis whole proceedings." These writers upheld Campion and the two priests convicted with him, saying that there was no proof of their guilt, that the witnesses, judge, and jury were corrupt, and that the three died as martyrs for their Catholic faith.

Mildmay continued:

To touch the reputacion or credit of any man by false and slanderous libells hath byn accompted in all well governed commonwealthes for such an offence as hath deserved great punishment, and so hath yt byn judged often in this place according to the qualyties of the persons slandered. But this kinde of libelling is of another nature, for this doth not touch only perticuler persons, but reacheth to the whole state of the realme, sounding out maliciously to the whole world.

That this noble kingdome, so much reputed heretofore amongst all nations for just and upright government, is no more worthie the name of a monarchie ruled by law and order, but is become a mere anarchie without law, without justice, without equity, without regard of conscience towards God or honest fame towards men: that this slander is in the highest degree of ympudency that may be is apparent, and that it is most false who can deny that beholdeth continuall experience of the justice used in this land?

After praising the order and impartiality of the English judiciary system, Mildmay returned to the question of the priests' offense. He recalled that the Jesuits, when asked if the Pope possessed the authority to deprive the Queen or absolve subjects of their allegiance to her, answered that it was "a question of divinity, and disputable, meete for schooles, by which they do bewray the treason of their heartes in advauncing the power of a forreyne usurper above the lawfull possession of our gracious Quene."

A dutiful and loyal subject, Mildmay said, would have replied:

The Pope is a forreyne potentate and may command within his owne territoryes where [he] hath jurisdiccion; but here in England he may command nothing, for maugre his head[ship] or anything that he hath or can do, we Englishmen do hold him as a false bishopp and do reverence and obey our Quene as a lawfull and rightfull princesse, so firmely stablished in her seate, by God first, and next by the love of her subjectes, that no Pope nor other enemy shalbe able to prevaile against her.

What difference there is betweene such an answere, which no good subjecte will refuse to make, and the answere of the Jesuites and preistes, making a dowbt of her Majesties lawfull estate, is easie to be seene; and thereby also it is evident enough whether theis men dyed for religion or for treason.

Vallenger stood before the court charged with writing and spreading such libels. Although he stoutly maintained his innocence, Mildmay showed the court a book, written in Vallenger's hand and found in his lodgings, containing a libelous account of the trials. This account had been printed in February, anonymously; since Vallenger confessed writing out his copy in January he was presumably its author. Another libel, this one in rime, was also produced. Since he could not prove that Vallenger had written the tracts, Mildmay attempted to discredit Vallenger's denial by attacking his character, calling him "a vayne man, . . . knowne . . . to be a maker of rymes and such vayne thinges; a masterles man without any livelyhood to maynteyne himselfe withall; making a trade by . . . hyring of felowes to wryte coppyes of such things and uttering them agayne for advantage." Mildmay could not doubt that he was the principal author and publisher of the libels.

There remained only to fix the penalty. Mildmay advocated imprisonment during the Queen's pleasure, a fine of £100, and, "to make him a publique example for so publique an offence, to stand on the pillory one day in the pallace at Westminster and one other day in Cheapeside, and to leefe at each place one of his eares, to remaine as a perpetuall marke of his lewd dealinges."

It is painful to see Mildmay, admirable in so much else, descending to such oratorical trickery as defamation of character. His purpose, of course, was fulfilled—the government obtained Vallenger's conviction —but the matter hardly demanded so forceful a speech. It was an artillery barrage directed at a mouse. In broad perspective, as a statement of the Privy Council's position on Campion's execution, it may have been more needed, and again, no doubt, effective. But one is left wondering whether Mildmay realized how partisan a stand he elaborated, and perhaps wishing that he had not served the Crown quite so well.

While the government was thus punishing the Papists there occurred a conspiracy, not based on religious motives, to blackmail the Archbishop of York. Were it not so disgusting it would be one of the most amusing episodes of the reign.

Although the matter remained secret until 1583, it had in fact begun May 10, 1581, when Archbishop Sandys, conducting a visitation of his diocese, had lodged at the Bull Inn in Doncaster. The hostess, one Ann Sisson, had formerly been a servant of Sandys' wife and hence knew the Archbishop; Sir Robert Stapleton, a prominent North Country gentleman and long-time acquaintance of Sandys', also happened to be spending the night.

After Sandys, aged at sixty-five and now tired from his journey, had retired, Mistress Sisson entered his room to bring his accustomed hot drink, or caudle. She straightaway threw off her smock and crept naked into the Archbishop's bed, where she was shortly discovered by her husband. He drew his dagger on poor Sandys and sent a serving man, Alexander Furboys, to summon Stapleton, who soon appeared to witness the scene. Pretending to act as the Archbishop's friend, Stapleton advised Sandys to keep the matter quiet by judicious bribes to all concerned. Thus began a systematic milking in which the prelate paid £ 700 to the Sissons and Stapleton and also cancelled a debt owed him by his former servant Bernard Maud.

By January, 1583, Sandys could bear it no longer. He wrote the Queen and Burghley explaining the whole affair and offering to resign rather than submit to continued extortion. Stapleton, the Sissons, Maud, and Furboys were examined, first by Burghley, Hatton, and Leicester, then—after they had been imprisoned—by the Lord Chief

Justice and the Master of the Rolls. Finally it was decided to try them in the Star Chamber.

The case was heard May 8. Once again Mildmay delivered a long prepared speech, summing up the evidence, emphasizing the gravity of the offense, and recommending severe punishment.[11] He began by stating the "foule and horrible facte, the some whereof is, that by . . . most detestable practice an impudent harlott was conveyed into the chamber, yea into the bedd of the Archbishop, to bring upon him this horrible slander and abuse." So much had been confessed.

But to extenuate the fault, Sir Robert Stapleton hath found two thinges to serve him, as he thinketh to great purpose, the one that the devise came from Sisson and his wife, and not from him, but that he did only assent unto yt to have yt put in exeqution, not being made acquainted therewith past three howers before. Th'other he leaveth as a blott upon the Archbishop, by saying that he alured the woman, as she told Sir Robert, whereunto he gave creditt.

Neyther of theis are sufficient to helpe him or to hurt the Bishopp.

For is yt likely or probable that so base folkes as Sisson and his wife are, so well knowne to Sir Robert Stapleton, would adventure to breake such a matter with him whom they knew to be none other then well assured in frendshipp to the Bishopp, for so he did pretend; whereby those lewde persons might have had their practices discovered and have receyved also greate punishment? But rather yt is likely that Sir Robert Stapleton, malicing the Bishopp in his heart though he made shew of frendshipp, knowing this woman for her ympudency to be a fitt instrument to serve such a turne, did first himself conceyve and after disclose the practice to her, whom he had power enough over to command in such a matter, which afterward he directed to be followed as it was. A thing that otherwise neyther shee nor any of the other durst once have meddled in.

Since the parties in the conspiracy were of so base reputation and the Archbishop so elevated, the charges against him might well be dis-

---

[11] Copies of Mildmay's speech are Sloane MS 326, fols. 56–70, and Harl. MS 6265, fols. 89–92. Harl. MS 4990, fols. 80–85, is a copy of the Star Chamber decree and contains a summary of the proceedings. See also Conyers Read, *Lord Burghley and Queen Elizabeth*, pp. 278–280; Eric St. John Brooks, *Sir Christopher Hatton*, pp. 261–262.

counted without further examination—as, Mildmay noted, the Romans had done in the case of a Senator, Marcus Attillius Scaurus. But, "for the more cleiring of the Bishopp," Mildmay proceeded to further analysis of the affair. He found the motives behind the conspiracy to be malice and gain,

. . . two meete foundacions to build so ill a work upon: for malice did so boyle in Sir Robert Stapletons heart against the Bishop, as to be revenged and to have the Bishops head under his girdle, he was contented to cast of[f] all feare of God and all respect of his honesty and creditt in the world, and the hope of gayne did so entice th'other needy folkes as they were content to adventure conscience, credit, honesty and all.

Stapleton's crime was especially odious since he was a gentleman born and was serving as sheriff of Yorkshire at the time. Indeed Mildmay himself had previously respected Stapleton; he once called him "a gentleman whom I . . . like of as well as any in the North parties."[12]

Mildmay dilated upon the damage caused by the conspiracy. It was, first, "a greater hurt then which could no way light upon [Sandys]."

For if we accompt such amongst the worst sort of people that by vyolence take mens goods from them: what is . . . to be thought of those that by malicious and covetuous fraud take from any, specially such as be of great calling in the Church or Commonwealth, their good name, a thing more precious then any worldly good can be, the rather for that, though the wound of a slaunder may be cured, yet the scarr doth often remayne long after.

But the personal injury was not the worst. Mildmay emphasized the damage to the Church and State and, fittingly enough for the time, the benefit to the Papists:

There hath followed also a greate touch to her Majesty and the whole realme in honor and reputacion, and a great slaunder to the Religion of the Gospell, which we enjoy under the most Christian government of our gracious Quene.

A great advauntage also to the enemyes of our religion both at home and abrode: for as you may be sure that ill disposed men at home, glad of every

[12] Add. MS 15,891, fol. 90. Mildmay made the comment in 1582, when he obtained the favor of the Queen and Hatton for Stapleton's marriage to Olive Talbot.

occasion to do evill offices, have spared no diligence to advertice this slaunder as acceptable newes to Rome and Reymes and other seminaries of Popery, so we are to looke for from thence, by the slaunderous pens of freers and Jesuites and such other, a malicious defamation of our Church and Religion, to sound through the world in reproach of her Majestie and of all us that lyve under her proteccion.

After a good deal more in the same vein Mildmay suggested penalties. Furboys, the chamberlain, should be committed to the Fleet for three years and exiled; he should pay a fine of £100, stand on the pillory one day at Westminster and another day during the assizes at York, and leave one of his ears at each place. Sisson and Maud were to be spared their ears because they had confessed their guilt, but they should be imprisoned and likewise set on the pillory, and be fined: Sisson £500, Maud £300. Stapleton's offense was the greatest, but since the Queen intended to proceed against him by the law of arms, degrading him from his knighthood, Mildmay recommended merely imprisonment and a staggering fine of £3,000. Finally, all should be obliged to repay the money they had wrested from Sandys, and should publicly ask the Archbishop's forgiveness in the next assizes at York. The judges, including all the principal Privy Councillors, concurred in this judgment.[13]

This should have been the end of the matter, but it was not. Stapleton and Maud went through the ritual of submission at York, but in such a manner as to make a mockery of it. (One wonders why Mildmay suggested it at all; surely the best plan would have been to drop the matter as quietly as possible.) Sandys was enraged: he said that, as Burghley advised him, he had "followed the example of my Master Christ [and] forgiven my persecutors and enemies who have many waies crucified me," but clearly he had forgiven nothing. He wrote Burghley, on August 2:

The Knight [Stapleton] came to the barre in great bravery, with prowde lookes and disdainfull countenaunce and gesture, having a greate white ribbaunde in bawdricke sorte cast uppon a blacke sattyn doblett. [This was taken by the people as a sign of his innocence.] He read his submission with so lowe a voyce, and so runningly, as one reading a lettre so fast as he

---

[13] The decision was handed down June 21, 1583 (Harl. MS 4990, fol. 85).

coulde; of the presence he could not be heard, neither understood. It was most scornefully done withowt any token of repentaunce, and when he had made an ende he saied thus: "Nowe I have read it verbatim, and fulfilled her Majestes commaundement." . . . Mawde abused the judgement of the Starre Chamber and the whole presence here most lewdly. He came in with a blacke sattyn doblett with a white ribbande fast abowt his right arme, spake so lowe and read so disorderly and disdainfully that the Justices of Assize rebuked him sharpely.

Perhaps the thing that angered the Archbishop most was a statement made by Stapleton after his submission, charging Sandys with being a Papist. "I will stande against any man in that quarrell," Sandys wrote, "for I earnestly favour the Gospell and defie all Popery, and will be ready to adventure my liefe for the Gospell." He was also irritated by a letter from the innkeeper urging him to clear Mistress Sisson's reputation by confessing that he had allured her. Sandys understood both Sisson's motives and his own frailties; he thought the letter intended "to put me in suche anger that I shoulde be moved to speake unadvisedly, that advantage might be taken of me." But he could not overcome his desire for vindication, or indeed his bitterness at the whole situation. "I see now," he concluded, "that while I lyve here I shall lyve bothe in greate misery and great daunger, and shall labour unprofitably, hurlinge pearles before swyne, and bestowe all my labours uppon an unthankfull people."[14]

On August 17 Sandys wrote again, referring to "the late disordered and scornefull submission here made by the aspiring Absalom and his confederat craftie Achitophel" long before the characters were immortalized in Dryden's satire.[15] After further interrogations—descending to a ridiculous level[16]—Stapleton was again jailed, first in the Tower, then at the Fleet. He remained in prison until 1584, when

[14] Lans. MS 38, fol. 190. Further details of the scene at York, including the laughing and jollity of Stapleton and Maud after their submission, are in an account on fols. 191–192.

[15] *Ibid.*, fol. 194.

[16] Stapleton and Maud were asked where they obtained their white ribbons, and Stapleton and one of his servants were interrogated at length concerning a whetstone which Stapleton allegedly had worn to signify that his submission was a lie (*ibid.*, fols. 196–202).

Burghley persuaded Sandys to intercede with the Queen for his release so that the Archbishop might not be blamed for taking undue personal revenge.[17] Throughout it is pathetic to see Sandys so disturbed, wasting energy on such a matter when so much remained to be done in the Church. He was, no doubt, fast approaching senility. Although still capable of brilliant expression, the telling phrase, the Biblical allusion, he had lost his judgment and sense of proportion.

Meanwhile Walsingham had uncovered a really serious conspiracy, the famed Throckmorton plot. Francis Throckmorton, a hitherto little noted member of that perverse family, had returned to England in 1583 after some months in Spain, where he had talked with Charles Arundel and other English exiles. He was immediately taken up by Bernardino de Mendoza, the Spanish ambassador, who had been putting together plans for an invasion led by the forces of the Duke of Guise, financed by the Spanish King and the Pope, intended to free Mary, Queen of Scots, and place her on the throne as the rightful Catholic ruler. In October Throckmorton was seized in the very act of writing Mary a ciphered letter; under torture he confessed all he knew and was executed in July, 1584. At the discovery of the plot Mendoza was ordered out of the realm, and the Council instituted further investigations.

One of the men suspected of complicity was Philip Howard, Earl of Arundel, son of the Duke of Norfolk who had been executed in 1572. Mildmay and Hunsdon, apparently too worried to take much of a Christmas holiday, questioned Arundel December 24, 1583. They were primarily concerned with establishing his connections with known or suspected conspirators: Charles Arundel; Lord Paget, who had returned from the continent early in the year to organize the recusant noblemen; Henry Percy, eighth Earl of Northumberland, brother of the seventh Earl who had been executed in 1572; Lord Henry Howard, Arundel's uncle, one of Mendoza's chief informants. Naturally enough Arundel denied any conversations of consequence. He admitted visiting Northumberland in London, but he "had no conference with him but of ordinarie matters." He had not received any recent correspondence from the Queen of Scots or the French am-

[17] Read, *Burghley*, p. 280.

bassador. His chaplains, he said, were blameless, although he had been obliged to discharge a bailiff whom he suspected of being a Jesuit in disguise. He had never "heard of any Jesuite or seminarie priest that ever cam to the Lady his wief, or resorted to his L. howse."[18]

No action was taken against him at the time, but the following September Arundel and Northumberland were implicated in some spectacularly obtained Jesuit papers and were sent to the Tower.[19] There they were to die, Northumberland presumably by his own hand in 1585, Arundel a natural death ten years later.

Although Mildmay and his fellow Privy Councillors were primarily concerned during these years with the growing Catholic menace, they found time for a host of minor matters. Mildmay seems to have been too busy to attend the Council meetings regularly—he was present on only thirteen occasions during the year and a half ending in June, 1582, when a four-year gap in the defective register begins—but he was delegated responsibility for investigating various affairs.

In May, 1581, for instance, he was ordered to adjudicate a dispute over lands leased by George Freville from the dean and chapter of Durham. Apparently he effected a skilful compromise, for the Council heard no complaint from either party and ordered his settlement to be observed.[20] In June he was busy examining the tenements and the highway illegally erected in the former cloister of the Black Friars in London; the following April he was interrogating John Rogers, who had been charged with neglect of duty in his negotiations at Ebling on behalf of the Eastland merchants.[21]

---

[18] SP 12/164/52–55. Charles and Matthew Arundel were members of the prolific Cornish recusant family, on whose activities see A. L. Rowse, *Tudor Cornwall*, pp. 342–379.

[19] William Waad, clerk of the Privy Council, had managed to piece together some documents which William Creighton, the Scottish Jesuit, had torn up and attempted to throw overboard at the time of his capture at sea (A. F. Pollard, *History of England from the Accession of Edward VI to the Death of Elizabeth*, p. 386).

[20] *APC, 1581–82,* pp. 51, 65.

[21] *Ibid.,* pp. 76, 401.

In January, 1583, Mildmay joined with other Councillors in asking the bishops to obtain contributions for the relief of Geneva, "in this latter age a nursery unto Gods churches," which had been attacked by the Duke of Savoy.[22] Two months later he opposed granting Edward Seymour, Earl of Hertford, a prebend formerly held by the Poor Knights of Windsor; it would be better for that "honorable foundation," he wrote Burghley March 29, that Hertford should "accept a lease for a good number of yeres, leaving the inheritance in the College." "I wold have wayted uppon your Lordship myself," he added, "but that theis three dayes I have been ill at eas."[23] We do not know the nature of his indisposition; Mildmay virtually never complained of ill health.

In March the inhabitants of Marsham, Norfolk, wrote to Mildmay and Walsingham lamenting their oppression by James Brampton, who held the farm of their traditional rents and dues; presumably some investigation followed.[24] We know more about a dispute of 1584 over the ownership of two mills, Le Moulin de l'Eschelle and Le Moulin du Millieu, in the Isle of Guernsey. The Council wrote Mildmay,

Forasmuch as at this time we cannot convenientlie attend the hearing therof at such length as were requisit, we have thought good to intreate you (being allreadie partlie acquainted with those causes by reason of your travell hertofore used therin) . . . to heare the matters at large, to view thir severall grauntes on bothe sides and to consider of the validities of them in law, and to examine all such circumstances, writinges and particularities as shalbe alleaged and produced by the parties uppon their oathes, and with as much convenient speed as you maie to certifie us in writing what you shall have founde, together with your opinions therof, that we maie take order therein accordinglie.[25]

Naval administration also required Mildmay's attention. It had

---

[22] Harl. MS 767, fol. 107ᵛ, printed in Henry Ellis, *Original Letters Illustrative of English History*, second ser., III, 83–85. In appreciation of his concern the ministers of Geneva gave Mildmay a French Bible, now in the Emmanuel College Library, shelfmark 311. 3. 2.

[23] Harl. MS 6993, fol. 41.

[24] SP 12/161/10.

[25] Egerton MS 2603, fols. 43–44. The letter is signed by Bromley, Burghley, Knollys, Croft, Hatton, and Walsingham.

been greatly improved after 1577, when John Hawkins, the famed navigator, was made treasurer of the Navy; but Hawkins was opposed by the Navy Board, particularly by Sir William Winter, who had profited from the laxity of earlier years. By the autumn of 1583 Winter's complaints grew so tiresome that the Council decided to appoint a commission of inquiry. Five men were named—Burghley, Walsingham, Hunsdon, Mildmay, and Lord Admiral Clinton—but probably only the last three served. The loss of the commission's papers is one of the minor tragedies of the reign, for they would have told us much about the Navy; but obviously the examination vindicated Hawkins.[26]

Still bitter, Hawkins scribbled a letter to Mildmay in March, 1584. He began:

Syns I wrote unto your honour I have had many occasyons to busye my person, for syns . . . the officers have taken courage and hardines to oppose themselves agaynst me, dyvers matters have byne omyttyd, delayed, and hyndryd by many subtyle practyses, which now with some travayle and dyllygence I mynd with Gods favour to put in order, and I hope wyll not requyre above fifteen dayes of my service.

Hawkins's purpose in writing was to send Mildmay a new plan for the maintenance of the fleet. For years naval expenditures had been divided into two categories, the "ordinary" charges for routine repair of ships and the "extraordinary," for major alterations and renovations. In 1579 Hawkins had contracted to provide ordinary maintenance for £ 4,000 annually, but the extraordinary repairs had remained on a piece-work basis. This led to confusion and extravagance; as Hawkins wrote in a memorandum which he forwarded to Mildmay:

There do growe in the office sondrie controversies in devyding the ordinarie and extraordinarie for carpentry, wherby her Majestes service is hindered. The shippwrightes denye some matters to be ordinarie and refuse to do the service. The officers on th'other side denye to give allowance for sondrye matters, alleadging them not to be extraordinarie, and by these meanes the strife continueth, and divers thinges [are] omitted that otherwise wold be done.

26 J. A. Williamson, *Hawkins of Plymouth*, pp. 265–268.

To allay this confusion Hawkins proposed that the ordinary and the extraordinary be combined, and he agreed to see that the extraordinary repairs were undertaken and new ships built, "yerlie one in place of another that can no more be repayred," for £ 1,714 annually.

Hawkins asked Mildmay to consider whether his memorandum "hathe sufficient order to be presentyd to my Lord Treasorer and my Lord Admyrall, and yf your honour shall have lykynge of yt I will putt the same in order and present yt, for yt shall not only end all objections, make a safe, a sure, and a proffytable service, but declare that ther ys £ 3,231 charge yerely savyd of the expence in tyme past." He added, in a postscript, "The officers wyll hold this for a myracle at the first syght." They were still not reconciled to his schemes.[27]

After a series of discussions in which Mildmay acted as Hawkins's champion his bargain was accepted. The new agreement considerably reduced expenses, thus gladdening the heart of the Chancellor of the Exchequer, and it helped put the Navy in readiness for the great conflict with Spain.[28]

[27] Egerton MS 2603, fols. 39–42.
[28] A less important naval order had been issued in September, 1583, when Mildmay and several other Councillors authorized Richard Bingham "to repayre with two of her Majestes shippis unto the seas for the takinge of suche pirates as infest the coastes of this realme," especially the South coast from the Isle of Wight to Land's End (Add. MS 35,831, fols. 299–300).

## 13. THE KING AND QUEEN OF SCOTS
### 1582–1586

As THE CATHOLIC THREAT mounted, Elizabeth's government naturally became increasingly concerned with Scottish affairs. The possibility of a Catholic revolution in Scotland, or of a Catholic attack
across the border into England, loomed larger after Morton's execution
in 1581 and the rise of D'Aubigny, soon created Duke of Lennox.
With his chief lieutenant, James Stuart, Earl of Arran, Lennox dominated James VI and the Scottish government, broke diplomatic relations with England, and generally instituted pro-French policies. To
make matters worse, the Jesuits began infiltrating the Northern realm,
attempting to kindle Scottish zeal for an invasion of England. Elizabeth, it is true, had the support of the Kirk and of a group of Scottish
noblemen led by Archibald Douglas, Earl of Angus, Morton's nephew,
whom Mildmay regarded as England's best hope north of the border;
but Angus was not safe within Scotland and in fact spent the earlier
months of 1582 at the English court.

A ray of hope pierced the clouds in August, 1582, when James was
captured, while hunting, by a group of Protestant lords. Probably
contrived by Angus, this famous Ruthven Raid precipitated Lennox's
fall and finally his flight to France, where he died the following May.

Mildmay was summering at Apethorpe, as was his custom, when
news of the Scottish revolution reached London, but Walsingham immediately sent him word and sought his advice. His reply, written
September 3 and marked "hast, hast, hast" for the postrider, called
the change "a mercifull worke of God towardes us, if we have heart
to be thankefull to hym and to lay such hold uppon yt as the cause
requireth." Although confident that Walsingham would not fail to

take appropriate action, Mildmay commented, "yt is straunge that every man fynding the same so necessary for us, there is no more regard had of it"—another expression of his lifelong concern for Anglo-Scottish amity. He added, "If I might heare of the Erle of Angus reatorne thether with surety, I wold hope the better, and specially in the direction of that Kinges marriage, of all other the most principall peryal for us, as I thinke."[1] He feared that James would be betrothed to a Spanish or French princess, thus preparing the way for enduring Catholic domination.

Walsingham and the Council did seize the opportunity, swiftly dispatching Robert Bowes as resident ambassador in Scotland and Hunsdon's son, Sir George Cary, as a special envoy to James. Bowes and Cary recommended that the Scots be bound to England by the grant of substantial pensions, a policy which the frugal Elizabeth was not willing immediately to implement. While she dallied the French King sent La Mothe Fénelon, a former ambassador to England, as an envoy to James, certainly to protect the French interest and perhaps to advocate a French marriage. That at least was what Mildmay suspected; on December 30 he wrote Walsingham that, unless the English bestirred themselves, Fénelon would work all manner of mischief and the French would carry Scotland.[2]

There was no need to stir up Walsingham; he shared Mildmay's anxiety and worked frantically to secure a decision on the pensions. In January, 1583, he wrote Burghley, "I howld Scotland for lost unles God be mercyfull unto this poore ilande. . . . God open her Majestes eyes to see her peryll."[3] A month later Walsingham, Mildmay, and Chancellor Bromley met with Burghley at his house, where the elder statesman was confined by an attack of the gout, and agreed to urge the expenditure of £ 10,000, half for James himself, £ 3,000 to buy the support of the Scottish noblemen, the remainder for the expenses of the English ambassador.[4]

---

[1] SP 12/155/36. Mildmay reiterated his views in another letter of September 14 (*CSP, Scot.*, VI, No. 166). He seems to have spent an unusually long time at Apethorpe in 1582; he was still there on October 14 (SP 46/32/283).

[2] *CSP, Scot.*, VI, Nos. 233–234.

[3] SP 12/158/33.

[4] Conyers Read, *Lord Burghley and Queen Elizabeth*, p. 283.

James, still dominated by the Anglophile lords, was eager for some such treaty. Early in the year he dispatched John Colville and William Stewart as representatives to the English court, and on April 23 he wrote Mildmay soliciting support for them.

We ar very desyrous to know [the Queen's] favorable myndie and gude will at this tyme speciallie, as hertofore we have had large pruif of it, and thairfore will affectuuslie requyre yow that in geving advyse according to the place and credite which ye occupy, ye will bie a furdirar to . . . our causes, . . . which we doubt not sal be to hir gude service, and we will accept it for right thankfull pleshr.[5]

The embassy, however, accomplished little; the treaty hung fire for several years while Elizabeth sought a solution less costly than the pensions.

Meanwhile the center of attention shifted to Sheffield Castle, where Mary, Queen of Scots, was being guarded by the Earl of Shrewsbury. In April, 1583, Elizabeth decided to reopen negotiations aimed at granting Mary her liberty in exchange for suitable guarantees of good conduct. Apparently she hoped that this move would please James and would contribute to Anglo-Scottish accord, while relieving England of the expense of maintaining Mary's household.

Robert Beale, clerk of the Privy Council, was dispatched to aid Shrewsbury in the preliminary talks. He reached Sheffield April 12 and, after several interviews with Mary, sent letters to the Queen and to Walsingham on the sixteenth. Mary, he found, "coulde not bee brought by anie meanes that wee coulde use to declare anie farther particular matter then onelie desire of libertie";[6] he was at a loss to know "what to saie to this Ladies answeres and demaundes, considering her wylenes on the one syde and her Majesties suspicion and irresolution that maie be conceaved to goe through with this greate accion."[7] The difficulty of negotiation was increased by Shrewsbury's ignorance of French and by Mary's ill health—"she is waxen farre

[5] Westm. MSS, 2, XII, 1, D4.
[6] Cot. MS Caligula C. IX, fols. 70–75; the papers cited in this and the following eleven notes are calendared in *CSP, Scot.,* VI, Nos. 400–530, *passim.*
[7] *Ibid.,* fol. 75.

grosser then ever I sawe her, rayther puffed up in myne opinion then otherwyse," Beale wrote;[8] but finally a number of definite statements were dragged from her. She would not demand liberty to return to France or Scotland, but would be satisfied to remain honorably in England; she would insist that any treaty should be made "with her sonne joyntlye, seing they were all one"; she and James would agree to enter into a league of friendship with Elizabeth in return for her freedom.[9]

On April 22 Beale, having extracted no further matter during several walks with Mary in the Castle gardens, began his journey back to court.[10] Walsingham next attempted to ascertain James's attitude toward a joint treaty. Bowes, to whom the task was entrusted, found the King eager for the alliance with Elizabeth and willing to see his mother freed but quite unwilling to join with her in any agreement. No love was lost between son and mother; James resented Mary's attempt to speak for him and could not forget her Papistry, her French connections, and her desire to secure the English throne for herself rather than for him.[11]

Despite this dampening news Elizabeth was determined to proceed. Perhaps she thought that separate but complementary treaties might be effected. In any case she ordered Mildmay, an old hand at managing Mary, to assist Shrewsbury in formal negotiations, and she presented him with detailed instructions, no doubt framed by Walsingham.[12] Mildmay and Shrewsbury were to remind Mary of her previous offers, ten of which were listed—"to repeate them in order unto her and to knowe of her whether they be rightly conceved or not." If she dissented in any point they were to notify Elizabeth; if not, they might open negotiations for a treaty. They should, generally, signify Elizabeth's pleasure at Mary's concessions and urge her to state more specific terms.

The instructions dealt at length with the question of James's in-

---

[8] *Ibid.*, fols. 76–77.
[9] *Ibid.*, fol. 76.
[10] *Ibid.*, fols. 77–79.
[11] *Ibid.*, fols. 80–81.
[12] *Ibid.*, fols. 81–83; the instructions are dated May 24, 1583.

clusion. Mildmay and Shrewsbury were to inform Mary that no article affecting the King could be concluded without his assent.

And in case she shall thereuppon urge that a minister of hirs maie bee sent to her sonne for that purpose together with another from us, you shall then lett her understand that you will advertise us of that request, perswadinge her to sett downe such articles whereuppon shee shall thinke meete that her sonne be treated withall towching this matter, as also faithfullie to promise that her saide minister, wee allowinge of the saide articles and assenting to his repaire thether, shall have no dealinge underhande for anie other matters, but shall carrie himselfe sincerelie during the time of his beinge in Scotland.

If James's assent could not be obtained Mildmay and Shrewsbury were to discuss the portions of the draft treaty which concerned Mary alone.

Mildmay arrived at Sheffield June 1. That evening (as he wrote Elizabeth on the fourth) he and Shrewsbury "delivered . . . your Majestes lettres to the Scottyshe Quene, which as it semed unto us she receaved verie gladlie, and when shee had red them, she saide that nothinge coulde be more welcom to her then so much from your Majestie as was contayned in them; protestinge before God shee woulde deale plainelie and sincerelie in all thinges."

Since the hour was late, Mildmay and Shrewsbury delayed further proceedings until the following day.

And then resortinge to her agayne wee entred into the matter and tolde her that your Majestie havinge receaved advisement of certain offers made by her to your Majestie, and of her desire that some from your Majestie mighte be appointed to treate with her uppon the same; it hath pleased your Majestie to authorise us to deale with her therein.

And because th'offers were taken onlie from her speache and not sett downe by her in writinge, therefore least anie thinge might bee misconceaved and misremembred that shee spake, wee thoughte good to repeate the same unto her, and knowe of her whether they were rightlie conceaved or not.

Which course she liked well of, renewinge agayne her former protestacion of her playne and uprighte meaninge in all thinges towardes your Majestie.

Whereuppon those offers as they be digested into articles [we read] unto her, which she harde deliberatelie, and did acknowledge that the same were rightlie conceived, as she delivered them, nor varienge in anie thinge materiall as by her answers to them it shall appeare.

Which don wee began at the first article and so in order declared unto her your Majestes answere to everie of them, accordinge to your Majestes commaundement conteyned in our instruccions signed by your Majestie.

Mary willingly accepted virtually all of Elizabeth's emendations to her offers. In the article containing her promise not to aid the Pope, the Jesuits, or seminary priests in any activity "tending to the alteracion of the state of religion in this realme" she wished to substitute the wording " 'tending to the alteracon or unquietinge of this estate under the colour of religion,' because that otherwise it might be taken that she would be a partie against anie of her owne religion for the matter of religion onelie, alleadginge besides, that your Majestie havinge lawes sufficient to punysh them for suche offences, there is no necessitie of anie thinge to be don by her therein."

Mary also spoke at length of her son's position. She thought that Elizabeth's security would be the greater if she and James joined in the treaty; she maintained that James held his right to the Scottish throne from her "and further that he be associate with her in title" although the government was, for the time being, in his hands alone. James, she added, would acknowledge the association "if [he] had not fallen into their handes that she saieth detayne him against his will." Although eager to send ministers to talk with James, Mary agreed that she would give them "no other instruccions but suche as shall concerne [the treaty], and the same to bee first seene and allowed by your Majestie; she doth also faithfullie promise that her ministers shall not deale underhande nor in anie other thinge there, but onelie for this cause plainelie and directlie."

Mildmay and Shrewsbury concluded their dispatch:

Onelie this wee are to add, that she desireth us to recommende unto your Majestie her great and earnest affection to doe all thinges that maie content you, and that she doth desire above all thinges in the worlde that shee maie have your Majestes assured good will and favour, and that your Majestie will receive her into your proteccion, withowt the hope whereof she should thincke all to be in vayne that maie bee don in theis matters, and coulde looke for no good successe in them.[13]

In a private letter to Walsingham Mildmay wrote, "I praie God our proceadinges be as well accepted as wee have meant, and I praie God to procure us a spedie answere." He found Mary "much decayed in health" and "greatlie wearied . . . with her longe captivity; she understandeth well what is fitt for her [and] speaketh francklie to content her Majestie in all thinges." Although "doubtfull least she shalbe delayed, as she saieth she hath bine heretofore," she was "relieved by this commission to my L. [Shrewsbury] and me, and thereby in hope of good to follow her."[14] Clearly Mildmay, too, hoped for speedy success in the negotiations.

By the tenth, however, Elizabeth had decided that nothing further could be done until James had been consulted. She liked Mary's conciliatory attitude and would have proceeded to some full resolution, she wrote,

had wee not bine latelie advertised owt of Scotlande that suche of the noblemen as stand not best devoted towardes us have sought to breade in the Kinges head a doubte and jealousie that our dealinge with the said Queen tendeth to the abridgement of his authoritie and the callinge in question the validitie of his present government, which hath engendred especiallie in his subjectes verie strange conceiptes which wee thincke meeter to be suppressed then anie waie nouryshed, and therefore do hold it best that our further proceeding in the treatie shoulde be stayed untill the King her sonne maie be throughlie informed that their informacion be untrue and voide of ground.

Since she wished the treaty to "proceade imeadiatlie after wee shall heare owte of Scotlande," Elizabeth ordered Mildmay not to return to London but to retire to Apethorpe, which was much closer to Sheffield, until he received further instructions.[15]

It is doubtful that Mildmay had received Elizabeth's letter by the eleventh, but he had somehow learned of the stay in negotiation. He vented his disappointment and irritation in a letter to Walsingham;

[13] *Ibid.*, fols. 83–84.
[14] *Ibid.*, fol. 84.
[15] *Ibid.*, fols. 84–85.

he attributed Elizabeth's change of heart to the news of Lennox's death, which had just reached the court. Although the pro-French faction in Scotland might thereby be weakened, Mildmay feared that the respite would be short. "If thinges be so tickle in Scotlande," he concluded, "it is good for her Majestie to take that good she maie by this Ladie, who nowe pretendeth to seeke her Majestie above all the worlde."[16]

By the seventeenth Mildmay and Shrewsbury had informed Mary of the delay. They wrote the Queen:

Wee founde her verie much greived, saienge that where she had alwaies required that she mighte sende a minister of hirs to be accompanied with one of your Majestie into Scotlande to bringe all those matters to the better conclusion, if your Majestie doe nowe sende alone thether withowt her, she cannot but holde this treatie as broken. For there will come thence none other thinge from her sonne but suche as shall like those nowe aboute him, whome she termeth to be rebelles and her enemyes, and such as are willinge to interrupte anie good course betwene your Majestie and her.

Not only did Mary take the delay "to be as good as a refusal"; she also flew into one of her fits of passion. "All theis speaches and more to that effect she uttered with great greife of mynde, and with teares, sheweing herselfe greatlie trowbled that she coulde receave no certaine resolucon." Mildmay's efforts to quiet her failed.[17]

Mildmay and Shrewsbury dispatched Beale, who had been with them at Sheffield, to give Elizabeth a fuller account of the situation. Mildmay also wrote melancholy letters to Burghley and Walsingham. "We left [Mary], but veary difficultely, in some hope that [the treaty] shall proceade," he told Burghley.[18] His letter to Walsingham reveals that the Secretary had anticipated Mary's attitude: "You judged rightlie of this Ladies interpretacion of theis thinges," he wrote, "all in the worst sense that maie bee, thinckinge herselfe utterlie abused by faire wordes and wynninge of time, which she saieth she can no longer

16 *Ibid.*, fol. 85.
17 *Ibid.*, fols. 85–86.
18 Harl. MS 6993, fol. 46; *CSP, Scot.*, VI, No. 528, where the sentence "I do not retire to my house at Apethorpe" should read "I do now retire to my house at Apethorpe."

endure but will seeke some other waie," presumably renewed plotting. "I mervaile that finding the situation in Scotland so tickle as you righte, and this woman offringe so much to her Majestie, there is no more regarde had of it," he reiterated; "I doubte the death of Lennox hath brought so great a securitie."

Mildmay still thought that the treaty should proceed through tripartite negotiations between Elizabeth, Mary, and James "and be dealt in by men of quallitie and degree, for otherwyse I looked for no good of yt." He suggested Shrewsbury, Huntingdon, Lord Evers, and Lord Gray as the English negotiators, "matched with the like of Scotlande, some for this Quene and some for the Kinge."[19]

Hoping to mollify Mary, Elizabeth wrote Shrewsbury on the sixteenth that she would send no special envoy to Scotland but rather would conduct negotiations through her resident ambassador.[20] Shrewsbury and Mildmay were riding together near Sheffield when the messenger arrived; they replied on the eighteenth:

Wee doe both thincke [it] most convenient . . . for the present not . . . to lett her knowe that her Majestie had or meant to send her ambassador there touchinge these causes, for that wee knowe woulde as much trouble her as yf her Majestie would send one expresslie thether; and suerlye yf her Majestes pleasure be to graunt that one from her Majestie and another from that Queen shall goe together, it were good the same shoulde be don with some speede.[21]

By June 27 both Mildmay and Walsingham had despaired of any good outcome. Mildmay, at Apethorpe, wrote his brother-in-law, "I finde you growe to an opineon that this treatie is at the farthest, and then better never begonne. And I am sorrye to have bine employed in so unfruitefull a jornye. . . . This woman was in good time before this interruption," he commented, noticeably irritated, "but nowe I have not so good hope of her conformitie, and it cannot bee but she will do her best to see revenge. If her sonne be caried into Fraunce, which I alwaies doubted, then farewell all likelihood of anie good from Scotlande; he wilbe maried there and corrupted with the deli-

---

[19] Cot. MS Caligula C. IX, fol. 86; *CSP, Scot.*, VI, No. 530.
[20] *CSP, Scot.*, VI, No. 524.
[21] Cot. MS Caligula C. IX, fol. 86; *CSP, Scot.*, VI, No. 533.

cates of that lose countrie. I am woe in my harte that it is no more regarded."[22] On the twenty-eighth he added, "Yf [Mary] gett knowledge that Mr. Bowes is advertised of our dealinge with her, suerlie all is broken, as I thincke, and howe it canne be kept from her I see not."[23]

Meanwhile Bowes, in Edinburgh, had felt out the King and "some fewe persons of best judgement, affection, and secrecie." He found James "nothinge well pleased" that his mother "should seeke to bynde him to joyne with her in this treatie," although he agreed to the articles designed to safeguard Elizabeth's security. He thought the article intended to preserve Mary's claim to the English throne "worthye deepe consideracion"; his position was that, by her abdication, she had passed to him both the Scottish Crown and her right of succession in England. Although James protested that he would be happy to see his mother given greater freedom, the chief Councillors were opposed. They feared that she would use her liberty to stir up rebellion against their government.[24]

Rebellion, indeed, occurred much sooner than they anticipated. On the very day of Bowes's dispatch, June 29, James was spirited away from Edinburgh to St. Andrew's. Angus and Mar, who had been friendly to Elizabeth, fell from power and were ultimately exiled; William Stewart, Huntly, Crawford, Montrose, and finally Arran— the remnants of Lennox's party—assumed control. Although Bowes did not immediately appreciate the seriousness of the situation, he realized by July 13 that the palace revolution worked to the advantage of the French and the King's mother.[25] Mildmay had been right: the fall of Lennox had not produced a stable Anglophile Scotland.

Although still uncertain what course to follow in Scotland, Elizabeth wrote Shrewsbury July 7 that the treaty with Mary, "so farre forthe as concerneth herselfe" alone, should proceed. Mildmay would be sent to aid in the negotiations. Mary was to be told of James's refusal to enter into a joint agreement; if she objected that he was dominated by Councillors opposed to her she should be informed that they had been removed "and such others newlie called to counsell and

<hr/>

[22] *Ibid.*, fol. 86.
[23] *Ibid.*
[24] *Ibid.*, fols. 86–88; *CSP, Scot.*, VI, No. 546.
[25] *CSP, Scot.*, VI, No. 563.

creditt aboute the King whome she hath ever thoughte to bee no un-frendes."[26]

Mildmay did not, however, return to Sheffield. Instead, Walsing-ham suggested that Mildmay and Hunsdon be sent to Scotland, to survey the situation and, if possible, to avert the dangerous effects of the revolution.[27] Finally this idea, too, was dropped; Walsingham himself set out for Edinburgh, authorized to offer substantial pensions in return for an alteration in Scottish policy. Pending his return the Marian negotiations dissolved into irresolute flux. On July 25 a per-plexed Shrewsbury wrote Elizabeth asking what he should do and why Mildmay had not returned.[28] In August the treaty was permanently tabled. Elizabeth's position, acknowledged by Shrewsbury in a letter of August 16, was that the alteration in Scotland had been effected by forces favorable to Mary and perhaps in league with her; the treaty could not proceed until James showed himself favorably disposed toward England and before Mary cleared herself of all suspicion.[29]

Elizabeth's government, characteristically, spent several months without formulating a new policy. Perhaps the Queen felt that, through the pressure of external events, the Marian problem would shortly re-cast itself in a new form. If so, she was right, for Walsingham had scarcely delivered his gloomy account of the Scottish situation when he uncovered the Throckmorton plot.[30] The reaction against Mary was immediate: far from desiring her liberty, the Council now contem-plated her execution. All hope for an amicable settlement between Elizabeth and Mary was irrevocably lost.

Yet hope had existed. Elizabeth was not merely play-acting or winning time; as in 1570, she had seriously desired a compromise settlement, but the flow of events had made it impossible. Indeed one is struck by the parallels between the discussions of 1570–1571 and those of 1583: in both cases Mary was originally yielding and con-ciliatory; in both cases James's councillors blocked a settlement; in both cases negotiations were finally cut off by the discovery of a Catho-

[26] Cot. MS Caligula C. IX, fol. 88.
[27] *CSP, Scot.*, VI, No. 557.
[28] Cot. MS Caligula C. IX, fol. 88.
[29] *CSP, Scot.*, VI, No. 602.
[30] See above, Chap. 12.

lic conspiracy. There was no third chance. After 1583 matters moved inexorably toward the Babington plot, Mary's execution, and the Spanish war.

Scottish affairs, however, were brought at length to a satisfactory conclusion. James, now nearing twenty, showed an increasing inclination to rule himself and, with an eye on the English throne, to favor Elizabeth. Arran grew less popular as his Catholic connections appeared more openly. Elizabeth and Walsingham exploited the situation; they sent Edward Wotton to Edinburgh in March, 1585, with proposals for an Anglo-Scottish alliance. Arran's ruin followed, and in July, 1586, Elizabeth and James signed a formal treaty. James agreed not to support Elizabeth's enemies and to send her military aid in case of attack; the Queen, for her part, finally granted him a pension of four thousand pounds a year.[31] Mildmay must have rejoiced.

---

[31] Mendoza thought that Mildmay was the envoy sent to Edinburgh to pay the pension and conclude the league (*CSP, Spn., 1580–86*, No. 443), but in fact it was Thomas Milles (*CSP, Scot.*, VIII, Nos. 386, 394). The treaty was concluded on July 5, 1586 (*ibid.*, No. 562).

## 14. EMMANUEL COLLEGE

W ITH HIS POSITION SECURE, his family established, and his fortune growing, Sir Walter Mildmay was free to turn his thoughts
to the advancement of good learning and true religion. In his decisions
at the Exchequer, as has been seen, he had favored scholars and clergymen; now, perhaps with some intimation of his mortality, he prepared
to erect the capstone of his philanthropic edifice, Emmanuel College,
Cambridge.

Mildmay had earlier demonstrated his concern for higher learning
through his donations to Christ's College. In 1569 he granted Christ's
an income of £ 20 a year derived from the manor of Farcet, Huntingdonshire, which he had acquired in 1553. The endowment was to
provide for a lectureship in Greek—interesting evidence of Mildmay's
regard for the study of the ancient language which the Humanists
thought so important—as well as six scholarships and an annual sti-
pend to a preacher who was a member of the College.[1] Perhaps at about
the same time he gave a number of books to the College Library; the
catalogue of donations compiled in 1623 lists as his gifts a Latin Bible
and a Greek Testament; the works of Plato, Aristotle, Dion, and
Plutarch, all in Greek; Averroës's commentary on Aristotle; the writings of Cicero, Demosthenes, and Dionysius of Halicarnassus; and
Nizolius's Latin dictionary. Of these the Aristotle, Averroës, Plutarch,
and Nizolius remain in the Library; the volumes of Aristotle and
Plutarch, interestingly enough both in Greek, are signed by Mildmay
and bear the dates 1556 and 1559 respectively.[2]

[1] C. H. Cooper, *Memorials of Cambridge,* II, 32. The original grant, in the
College muniment room, is written on vellum in English and Latin, is signed
and sealed, and bears the date March 10.

[2] The College also has several Latin Bibles and Greek Testaments which, by

Thomas Fuller, in his charming seventeenth-century *History of the Worthies of England,* says that Mildmay "began with his benefaction to Christ's-Colledge in Cambridge, only to put his hand into practice; then his bounty embraced the generous resolution (which the painfull piety of St. Paul propounds to himself, viz.) 'not to build on another man's foundation'; but, at his own cost, he erected a new Colledge in Cambridge, by the name of *Emanuel.*"[3] A less pious account suggests that Mildmay chose not to continue his bounty to Christ's because its master had been elected contrary to his advice and was suspected of holding insufficiently Calvinistic views in theology.[4]

Whatever his immediate motivation, Mildmay had determined by 1583 to found a new college. Aiming to train preaching ministers, he appropriately chose the site of the dissolved priory of the Dominicans, or Friars Preachers; on June 12 it was bought for him, for £ 550, by Laurence Chaderton, who was to become the College's first master, and Richard Culverwell, a London mercer and Chaderton's brother-in-law.[5] We do not know how the buildings had been used since the dissolution of the house in 1538, or what portions were in decent repair when Mildmay acquired them. He did, however, succeed in utilizing several: the friars' chapel was converted into the College hall, and another building—probably not, as if often said, the refectory—was made the College chapel. Its north-south orientation does not seem to have worried Mildmay; indeed it has been suggested that he intentionally avoided using a building with Catholic connections, or

---

their dates, could have been given by Mildmay, although they do not bear his signature. I am greatly indebted to Dr. A. L. Peck, librarian of Christ's College, for communicating this information to me.

[3] Thomas Fuller, *The History of the Worthies of England,* I, 356. The first edition appeared in 1662.

[4] E. S. Shuckburgh, *Emmanuel College,* p. 26. The master in question was Edmund Barwell, elected in 1582, on whom see H. C. Porter, *Reformation and Reaction in Tudor Cambridge,* p. 236. Mildmay did succeed in securing the election of his candidate for fellow in 1583, although Burghley opposed the choice (see Mark H. Curtis, *Oxford and Cambridge in Transition,* pp. 46–47).

[5] Robert Willis and J. W. Clark, *The Architectural History of the University of Cambridge,* II, 687–688.

indeed one properly oriented liturgically, in order to demonstrate his Puritan convictions and his contempt for medieval tradition.[6] What is more likely is that he used the facilities he found available in the most reasonable way, so as to provide the maximum accommodation at the minimum cost.

The original arrangement of the buildings may be discerned by studying David Loggan's print of about 1688 (Plate 9).[7] The present entrance from St. Andrew's Street had not yet been constructed, nor had the fine chapel by Wren or the range of chambers at the extreme right been raised. The College of Mildmay's time was entered through a gate inscribed *Sacrae Theologiae Studiosis posuit Gualterus Mild-maius*, A.D. 1584.[8] To the left as one entered was the chapel, marked *B* in the print; to the right, the kitchens; straight ahead, separating the two courtyards, the hall and master's lodge, forming together the most imposing building of the original College. The second courtyard was open to the east, where Wren's chapel now stands. On the west Mildmay built a range of chambers, probably utilizing what remained of the friars' dormitory, and on the south he erected his one wholly new building, the so-called Founder's Range, which provided rooms for fellows and scholars.[9]

The architect for Mildmay's buildings was Ralph Symons. Although he was to do a good deal of work at Cambridge in the 1590's—he built Sidney Sussex and considerable parts of St. John's and Trinity—Emmanuel was his first essay in collegiate architecture. We do not know how Mildmay happened to select him; perhaps the two men had become acquainted in London, for Symons is styled a stonemason of Westminster in the contracts for the second court of St. John's.[10] Certainly Mildmay chose well: as a lease of 1586 records, Symons "shewed

[6] *Ibid.,* p. 694.

[7] Reproduced from one of the volumes of Loggan's prints in the University Library, Cambridge (classmark Ii. 9. 8), by kind permission of the librarian.

[8] The Rev. J. C. Dickinson, "Emmanuel College," in *Victoria History of the Counties of England, Cambridge,* ed. J. P. C. Roach, III, 474.

[9] Willis and Clark, *Cambridge,* II, 689–692.

[10] *Ibid.,* p. 250.

himselfe verie dilligent and carefull" in workmanship,[11] and the buildings, although not elaborate, were attractive.[12]

At about the time that building operations were commenced Mildmay obtained the Queen's license for the foundation of the College. It is an elegant document, not unusual in content but ornamented with a charming portrait of Elizabeth surrounded by muses and playful representations of flowers and animals, among them a snail, a dragonfly, and a serpent (see Plate 5).[13] Mildmay also secured the Queen's financial aid; in 1585 she gave the College an annuity of twenty marks drawn from the former estates of Glastonbury Abbey to be used for the maintenance of scholars and exhibitioners.[14] Originally the monastery had used the funds to support scholars at Oxford; it is pleasant to suppose that Mildmay himself chose the source of the grant with a view to continuing an educational tradition.

Other benefactions, too, were forthcoming. Sir Henry Killigrew, the courtier and diplomat, contributed £140 for the purchase of St. Nicholas's Hostel, which was pulled down and its materials utilized in the construction of the master's lodge. Sir Wolstan Dixie, the Lord Mayor of London whose name has been immortalized in the Dixie Professorship of Ecclesiastical History, gave £650 toward the buildings, and Dr. Edward Leedes, rector of Croxton and a former master of Clare Hall, contributed 1,000 marks for the same purpose.[15] The College also accumulated a number of advowsons during Mildmay's

[11] *Ibid.,* p. 693.

[12] They did not, however, last very well, probably because the brick began to crumble. The only portion of the original buildings to remain is the hall range, which was repaired and cased in stone by James Essex in 1760. The Founder's Range had shown defects earlier and in 1719 was pulled down and replaced by the present Westmorland Building. The building forming the west side of the south court was replaced by Essex's impressive façade and building in 1769.

[13] The illuminated charter is in the library of Emmanuel College; the text is also enrolled on the Patent Rolls for 26 Elizabeth and is printed in *Documents Relating to the University and Colleges of Cambridge,* III, 479–482.

[14] EC Lib. MSS, COL. 9. 10. The College still receives this payment from the Exchequer, although certain charges have reduced it by about £3 a year.

[15] Willis and Clark, *Cambridge,* II, 692–693.

lifetime: Stanground with Farcet, Huntingdonshire, given by Mildmay himself; Little Melton, Norfolk, given by Francis Chamberlain; Thurcaston, Leicestershire, given by Walsingham; Brompton Regis and Winsford, Somerset, given by Henry Neal; and Loughborough, Leicestershire, and North Cadbury and Aller, Somerset, given by Henry Hastings, the Puritan third Earl of Huntingdon.[16] These rights of presentation to ecclesiastical livings were of great importance because they enabled the College to spread the Puritan zeal of its graduates throughout the realm.

An oft-told tale has the Queen remarking to Mildmay, soon after the foundation of the College, "Sir Walter, I hear you have erected a Puritan foundation." Mildmay is said to have replied, "No, madam, far be it from me to countenance anything contrary to your established laws; but I have set an acorn which, when it becomes an oak, God alone knows what will be the fruit thereof."[17] Like most apocryphal stories this contains an element of truth; Mildmay was too loyal to the Queen and her government to favor subversion of the established Church, but he was keenly concerned for its improvement, especially through the supply of a learned, preaching ministry. He later wrote: "The one object which I set before me in erecting this College was to render as many as possible fit for the administration of the Divine Word and Sacraments; and that from this seed ground the English Church might have those she can summon to instruct the people and undertake the office of pastors, which is a thing necessary above all others."[18] Its very gate indicated that the College had been erected for the study of sacred theology.

Further proof of Mildmay's intention is supplied by his statutes for Emmanuel.[19] Dated October 1, 1585, they are in the main closely

[16] Dickinson, "Emmanuel," *Victoria History,* III, 479–480; Huntingdon's deed, Emmanuel College Treasury, Box 1, A.2.

[17] C. H. and T. Cooper, *Athenae Cantabrigienses,* II, 54; Shuckburgh, *Emmanuel,* p. 22.

[18] Shuckburgh, *Emmanuel,* p. 4.

[19] Copies of the statutes, in Latin, are held in the College Library and in Sloane MS 1739, fols. 1–47; they are printed in *Documents Relating to the University and Colleges of Cambridge,* III, 483–523.

modelled on those of Christ's; since the statutes of Christ's were based on those of God's House, which were in turn derived from those adopted for Clare in 1359, and since the statutes of Sidney Sussex are founded on those of Emmanuel, a whole line of filiation can be traced.[20] In the case of Emmanuel, however, Mildmay's own views and purposes are clearly interjected. He broke from tradition in making no provision for fellowships in law and medicine. Indeed he wrote, "Let fellows and scholars who obtrude into the College with any other design than to devote themselves to sacred theology, and eventually to labor in preaching the Word, know that they are frustrating our hope and occupying the place of fellow or scholar contrary to our ordinance."[21] The master and all fellows were required to take an oath against Papistry and other heresies and superstitions; the master and at least four fellows were to be ministers; students were enjoined to attend divine service without exception.

Other statutes were designed to prevent luxury and nonresidence and to encourage industrious study. Fellows, for instance, were not to be absent from the College for more than twenty days a year without special permission; no scholar was to occupy more than one room; students were directed not to gather for "collocutiones de rebus inanibus," such vain talk being a great hindrance to progress in good letters. All masters of the College were to be Englishmen of fidelity, industry, and good conscience who had publicly professed the study of sacred theology for eight years and who abhorred Popery and superstition. Fellows were to be poor men of pure religion who had held the bachelor of arts for at least three years or were masters of arts. All scholars were to be candidates for the ministry, poor and able. In selection of masters preference was to be given to members of Christ's, Mildmay's old College; students from Essex or Northamptonshire, Mildmay's native and adoptive counties, were to be preferred for fellowships and scholarships.[22] Mildmay's interest in the Latin and Greek classics—apparently the only study besides religion which he

---

[20] C. H. Rackham, *Early Statutes of Christ's College, Cambridge, passim.*

[21] Statute XXI; translation from Dickinson, "Emmanuel," *Victoria History,* III, 474.

[22] A letter of 1641 to Benjamin Whichcote states that this clause was always

thought worth while—is evinced by the provision for a lecturer to expound the writings of Plato, Aristotle, or Cicero.

The most controversial statutes were those designed to prevent fellows from regarding themselves as having perpetual domicile within the College. One of the original statutes requires fellows to resign if they receive an ecclesiastical living worth £ 10 a year or more, since Mildmay would not countenance pluralism and nonresidence; a supplementary statute of 1587 states that fellowships are to terminate within a year after the fellow proceeds to his doctorate in theology. The latter was suspended in 1627 as being too rigid, since fellows might not have been able to find suitable positions in the Church during the first year after taking their doctorates, but it was declared still valid by a committee of the Long Parliament. Opposition continued, leading to permanent suspension at the Restoration. The only other college to attempt such a rule, Sidney Sussex, also soon abandoned it.[23]

Mildmay's successors might be less strict than he—indeed the second master, John Preston, was a chaplain to Prince Charles and obtained an interpretation of the statutes allowing him to spend most of his time at court.[24] But in his first master, Laurence Chaderton, Mildmay found a learned linguist and zealous Puritan with whom he could be in full sympathy. Chaderton, son of a wealthy Roman Catholic gentleman of Lancashire, had accepted Protestantism while a student at Christ's in 1566. His father disowned him; but Chaderton, with the fervor of a convert, continued to study and, later, to preach. He had been a fellow of Christ's and preacher at St. Clement's Church, Cambridge, when Mildmay selected him as master of Emmanuel. A member of the Puritan delegation at the Hampton Court Conference in 1604 and one of the four members of Emmanuel to help translate

---

taken to mean that they were preferred only "*caeteris paribus*; more respect was had to merit than to either of those counties" (Harl. MS 7033, fol. 106).

[23] Harl. MS 7033, fols. 91, 101–106.

[24] Dickinson, "Emmanuel," *Victoria History,* III, 475. One also notes that in 1610 four students were admonished "for misdemeanour in drinking wine, and clamorous singing to the disturbance of the College, . . . and going after to the Rose, and drinking more wine, and lying out of the Colledge all night contrary to the statutes of the said Colledge" (EC Lib. MSS, CHA. 1. 4).

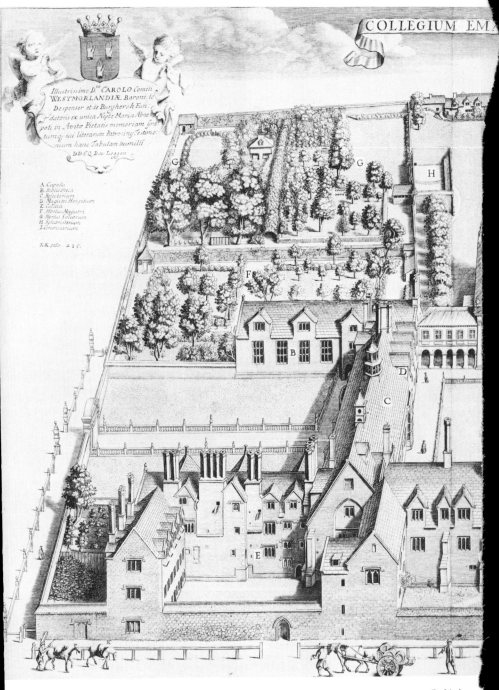

9. Emmanuel College, print by Dav
*(Reproduced from University Library,*

NUELIS

A

id Loggan, about 1688

Cambridge, Volume Ii, 9.8).

the "King James" Bible, he did not resign the mastership until 1622, when he was 86. He lived to the amazing age of 103.[25]

Of the original fellows perhaps the most notable was John Richardson, formerly a fellow of Clare, who later became professor of divinity and master, in succession, of Peterhouse and Trinity. But Richardson's colleagues, if not so distinguished, were no less zealous in their Puritanism. Eleven of the twelve fellows of Emmanuel in 1589 were signers of a petition favoring Francis Johnson, a fellow of Christ's who had been imprisoned for public advocacy of the Presbyterian form of ecclesiastical government.[26]

Chaderton and some of the fellows must have taken up their residence by November, 1584, when twenty-six students matriculated.[27] Mildmay was perhaps present to greet them; we know that the townspeople of Cambridge gave him a present which cost 23s. 4d. during a visit of that year.[28]

The College was not complete, however, until 1587, when an elaborate "dedication festival" was held. Mildmay sent two does for the banquet, and the College bought a "crag of sturgeon"; the chambers were "dressed" at some cost, and the street in front of the College was specially cleansed.[29] Mildmay was almost certainly present: the remaining documents are frustratingly vague, but it is recorded that the town gave him another gift, which he presumably accepted in person. Our best description of the dedication is in a letter to Mildmay from Thomas Legge, Regius Professor of Civil Law, master of Caius, and Vice-Chancellor for 1587. He wrote, on December 20:

What joye and comforte we received at the late dedication of Emmanuel

[25] Cf. Porter, *Reformation*, pp. 239–240, and the article in the *DNB*. According to an unsubstantiated story in the *DNB*, Chaderton was reluctant to accept Mildmay's appointment, having been offered more lucrative ecclesiastical preferment; but Mildmay refused to found the College unless Chaderton accepted its mastership, and Chaderton yielded.

[26] Porter, *Reformation*, pp. 157–159, 210.

[27] EC Lib. MSS, CHA. 1. 4.

[28] C. H. and T. Cooper, *Athenae Cantabrigienses*, II, 54.

[29] Shuckburgh, *Emmanuel*, p. 7. Shuckburgh and a number of other printed sources incorrectly give 1588 as the date of the festival.

Colledge, fownded by your honour, and brought to suche perfection in so shorte a space, I may not seeke to expresse sufficientlie by theise my lettres. As then we joyned togither in humble prayers that God might blesse the same, to his honour and the benifite of his churche and the common wealthe, so we rejoysed not a litle that by the erection of that Colledge, such a beautye and ornament also is added to the Universitie. Wherfore I thought it my humble dewtie, to whom a more particular charge is committed of the University this yeare, not onlie to gyve my humble thankes to your h[onour] for the same, but also to shewe our dewtifulnes in accepting it, and to declare how willing I shall be to shew such favoure to the said Colledge as shall lye in my poure.[30]

The College Library was probably decently furnished and supplied with books by the time of the festival, although the accounts for 1592 do record the purchase of two additional tables at a cost of 8s.[31] Mildmay himself gave a number of volumes to form the nucleus of the collection. No complete list of his donations remains, but a general impression can be obtained from a fragmentary seventeenth-century inventory and from an examination of the Library's present holdings. In addition to a copy of the Vulgate and the French Bible given Mildmay by the ministers of the church in Geneva, Mildmay donated a theological treatise by Theodore Beza, Calvin's successor; a volume on commerce and exchange by Carolus Molinaeus (Charles Dumoulin); *De inventione dialectica* by Rudolf Agricola, the German humanist; the works of Isocrates, Appian, and Livy; a Greek *Iliad* and *Odyssey*; and a number of mathematical treatises: Orontius's *Cosmographia* and *Commentary on Euclid*, Dürer's *Institutiones geometricae*, and Bishop Tunstall's *De arte supputandi*.[32] A number of these volumes bear annotations in Mildmay's own hand; some of them he probably used during his own student days at Christ's.

Mildmay may have contributed a number of other volumes, and he may have persuaded his friends to follow suit. Certainly the Library

[30] EC Lib. MSS, COL. 9. 10.

[31] EC Lib. MSS, BUR. 8. 1, p. 4.

[32] I am indebted to Dr. F. H. Stubbings, the librarian of Emmanuel College, for supplying me with a list of Mildmay's donations and allowing me to examine a number of the volumes. The College also has two books once owned by Mildmay and acquired at later dates.

grew rapidly; by 1610 it included more than five hundred books.[33] Mildmay also gave the College more mundane items, including the "great brass pott geven by our Founder" recorded in an early inventory of kitchen equipment.[34]

That Mildmay's acorn did become a Puritan oak is well known. Considerable evidence of its growth may be found in the extensive records relating to the services in the College chapel. They reveal that the first Communion was not held until May 26, 1588, and that during the early years Communion was administered only twice yearly. All members of the College were expected to communicate unless incapacitated by ill health or lack of knowledge—one wonders if this last provision reflects strict standards for admission to the Lord's Table or is merely a ruse to cover the nonparticipation of those not in sympathy with the Prayer Book service; offerings, usually amounting to something more than £ 3, were received for the aid of the poor.[35]

It is not unusual to find the Holy Communion seldom celebrated during the Elizabethan and Jacobean ages, but it may be that this situation at Emmanuel reflected particularly the Puritan belief in a preaching rather than a sacramental church. Other signs of "publick disorders as touching church causes in Emmanuel Colledge" shortly became apparent and were spelled out in a paper of 1603. The very orientation of the chapel the anonymous writer thought "a prognostication of disorder," for, although "all the chappells in the University are built with the chancell eastward, according to the uniform order of all Christendome, the chancell of that Colledge standeth north, and their kitchen eastwarde." Still worse, the College did not use the Book of Common

---

[33] EC Lib. MSS, BUR. 8. 1.

[34] *Ibid.*

[35] Harl. MS 7033, fols. 78–85, one of the forty-two volumes of Cambridge materials collected by Thomas Baker, an eighteenth-century antiquarian of St. John's College. Mildmay had intended that there should be administration of the Holy Communion at least once a term; Statute XX reads in part, ". . . cuiusque termini initio ad minimum ad socios et scholares eiusdem Collegii sacello publice coeuntes [magister] sacram concionem habebit in propria persona, et una etiam sacram Eucharistiam eodem tempore administrabit; ut autem utrumque saepius faciat, in Domino adhortamur."

Prayer but followed "a private course of publick prayer, after their own fashion, both Sondaies, Holy Daies, and worke days." At Holy Communion "all other Colledges do use one manner of forme in celebrating . . . according to the order of the Communion Booke; . . . but in Emanuel Colledge they receive that Holy Sacrament sittinge upon forms about the Communion Table, and doe pull the loafe one from the other, after the minister hath begon. And soe the cupp, one drinking as it were to another, like good fellows." Surplices had never been worn in the chapel, and members of the College did not wear gowns and square caps in keeping with the custom of the University and the specific order of the Queen. Nor did they fast on Fridays and Ember Days, but had "suppers every such night throughout the year, publickly in their Halls: yea upon Good Fridaye itself."[36]

At the Hampton Court Conference, Chaderton admitted that there were "sitting communions in Emmanuel College, which he said was so, by reason of the seats so placed as they be, yet that they had some kneeling also."[37] But the reason did not satisfy; the canons of 1604 ordered kneeling and the use of the surplice and Prayer Book. Samuel Ward, a fellow of Emmanuel who became more famous as master of Sidney Sussex, recorded in his diary that on Wednesday, January 18, 1605, "the surplice was first urged by the Archbishop to be brought into Emmanuel."[38] Reverence for Mildmay's memory had staved off the evil day for twenty years, and the respect in which even his opponents held Chaderton continued to help avert trouble. But the College still did not conform, thus becoming a particularly sharp thorn in William Laud's side. As late as the Restoration half the fellows favored the established liturgy and half opposed it, so that the Prayer Book service was read one week and the Genevan directory of worship the next.[39]

---

[36] *Ibid.*, fol. 98.

[37] Quoted in Porter, *Reformation*, p. 240.

[38] Quoted in *ibid.*

[39] Harl. MS 7033, fol. 77, a letter from Thomas Smith to William Sancroft. As the directory was the approved form of worship during the Interregnum, the College appears not to have conformed entirely to nonconformity!

It was perhaps mainly in order to provide a more seemly environment for the sanctioned ceremonies of the established Church that William Sancroft during his mastership from 1662 to 1665 planned the erection of a new chapel, properly oriented and fitted up. Although he soon left Emmanuel to become Dean of St. Paul's and, later, Archbishop of Canterbury, Sancroft actively supported the construction and was responsible for the selection of Sir Christopher Wren as architect. We know that Mildmay's descendants provided timber, probably from the woods at Apethorpe, for the chapel, which was dedicated by Bishop Gunning of Ely in 1677.[40]

By its fruits—to change the metaphor from oaks to students—the progress of the College can best be judged. In purely numerical terms its success was obvious: in 1624, for instance, Emmanuel admitted seventy-four new students, the highest number in the University.[41] Nor can there be doubt of the learning and zeal of many of the early graduates.

As might be expected from its Puritan tone, Emmanuel supplied a disproportionate number of the early immigrants to New England. Thirty-three Emmanuel men—about a third of the Cambridge graduates, and more than the entire number from Oxford—fled from the personal rule of Charles and Laud between 1629 and 1640. Among them were two former fellows of the College, Thomas Hooker and John Cotton; Thomas Shepard, whom Professor Morison calls "the most noted evangelist of early New England";[42] Samuel Stone, for whose English birthplace Hartford, Connecticut, was named; Richard Saltonstall, progenitor of the distinguished Massachusetts family; Simon Bradstreet, governor of the colony; John Harvard, who, dying at the age of thirty, acquired undying fame as a benefactor of American education; and William Mildmay, great-grandson of Sir Walter, who began his studies at Emmanuel and completed them at Harvard in 1647.[43]

[40] *Ibid.*, fol. 100; Willis and Clark, *Cambridge*, II, 703–709.
[41] Dickinson, "Emmanuel," *Victoria History*, III, 476.
[42] S. E. Morison, *The Founding of Harvard College*, p. 400.
[43] Porter, *Reformation*, pp. 241–242. The Mildmay family was also con-

Not all the early Emmanuel men, however, were Puritans. Indeed the principal latitudinarian movement of the early seventeenth century, that of the Cambridge Platonists, centered at Emmanuel, where Ralph Cudworth, Nathaniel Culverwell, John Smith, and—greatest of them —Benjamin Whichcote developed their rational, humanistic philosophy. During the 1630's and 1640's these scholars formed what a later master referred to, somewhat disapprovingly, as a "company of very learned and ingenious men, who, I fear, at the least some of them, studied other authors more than the Scriptures, and Plato and his scholars above others."[44] They provided a sorely needed liberalizing influence.

Nor did the College breed only philosophers and divines. Following Mildmay's example more than his statutes, it fostered several mathematicians, including John Wallis, the inventor of differential calculus, and Jeremiah Horrocks, the astronomer.[45] Scientific studies were still unorganized, however; although the Emmanuel Library possessed a number of mathematical treatises, the College offered no formal instruction in the subject. As Wallis wrote, "Amongst more than two hundred students . . . in our College, I do not know of any two (perhaps not any) who had more of mathematics than I, . . . which was then but little; . . . for the study of mathematics was at that time more cultivated in London than in the Universities."[46]

Although Mildmay's sons had completed their education before the foundation of Emmanuel, a number of his grandsons and other rela-

---

nected with New England through the Winthrops, for Agnes Winthrop married Thomas Mildmay, son of Sir Walter's brother William, of Springfield Barnes, Essex.

[44] Anthony Tuckney, writing to Whichcote in 1651; quoted in Porter, *Reformation*, p. 423. On the Cambridge Platonists see Ernst Cassirer, *The Platonic Renaissance in England,* trans. James P. Pettegrove. The Platonists were acceptable to Cromwell and his followers, Whichcote being made provost of King's and Cudworth master of Clare to replace royalists or high churchmen who had been ejected. At Emmanuel itself the master, Richard Holdsworth, was removed because of his royalist sympathies, and learning seems to have receded, although in the chapel the contemporary iconoclasts found "nothing to amend."

[45] Curtis, *Oxford and Cambridge,* p. 243.

[46] Quoted in *ibid.,* pp. 244–245.

tives attended the College. The first to enter was Thomas Mildmay, probably the grandson of Sir Walter's older brother Thomas, the auditor of Augmentations. He matriculated fellow-commoner in 1589. Seventeen other members of the family attended Emmanuel during the seventeenth century, although none achieved distinction in scholarly pursuits.[47]

Mildmay's concern for education did not end with the foundation of Emmanuel. It may also be seen in a Star Chamber suit of 1584 concerning the endowments of the grammar school of Godmanchester, Huntingdonshire. The school had been refounded early in Elizabeth's reign by Richard Robbins, who left lands to the annual value of £ 20 for its support. Litigation arose when Robbins's heirs contested the will and sought to obtain the revenues for themselves. The Court's decision awarded the disputed lands to Mildmay, who was apparently cast in the role of a disinterested but benevolent third party; he then granted the governors of the school an annual income of £ 20 drawn from the estates.[48]

He also gave an annuity to Christ's Hospital, stone for the tower of Great St. Mary's, the University church in Cambridge, and a scholarship to Hugh Broughton, the linguist and radical Puritan of Christ's.[49] How much aid he gave to other deserving students there is now no way of knowing, but it may have been considerable.

As these philanthropic endeavors bore their fruit Mildmay must have felt warm satisfaction, if not that pride which Puritans counted sinful. Few men of Tudor times, and certainly no other Elizabethan civil servants, so deserve the gratitude of those in every age who cherish knowledge and the faith.

[47] EC Lib. MSS, COL. 9. 14 (b). 1. In 1587 Mildmay had set aside one of the chambers in the Founder's Range for the use of his descendants who might be studying in the College.

[48] *Victoria History of the Counties of England, Huntingdon,* ed. William Page, Granville Proby, and S. Inskip Ladds, II, 111–113.

[49] C. H. and T. Cooper, *Athenae Cantabrigienses,* p. 55; M. Claire Cross, "Noble Patronage in the Elizabethan Church," *Historical Journal,* III (1960), 12–13.

## 15. THE PARLIAMENT OF 1584–1585

A NUMBER OF CONSIDERATIONS combined to move Elizabeth to summon Parliament in October, 1584. The negotiations aimed at restoring Mary to guarded obscurity in Scotland had, finally, collapsed. The Throckmorton plot, following closely on the heels of the abortive talks, had demonstrated the continuing menace of the Catholics in England. And the assassination of William of Orange in July, 1584, removed the ablest Protestant leader on the continent and served as a grim reminder of the English Queen's mortality. Her Councillors felt the need of new legislation to insure Elizabeth's safety.

The elections, the first since 1572, returned an unusually young House of Commons, and an unusually fresh one. Nearly three-quarters of the 460 Members had never before sat in Parliament, and only 97 had been Knights of the Shire or Burgesses in 1581.[1] The lack of experience and continuity made leadership all the more important. Again it was provided chiefly by Mildmay and Hatton, the two county Members for Northamptonshire. Unlike Hatton, a childless bachelor, Mildmay had the support of his two sons—Anthony sat for Wiltshire, Humphrey for the borough of Higham Ferrers, Northamptonshire— and of a number of other relatives. William Brounker, probably his son-in-law, was a Member for Westbury, Wiltshire, and another Brounker was returned for Devizes. William Fitzwilliam, son of the great Sir William and husband of Mildmay's daughter Winifred, sat for Peterborough. Secretary Walsingham, Mildmay's brother-in-law, again won election for Surrey; another of Walsingham's brothers-in-law, Robert Beale, sat for Dorchester and, like Mildmay and Walsingham, appeared in the Puritan front ranks. Two Exchequer officials,

[1] Sir John Neale, *Elizabeth I and her Parliaments, 1584–1601*, p. 23.

Thomas Randolph and Peter Osborne, also were present in the House. Sir Richard Knightly, Member for the borough of Northampton who later was found harboring the Martin Marprelate press, may or may not have been under Mildmay's patronage.[2]

Other links with the Council were provided by Sadler and Knollys, the latter's position bolstered by the presence of four sons. Burghley was of course in the Lords, but his older son, Sir Thomas Cecil, found a seat in Commons as a Knight for Lincolnshire. As the number of second-generation Members suggests, the leaders were aging. Mildmay and Burghley, almost exact contemporaries, were about sixty-four, Walsingham a decade younger. Hatton, at 44, was the youngest member of the front bench; Sadler, now 77, its grand old man.

To Mildmay's son-in-law, William Fitzwilliam, we probably owe our best account of the session.[3] Recently deposited at the Northamptonshire Record Office, the anonymous journal survived among the Fitzwilliam Papers at Milton and has been confidently ascribed to Fitzwilliam by Sir John Neale.[4] The journal's internal character lends considerable support to Professor Neale's argument, which is based primarily on provenance. The historian is doubly indebted to Fitzwilliam because of the scarcity of other sources: the Commons' journals for the period from 1581 to the end of the reign have been lost; the Lord's journal is incomplete, lacking the usual listing of bills accepted or vetoed by the Queen; and Thomas Cromwell's diary for 1584–1585, although useful, is briefer than his earlier accounts and has faded badly.[5]

The Parliament gathered on Monday, November 23. So many of the Members being new, there was considerable disorder; but at length they were sworn and, under Burghley's direction, named as their Speaker John Puckering, a serjeant-at-law, Member for Bedford, and future Lord Keeper. Like so many others, Puckering was a new man: this was his first Parliament.

Puckering's first duty, after his *pro forma* declaration of inability, was to petition the Queen for the usual liberties of the House. The matter of freedom of speech was unusually slippery, since the Puritans

---

[2] *Return of Members of Parliament,* I, 413–416.
[3] F(M)P 2.
[4] Neale, *Parliaments, 1584–1601,* p. 24.
[5] Crom. d., fols. 73–94.

could be counted on to press for religious reform while the Queen would just as certainly disallow the discussion. Indeed when Chancellor Bromley answered for Elizabeth he made it clear that "shee restrained the cause of religion to be spoken of amonge them," although in all other respects she "willinglie condescended" to their request.

As usual the reformers, among whom we may number Fitzwilliam, objected. He wrote,

It was thought verye straunge that the Nether House should be restrayned in anie matter, but especiallie to speake or move that which heretofore had his beginninge veraie often from that place, which was the cause of religion: for by searchinge of the recordes it appearethe that from xxj$^{mo}$ H. 8 [1529] and a yeare or two after, when the Pope first begann to stagger in England, veraie manie of the Church matters tooke theire beginninge from the Nether House.[6]

Fitzwilliam had even "gethered out of the Parliament roles" a number of statutes dealing with ecclesiastical affairs. Had his party paid less attention to antiquarian research and more to the events of Elizabeth's own Parliaments, they would perhaps have understood better.

Although unconvinced and unrepentant, the Puritans let the matter drop for the time being, and the House proceeded to its principal business on Saturday, November 28. It had by now become something of a tradition for Mildmay to open the session with an oration setting out the condition of the realm and the government's program for parliamentary action. In 1584, for once, nothing intervened to delay his address.[7] It was a long speech—William Fleetwood, recorder of London, wrote that it lasted more than an hour—and demonstrated the order and logic which seasoned Members had come to expect.

Sir Walter marshalled his remarks under four heads: "First, of the present state and condytion of this tyme; next, what enemyes we have

[6] F(M)P 2, fol. 1$^r$.

[7] Copies of the oration are in the Fitzwilliam journal, fols. 2–4; in Sloane MS 326, fols. 71–83; and in Harl. MS 6265, fols. 92–94. I have taken my text from Fitzwilliam, considering his rendition closest to the original; it is possible that Fitzwilliam was acting as private secretary to his father-in-law during these years, and in any case he would have had access to Mildmay's notes.

that doe envye the felicytie thereof; thirdlye, what they desire and looke after; and lastly, what it behooveth us to doe." His first section gave him opportunity to praise the Queen's wise and gracious government, the realm's deliverance from the superstition and tyranny of Rome, the free preaching of the true Gospel, and the maintenance of peace. To old Members Mildmay gave little that was new, but his rhetoric must have impressed the novices as he eulogized "the blessednes of this our happie peace," comparing it with "the miserable state of our neighbours, longe afflicted with cruell warrs": "We possess in all freedome and libertie our religion, which is the cheife: our landes, lives and goodes, our wifes and childeren. They on the other side through civill and intestine troubles are bereaved of all those good thinges that we enjoye, in daunger to fall at the lengthe into the grevious yooke of perpetuall servitude." He cited specifically the continuing efforts to preserve amity with the Scots.

To tye them . . . more suerlie in frendship to this Crowne, you knowe how that at hir great charges hir Majestie hath delivered them from the tyrannye of straungers that sought utterlie to oppresse them [in a marginal note Fitzwilliam wrote, "Fraunce"] and by puttinge out also the fire of civill warrs emongst themselves [she] hath brought peace to that contrye, and preserved their yonge Kinge from his cradell more carefully then any mother doth hir own childe.

But this fortunate realm of England did not lack enemies who, envying her felicity, sought her utter overthrow. Turning to his second point, Mildmay named as "the most mortall and capitall enemye" the Pope, who "both hateth us and the verye soile that we treade on." As proof, he cited the bull excommunicating Elizabeth and absolving subjects of allegiance to her, the rebellion in the North, the invasion into Ireland, the activities of the Council of Trent, and the recent plots of Campion and the Jesuits. He was particularly concerned, as he had been in Vallenger's trial, to show that Campion and his followers had been executed, not merely for supporting Rome, but for capital offenses and conspiracies: they sought the "deposinge of our gracious Queen, advauncinge another in hir place, alteration and subversion of this whole state and government, wherof thei were justly condemned *foro publico* by orderly and lawfull proceedinge accordinge to the lawe of this lande."

Mildmay mentioned also two recent Catholic tracts, William Allen's *Defence of English Catholics* and Robert Parson's *De persecutione Anglicana*. The former maintained the right of the Pope to depose princes, adducing the instance of King John as support. In reference to Parsons's work Mildmay exclaimed:

Will you heare further of another notable libell . . . wherin thei have sett forthe the greate and extreame persequutions used towardes the Catholickes, as thei call them, amplifying the same with a number of false and impudent lyes, as though we lived here in England under Nero, Domytian, Caligula, and such other tyrauntes, and not under a most gracious and mercyfull Queen; they forgettinge in the meane tyme that great favoure and clemency shewed to all Papistes, even to those that be most obstinate, and forgettinge also the cruell persequutions used in the dayes of Queen Marye by preistes against great number of good subjectes that with their bloud sealed the profession of their faith.

These lies were effectively taught the English Catholics at their two seminaries, "the one at Rome, the sinke of all evill and the nest of all treasons," as Petrarch had called it, the other "begonne by the Cardinall of Lorayne, a deadly enemye to religion and this realme," now moved from Douai to Reims. What a contrast between the diligence of the Catholics and the negligence of true Englishmen "to sett up and cherishe schooles for the suppressinge of Popery and the mayntenaunce of the Ghospell which we professe and make so great a shewe to love"! It was a weakness that Mildmay even then was trying to remedy through his foundation of Emmanuel College.

If Parliament did not make preparations to withstand the Catholic menace, Englishmen could expect at the best the loss of their monastic lands—how shrewd of Mildmay to arouse the gentry's fear of confiscation!—and at the worst an invasion, "devastation of whole contryes [counties], sackinge, spoylinge and burninge of cytties and townes and villages, murderinge of all kinde of people withowt respect of persons, age, or sexe: and so the ruine, subversion, and conquest of this noble realme, the utter rootinge out of the whole nobilitie and people of this land, and the placing in of strangers."

This terrifying scene, more dreadful than the Norman conquest, was prelude to Mildmay's proposals. Chief among them was the enactment of "the strongest lawe we can make" to insure Elizabeth's safety from all malicious enemies. Mildmay used a favorite Tudor simile to point up her importance to the realm:

Like as in a naturall bodye the head is the principall member, by which the rest are directed, even so in a pollyticall bodye of a Commonwealthe, the prince is the head, chiefe director of all thinges done in the same: and like as for the preservation of the heade in a naturall bodye, all the members are readie to adventure any daunger to save that without which they cannot contynewe, even so al the subjectes of a realme ought bothe to be carefull and shunne noe hazarde to preserve the prince their heade without whom all they must needes perishe.

He suggested three specific ways of strengthening the Queen's surety: "straight lawes . . . against troublers of this state under pretence of titles either present or future" (that is, against Mary, Queen of Scots), excluding them from the succession if they engage in any conspiracy or plot; straight laws to prevent "these malycious raginge runnagates, these Jesuites and priestes" of Rome from troubling the peaceable kingdom; and finally, "straight lawes . . . against the usurped authorytie of Rome, that it never rise againe in England."

His conclusion was brief and pointed.

Seeinge the present state and condycion of this tyme is suche and so blessed as we all desire the contynuance therof; and seeing our daungers be so many, so mightie, and so malicious; and seeinge that which they seeke and looke after is no lesse then the overthrow of hir Majestie and this whole state: I leave it to your considerations to thinke uppon these matters as of thinges of the greatest weight that can be spoken of. And therewith to provide suche remydyes in tyme as may be hable to prevent and withstand so many and so present daungers.

With Mildmay's oration ended, Sir Christopher Hatton took the floor. His address ran even longer than Mildmay's; Fleetwood timed it at more than two hours, but praised its contents as being unlike anything ever before uttered in Parliament.[8] Fitzwilliam was evidently not so greatly impressed, for he refers merely to the "long course of

[8] Neale, *Parliaments, 1584–1601*, pp. 28, 31.

speache" and summarizes only one section, that in which Hatton gave a history of Anglo-Spanish relations and warned of Philip II's "dishonorable dealinge." No doubt the two Councillors' speeches were effective complements to each other.

Their spirits thrilled but their flesh weary with long sitting, the members of the House resolved that a committee should meet the same afternoon in the Exchequer Chamber to "consider of some poyntes and forme of lawe for the preservation of hir Majesties saiftie."[9]

Fitzwilliam does not name the committeemen or give their number. Apparently the group was large, although not a committee of the whole House.

Mildmay acted as their leader, opening proceedings by reminding them "what greate enemyes hir Majestie had that did envie this state." They were, as Fitzwilliam enumerated them, "(1) Pope, (2) Jesuites, (3) Papistes at home, (4) Rebells fledd, (5) Fugitives; all which did shoote at one marke, namely subversion of the present state of this governementt." Their aim was to displace Elizabeth and set up a Catholic sovereign.

The objective of the ensuing discussion in the House was to provide that invaders, rebels, and conspirators "might feele a penaltie, and that in the highest degree." Although Mildmay had spoken of conspirators and claimants to the throne impersonally, without mentioning Mary, several Members were quick to name her as the greatest source of danger, proposing her death as the best surety for Elizabeth's life. This the Queen, as she had shown in previous Parliaments, could not stomach. But an impersonal bill might still be drawn so as to include Mary, if she were a party to further plots. A subcommittee of five was named to draft the specific provisions.

The principal problem was that raised by the famous Bond of Association. This document, which had circulated throughout the realm during the autumn months and which had acquired thousands of signatures, bound signatories to withstand and pursue, even to the death, all persons who might conspire against the Queen or plot her deposition or murder. It further committed them never to accept as Eliza-

[9] Fitz. jour.

beth's successor anyone by whom, or for whom, any such plot might be contrived, or anyone inheriting title through such a claimant. Mary and her son, James, were thus to be barred from the throne in the event of another Catholic plot, even though they themselves were not parties to it.

Any bill for the Queen's safety had to take cognizance of the Bond, to give it some sort of legal status. This was done in the draft presented to the committee December 1. It provided for the summary trial of any claimant clearly involved in an unsuccessful rebellion, and for the exclusion from the throne of any claimant in whose behalf a rebellion might be raised, whether a party to it or not. The claimant's heirs were similarly disabled, but they could not automatically be pursued and killed—by, presumably, any member of the Association—as could the claimant and conspirators. Heirs might even, according to a proviso, be pardoned fully by action of the Queen.

At such leniency Members boggled. They wished any conspiring claimant to have a fair trial. Indeed, they inserted a clause guaranteeing the accused the right to defend himself. But they could not—to use the personal terms which the bill so scrupulously avoided—swallow the concessions regarding James VI. Many Members had bound themselves to pursue and kill him in the event of a conspiracy; how were they to reconcile their solemn oath with the provisions of the bill? Mildmay and his fellow Councillors could only resort to sophistry, stressing the intent of the Bond rather than its precise wording.

In the end the government's draft bill passed the committee, appearing on the floor of Commons for first reading on Monday afternoon, December 14. It was not long discussed. Indeed the House spent most of its time arguing over, and in the end rejecting, a bill for the better collection of tithes in corporate cities and towns. Apparently Members found the bill little to their liking but hesitated to oppose the government or question the work of the committee. After its second reading on March 15 it was sent to be engrossed.[10]

So matters stood on Friday the eighteenth, an Ember Day, just a week before Christmas. Then Hatton announced that he had a message from the Queen. She had "desired t'understande the penalties of the

[10] Crom. d., fol. 78$^r$.

byll which wee had in hande," and when he declared them to her she "did verye thankefullye accept the greate care we had of her preservacion, which he seyed that her Majestie seyed (but he myght not so seye) was more then her merites." Still, she wished some changes in the bill: she had heard of the "scruple conceaved in soome here" regarding the proviso that the Queen might restore to the succession innocent heirs of a conspiring claimant, which some thought contrary to their oath, and so wished "that the proviso myght be lefte out." Although one might think this deletion would strengthen the bill, the Queen's purpose was the reverse. She did not wish any of its penalties to apply to James unless he proved personally guilty; "the acte," she said, "sholde not extende to th'issue of th'offender excepte th'issue were also fownd fawltye."[11]

The message was "verye thankefullye accepted," according to Cromwell—the Commons were likely too happy at the sign that Elizabeth would accept action against Mary to stick at her saving of James—and the bill was referred back to committee for suitable alterations. Here trouble again struck. Objections that the bill was incompatible with the Bond continued to be heard, perhaps primarily from George Ireland, who had just been added to the committee and who was a staunch foe of the Scottish Queen and her offspring. Mildmay and Hatton did their best to set minds at rest, but without conspicuous success.

In the face of such determined opposition Elizabeth decided, typically, to play for time. The approach of Christmas made this course easy: the session might be adjourned over the holidays, until scruples died or new programs of action were formed. The idea of a recess may well have been advanced by Mildmay, who—with Hatton—could judge the temper of the House better than could any other. Thus Hatton announced on Saturday morning, December 19, that the session would be interrupted for the better ease and recreation of Members at the festive season. The grateful Knights and Burgesses directed Hatton to tender their thanks for the Queen's comfortable message.

At this point Elizabeth seized the opportunity to bind the Commons to her through one of her love tricks, and on Monday Hatton returned to the House with the Queen's gratitude for "the greate thankes we

---

[11] *Ibid.*, fol. 78ᵛ.

had sent her, which she woulde not consider to have deserved."[12] Another source says that she redoubled to them their thanks ten-thousand-thousand fold.[13] The romance between the sovereign and her faithful Commons may have cooled since 1576, but it was not dead.

After Hatton had spoken, a group of judges came down from the Lords to announce a recess until February 4. Cromwell comments merely that at this point "our Howse brak up," but Fitzwilliam hints at some dissatisfaction. "This was thought straunge," he wrote; "it had bene used heartofore that the too Howses by consentt for a weeke in Christmas or at Shrovtide have adjourned the Parliamentt," but "so longe a vacation as six weekes" had never been ordered "without the presence of the Prince's persone."[14] Had it not been for Elizabeth's politic romance, real opposition might have developed; as it was, the day ended with Hatton's leading the House in prayer for the long preservation of the Queen's prosperous government.

Several other significant bills launched in December also encountered stormy seas. The most important was the bill against Jesuits and seminary priests advocated in Mildmay's opening oration. Doubtless drafted by the Privy-Councillor Members, the measure was examined by the same grand committee which debated the bill for the Queen's safety. It provided that all Jesuits and others who had entered the Catholic priesthood since 1559 should quit the realm within forty days following the end of the session or be adjudged traitors. Those who harbored or aided such priests also would commit treason, as would English students in continental Catholic seminaries if they returned to England after a brief period of grace. The lesser penalty of praemunire—forfeiture of goods—was imposed on those who sent aid to priests or Catholic schools outside the realm.[15]

The bill passed its first and second readings uneventfully on December 12 and 15. Two days later, however, its third reading precipitated a tempest. William Parry, an unbalanced doctor of laws who had acted as an English spy on the continent and who was now probably a Catho-

---

[12] *Ibid.*, fol. 79ᵛ.
[13] Neale, *Parliaments, 1584–1601*, p. 42.
[14] Crom. d., fol. 80ʳ; Fitz. jour., fol. 26ʳ.
[15] On this bill see Neale, *Parliaments, 1584–1601*, pp. 37–41.

lic agent in England, attacked the bill as being "very perilouse" to all English subjects, since there was "nothinge therin but blood, nothing but confiscation of ower goodes, not to the Queene but to others, nothing but dispeyre and terror to us all." He thought that the bill would pass both Houses, but he intended to vote "no," and he hoped that the Queen would veto the act. He would not disclose his reasons to the House—a curious course, if he hoped to carry any other Members with him—but reserved them to show the Queen.

This speech, Cromwell tells us, was "greatly mislyked," and there was debate about committing Parry to prison. Several examples were adduced to prove that the House had authority to imprison its Members: it had sent John Story to custody under Edward VI, Sir Thomas Copley under Mary, and Arthur Hall and Peter Wentworth ("a good member of the House") during Elizabeth's reign. After much discourse Parry was committed to the serjeant-at-arms, then recalled and interrogated. When he refused to alter his opinion or disclose his reasons he was left in the custody of the serjeant.[16]

The Queen and Council retained a misplaced trust in Parry. He was allowed access to Elizabeth and—as Hatton told the Commons December 18—"declared his reasons to the satisfaction of her Highnesse wherfore he refused to give his consent to the byll and why he refused to declare his reason in the House." The Queen "commended and alowed verye well of th'order of our proceedinge ageynst him" but hoped that "yf he submytted himselfe humblye to the House and acknowledged his offence" the Commons would pardon him. Parry was again summoned; after confessing that his words were "rashe, undiscreete, and unconsiderate," he was discharged.[17]

Despite Parry's outburst the bill had passed the Lower House. It was received by the Lords on the nineteenth but was not read in the Upper House until after the recess.

A bill "for the better and more reverent observing of the Sabbath Day" ran a similar course. Although the subject was dear to Puritan hearts, the bill was apparently not theirs; rather it was a milder measure conceived by some bishops and Privy Councillors, whose consciences

---

[16] Crom. d., fols. 78ᵛ, 79ʳ.
[17] *Ibid.*, fol. 79ʳ.

had been pricked when, a year before, eight persons were killed by the collapse of scaffolding at the Paris Garden during a Sunday bearbaiting. Probably introduced by Mildmay, the measure was read as the first bill of the session. After second reading it was committed to a group of thirty-three Members, among them some staunch Puritans, presided over by Mildmay. There was much talk but no action, so that the meeting dragged on until night and, as Fleetwood tells us, "Mr. Chancellor was weary."[18] Poor Mildmay!

By December 3 the committee had produced a new bill, apparently a stronger one which gave the Puritans greater comfort. It ran through three readings in as many days and was sent up to the Lords, who first committed it to Whitgift and Burghley, then passed it "with certain amendments." Probably they wished to tone it down again, so as not to ruin its chances of royal approbation. Back went the bill to the Commons, where new amendments were piled on the Lords' changes. Committees of the two Houses conferred, but without much success: the Lords (so reads their *Journal*) "thought it not to stand with the order of the House to pass the same bill again with the . . . new amendments," so they returned the bill to the Lower House untouched. In this procedural deadlock the Christmas recess overtook the measure.[19]

Another Puritan skirmish was more serious. On December 14 "diverse bylls of compleynte were exhibited to the House bye Sir Thomas Lucy and others conteyninge grief conceaved by the subjectes of the restreyninge of so many good preachers"—a blow at the disciplinary measures of Whitgift, who had become Archbishop of Canterbury in 1583—"of th'insufficiencye and wante of preachers, for their non-residence, and requyred that a petition myghte be made to the Queene for reformation." Next the impetuous Dr. Peter Turner pressed for the adoption of his "bill and book"—the book a Genevan directory of worship to replace the Prayer Book and the bill an act to provide for its uniform use and for a Presbyterian system of ecclesiastical government. As Knollys and Hatton pointed out, such a drastic suggestion clearly ran counter to the Queen's charge at the beginning of the session; Turner's proposal came to naught, and the motion for a petition

[18] Lans. MS 41, fol. 45.
[19] Crom. d., fols. 76–78; *LJ*, II, 70–76.

to the Queen was also stayed, "in respect the Queene had promised to have a care therof."[20]

The matter was not, however, disposed of so easily. Two days later there were further motions and arguments, and Mildmay himself "spake exceeding well touching this business."[21] He proposed that a committee study the complaints and consult with the Lords regarding the possibility of joint action. It is amazing to see a Privy Councillor so flatly disregarding his sovereign's ban: a significant prediction of trouble to come.

On December 21 the delegations of the two Houses met, Mildmay acting as spokesman for the Commons. He reminded the Lords of the Queen's earlier promises of reform but said that nothing had been done; the petitions and complaints showed that the situation had, indeed, worsened. At length the Lords acknowledged the need for redress, finally deciding that the most politic course would be to approach the Queen through the Privy Councillors. News of this decision mollified the Commons for a time; they were assured that "at the next session we sholde have answer."[22]

Before the next session, during the Christmas recess, Mildmay and Burghley spent considerable time examining proposals for an ordered interregnum in case of the Queen's death or assassination. The ideas had originated with Thomas Digges, Member of Parliament for Southampton and a mathematician of some note. Digges was gravely concerned at the prospect of anarchy or of civil war; he suggested that all governmental officers should retain their powers following the death of the sovereign and that Parliament should immediately be assembled to judge the various claims to the throne and name the new monarch. Since Elizabeth steadfastly refused to designate her heir, it seemed the only reasonable solution to a serious problem.

Digges elaborated his notions in a long tract, somewhat ironically entitled *A Briefe Discourse*. Directed to the Queen herself, it aimed at "discoveringe a most assured meane for your Majestes saftie and to

---

[20] Crom. d., fol. 77ᵛ; Neale, *Parliaments, 1584–1601*, pp. 61–64.
[21] Fulk Ownslow, clerk of the House, quoted by Neale, in *ibid.*, p. 63.
[22] Crom. d., fol. 79ᵛ.

cut of[f] all searchinge for anie other heire or successor duringe your Majesties lyfe and yet fully to content all suche faythfull dutifull subjectes as desire the safetie of the realme joyned with the service of your royall person." Mildmay evidently studied the treatise closely, for a copy of it survives with his papers.[23] Also among his papers is a speech, obviously intended for delivery in the Commons, containing the essence of Digges's proposals and, to a considerable extent, his very words.[24] Had Digges, one wonders, persuaded Mildmay to introduce his measure into Parliament, and supplied him with an appropriate oration? Or had Mildmay, moved by the force of Digges's arguments, espoused the cause and written the speech himself? We shall never know. What we do know is that the words were never spoken: Elizabeth, less frightened than her subjects and less ready to tamper with the constitution or to give Parliament additional powers, refused her consent. The measure did not proceed, and the hopes of Digges, Mildmay, and Burghley were dashed.[25]

Parliament reconvened on Thursday, February 4, 1585. Members, perhaps feeling their way, made a slow beginning. The bill against Jesuits was read in the Lords on February 6 and committed to a group led by Burghley and Whitgift; in the Commons, routine matters occupied the first week. A bill to tighten up licensing requirements on books and printers—probably a government measure—was read "and very much misliked" on the tenth, and on the eleventh the House was busy examining one Kerle, who had obtained a subpoena and an attachment from the Star Chamber against a Member of the House. Kerle was held to have "committed two contempts," one for the subpoena and one for the attachment, both obtained against a Member during the session in violation of parliamentary privilege, and was ordered

[23] F(M)P 96. SP 12/176/32 is another copy of the discourse. Cf. Neale, *Parliaments, 1584–1601*, pp. 44–48. F(M)P 184, dated January 21, 1584 [1585], is a memorandum on the same subject.

[24] F(M)P 4, a beautifully written fair copy.

[25] Burghley had gone so far as to draft an addition to the bill for the Queen's safety, incorporating Digges's ideas (SP 12/176/22). Earlier stages of the draft addition are SP 12/176/29, 30, 31. On Burghley's role see Conyers Read, *Lord Burghley and Queen Elizabeth*, pp. 299–300.

into the custody of the serjeant-at-arms for six days, or longer should he fail to pay the Member's costs in the matter.[26]

After such minor skirmishing, great excitement: by Monday, February 15, Members must have known that Dr. Parry, so recently pardoned, had been apprehended for plotting the Queen's death. Edmund Neville, whom he had tried to lure into the conspiracy, had betrayed him to the authorities. The details remained obscure (as indeed they do to the modern historian), but the fright was no less for that.

Perhaps emboldened by anxiety, the Puritans opened Wednesday's business by presenting petitions from three parts of the realm listing ecclesiastical abuses and calling for reform. After considerable discussion Mildmay rose to remind Members of the conference with the Lords and to urge patience until the next day, when the Upper House would make answer. Thus frustrated, the reformers must have been uncooperative that afternoon when Mildmay presided over the committee considering the bill for the Queen's safety—its first session since Christmas. It yielded much talk but little action; the Oath of Association still seemed irreconcilable with the Queen's order sparing the issue of a conspiring claimant. At length the committeemen decided merely to apprise Elizabeth of the impasse and ask her advice.[27]

Next day, on the Thursday, the Commons awaited word from the Lords about religion. Instead of that, they heard that the Upper House was angry at their treatment of the bill against fraudulent conveyances. This government bill, providing remedy in the Star Chamber against those who sold land without disclosing hidden encumbrances upon it, had passed the Lords before Christmas. But at its second reading in Commons, on February 8, it was "longe debated and greatlye impugned," and the House on division refused, in an unusual move, even to send the measure to committee.[28] If the Commons would not deal favorably with their bill, the Lords would not act in the Commons' religious projects.

Mildmay now suggested that if the House still refused to commit the Lords' bill it might either pass it as it stood—unlikely thought!—or

[26] Crom. d., fols. 81, 82r.

[27] Fitz. jour., fols. 28–29. Cromwell "was sicke from the xjth of February untill the xxijth of the same," giving no account of occurrences in his absence.

[28] Crom. d., fol. 80v.

frame an entirely new measure. When nothing had been done by February 18, he recalled Members to the task; they agreed to turn away the wrath of the Upper House by a soft answer while at the same time writing a new bill. In the end—to finish the tale—they provided redress against fraudulent sales, but through the common-law courts rather than the court of Star Chamber. The new bill passed the Commons March 5 and was ultimately accepted by the Lords, albeit with a proviso that nothing in the act should be interpreted as impairing the authority of the Star Chamber. The Commons' fear of the prerogative courts is an interesting portent of the further troubles to come under the Stuarts.

Somewhat mollified, the Lords agreed to discuss religion with a deputation from the Lower House on February 22. Burghley, spokesman for the Lords, told them that certain Privy Councillors had mentioned the matter to the Queen, who said that "soome of th'actions requyred were alreadye considered of to be reformed; soome other her highnesse by her supreme auctorytye meante to reforme; and soome were not fit to be reformed, as requyringe none action and impugning the Booke of Common Prayer." If offenses occurred within a diocese, the bishop should be notified, and "only yf that wolde not serve" should further complaint be made.[29]

After Burghley, Whitgift spoke. He "made particular answer to every article," generally upholding the independence of the Church and denying Parliament's right to meddle in its affairs. His draught was but gall and wormwood to the reformers, and much was to be made of it in the Commons.

One wonders if the Members had anticipated the prelate's hauteur: they had, earlier in the same day, given first reading to an amazing bill "that every Archebishop and Bishop do in the Chauncery take an oth for his dewe obedience to the Queene and for equall and dewe administration of such thynges as do apperteyne to his office, [and] that no Bishoppe shall sweare any canonicall obedience to anye Archebishop."[30]

Little was done on the twenty-third; Members were no doubt busy conferring about appropriate action, and the committee which had met

[29] *Ibid.*, fol. 82ᵛ. Cromwell was a member of the Commons' committee.
[30] *Ibid.*, fol. 82ʳ.

with Whitgift was engaged in setting down an account of his answers. But on the twenty-fourth—Ash Wednesday—the House rang with oratory, and religious reform was, for the time, forgotten. Mildmay began with a carefully constructed speech for supply. His timing merits attention. Presumably he had originally planned, first, to obtain the bills for the Queen's safety and against the Jesuits, then to approach taxation. Now he must have concluded that he could wait no longer for passage of the other major bills, and he may have hoped that he could draw Members' attention from ecclesiastical wrangling to the principal work of the session.

"In the beginning of this session," Mildmay reminded the Commons, "I troubled yow withe the remembraunce of some such thinges as I thought woorthie of consideration in this assembly of Parliament, emongest which I noted unto yow how manye and how malicyous enemyes we have that doe envie this state and tyme." These Papistical foes aimed at the deposition of England's most gracious sovereign, the alteration of its true religion, and the subversion of the entire state. So far, it was true, God had disappointed them.

Yet as men that see a daungerous tempest coominge doe not leave all to hope, but laye to theire owne handes and industries how to avoyde it: so we, being threatned and seeing so darke a cloude of perill like to fall uppon us, ought not bee negligente, but with all the care and circumspection we can, provide aforehande suche thinges as shalbe hable to preventt or resist the same, that we be not to seeke when we shall have neede.

The crisis required, first, laws to protect the Queen and to punish her secret enemies—these were "put in suche forwardnes alreadie as there is no doubte of their good successe"—and, second, a military establishment adequate "to defende the realme, both by lande and by sea, . . . and to withstande anie attempt that may be made either abroade or at home."

The Queen and her advisors had already seen to the military preparations and had thus preserved the realm from many dangers, but not without great cost. Ireland alone, Mildmay reported, had consumed the entire subsidy granted in the previous session. Further, fortifications had been constructed at Berwick and at diverse port cities, and large stores of powder and munition had been laid by. These last were "more to be accompted of then monie itselfe, for suche thinges cannot at all tymes be gotten for monie." Finally, the Navy had been put "in better strength and better readiness then at any tyme before this: a matter of greate importance, for the Navie, beinge justlie termed the wall of Englande, is a thinge of all other principally to be cared for."

These expenses had proved so great that the Queen had been forced to spend "of hir owne revenue, for the defence of the realme, allmost as muche more as the ayde graunted by the last Parliament did amount unto; which I doe not speake unto yow by gesse or by conjecture, but by vewe of hir Majesties recordes that conteine hir receiptes and pay-mentes." The Queen had done this willingly, bestowing her treasure "upon the publique affaires of the realme and never a whitt uppon vaine expences for pleasure or delight, as other princes use." She had thus been able to avoid borrowing upon interest, a perilous canker able to eat up even the estates of princes.

Some men might think it strange—perhaps a sign of waste or extravagance—that the subsidy and two tenths and fifteenths so recently voted were exhausted. Mildmay, bidding for their support, explained that he would marvel at it himself "if two thinges did not move me, which I thinke will move yow also." One was the costliness of the wars and the continuing inflation of prices; the other, "the easines of the taxation," in which many rich men were very favorably assessed. The last subsidy, in fact, had yielded "farre lesse then that which went before," although costs had risen.

Money was therefore urgently required, and Mildmay was confident that the House, recognizing the need, would gladly vote it.

He summed up glowingly:

It behoveth us in time to consider both of hir Majesties greate charges alreadie bestowed and of those which of necessitie she must bee at for the saufegarde of hir realmes and subjectes: and theruppon to offer hir such an aide as maye be aunswerable to the greatnes of the charges incydent to matters of this weight and importaunce.

Wherin we shall shew ourselves deutifull to so gratious a Queen that governs us with justice and keeps us with peace; and carefull also of the preservation of hir Majestie and of this noble realme and of the maynteinance of Godes trewe religion now taught amongst us, which ought to be more deare to us then life, landes or goodes, or anie thinge that we have.[31]

Mildmay had done his work well, arousing sufficient fear and patriotic zeal to overcome the natural resistance to voting taxes. No sooner had he concluded than a committee composed of all Privy-Councillor Members of the House and one Knight from each shire was charged with bringing in a supply bill.[32] There was a minor crisis: an unidentified Burgess suggested that the House should not vote taxation until the Queen made an acceptable answer to the petition for ecclesiastical reform—redress of grievances before supply. This speech, another portent of seventeenth-century parliamentary maneuvering, made "a deepe impression into the myndes of the whole assemblie."[33] But in the end the tactic was, mercifully, abandoned. The committee reported on February 25, recommending as usual one subsidy and two tenths and fifteenths. The Attorney General then wrote out the bill. It passed the Commons, with no record of opposition at any stage, on March 12, and it was through the Lords within the week.[34]

Tracking the uneventful course of the subsidy bill has led us ahead of our story. We must now return to the Commons chamber on Ash Wednesday. Following Mildmay's speech Sir Christopher Hatton discoursed at length on Dr. Parry's intrigues. Parry had already been "disburgessed"—ejected from the House—and several Members had requested that, in view of his horrible crimes, horrible tortures be used at his execution. This desire Hatton had communicated to the Queen, who took their concern very thankfully but "wolde not agree to other dealinge with hym then th'ordinarye course of law." Sensible woman! To moderate the unpalatability of this cold news, Hatton did give Members a full account of Parry's conspiracies, hatched in Catholic nurseries at Paris, Venice, and Rome, and of his plan to murder the

---

[31] Copies of the speech are in the Fitz. jour., fols. 30–31; Sloane MS 326, fols. 83–87; and Harl. MS 6265, fols. 94–95. My text is derived from Fitzwilliam, with occasional readings from Sloane MS 326.

[32] Crom. d., fol. 83ʳ.

[33] Fitz. jour., fol. 31ᵛ.

[34] Crom. d., fols. 88–90; LJ, II, 98–101.

Queen either in her coach or her barge, when few were about her. Finally, as proof of Parry's guilt, he showed the Commons a letter written by Cardinal Como on January 30 setting out details of the enterprise.[35]

After two such speeches the day must have been far spent; the House adjourned. On the morrow there was further excitement. "This daye," Cromwell noted, "Mr. Chauncelor [of the Exchequer] opened to the Howse the contents of the Archbishoppes answers to our petitions, wherin the Howse were nothing satisfeyed and agreed that commyttees shulde be apoynted to set downe th'insufficiency of the same; of the which I was one," Mildmay being another.[36] February 26 seems to have been quiet enough; the committee met, and the bill for the swearing of archbishops and bishops passed its second reading. But on Saturday, the twenty-seventh, came another explosion. Outside the House, at court, the Queen met with Whitgift and some other bishops to receive the clerical subsidy. She seized the opportunity to compare the loyalty of the clergy to the disobedience of the Commons, who violated her command by meddling in religious matters far above their capacity. "And we understand they be countenanced by some of our Council," she added, evidently referring to Mildmay, "which we will redress or else uncouncil some of them."[37]

Indeed, at that very moment, Mildmay was preparing further irritation for the Queen, as he met with the committeemen drawing up the rebuttal to Whitgift. They rapidly produced an amazing document exalting Parliament's authority to determine ecclesiastical affairs by statute, disregarding Canon Law and, of course, the Queen's will. The committee seems to have been dominated by Puritans, angry at Whitgift and eager to achieve their ends through Parliament; and Mildmay seems to have gone along with them.

The Commons, who would greatly have relished the committee's manifesto, were never able to hear it. They did not meet on Monday, March 1, because the Speaker was sick—he had taken physic the day

---

[35] We have an unusually full account of the speech in Crom. d., fols. 83ᵛ–86ʳ; Cromwell, who reported Mildmay's address only briefly, was obviously fascinated by Parry's conniving.

[36] *Ibid.*, fol. 86ᵛ.

[37] Quoted in Neale, *Parliaments, 1584–1601*, p. 69, from SP 12/176/68.

before and dared not venture out. Puckering was forced from his bed, however, by the Queen's command: "some faulse brother amonge the reste," Fitzwilliam thought, had let news of the committee's work slip, and Elizabeth had decided to put an end to such foolishness. On Tuesday the Speaker explained to the House how he had been summoned to attend upon the Queen, who was "greatly agrieved that we still proceeded in such cawses as we understood her pleasure to be that we sholde not deale, namely our petitions, the bill for swearing of archbishoppes and bishoppes, and the bill concerning bishoppes visitations." She "liked not this publique usage" and reiterated that the appropriate channel was "admonityon to the bishoppes," then "compleynct to her Privy Counsell or herself."[38] Here Cromwell ends, but Fitzwilliam adds that Elizabeth greatly blamed the Privy Councillors in the House—again, Mildmay chiefly—for allowing proceedings to reach such a state.

Fitzwilliam also tells us that the House was amazed and deeply wounded at Elizabeth's chiding. Members thought that their liberties were touched, and—rather than send a delegation complaining to the Queen—they determined to assert their privileges by deliberately drawing another bill of religion.

The new measure, fortunately, did not appear on the floor for several weeks, and in the meantime there was opportunity to settle some major issues. A new bill for the Queen's safety was introduced by Hatton on March 3; as Cromwell noted, it provided

. . . that yf anye make anye invasion into this realme or stirr upp rebellion or sedition or anyything to the hurte of the Queene, that then xxiiij of the Counsell, callinge to them certeyne of the judges, maye heare and examine the cause; theruppon all such persons for whom such offence shalbe commytted and all other privies shall be disabled to have or pretend to have any title to the Crowne, and that theruppon yt shalbe lawfull to all persons to pursewe suche offendors, theyr aydors and confederers to the death; yf the Queene be sleyne they and theyr yssewes prevye to be lykewyse disabled.

The bill had not been greatly altered, for it still spared James VI unless he were privy to a plot. "The Othe of Association," the bill added,

---

[38] Crom. d., fol. 87r.

was "to be expounded accordinge to this lawe." It was a feeble solution, but perhaps the only available compromise. The bill received only minor amendments in committee and passed easily, clearing the Commons March 9 and the Lords four days later.[39]

The bill against Jesuits and seminary priests also went forward. Having been passed by the Commons before Christmas, it began its course through the Lords in February and was passed by the Upper House March 3 with amendments reducing the charge for aiding Catholic priests from treason to felony. Thomas Digges spoke against the bill in the Lower House—it was, he thought, too mild already—but the real difficulties turned out to be procedural rather than substantive, with Commons amending the Lords' amendments, committees conferring about amendments to amendments, and the Lords making a final addition. By March 19 the conglomerate had passed both Houses.[40]

A week earlier—March 12—the Commons had completed their work on the three principal measures of the session, the bills for the Queen's safety, for the subsidy, and for punishment of the Jesuits. Surely, with the Queen so eager to keep religion out of Parliament, a speedy end of the session might be expected.

So thinking, apparently, the Commons made haste to pass a number of ecclesiastical measures. There had been difficulties with the Lords over amendments to amendments in the bill for more reverent observing of the Sabbath, but they were finally cleared away and the measure passed on March 17. The previous day the Commons had passed a bill allowing marriages at all times of the year: a Puritan proposal, designed to abolish the Popish prohibition during Lent. They also concluded a bill providing that parsonages impropriate might be devoted to godly and charitable uses. But their chief interest was in the bill framed after Hatton's report of the Queen's anger, the bill intended to vindicate the liberties of the House. It provided for the punishment of any minister who accepted a benefice without being properly qualified under the terms of a statute passed in the thirteenth year of the Queen's reign. Behind this seemingly innocent façade were hidden trial

---

[39] *Ibid.*, fols. 87ᵛ–89ᵛ; *LJ*, II, 95–97.
[40] For some of the details see Neale, *Parliaments, 1584–1601*, pp. 53–54.

of the minister's sufficiency by twelve laymen, a horrifying invasion of the bishops' authority, and penalties including a fine of £ 20, imprisonment for a year, and disablement forever.

This provocative measure was brought in on March 18 and given first reading, with only one Member arguing that it could not be discussed because of the Queen's prohibition. At second reading it was committed to Knollys and others; it returned as a new bill which sailed through the House. Mildmay seems to have been active in the debate on the nineteenth and twenty-second, blaming the bishops rather than lay patrons for the defects of the ministry and answering such moderates as Francis Alford and James Dalton, who hesitated to eject several thousand ministers when a supply of more qualified replacements was not at hand. Better no ministers than those who disgrace their calling, Mildmay seems to have thought.[41] His total opposition to the Queen and Archbishop amazes us as much as it must have infuriated them.

Nor was this all. The Commons, in the face of a specific prohibition from Elizabeth, gave a second reading to their bill against excessive fees in ecclesiastical courts. They then brought out a measure designed to protect Puritan ministers who could assent to the doctrinal articles of faith, as prescribed in the act of 1571, but who would not subscribe to all thirty-nine, in spite of Whitgift's efforts.[42]

Small wonder that Elizabeth hastened to end their sitting. She was expected "to have come to the House" on Saturday, March 27, Cromwell wrote, but "cam not." At least no business was put in hand; the session ended after a prayer from the Speaker. Next came Passion Sunday, and then the prorogation on the twenty-ninth. Lord Chancellor Bromley spoke for the Queen, saying that "her Majestye mislyked greatly . . . that we had dealt in cawses of religion notwithstandinge her commandment given to the contrary." She disapproved also of the Commons' harsh treatment of the bill for fraudulent conveyances,

[41] *Ibid.,* pp. 78–81; Crom. d., fols. 91ᵛ–92ʳ.

[42] Mildmay may have been particularly interested in this bill, for his papers include several memoranda dealing with the deprivation and trial before the High Commission, in January, 1585, of Eusebius Pagett, the learned Puritan minister of Kilkhampton, Cornwall. Pagett did not use the Prayer Book because, he said, he did not have a copy; he refused to wear the surplice or use the sign of the cross in baptism. See F(M)P 55–57.

which had been carefully drawn by the Lords and the judges. She grate-
fully accepted the subsidy and the bills for her safety and against the
seminary priests, but she vetoed the bills for better keeping of the
Sabbath and for parsonages impropriate. She would doubtless have
rejected the other religious measures also, but fortunately they had not
passed the Lords and so were dead. Perhaps the Lower House had expected as much; it had, at least, done its part.[43]

Although the Commons had proved recalcitrant, the Queen did not
dissolve the Parliament, merely proroguing it to May 20. With so
many threats to the realm, it was necessary to have the Members on call
without the time-consuming formality of fresh elections. But in fact the
Parliament did not meet again. After a series of further prorogations
it was dissolved in September, 1586.[44]

Mildmay's role in the Parliament of 1584–1585 is new and intriguing. In earlier sessions we have seen him skilfully moderating between
the Queen and the Commons, between the Church and the Puritans.
Now he seems to have countenanced all the Puritan scheming and disobedience: indeed, to have led it. One can only wonder at his motives.
Did he feel the need of ecclesiastical reform so strongly that he could
not in conscience obey his sovereign? Or did he fear that he would forfeit his position of leadership if he swam against the Puritan stream?
Or, as is more likely, were both considerations—and others—subtly
blended? Since he did not commit his inmost thoughts to paper, we
shall never know.

We can be fairly certain, however, that his position at court suffered,
at least temporarily. Bromley had told the assembled houses that the
Queen would see to the punishment of "some particular persons" in
the Lower House who, "in a heady and violent course, forgetting the
bounds of modesty and good manners, most audaciously and arrogantly
did forerun their elders [the Lords and the Queen], to the derogation
of her Majesty's authority, to the contempt of the honorable assembly

---

[43] Crom. d., fols. 93ᵛ–94ʳ; Neale, *Parliaments, 1584–1601*, pp. 95–101. It
may be of interest to note that the Parliament considered, but did not pass, a
bill to adopt the Gregorian calendar, and that the Commons refused to continue "Cecil's fast" by keeping Wednesday as a fish day.
[44] *LJ*, II, 109.

of the Upper House, and to the breach of the orders of their own House."[45] Mildmay can hardly have escaped inclusion in the group.

He did not, of course, lose his offices, and, although he grew less active in the Privy Council as he aged, there are no dramatic signs of his altered status. But Thomas Fuller, setting down tradition some three-quarters of a century later, may well have understood the situation aright. Elizabeth had become convinced, he wrote, that Mildmay "was a better Patriot than Subject; and that he was over-popular in Parliaments. . . . His life . . . did set *sub nubecula,* under a cloud of the Royal displeasure."[46]

[45] Quoted in Neale, *Parliaments, 1584–1601,* p. 97.
[46] Thomas Fuller, *The History of the Worthies of England,* I, 356.

## 16. THE PRIVY COUNCIL AND THE
## DUTCH WAR, 1584–1585

APART FROM 1559, when the Elizabethan religious settlement was hammered out, 1585 was perhaps the most decisive year of the Queen's reign. In it Elizabeth and her Councillors committed the realm to intervention in the Netherlands, thus beginning the war with Spain which was to outlive the Queen.

The revolt of the Low Countries against Spanish rule had begun in 1568. Despite the antagonism between Elizabeth and Philip II, England originally held aloof, although English volunteers were in Flushing as early as 1572. Elizabeth did grant financial aid in 1578, but until 1585 she refused to take overt action, leaving the Dutch dependent on the strong leadership of William of Orange and the unhelpful alliance with the Duke of Anjou.

The situation was dramatically altered by the death of Anjou in June, 1584, and the assassination of William in July. Now there appeared to be no salvation for the Low Countries without aid from Elizabeth and, conversely, nothing standing between Philip and England but the Netherlands. The question of open English intervention was therefore the subject of several meetings of the Privy Council, the most important being held October 10, 1584, and March 8, 1585.

Mildmay's role in these discussions has been variously interpreted. John Clapham, a servingman to Burghley who set down his observations on Elizabeth's reign in 1603, wrote:

I have heard it reported that the Lord Burghley, then Treasurer of England, and Sir Walter Mildmay, men of great judgment and integrity, apprehending at that time some of the inconveniences that have since accompanied those wars, declared their opinions directly against [English intervention].

Howbeit, the Earl of Leicester, being in great favor with the Prince, and desirous for his own glory to have the government of those countries, urged the . . . considerations in behalf of the United Provinces so far as in the end he swayed the balance on the left side.[1]

William Camden's *Annales* similarly testify to a divergence of opinion but do not name the antagonists: "Some were of advice," he wrote, "that [the Dutch] should be received [into English protection], and ayde forthwith sent them; . . . other some advised, that they were to bee esteemed as rebels, and unworthy of succours."[2] One assumes that he viewed Leicester and Walsingham as the principal proponents of involvement, Burghley and Mildmay as the chief foes.

In direct contradiction is the statement of Sir Sidney Lee, writing Mildmay's life in the *Dictionary of National Biography*, that Mildmay "often urged the queen to intervene on behalf of the protestants in the Low Countries." Conyers Read also classed Mildmay and Hatton with Walsingham as partisans of Leicester, speaking only of "Burghley and the more conservative element in the Council" on the other side.[3]

The positions of Leicester and Walsingham are plain enough: they both argued for intervention. Their reasons, however, differed, Walsingham seeking to promote Protestantism and Leicester seeking to promote Leicester. Of the Earl's stand there is little direct evidence— he was, like most men of action, not given to writing memoranda —but contemporaries agreed that he was motivated mainly by "an itching desire of rule and glory."[4] Walsingham, too, failed to leave a formal statement of his views, perhaps because they were so well known as to render repetition ridiculous, but his correspondence amply reveals his feelings. He hoped, as he wrote the English ambassador in Paris, that Elizabeth and Henry III of France would jointly "enter into some course for the bridling of the King of Spain's greatness, which it doth so much import both her Majesty and him to agree presently

---

[1] John Clapham, *Elizabeth of England,* ed. Evelyn Plummer Read and Conyers Read, pp. 60–61.

[2] William Camden, *Annales: The True and Royall History of the famous Empresse Elizabeth,* Book III, pp. 98–99.

[3] Conyers Read, *Mr. Secretary Walsingham and the Policy of Queen Elizabeth,* III, 80–81.

[4] Camden, *Annales,* p. 109. Cf. the quotation from Clapham.

on as I do not see how they can any longer defer the same without manifest danger and peril to grow thereby, first to themselves and next to the whole state of Christendom."[5] Without intervention there was "no appearance, in any worldly possibility, but that, being left to themselves, [the Dutch] shall be forced, ere Christmas next, to become Spanish."[6]

The real problem, then, is twofold: what were the views of Mildmay and Burghley, and how much influence did they have in shaping the final course of action?

Fortunately we have positive evidence of their opinions, for both wrote memoranda of their speeches at the October 10 meeting. Burghley's comments probably opened the session; they consider the problem generally and present arguments on both sides. The chief point in favor of intervention was obviously fear of what Philip might do to England if he succeeded in subduing the Netherlands: his inextinguishable hatred of Elizabeth had been manifest in his support of rebellions in England and Ireland—Burghley mentioned specifically the Ridolfi conspiracy and the Northern Rebellion of 1569—and his means had recently been augmented by his accession to the Portuguese throne. Some color of legality, too, could be cast on intervention by ancient treaties with Burgundy, binding England to defend the Low Countries against Spain.

But Burghley saw more reasons for abstention. The Dutch lacked an able leader, and being "popular states" without a ruling dynasty they were particularly subject to mutiny and corruption. England, if she undertook to aid them, would be virtually alone, since the French were unlikely to join the enterprise. Indeed Burghley thought France favorable to Philip, the Emperor his sure ally, James VI willing to aid him. Many of the Dutch states themselves had returned to his allegiance. The cost of a war would have to be borne by England alone, since the Dutch were poor and had a bad record of defaulting on their obligations. Finally, a war would impair trade, reducing revenues at a time when money was most needed.

[5] Walsingham to Sir Edward Stafford, July 6, 1584, quoted in Read, *Walsingham,* p. 76.
[6] Walsingham to William Davison, July 12, 1584, quoted in *ibid.*

Having thus weighed the opposing considerations, Burghley proposed alternative policies. If the Queen and Council resolved to enter the fray, they should keep expenses to a minimum, demand binding promises and sureties from the Dutch leaders, guard England's "postern gate" by concluding a sure alliance with James VI, and explain the matter to Parliament so as to obtain the requisite grants of taxation. If, on the other hand, England remained aloof, security should be sought by strengthening the realm's defenses and by close surveillance of the "Popish faction." In either case Burghley trusted in divine support: "Si Deus nobiscum, quis contra nos?"[7]

The Lord Treasurer, then, hovered in judicious indecision. On balance he appears to have opposed the enterprise. Certainly he cited more arguments for abstention than for intervention, and his discussion of them seems to carry more conviction.[8]

Mildmay, too, presented a reasoned analysis of the considerations on both sides.[9] If Elizabeth failed to aid the Low Countries, he thought that Philip would shortly menace her directly:

The King of Spayne will overrunne all those Contres and so gett himselfe *merum imperium,* which will bringe the alteracion and overthrowe of religion, the breaches of their ancyent priviledges, the subjection of those Countreis to his will. And being thus settled there, then the malice that he beareth her Majestie will easelie move him to pike quarrells to her and this cuntrie, provoked thereunto by the neerenes of those Countries to this. . . . Of all which will followe a daungerous warre to the perill of her Majestie and her estate.

Philip had great wealth from the Indies, and after subduing the Netherlands he could command the considerable Dutch fleet. His naval

[7] A contemporary copy of Burghley's memorandum is in the BM (Cot. MS Caligula C. IX, fols. 64–66); it is summarized in HMC, *Cal. Salisbury MSS,* III, Nos. 108–110, and in *CSP, Dom., 1581–90,* p. 205.

[8] Professor Read seems to have shared Burghley's ambivalence. Considering this document, he wrote that Burghley had "concluded that Elizabeth should intervene" but, on the following page, that "if [the memorandum] leaned one way or the other, it leaned against intervention" (Conyers Read, *Lord Burghley and Queen Elizabeth,* pp. 307, 308).

[9] Cot. MS Caligula C. IX, fol. 66, summarized in *CSP, For., 1584–85,* pp. 96–97.

strength would then bring about, not only war, but "an interruption of the whole traffique of this realme by sea, to the intollerable losse of her Majesties revenues, and perillous for mutinies at home by the subjectes lacking trade and vent."

Mildmay also feared that if the Queen let this opportunity slip she would "never have the like occasion to stoppe the King of Spaynes malicious course against her: and much better for her to keepe him occupied abroade . . . then by passinge over this occasion to beare the warre at home."

There were, however, grave dangers inherent in intervention. Mildmay dreaded the consequences of breaking the ancient "league" with Spain, especially since Philip had given England no sufficient cause for war. It was "not just to ayde subjectes against their King, and therefore against honnour and conscience." War with Spain would bring "not onelie daunger, but also inestimable charges, . . . the burthen whereof her Majestie is not able to bear herselfe, and doubtefull howe her subjectes will like to contribute to the mayntenaunce of such an unnecessarye warre as the most of them will take yt." Philip's resources and staying power were greater than Elizabeth's, and she could count on little from the Dutch themselves, "the small certaintie of contribution by them beinge seene by experience howe slacklye they have delt with the Prince of Orange therein heretofore." There was also "small suertie to fynde in the Lowe Countries eyther a sufficient partie or stedfastnes in them, seinge they are in effect but a popular state without an head, the most part of the noblemen beinge severed from them." If Elizabeth entered the war and subsequently found its expense unbearable, the Dutch would be in greater jeopardy than if she abstained altogether.

Although such a balanced memorandum leaves Mildmay's position in some doubt, he seems, like Burghley, to have felt intervention the more perilous course. His last sentence suggests that he still hoped for a negotiated settlement: "It is like [the Dutch] maie make reasonable composition by such offers as the King [of Spain] hath or will make them both for their priviledges and religion; which yf they might obtayne then those countryes shoulde bee as before the revolt, and her Majestie have traffique and neighborhoode with them as before, and no more daunger thence then heretofore." In any case we cannot number

Mildmay among the strong advocates of intervention. His own staunch Protestantism and his kinship to Walsingham evidently did not determine his stand.

Some further information is given us by Camden. After summarizing the objections to intervention which we know to have been raised by Burghley and Mildmay, he commented: "Such as were of this opinion, as men degenerate, slothful, and addicted to the Spanish party, moved the men of warre to much indignation."[10] Leicester and Walsingham, perhaps because of their stronger convictions, carried the day. "In the end"—to quote Burghley's memorandum again—"it was concluded to advise her Majesty rather to seek the avoiding and diverting of the great perils than, in respect of any difficulties, to suffer the King of Spain to grow to the full height of his designs and conquests." This policy meant engaging Philip in the Low Countries rather than allowing him to overrun them and strike directly at England. The Council agreed to open the matter to Parliament, hoping for a grant of supply, and to send a "wise person" to discuss terms with the Dutch.[11]

As we have seen, Parliament met November 23. Surprisingly, however, intervention in the Netherlands was not discussed during the session. Perhaps Mildmay was loath to vex an already unruly House of Commons by introducing what he regarded as an unpopular subject. Perhaps, too, negotiations had not progressed far enough for Parliament to be informed of their aims.

Diplomatic discussions were, nevertheless, in progress. William Davison was dispatched to the Netherlands in November, and in January, 1585, Lord Derby was sent to Paris to help the resident ambassador, Sir Edward Stafford, sound out Henry III on the possibility of joint Anglo-French action. Affairs proceeded slowly, partly because the energies of Burghley and Mildmay were occupied in managing the Parliament, partly because Walsingham was taking physic and thus absent from court for some time. On March 3, however, Derby and Stafford reported that Henry positively refused to become involved,[12] and although Parliament still required attention the

10 Camden, *Annales*, pp. 99–100.
11 *CSP, For., 1584–85*, p. 97; Read, *Walsingham*, III, 82.
12 *CSP, For., 1584–85*, pp. 315–319.

Council could no longer defer the Dutch question. A consultation was held at Burghley's house near the Savoy March 8.

Eleven Privy Councillors, including Burghley and Mildmay, Walsingham and Leicester, were present. Unfortunately we do not have an account of the deliberations, but we do possess an oration that Mildmay prepared for the meeting.[13] It reveals that he had now come to oppose intervention unequivocally.

In his usual systematic fashion he noted four things "meete to be considered: first, whether the enterprise be just; next, for whom yt shalbe taken in hand; thirdly, against whome; and last, what is like to follow." His arguments, all directed against involvement, largely repeat his earlier objections. The enterprise was not just, he thought, because the Queen laid no claim to the Netherlands and had no grounds for meddling in their affairs. The Dutch, for whom the project would be essayed, were subjects in revolt against their King, "common people, . . . popular states without a head," unwilling to contribute to their own defense, "inconstant, ingratefull, and subject to mutynies and corrupcion." Philip, against whom England would be fighting, sought merely "to reduce his subjectes to their former obedience: a thing that any prince would do, and as her Majestie did upon like occasion, both in England and in Ireland, wherein she could not have indured that any forreyne prince should have medled." Intervention could only bring "a present warre with the King of Spayne, that will seeke to invade both England and Ireland," and charges "too greate for her Majestie to beare without support of the realme, whereunto yt is hard to thinke that the people wilbe willing to contribute."

What, Mildmay inquired, would become of the Low Countries if Elizabeth did deliver them from Philip? Since she did not intend to assume their rule, they would be left alone although not "able to maynteyne and continue their state in that good sort which her Majestie may leave them in," or else they would in the end revert to Philip. In either case it was difficult to see how anyone would benefit.

---

[13] Sloane MS 326, fols. 88–94; Harl. MS 6265, fols. 95–96. F(M)P 211 is a copy of the concluding portion of the speech with brief notes on its beginning taken "by report from [Mildmay's] owne mouth," probably by William Fitzwilliam. Professor Read seems to be in error in assigning this speech to Burghley and dating it March 18 (*Burghley,* pp. 311–312).

In conclusion Mildmay wrote:

It shalbe meete to consider whether yt were not better to advise her Majestie to forbeare the enterprize, accompanyed with so many difficultyes and dangers, and rather to proceed with effect in the treaty with the King and Realme of Scotland, for a certeyne and firme peace. . . . This done, and her Majestie putting her owne realmes in that ordre and strength which she may and is able to doe, there wilbe little cawse to dowbt any perill from the King of Spayne though he should possess all the Lowe Countreys in safety. . . . And finally, whether yt were not better for her Majestie to shunn this unnecessary warr, and to keep her treasure for her owne defense in tyme of need, then consuming yt this way, to lacke when she should have cause to use yt. Which together with the other necessary preparacion of all things here, whereof care is to be had, will deliver her from any perill that may come by any forreyne attempt or by sedition at home.

Burghley's sentiments may well have been similar. It is worthy of note that he and Mildmay—not Leicester and Walsingham—were responsible for the realm's financial stability. They doubtless realized England's inability to sustain a long, costly engagement.

After this meeting, the outcome of which we do not know, the center of interest shifts to the court. Camden tells us how "the Queen deliberateth with herselfe," and his account has the ring of accuracy. She perceived, he wrote, the cruelty of the Spanish to the Dutch and Spain's great hatred of England. She thought that "the Spaniards were verily perswaded that they could never reduce the Netherlands to order, if they first subdued not England." She trusted that her own mighty Navy, joined with the "men of valiant spirits" in the Netherlands, would easily achieve command of the seas. Finally,

. . . she resolved that she was bound in Christian charitie, to succour the afflicted Dutchmen, being professors of the same religion, and wisedome to provide for the conservation of a people, which God had committed unto her, by cutting through the ruinous complots of their enemies, not for any desire of glory, but for the necessitie of goodnesse. Whereupon shee openly tooke upon her the defence of the Netherlands.[14]

One imagines Walsingham's hand behind the pious phrases attributed to the Queen.

[14] Camden, *Annales*, pp. 101–102.

The war party thus triumphed. Elizabeth reached her decision in May. In June deputies from the Estates General arrived in London to negotiate a treaty. It was concluded August 12, when Elizabeth bound herself to provide four thousand infantrymen, four hundred cavalry, and seven hundred men for garrison duty, all to serve at her expense until the end of the war. The Dutch were to repay her following the cessation of hostilities, and she was to hold Flushing and two other towns as surety.[15] In October Elizabeth ordered the publication of a tract setting out the reasons for English intervention.[16] In December Leicester "passed with great pompe and state into the Netherlands."[17]

One more document belongs to the period of deliberation, although it cannot be dated precisely. It is a brief note containing Mildmay's advice to the Queen, apparently written after she had decided to intervene but before the signing of the agreement. Mildmay thought that Elizabeth, once entered into the war, should "houlde fast uppon too pointes: the one to bee constant in cause and not wavering, th'other to sett on it with a lustie force such as weare sufficientt to determine; the cause in shorte time." He well knew his mistress's inconstant nature, and he feared that it would produce a long, ineffectual war which would breed hope in the adversary and despair in the ally. Finance again was a major concern: "if hir Majestie shoulde make a lingering war of it, then woulde the charge bee greater then the realme coulde endure."[18]

Historians have generally assumed that English intervention in the Dutch revolt was desirable, even inevitable. Certainly one has difficulty imagining the closing decades of the sixteenth century without it. Yet our sources have shown how far intervention was from being the only possible course, or indeed a program generally supported by the Privy

---

[15] Cf. Read, *Walsingham*, III, 109–110.

[16] "A Declaration of the Cawses Mooving the Queene of England to give Aide to the Defence of the People afflicted and oppressed in the lowe Countries," in John Somers, *A Third Collection of Scarce and Valuable Tracts*, I, 91–111. Translations into Latin, French, Dutch, German, and Italian were issued at about the same time.

[17] Camden, *Annales*, p. 109.

[18] F(M)P 186.

Council. While it is fruitless to conjecture what might have happened had Elizabeth retired to a "fortress England," one may suggest that Mildmay's own program had at least as much merit as did the policy which was actually followed. By the end of the reign large quantities of money and manpower had been poured into the Dutch wars, but nothing positive had been accomplished.[19] The Spanish, true, had been kept occupied; nevertheless they found the energy to mount the Armada and to foment rebellion in Ireland. It is hard to avoid the conclusion that England could have done better, either by remaining at peace or by pursuing war more vigorously.[20]

[19] Sir John Neale ("Elizabeth and the Netherlands, 1586–7," *EHR*, XLV [1930], 373–396) attempts to exonerate the Queen from the charge of parsimony by examining the amounts actually spent in the war. He blames Leicester and the Dutch for its large cost and small success.

[20] During these months of deliberation Mildmay was also involved in a ridiculous but fascinating bit of religious foolery. Henry Caesar, the popishly affected Vicar of Lostwithiel and a believer in second sight, claimed "that Sir Walter Mildmay was desyrous to see Cardinall Poole after his death, and [when] one by conjuration cawsed the said Cardinall to appeare unto Sir Walter," Mildmay affirmed that he saw "a man much like the Cardinall." Although Caesar, when examined, regretted that he had ever mentioned Mildmay, he was tried, ordered to make a public retraction, and expelled from his benefice. Only under the Stuarts did he regain favor, ending his days as Dean of Ely. On the episode see SP 12/173/61; SP 12/176/46; Cot. MS Titus B. III, fols. 83–84; and A. L. Rowse, *Tudor Cornwall*, pp. 334–336.

## 17. BABINGTON, MARY, AND PARLIAMENT
### 1586–1587

WITH ANTHONY BABINGTON'S PLOT to assassinate Elizabeth and substitute Mary on the throne Mildmay was not directly concerned. That episode, with all its intriguing features—letters concealed in beer kegs, forged postscripts, spies and counterspies—was ably handled by Walsingham.[1] The aging Chancellor of the Exchequer could not, however, avoid being involved in its aftermath.

Babington himself was apprehended August 14, 1586, tried along with several confederates, and executed in September. Meanwhile the Council deliberated about Mary. She was in the custody of Sir Amias Paulet at Chartley, one of the Earl of Essex's houses near Stafford, but this was thought too far from London for Mary's interrogation and trial. When Elizabeth rejected the Councillors' recommendation that the Scottish Queen be lodged in the Tower there was a frantic search for other secure accommodation. Finally Fotheringhay, hard by Mildmay's Northamptonshire estate, was suggested. Late in August Mildmay was asked to consider ways of supplying it with wood, coal, and beer, and on September 3 he wrote Burghley from Apethorpe that he had consulted with the messenger sent by Paulet to view the castle.[2]

---

[1] For accounts of the conspiracy see Conyers Read, *Mr. Secretary Walsingham and the Policy of Queen Elizabeth*, III, 1–70; J. A. Froude, *History of England from the Fall of Wolsey to the Defeat of the Spanish Armada: The Reign of Elizabeth*, VI, 226–269. It is interesting to find Bernard Maud (or *Mawde*), who had aided in the conspiracy to blackmail Archbishop Sandys, acting now as a spy for Walsingham (see Read, *op. cit.*, p. 18; Samuel Hopkins, *The Puritans and Queen Elizabeth*, III, 79–80).

[2] *CSP, Scot.*, VIII, pp. 631–632; Harl. MS 6994, fol. 31.

Although the Queen thought it too distant, Fotheringhay was in all other respects satisfactory for Mary's confinement, and on the fifteenth Burghley wrote Paulet and Mildmay, "the one to carry her away, the other to provide for her bestowing."[3] Mildmay thus presumably helped arrange her transfer, which was completed on the twenty-fifth.

The act of 1585 provided for a conspiring claimant's trial by a commission of at least twenty-five, including all the Privy Councillors. Actually more than forty were summoned by the Council early in September. After a preliminary briefing in the Star Chamber on the twenty-seventh, they set out for Fotheringhay, arriving October 11. Since the castle was crowded with Paulet's soldiers and Mary's retainers, the commissioners had to find lodging in the village or at nearby country houses; Hatton, we know, stayed with Mildmay at Apethorpe.[4]

The commissioners brought with them a letter from Elizabeth urging Mary to confess her guilt and notifying her that the commissioners were to try her if she refused. Mildmay, perhaps because of his long acquaintance with Mary, was chosen to present the missive on the morning of the twelfth. There seems to have been some hope that she would open her heart to him in this private meeting, but she adopted the tone of injured innocence and admitted nothing. The next day she appeared before the commissioners—under protest, since she refused to acknowledge their jurisdiction. Although confronted with the confessions of Babington and of her secretaries Nau and Curle, she continued to protest her blamelessness. Little had been accomplished by the fifteenth, when a messenger arrived with word that Elizabeth had prorogued the trial to the Star Chamber so that she could better follow its progress.[5] There the commissioners reassembled on the

---

[3] Burghley to Hatton, quoted in Read, *Lord Burghley and Queen Elizabeth,* p. 349. Anthony Mildmay is listed in a memorandum of September 8 as one of the gentlemen of Northamptonshire to attend Mary during her journey (*CSP, Scot.,* VIII, p. 702).

[4] Eric St. John Brooks, *Sir Christopher Hatton,* pp. 306–307.

[5] M. M. C. Maxwell Scott, *The Tragedy of Fotheringhay,* pp. 23–82, based on the journal of Mary's physician Bourgoing; Add. MS 48,027, fols. 579 ff.

twenty-fifth and "gave their sentence against Mary, finding her not only accessory and privy to the conspiracy but also an imaginer and compasser of her Majesty's destruction."[6]

Although the commissioners' verdict was final, it remained for Elizabeth to authorize Mary's execution. Sensing her reluctance to take this irreversible step, Burghley and the Councillors decided that Parliament should be summoned, partly to put pressure on Elizabeth and partly to help justify her actions to the world. The Parliament of 1584 stood prorogued to November 14, but that was too late. In mid-September it was dissolved and fresh elections ordered; the new Parliament was to assemble one month later.[7]

Mildmay and Hatton, the Knights for Northamptonshire, remained the Privy Council's principal spokesmen in the Commons. The Council had urged electors to return members of the previous Parliament where possible, and a number of Mildmay's relatives and associates—Humphrey Mildmay, William Fitzwilliam, Walsingham, Beale, Peter Osborne, Thomas Randolph—took their accustomed places. For some reason Mildmay's older son, Anthony, was not named for Wiltshire as he had been two years earlier; his seat was taken by Mildmay's son-in-law William Brounker, a former Member for Westbury.[8]

Although summoned for October 15, the Parliament was prorogued because of delays in Mary's trial and did not finally assemble until the twenty-ninth. Elizabeth, unwilling to associate herself with proceedings against her cousin, did not attend the opening ceremonies, Burghley, Whitgift, and Derby deputizing for her.[9] Serjeant Puckering was

---

[6] Walsingham to Stafford, October 27, 1586, quoted in Read, *Walsingham*, III, 55.

[7] On the Parliament of 1586–1587 see Sir John Neale, *Elizabeth I and her Parliaments, 1584–1601*, pp. 103–191. This Parliament is unfortunately poorly documented; if either Cromwell or Fitzwilliam kept a diary it is not now known to exist, and there is no Commons journal. Part of a parliamentary roll at Hatfield has been printed by Neale: "Proceedings in Parliament Relative to the Sentence on Mary Queen of Scots," *EHR*, XXXV (1920), 103–113.

[8] *Return of Members of Parliament*, I, 417–421.

[9] *LJ*, II, 116.

again elected Speaker, and by November 3 Members were ready for their principal business.

That, as Lord Chancellor Bromley had said in his opening oration, was not the enactment of laws or the passage of fifteenths and subsidies. Parliament had been summoned because of "a rare and extraordinary cause," the monstrous conspiracy of Babington and his associates. "Although some of them had suffered according to their demerits," Bromley had continued, "one remained, that, by due course of law, had received her sentence, which was the chief cause of this assembly, and wherein her Majesty required their faithful advice."[10]

Hatton and Mildmay spoke to the same theme in the Commons. Rising first, Hatton systematically set out Mary's "horrible and wicked practices" since her return from France in 1559; he concluded that the realm could never be safe so long as she lived. "Ne pereat Israel, pereat Absalom."[11]

Mildmay's speech was another of his model orations, expounding three points: against whom the conspiracy was raised, by whom, and to what end.[12]

First, it was intended against our most gracious Quene Elizabeth, a Quene annoynted, the daughter of that most noble and famous King Henry the VIII[th], . . . a most Christian Princes, . . . a noble Quene, renowned through the world, and knowne to be religious, vertuous, faithfull, unspotted in word or deed, just in all her accions, mercifull, temperate, bountifull, beloved of her subjects, good to all, hurtfull to none.

Mildmay dilated upon the benefits of her peaceable rule:

What a singuler blessing of God peace is, and how happy a thing yt is to lyve in quietnes and to enjoy freely our lands, lyves, and libertyes, is so apparant as it need not to be amplifyed. And if any man could not conceave this so greate a blessing except he felt the lack of it, lett him cast his eyes over the seas into our neighbours countreys, and there behold the miseryes and calamityes which thos people are brought into, by civill warrs stirred up by those that seeke to bring the like trowbles here.

[10] *Ibid.,* p. 117.

[11] Quoted in Neale, *Parliaments, 1584–1601,* p. 107.

[12] Copies of the speech are Sloane MS 326, fols. 95–104; Tanner MS 78; EC Lib. MSS, COL. 9. 14.

Many malicious enemies and traitorous subjects were involved in Babington's conspiracy, "yett the principal conspirator, and the very roote from whom all th'other lewd weeds do spring, is that Lady whom we do commonly call the Quene of Scotts." She had been deposed from the Scottish throne "for horrible and odious crymes" nearly twenty years before. Although she had "byn ever sithence honorably enterteyned at the Queen's Majesty's charges with all curtesy and humanity," she had conspired against Elizabeth

. . . without intermission of her practices, the most notable whereof are the Rebellion in the North raised by the Earles of Northumberland and Westmerland, the next the marriage intended betweene her and the Duke of Norfolk, meant to have byn strengthened with an invasion by forreyne forces to the overthrow of our Quene and this state, and lastly this most cruell and heynous conspiracy to take away the life of our sovereigne Quene.

For this final crime she had been tried by the Queen's commissioners, making no reply "except her single negation without any other ground" to the evidence against her or the confessions of Babington, Ballard, Nau, and Curle. It appeared that "neyther the feare of God, neyther respect to honor, neyther naturall affinity, nor infinite benefitts receyved, could stay her from continuall and malicious practices."

"Th'end whereunto theis practices tended," Mildmay continued, "is evident enough: to advaunce this Scotish Lady to the present possession of this Crowne, and thereby to overthrowe the Church of God, not only here but in all countreys where the Gospell is professed; and so to restore Popery and to bring us againe under the bondage of the Pope." Of his plotting "there is none ende, but as the waves of the sea, without stay, doe one rise and overtake another: so the Pope and his lewde ministers be never at rest, but as fast as one enterprice faileth they take another in hand, without lett of tyme, hoping at the last to prevaile."

Mildmay's description of this international conspiracy recalls the somber picture he had painted in 1584. Papal forces, he said, meant to

. . . bring upon all the good subjects of this land fyre and sword, effusion of bloud, burning, sacking, and spoyling of cittyes and townes, wasting and depopulating of whole provinces and countreys, with all other insolencies and crueltyes that necessarily follow eyther civill or forreyne warrs; and finally to make a plaine conquest of this noble realme, thereby to turne out all the subjects from their lands and goods, and to distribute the same to strangers, and so to establish here a perpetuall tiranny never to be re-formed.

Finally, calling for action, he urged the appointment of committees to recommend guarantees "that we may be out of the like danger here-after, what person soever the same do concerne, and that without delay."

After further speeches along similar lines a joint committee of both Houses was named to draw up a petition asking the Queen to publish the commissioners' sentence against Mary and to put it into effect. The petition was adopted by the Lords and Commons November 9, and was presented to the Queen at Richmond three days later. Mildmay may have been instrumental in shaping it; he was no doubt present, with the other Privy Councillors, when Elizabeth received it. She still stuck at Mary's execution, and sent back the Parliamentarians with an order "to consult and devise according to their wisdomes to the utter-most of their understanding and skill, yf any other meanes could be provided for her Majesties safety and the preservation of the realm and common weale, which yf they coulde doe, she woulde most gladlye followe and better like of."[13]

No alternative, however, could satisfy Parliament. Mildmay, Hat-ton, and others supported the original petition—and Mary's death— before the Commons November 18, and on the twenty-first the whole House concurred. The next day the Lords agreed unanimously.

On Thursday, November 24, Elizabeth received her answer from a large delegation of peers and forty-two of the Lower House, includ-ing all Privy-Councillor Members. Lord Chancellor Bromley and Speaker Puckering expounded the "invincible reasons" which had con-vinced the Houses, again asking the Queen to accept the petition and turn its requests to deeds. But this Elizabeth could not bring herself to do; she would "take yet somme further deliberacion before she would make direct aunswere unto them."[14] The *Lords Journal* incor-

---

[13] Quoted in Neale, "Proceedings," *EHR,* XXXV, 109.
[14] *Ibid.,* p. 112.

porates the most famous sentence of her address: "If . . . I should say unto you, that I mean not to grant your petition, by my faith, I should say unto you more than perhaps I mean; and if I should say unto you, that I mean to grant your petition, I should then tell you more than is fit for you to know; and thus I must deliver you an answer answerless."[15]

Further parliamentary prodding could only increase the Queen's agony. She originally planned to prorogue the session to March 6, but in the end sent orders for its adjournment from December 2 to February 15. She also yielded to one request of the petition: the sentence against Mary was formally proclaimed throughout the realm.[16]

So far as surviving documents allow us to know, Mildmay was not directly involved in the next stages of the drama. Elizabeth, after much soul searching during the Christmas holidays, signed Mary's death warrant February 1, giving it to Secretary Davison. He told Burghley, then had the warrant sealed before the Queen could reconsider. On the authority of the Privy Council—given at a meeting which Mildmay apparently did not attend[17]—the warrant was carried by Robert Beale to Fotheringhay, where Mary was beheaded February 8.[18]

Elizabeth, as is well known, flew into a rage at the news of Mary's death: she had signed the warrant, she said, but had given no order for it to be executed. Her anger centered on Davison, who was sent to the Tower, and on Burghley, who continued to act in the government but who was out of favor for nearly six months. Walsingham, who suffered from an opportune illness in February and so was not implicated in the affair, wrote Stafford that Elizabeth was offended at the entire Council but blamed Burghley chiefly.[19]

Burghley's desperate state of mind is revealed in a series of appeals

---

[15] *LJ*, II, 123–125; cf. Neale, *Parliaments, 1584–1601*, pp. 126–129.

[16] Neale, "Proceedings," *EHR*, XXXV, 113.

[17] Mildmay was not among the ten Councillors who wrote the Earl of Shrewsbury on February 3 to credit and assist Beale. See Henry Ellis, *Original Letters Illustrative of English History*, second ser., III, 111–112.

[18] Among the numerous accounts of the execution may be mentioned Add. MS 48,027, fols. 646–650, 654–658; Maxwell Scott, *Fotheringhay*, pp. 200–224, 249–256.

[19] *CSP, For., 1586–88*, p. 242.

to the Queen and in a remarkable letter he wrote one of his closest friends, probably Mildmay, on February 25.[20] It is a difficult document, since the distraught Treasurer used ciphers, left blanks, and employed masculine pronouns when referring to the Queen. He began,

I doubt not but you understand [her Majesty's] great displeasure for the [doing] of [the] thinges justly donne and most profitable for [her] surety. . . . Poore Mr. [Davison] is as you know in the [Tower], whose conscience doth only comfort him. . . . I am forbidden, or not lycenced, to come to [court] to answere for myself, which I can defend both *in foro conscientii* [*sic*] and *in foro humano.*

The Queen, he continued, had been informed by Sir Edmund Anderson, the Chief Justice of Common Pleas, that her prerogative was absolute and that she might order Davison to be hanged. "We may all be so convicted," Burghley lamented; "I thynk it a hard tyme if men for doing well afore God and man shall be otherwise punished then law may warrant." The Queen's reputation, as well as the Councillors themselves, would suffer. Burghley asked Mildmay to admonish the other judges, lest they follow Anderson's lead; he concluded, "I will leave my motion to your owne discretion, without any mynd to press you further then yourself shall thynk good. And when you have considered of my lettre I pray you return it to me, either now or a day hence by sum trusty messenger." In the margin is scribbled, "My cheif sicknes is grounded uppon ingratitude, which is wurse then a contynuall fever." Mildmay probably made a special effort to consult with the Privy Council about Burghley and Davison; his first attendance at the Council table in over a year was on February 28.[21]

Although not in the end hanged, Davison was tried in the Star Chamber March 28 for misprision and contempt. In these proceedings Mildmay was cast in the role of prosecutor for the Queen. It must have

[20] Lans. MS 104, No. 54. Read agrees that the letter, which bears no address, was intended for Mildmay (*Burghley*, p. 373). On the letters to Elizabeth see *ibid.*, pp. 371–373.

[21] *APC, 1586–87*, p. 358. The only recorded business of the meeting, which Burghley, Leicester, and Hatton also attended, concerned rents due the dean and chapter of Gloucester and the scarcity of grain in London, but the registers note only letters sent, not matters discussed.

been exceedingly unpleasant for him to speak against his colleague on the Council, but he was no doubt given orders which he could not disobey. Elizabeth's reasons for choosing him are simple enough: he was a skilled orator, highly placed, and probably less implicated in the warrant episode than any other Councillor save Walsingham.

Mildmay's carefully constructed speech began with a long account of the proceedings against Mary.[22] He described the conspiracy, Mary's examination by the commissioners at Fotheringhay, their sentence against her, and the activities of Parliament.

All of this [he continued] could not move her Majesty so farr, but like a wise and temperate Princesse she tooke a further pawse to resolve, in cause of that ymportance, and therewith tarried to heare the messages of such ambassadours as she understoode were comyng from two Kinges her neighbours [James VI and Henry III] to deale with her in that matter. Thoes she receyved and hearde most honorably and patiently, to see if by reason or sufficient offers they could move her Majestie to stay from doing that which her whole realme did fynde so necessary.

But as yt appeared, neyther their reasons nor offers were sufficient to perswade her Majestie, and so they were dismissed without hope to stay the exeqution.

And thereupon her Majestie, to satisfy the law and to satisfy her good subjects, did by her proclamacion notify both the justice of the sentence given against that Lady, and how thereby she was become uncapable of anything within this realme [i.e., of succession to the throne].

And though this was one degree further towards th'end, yet her Majestie according to her milde and temperate disposition stayed there untill shee might better advise upon the full conclucion of that which the Scottish Quene had so justly deserved, and which the realme so much looked for.

Then certain new conspiracies were discovered, and Elizabeth "thought it convenient to put in readiness that which was requisite for the end of the whole accion." She therefore signed the warrant and gave it to Davison.

[22] Copies of the speech may be found in the BM: Sloane MS 326, fols. 122–130; Harl. MS 6265, fols. 101–103; Stowe MS 296, fols. 3–6; Add. MS 48,027, fols. 668–670. Add. MS 48,027, fols. 398–401, 671–690, gives various accounts of the trial, including Mildmay's comment that Davison had "done nothing by mallice but rather by ignorance," a mitigating consideration which he omitted in the formal oration.

But before his returne to her Majestie she sent an expresse messenger to him, to have stayed it from the seale untill he knew further of her Majesties pleasure. This message comyng too late, he attended upon her Majestie with declaracion what he had done, shewing to her the commission [for the execution] under the seale, to whom she said, "What needed that hast[e]," which might have served him for a sufficient caution to understand that her Majestie was not resolved when the matter should be finished. Notwithstanding Mr. Davison of his owne hedd, without the privity or consent of her Majestie and contrary to her commandment for secrecy, imparted the same to divers Lords and Councellors, shewing them also the commission. Whereupon they, not knowing any ympediment, wrote their lettres to commissioners to proceed, which letters Mr. Davison sent away the next day after, together with the commission for the exeqution of the Scottish Quene, which within four or five dayes after was performed accordingly, her Majestie being altogether unacquainted with the matter.

Mildmay commented at some length on Davison's actions, concluding that he had "greatly offended her Majestie in the abusing of the trust commytted unto him," by not observing strict secrecy in her service, "and in contempning her commandement" not to send the warrant without further order. He might say "that he tooke it to be lawfull for him to communicate that matter, and to shew the commission to the Lords and other of her Majesties Privie Councell, then present at court, being such persons as had the maunaging and directing of all her Majesties greatest affayres," but Councillors ought not to be "any further privie or acquaynted with her Majestes affayres of state then it pleaseth her to make them: and so in reason it must be, for otherwise for lack of secrecy in the handling of greate and weightie cawses, the same may receyve great prejudice." Davison had "none authority to send [the warrant] to be exequted without her Majestes expresse ordre and comandement." He was also at fault in concealing from the Queen the actions which he had taken: "nothing of weight may be withdrawne" from her, even on the authority of the Council.

After further discourse underlining the serious nature of the offense, Mildmay recommended as appropriate punishment a fine of ten thousand marks and imprisonment during the Queen's pleasure. The fine was "much more, I confesse, then he is any way able to satisfy, knowing his insufficiency that way as I doe, but therein he is to seeke grace at her Majestes hands, whom every man fyndeth gracious and merci-full." Perhaps Mildmay hoped that she would remit the entire sentence after making an example of the Secretary.

The proposed penalties were duly adopted, but Elizabeth cancelled Davison's fine and ordered his release from the Tower after eighteen months. He enjoyed the Secretary's salary until Walsingham's death in 1590, although he was not allowed to perform the duties of the office, and he received an annuity of £ 100 for the rest of his life.[23]

Mildmay's prosecution of Davison may seem to us, as it perhaps did to him, the most degrading episode in his long public career. While Davison's biographer exaggerates in terming the trial "injustice and tyranny" and Mildmay's speech "sycophantic flattery to the Queen,"[24] the proceedings remain a blot on the memory of Elizabeth and her Chancellor of the Exchequer. There are certain mitigating circum-stances—a trial in the Star Chamber, where the sovereign might legiti-mately influence the outcome, was no doubt preferable to such royal intervention in the common-law courts as Burghley had originally feared; the Queen was mentally disturbed and oppressed; her diplo-macy probably profited from the attempt to shift the blame. Mildmay, for his part, was performing a peculiarly painful service with his ac-customed loyalty. Still the sorry affair will not down. Ingratitude was indeed worse than continual fever.

Even as the trial proceeded Parliament was making further troubles for the Queen and her advisors. Its second session was to have begun February 15, 1587, but it was adjourned for a week because of the absence of some leading peers and gentlemen. On the twenty-second Hatton and Mildmay directed the attention of the Commons to the continuing threats to the realm. The effect of Mary's execution was to increase the external menace of the angered Catholics; Hatton reported a vast force of Spanish and Italian ships and men prepared for the invasion of England and Ireland. The Queen required her subjects' aid in strengthening the realm's defenses and in furthering the assist-

[23] Add. MS 48,027, fols. 680–688; R. B. Wernham, "The Disgrace of Wil-liam Davison," *EHR*, XLVI (1931), 632–636.
[24] Nicholas Harris Nicolas, *Life of William Davison*, p. 138.

ance to the Netherlands, so necessary for the safety of England and the maintenance of Protestantism.[25]

Mildmay followed.[26] "That which hath byn spoken," he began, "may sufficiently informe us both of the perills hanging over this realme by malice of enemyes, and what in duety and for necessity we ought to do."

He amplified. "Because, as you heare, greate things are threatned against her Majestie and state from Spayne, we ought in tyme in this Greate Councell of the Realme to provide a sufficient resistance against so mighty a storme that is commyng upon us, and is likely to fall upon England or Ireland or both." In patriotic periods he eulogized England, "our native countrey, one of the most renowned monarchies in the world, against which the Pope beareth a speciall eye of envy and malice: envy for the wealth and peace that we enjoy through the goodnes of Almighty God, powred upon our most noble Queen and her realmes; malice for the Religion of the Gospell which we professe, whereby the dignity of his Triple Crowne is almost shaken in peeces."

If the Pope's forces could, they would invade England and "destroy us all, as we should be no more a nation in the world." Mildmay thought, however, that they might hesitate, "knowing how well we love our Queen and our countrey, and what a hard reckoning they shall fynde here." He imagined—incorrectly, as the Armada was soon to prove—that the Pope would pass over England and attack Ireland instead.

For Ireland being a great kingdome and a principall flower of this Crowne, having so continued above four hundred yeres, we may not suffer any part thereof to be touched except we will bring our owne into perill, for as Ireland is a large and fertile soyle, so is it furnished by nature with many notable havens, such as no land in this part of the world hath the like, so as if a mighty enemy should settle himself there, it is easy to see how dangerous such a neighboure would prove to the whole state of this realme.

[25] Cf. Neale, *Parliaments, 1584–1601,* pp. 166–167.
[26] Sloane MS 326, fols. 105–111, and Harl. MS 6265, fols. 98–99. The speech is incorrectly dated February 24 in Sloane MS 326 (see Neale, *Parliaments, 1584–1601,* p. 168 n. 1).

The Dutch war next occupied Mildmay's attention. Although he had opposed its beginning, he now supported its vigorous prosecution:

And as we ought to be carefull for our owne countrey, so we may not forgett the countreys of Holland and Zeland and other Provinces United, tyed unto us both by ancient amity and by religion, which of all other is the strongest bonde that can be amongst people. Theis her Majestie hath taken into her proteccion upon greate and necessary cawses, as you have heard. If shee should be driven to abandon and leave them now, then we are to looke for present danger to follow, both to the Queen and all her domynions: for theis countreys being so nere as they be unto this, if the Spanyard possesse them agayne and command all at his will, then consider-ing the great number of shipping that he shalbe able to make there, he may with little difficulty invade us when he list, and cutt of[f] and ympeach the whole trade of our traffique, which is one of the greatest parts of our politie and commonwealth, and will touch all the people of this land from the highest to the lowest.

To avert all these dangers it was necessary for the Queen to "make a greater preparacion," both at sea and on land, "then at any tyme heretofore shee hath done." She was already "furnished with great and good shipping for the warr," and she could count on "nombers of good, valiaunt, and faithfull people able and willing to adventure their lyves for the service of so gracious a Quene and defence of their countrey, so many indeed as none other prince is able to bring of his owne subjects." But it required "a greate masse of treasure" to put these forces in order; the burden was far heavier than the Queen could bear alone. "And therefore yt behoveth us with franck and willing mynds to offer unto her Majestie such an aide as may sufficiently sup-port her forces against thoes greate preparacions, entended to ruyne her and us all."

Some might wonder why another subsidy was needed only two years after the previous grant. "In reason this might be thought somewhat to[o] soone after th'other," Mildmay admitted, "were yt not for two cawses." One was the favorable assessment of the subsidy, "whereby not the sixth part of that which is given by the statute doth come to her Majestes cofers"; the other, the abnormally heavy cost of defense, "which hath byn so much as, I dare assure you, all that was given the last Parliament doth not amount much above th'one halfe of the whole charges, the rest being supplyed out of her Majestes owne revennewes, a thing that princes heretofore never used to doe." If prompt provision is not made, he warned,

... the burden wilbe greater hereafter, for if the enemye should take hold of any part of England or Ireland, or if he should be wholly master of the Low Countreys, as he seeketh, then of necessity her Majestie shalbe forced to maynteyne greate and continuall armyes, both by sea and by land, for the saufegard of her estate and of us all; the charge whereof must needs be so greate as yt will prove in th'end untollerable, and yett necessarily to be borne except we should suffer them to overrunne us at their pleasure.

For peroration Mildmay added:

And therefore to conclude, seeing that we lyve under so gracious a Queen that hath don so many and so great things for us, and seing that the ymplacable malice is such as we are to looke for at their hands all the mischeif they can bring upon us: it behooveth us now presently to thinke upon theis matters as the weight and necessity of them deserve: and so to shew ourselfes ready and willing towards our gracious Quene, as she be not unfurnished of that which is needfull to answere so greate forces intended against her and us: that our enemyes fynding her Majestie in such a readines may either stay their malicious purposes, or if they do proceed, they may feele sufficient resistance, to their owne confusion and the safety of us all.

A grand committee was straightaway appointed to consider supply and the other matters opened by Mildmay and Hatton. Mildmay need not have feared trouble over the subsidy; it was willingly granted.[27] Attention then turned to the Netherlands, with Job Throckmorton, a hotheaded admirer of Essex, pleading that the Queen should accept the sovereignty of the Low Countries rather than satisfying herself with limited aid to the Provinces. For his speech, in which he cast aspersions on James VI and Henry III, he was sent to the Tower; others, however, took up his line.

Mildmay opposed English sovereignty. As he told the committee on the afternoon of February 27, "her Majesty did make it known to all

[27] The Commons' bill for a subsidy and two tenths and fifteenths was sent up to the Lords March 7 (*LJ*, II, 132).

princes what she ment in taking the Lo Countries, not to seeke to gett oughte to herselfe, but to assist and defend her distressed neighbours, as appeareth in the printed booke put in severall languages to be knowne abrod to all the world."[28] He did suggest, however, that if Members wished to encourage her interest in the Netherlands they might offer a voluntary benevolence, over and above the subsidy, specifically for the war.

The Queen shortly made it clear to her Councillors that Parliament should not meddle in the question of sovereignty. Convocation, however, proceeded to offer a benevolence, equal to half the clerical subsidy, for the Dutch war. Mildmay apparently thought that the Commons should do likewise, attaching no conditions to the gift. At a committee meeting March 6 he urged Members to "falle to good consultacion heare how more should be levied: first t'agree the contribucion, and after to rate it."[29] Although we do not know precisely what was offered, it was probably a benevolence amounting to half a subsidy from those assessed at ten pounds and more.[30] Elizabeth, however, rejected the grant; she was unwilling to accept Dutch rule and probably resented the attempt of Parliament to bully her into it.[31]

Displeasure at the activities of royal purveyors, whose work in gathering provisions for the court was often tinged with corruption and tyranny, provides an interesting sidelight to the financial discussions of the session and a foretaste of the problems to face the Stuarts. Mildmay thought that "exaction of the purveyans" should be "well punisshed wher caus proved," although it was true that some "com-

[28] Harl. MS 7188, fol. 92, an anonymous parliamentary diary. Some further notes relating to the committee meetings are in Harl. MS 6845, fols. 34–39.

[29] Harl. MS 7188, fol. 101.

[30] Cf. Neale, *Parliaments, 1584–1601*, p. 182. The Lords, after conference with the Commons, proceeded to offer their own contribution of two shillings in the pound (*LJ*, II, 137).

[31] An amusing tract, probably written at about this time to encourage English sovereignty over the Netherlands, is Harl. MS 6845, fols. 71–86: "Brittano Belgicus: Shewinge and proveinge the necessitie of consolidatinge the English with the United States of the Lowe Countries in a perpetuall bond of amitie, Beinge A Dyalogue Held in a Barbors Shopp Betweene An Englishman bredd at Doway, A Dutchman brought upp in London, The Barbor of Ratcliffe, and his Boy."

playn for private displeasure," without just cause. If subjects were "free from vexacion," they would pay subsidies more cheerfully.[32] Partly under his guidance, a bill providing penalties against dishonest purveyors and limiting their power to call subjects to account at Whitehall passed both Houses. But it touched the royal prerogative too nearly; it was vetoed.[33] In this, as in the religious discussions of the previous Parliament, it is fascinating to see the Privy Councillor disregarding the wishes of his mistress.

The closing weeks of the session brought the greatest struggle of the reign for ecclesiastical reform. Chafing under the failure of their "bill and book" in 1584, the Puritans had been laying plans for a concerted attack. They attempted to influence the elections in 1586, and during the Parliament itself they met at least once in national synod.[34] A new bill and book were prepared, and on February 27 Anthony Cope sought to introduce them into the Commons.[35]

They are remarkable documents. The book, as before, was a Genevan directory intended to replace the Book of Common Prayer, but the bill was vastly expanded in scope. Meaning to establish a Presbyterian form of ecclesiastical government, it declared "utterly void and of none effect" all existing statutes, canons, and other regulations touching the Church. Whether the Puritans really appreciated the magnitude of their proposed revolution may be doubted—Mildmay later commented that the devisers of the bill were "of small judgment, small experience"[36]—but their ardor was intense.

Although Cope, Edward Lewkenor, Job Throckmorton, and several other members spoke glowingly of the need for such reformation, and although the contents of the bill and book were discussed, the documents themselves were not read to the House. The Queen ordered them delivered to her, ostensibly for study, actually for oblivion. This action led Peter Wentworth, on Ash Wednesday, March 1, into a famous oration for freedom of speech in Parliament. For his efforts

---

[32] Harl. MS 7188, fol. 95ʳ.
[33] Cf. Neale, *Parliaments, 1584–1601,* pp. 187–189.
[34] *Ibid.,* pp. 147–148.
[35] Harl. MS 7188, fol. 92ʳ.
[36] *Ibid.,* fol. 98ʳ.

he was sent to the Tower, where Cope and his supporters shortly joined him.

By March 4 the Privy Councillors had massed their counterattack. Hatton fired the opening salvo, noting chiefly that the Puritans would utterly abolish the Prayer Book: its familiar, comforting cadences would give way to extempore prayers and long sermons.[37]

The next round was Mildmay's. He had prepared an admirable address, the last of his parliamentary orations for which we possess a complete text.[38] "Both the bill and the booke," he noted, "do tend to the present alteracion of this government and state of the Church established amongst us, and to the planting of another forme; whereupon doth follow a generall repeale of all lawes and statutes heretofore made or used for matters or cawses ecclesiasticall." Such a proposal, to cancel with one stroke so many laws, "even from the statute of Magna Carta," had never before been offered in the House. Nor was it convenient now; it would abrogate the Act of Supremacy itself, thus presumably restoring the power of the Pope.

Statutes are often, and so may be, repealed as occasion doth serve, but to make voyde so many lawes, old and newe, in one generall short lawe before every of them be considered is utterly unmeete. . . . It shall suffice that you be remembred of some late statute made in her Majesties tyme, as the statute made the first yere of her reign for recognition of her supreme authority over all persons and cawses ecclesiasticall within her realmes and domynions, . . . due unto her by the law of God and so acknowledged by all the states and people of the realme, and whereby also is banished the usurped authority of Rome; whereunto all the subjects are bounde by oath sett forth in that statute, specially all persons ecclesiasticall, all officers and ministers in any court or place of service, all graduates of the universityes and students of the law.

Cope's bill would also annul the penalties against Jesuits and other recusants and the statute—desired by the Puritans themselves—"for the ordering and admitting of sufficient and learned ministers." It would abolish "not only . . . the names, but also . . . the authorityes

[37] Cf. Neale, *Parliaments, 1584–1601*, pp. 159–161.

[38] Sloane MS 326, fols. 112–121, and Harl. MS 6265, fols. 100–101. A long précis by the anonymous diarist is Harl. MS 7188, fols. 98–99.

and functions of bishopps and all other ordinary ministers and officers now used in the Church." Without ecclesiastical courts there would be no recourse in "cawses matrimonyall, cawses testamentary, cawses of tythes, and other, for which neyther this bill nor this booke provideth any remedy." It can easily be seen "what mervelous confusion, disorder, and losse will and must fall upon the subjectes of the realme, of all which the devisors of this new plott (as it seemeth) had noe consideracion."

Mildmay added that "by their devise there will fall to the ground all cathedrall churches, together with the members and officers of the same, as deans and prebendaryes, places and rewards for learned men, a thing that could hardly be spared." He doubted that the Puritans intended such a revolution: was he dissembling, or had he forgotten their articles of 1581?[39]

In place of bishops, rectors, vicars, and curates, the book "established in every church, or congregation as it is there termed, a pastor, a doctor, elders and deacons: the pastor to preach and minister the sacraments, the doctor to teach, the elders to governe, and the deacons to gather and distribute almes. All theis are to be chosen by the assent of the whole congregation and to be disposed by them as cawse shalbe given." There was no provision for incumbents or for the legal claims of patrons.

Mildmay discussed the question of patronage, a frequent target of Puritan criticism, at some length.

There is no dowbt [he admitted] but many evill disposed patrons, eyther by corrupcion or affeccion, do present unworthy men to benefices, upon whom it is requisite some greate penaltie were layd; but it is not to be dowbted likewise, but that many, specially such as feare God and love the Gospell, do take greate and singuler care to bestowe their guifts upon thoes that are sufficient, both for sincerity in doctrine and uprightnes in conversation. And amongst othere there is no feare that colleages in universityes should err in such a matter, both for their ability to judge and for the choyce they have of such as be meete within their owne houses.

His hearers must have realized that Mildmay had founded Emmanuel, and endowed it with advowsons, for just such a purpose. If patrons

[39] See above, Chap. 11.

erred, he added, bishops had authority to reject their nominees; "whether that election which the booke appoynteth, being meere populer, will reforme this fault is greatly to be dowbted."

Mildmay next considered how the new ministers would be maintained. "In the booke there is utterly no provision certeyne for them, for of tythes there is nothing spoken, and if they shall live upon the devotion of the people, what a bare and uncerteyne releif will that be!" Tithes could legally be collected only by rectors and vicars. Mildmay concluded that "the devisors of this plott . . . lacked judgment to consider what in such a matter was convenient and necessary."

Somewhat also [he continued] is to be said of the elders. Theis the booke woulde have to be godly and wise men. How such meete and able persons wilbe found, specially in countrey townes and small villages, is to be thought on. But such indeed they had neede to be, for their authoritie is very greate, not only in eleccions but also in excommunycacions and censures of the church, which they only are to doe, with the assent of the whole congregation. And yet if the parties excommunicate doe disobey, there is noe order in the booke how to compell them, as now in our Church is used by a wrytt *de excommunicato capiendo.*

Mildmay next noted certain miscellaneous objections. If annates and clerical subsidies are abolished, the Queen will lose at least two thousand pounds a year; Parliament will have to vote correspondingly heavier taxation. If Englishmen are obviously disunited in religion, the Papists will slander the Church "and the recusants may say that we have done them wrong to force them to come to our Common Prayers, which our selves do mislike." If Parliament intends to pattern the English Church on "the best reformed churches, it may be demanded which reformed churches we shall followe." Churches in Germany, Switzerland, Denmark, France, and Scotland had all forsaken the Pope, "and every of them thinketh that their churches be well reformed."

Drawing to a conclusion, Mildmay conceded defects in the English Church. "In all ages there have growne faultes, and so will do to th'end, . . . so long as the [Church] is governed by men subject to affections and corrupcions." But Parliament is not able to determine on new schemes of ecclesiastical polity without careful preparation by learned divines. When the Prayer Book was first framed, "Bishopp Cranmer, Bishop Ridley, and other excellent clerkes . . . did assemble by the Kinges authority and spent long tyme in the same, and so brought their labours to the Parliament." Grindal, John Jewel, and James Pilkington—Mildmay did not mention Parker, who was presumably too conservative for the Puritan taste—likewise labored under Elizabeth "for restitucion of our Church overthrowne in Quene Maryes tyme, . . . and so was the same exhibited and authorized by Parliament." If the Puritans wanted reform, let learned men consider its shape and effect more closely.

In the meane tyme, thankes be to God, we lyve here under a Christian Princesse, in a Church that professeth the trew Religion of the Gospell, whereof we are assured by thoes things which are the trew notes of the Church of Christ, and thoes are not the externall showes of the Church which the Romaynes stand upon, as universality, antiquitie, and successions of bishopps, being grounds false and uncerteyne, and such as the learned men of our side have sufficiently refuted. But the notes and markes of the trew Church of Christ are the sincere preaching of the word of God and the right administration of the sacraments. Thoes we have as purely and cleirelie taught and used in our Church as may be founde in Christendome, which is a greate blessing of God powred upon this realme, for the which we ought to be thankefull, first to Him and then to her Majestie that hath and doth maynteyne the same amongst us.

The oration is Mildmay's clearest statement of his own religious position. He had supported reform, even in opposition to the Queen's orders, and he had founded Emmanuel College in his attempt to remedy defects in the ministry. But he could not countenance ecclesiastical revolution. His thoughtful speech must have made a great impact.

Sir Thomas Egerton, the Solicitor General, followed with an anticlimactic list of the alterations involved in the Presbyterian program.

The character of the radical Puritan platform having been exposed, the moderates took the floor. Sir John Higham proposed, on March 8, that Whitgift's disciplinary campaign against nonconformists be curbed and that further steps toward securing a learned ministry be taken. Perhaps following Mildmay's advice, the House named a committee of able Puritans and Anglicans to study the matter and draft a petition to the Queen. But nothing came of it. Whitgift seems to have cut off all religious discussion with a sharp message to the House: "Her Majesty is fully resolved . . . upon the truth of the reformation which we have already; . . . Her Majesty thinketh it very inconvenient and dangerous, whilst our enemies are labouring to overthrow the religion established, . . . that we by new disputations should seem ourselves to doubt thereof."[40]

The session was brought to an end on March 23. There are signs that Elizabeth was angry with her Councillors and Parliament men: she did not attend the closing ceremonies; she omitted Burghley from the commission to deputize for her; she ordered the Parliament dissolved, even though—what with the continuing Catholic peril—it would have been convenient to keep it available by short prorogations. Sir Edmund Anderson, who, it will be remembered, had agreed that Elizabeth might hang Davison, substituted for the mortally ill Chancellor in declaring her assent or veto to bills. The Queen vetoed the bill regulating purveyance and two or three other minor measures. The really important projects which she opposed had been struck down earlier in their course.

The Puritans thus suffered another defeat. Parliament had helped press Mary's execution upon the Queen and, under Mildmay's guidance, had voted the usual subsidy. In its fascinating discussions of Dutch policy and religion it had been repulsed by royal proscription. The twin citadels of Anglicanism and prerogative survived unscathed.

Mildmay continued to tread the tortuous path between his own convictions and the Queen's commands.

[40] Quoted by Neale, *Parliaments, 1584–1601*, p. 163, from Lambeth MS 178, fol. 88.

## 18. THE LAST YEARS, 1587–1589

"GREATE THINGS are threatned against her Majestie and state from Spayne," Mildmay had told the House of Commons in 1587.[1] How great, he did not perhaps realize. It was evident when he spoke, in February, that Philip was gathering a fleet, either for the relief of Parma in the Netherlands or for an invasion of England and Ireland. Eager to singe the Spaniards' beard, Sir Francis Drake begged permission to lead the English Navy in "distressing their ships within their havens" and hampering Philip's operations in any possible way. It was granted in March; in April Drake's men destroyed thousands of tons of shipping in Cadiz harbor, and in May they burned vital barrel staves and hoops at Sagres.[2]

Philip's plans were delayed but not abandoned. By November Walsingham and Burghley knew of his intention to invade both England and the Low Countries; they took measures to strengthen the Navy, already in good form because of Hawkins's efficiency and Mildmay's support,[3] and to recruit an army. Philip proceeded with the irrational vigor of desperation. By April, Medina Sidonia had put together a force of some hundred and thirty ships in Lisbon harbor. The Invincible Armada set sail in May. By the end of August it had been vanquished.

We know little about Mildmay's role in the English preparations. He was probably involved in raising funds—£ 75,000 was borrowed from the wealthier subjects in January, 1588, £ 30,000 from the City of London in March, and nearly £ 30,000 more from the London

---

[1] Sloane MS 326, fol. 105ʳ; see Chap. 17.
[2] Cf. Garrett Mattingly, *The Defeat of the Spanish Armada*, pp. 95–122.
[3] See Chap. 12.

livery companies in August—although Burghley seems to have handled the negotiations.[4] Mildmay must also have borne the harassment of stretching totally inadequate resources to cover the most urgent needs of the admiralty and ordnance.

Added to these national problems were more personal worries. Mildmay, now about sixty-eight, was in failing health. Despite the emergency he had retired to Apethorpe in August; on the thirtieth he wrote Burghley,

. . . beseching your L. to beare with myn absence. I have not been above twies owt of my hous sithence my commyng hither, and that not twoo myles from hence to take the ayre. Myn infirmity doth so grow uppon me as I am worse and worse. Travaile is so paynefull to me as I can goe nowheare. . . . I am entred into somme phisike, hoping to fynd ease as I am promised, and yet I dowbt of it.

He had even begun to meditate upon death.[5]

Mildmay, in his letter to Burghley, mused also on the news of irregularities in the Exchequer. Raven, a deputy to Robert Taillor, one of the four tellers in the Receipt, had absconded with funds, and Richard Stanley, another teller, owed the Queen a considerable debt.

I am most hartely sory that your good L. is so moche trowbled, and I [have] so greate cause allso to be grieved, by the false and lewde dealing of Raven, to the disappointing of her Majestes service in such a tyme as this; and I cannot but mervayle greatly how the same shold be, the cheestes being, as I tooke yt, so fast locked and the keys with me. But for myn opinion, I see no reason but Taillor, hir Majestes officer, must aunswere for his deputy; neither is it to be thowght but that he toke sufficient bondes and assurance for his dischardge. And considering the present occasion of service, it is reason that Tayllor doe trye his credyt and frendes, to borow so moche as may furnishe the hole want or the most parte therof. And it is like allso that Raven, to avoyde the punishment justely due to hym, will make provision for the rest that Taillor shall not supply.

Stanleys debt . . . I trust . . . will be aunswered veary shortely. This debt of his was owing by hym before your L. was L. Treasorer or I Under-treasorer, as himself hath confessed to me, and how often and how earnestely he hath bee[n] called uppon your L. doth remember.

[4] Conyers Read, *Lord Burghley and Queen Elizabeth*, pp. 424–425.
[5] Harl. MS 6994, fol. 146.

The other tellers, "Freke and Mr. Killegrewes deputy, may well be trusted," Mildmay added; "I never understood of any defect in them." He advised against informing the Queen of Raven's defalcation; it would only "breede offence with hir Majestie" at a trying time.[6] Perhaps the troubles were natural enough in a department supervised by such aging and overworked officers as Burghley and Mildmay. One of the Queen's great weaknesses was her failure to enlist efficient young administrators as her long-reliable servants aged.

The burden of routine work in the Council and at the Exchequer did not lessen. Indeed Mildmay attended meetings of the Privy Council more frequently in 1587 and 1588 than he had in 1586, although still not so often as Burghley, Walsingham, or Hatton.[7]

During these years much of the Council's correspondence with Mildmay concerned the estate of Sir Thomas Gresham. The financier had perhaps overindulged his philanthropic impulses in the foundation of Gresham College; he died in 1579 leaving substantial debts and a contentious widow. These problems were assigned to Mildmay and Sir Gilbert Gerard, Master of the Rolls, in 1586. After a number of discussions, especially of a legacy to the daughter of Sir Henry Neville and of a debt to the widow of Sir John Rivers, the Council in May, 1588, ordered "a fynall and speedye end of the said controversyes." When, a year later, Lady Gresham was still at odds with Lady Rivers, "the cawse was hard again before theyr Lordships" in the Star Chamber, and Lady Gresham was ordered to pay without further delay. Presumably she did so; the matter was finally dropped.[8]

Mildmay and Gerard also examined the case of Thomas Wriglesworth, who had brought suit at the Queen's Bench against Thomas Hore, a college servant of Oxford. They concluded that the matter "infringe[d] the auncyent priviledges graunted by her Majesties pro-

---

[6] *Ibid.*

[7] He attended twelve meetings between March 26, 1587, and December 31, 1588, in contrast to only one session between February 19, 1586, and March 22, 1587 (*APC, 1586–87, 1587–88, 1588, passim*). The registers covering the period between 1582 and 1586 are lost.

[8] *APC, 1586–87*, p. 164; *APC, 1587–88*, p. 378; *APC, 1588*, pp. 8–9; *APC, 1588–89*, pp. 149, 159, 172.

genytors to the Unyversity"; Wriglesworth was "not to be permytted
to proceed any further in his said suyte," and "for the further indemp-
nitie of the said Universytie men" the Council entered the order in its
register and sent the judges a copy.[9]

The scarcity and high price of foodstuffs was a recurring problem
for Elizabeth's financial officers. In February, 1587, the Council asked
Burghley, Mildmay, Hatton, and Croft to seek a remedy; the matter
was "very requisite to be redressed."[10] On March 20 they ordered grain
to be brought to London from the Home Counties and had sheriffs
certify what quantities their shires could provide.[11] The Exchequer
was concerned in December with the case of Henry Page, a London
merchant who had illegally exported corn; Page wrote Mildmay that
he had shipped the grain to Calais only after it failed to sell in Ipswich
because it was "not very sweet."[12] An abundant harvest had relieved
the shortage at home.[13]

A few months before his death Mildmay heard the complaints of
certain soldiers who had served in the Netherlands, finally ordering
Captain John Wootton to pay them £ 123 in withheld wages, and
considered employing Flemish specialists to drain additional fenlands
near the Wash.[14]

At the Exchequer, Mildmay did what he could to relieve the ill and
overworked Lord Treasurer. Two letters from Burghley will tell the
story. In 1585, concerning the case of the delinquent collector of Lichfield and Coventry, he wrote, "Forasmuch as bie reason of my indisposition I am not so well able to take paines in hearing of the same,
I have thought good to desire you, at your convenient leisure, to informe yourself of the cause and take what order you shall thinke good
to sett downe uppon the hearinge thereof. I shall willinglie conde-

---

[9] *APC, 1587–88*, pp. 271, 285–287.

[10] *APC, 1586–87*, p. 342.

[11] *Ibid.*, p. 392.

[12] SP 46/34/287.

[13] Cf. Read, *Burghley*, p. 382. As the inflation was little understood, speculators were frequently blamed for shortages and high prices. In 1589 Parliament
attempted to enact legislation against forestallers and regraters but was dissolved before the bill could pass the Lords (*LJ*, II, 167).

[14] *APC, 1588–89*, pp. 43, 112, 114.

scende thereunto."[15] Two years later he commented, of another routine matter, "If I had leisure I would surelie enter into the full consideracion of the case myself, the which bicause I cannot presentlye attend, and for that it seemeth to require verie speedie redresse, I am bold to praie you to take sum paines."[16] Fortunately Mildmay could decide most matters himself, or refer them to his trusty Remembrancer, Thomas Fanshaw; but some agreements, especially those involving debts to the Crown, required the Queen's assent. "You knowe howe slowly all such matters bee here done," Walsingham lamented about an affair of 1584, "and therfore I hartely pray you [be patient] untill I may have opportunitie to knowe hir Majestes pleasure."[17]

Most of the Exchequer memoranda of Mildmay's last years deal with ordinary matters: debts, customs, title to lands, standardization of weights,[18] even the export of Barbary goat skins.[19] Of greater interest are some letters of 1587 from Robert Legge, the Remembrancer in Ireland. Bragging of his efficiency, Legge wrote Mildmay: "I have brought many thinges to better order then they have bene, and called in more debts and accomptes then were used in tymes paste to be. All thinges lay asleepe till I came and none durst call upon them for feare of displeasure, but without feare I wente roundely to work." He received little aid from the Queen's Attorney, a simple fellow who "dothe nothinge at all," but acknowledged the assistance of Sir John Perrot, the Lord Deputy. Indeed Perrot's rule was thorough, but ill-advised; after a quarrel with the Archbishop of Dublin he returned to England, disgraced, in 1588. He was committed to the Tower, where he died after being found guilty of treason. Legge's letter to Mildmay contains a hint of the troubles to come: "By my earnest dealinge for

[15] SP 46/33/322.

[16] SP 46/34/155; a copy of the letter is in the BM, Add. MS 24,459, fol. 191. "I allow hereof if Sir Walter Mildmay shall so thinke meete" is another typical note (Burghley to Fanshaw, SP 46/33/313).

[17] SP 46/33/176, Walsingham to Mildmay concerning the debts of Thomas Hanford. Attempts were made in the Parliaments of 1586–1587 and 1589 to force Hanford to sell lands in order to pay his debts; see Sir John Neale, *Elizabeth I and her Parliaments, 1584–1601*, pp. 188–189, and *LJ*, II, *passim*.

[18] See Add. MS 24,459, fols. 193–198, and SP 46/35/57, 59; all probably from May, 1588.

[19] See SP 46/33/311.

the Quene I have purchased myselfe great displeasure, for I have tutched great men in suche cases as lay hidden longe." Still the revenue collections were in arrears, and officials were able to make private profits. "I woulde Sir Thomas Myldmaye ware vice-treasurer here; it is a gaynfull place," Legge added in a postscript.[20]

Mildmay's last memorandum is dated March 21, 1589, little more than two months before his death.[21]

Two treatises were given to Mildmay in 1587. The more interesting is a presentation copy of William Lambarde's *Archeion,* the famous discourse on the English courts of law, especially the Star Chamber.[22] In a dedicatory letter dated June 21, 1587, Lambarde acknowledged "the grete debt of thankes" that he owed Mildmay "not onely for a rare bennifitt longe since bestowed uppon me, nether diservinge nor desyringe it, but allso for your later favour." In partial recompense he offered Mildmay, "by the hand of this your sonne-in-lawe [probably Sir John Leveson of Halling, Kent], my deare frende and beste neighbour, . . . this discourse that I penned some yeares agoe and revised not long since." Mildmay's copy, which has previously escaped notice, is of considerable interest because of its early date; heretofore it has generally been thought that the first datable manuscript of the *Archeion* was that presented to Sir Robert Cecil in 1591, although earlier undated versions exist at the Folger Library and among the Tanner Manuscripts in the Bodleian.[23] The treatise was not printed until 1635. No doubt Mildmay found "an hower or twayne at some tyme this sommer" to read it, as Lambarde hoped he would; with his experience in the Exchequer and the Star Chamber he would have understood and appreciated Lambarde's antiquarian disquisitions.[24]

---

[20] SP 46/34/221, 223, 228.

[21] SP 46/35/216. The memorandum is a routine order to delay process against Anthony Painter, whose father had failed to render proper accounts to the Exchequer.

[22] F(M)P 109.

[23] See William Lambarde, *Archeion,* ed. Charles H. McIlwain and Paul L. Ward, pp. 145–176.

[24] It was perhaps to aid Lambarde in revising the *Archeion* that Mildmay set down, in 1588, certain observations on the nature of Star Chamber cases; see HMC, *Third Report,* Appendix, MSS of the Duke of Northumberland, p. 49.

The second is a treatise "against lycences to buy and sell wulls in Englande."[25] Written on behalf of the Merchants of the Staple, it attacks the policy, adopted by the Council in May, 1587, of allowing export of cloth by both English and foreign merchants.[26] By thus abrogating the monopoly of the Staplers and the Merchant Adventurers the Council hoped to encourage the cloth trade, which had badly decayed as a result of the Dutch wars. The treatise maintains, however, that this policy "is not for the Quenes Majestes proffit; that it is hurtefull to the clothemakers; the realme dishonored thereby; the Merchauntes of the Staple in daunger to be ruyned thereby, and the Commonweale damaged." It would be better, the anonymous writer concluded, "that th'old aunccient lawes be restored and none suffred to buy wulles in Englande but the Merchauntes of the Staple and the Clothiers." It is unlikely that Mildmay was influenced by the muddled reasoning of the treatise, but the experiment in free trade proved a failure and the monopoly was re-established within a year.[27]

Mildmay's last Parliament met early in 1589. It had originally been summoned for the previous November, but—as its principal business was to be the granting of taxation, and as collection of the subsidies voted in 1587 would not be completed before the end of the year—it was prorogued to February 4. Even though less than half of the Members were new to the House,[28] there were significant changes on the front bench. Hatton, who had shared the leadership of the Commons with Mildmay for so many years, now presided over the Upper House, for Elizabeth had made him Lord Chancellor on the death of Bromley in 1587. Mildmay himself was ill; with all his physical and mental stamina he attempted to manage the Commons but he could not fill the void. Nor was the House so well furnished with his followers as

[25] F(M)P 161.

[26] SP 12/201/19, notes of the Council meeting May 15. Cf. Read, *Mr. Secretary Walsingham and the Policy of Queen Elizabeth*, III, 259–260. Walsingham was among those licensed by the Queen to export cloths (*ibid.*, pp. 380–381), but the writer did not think that his license brought "ruyne or hurte . . . to the Staple."

[27] Read, *Burghley*, p. 381.

[28] Neale, *Parliaments, 1584–1601*, p. 194.

in the past: neither of his sons was a Member, although William Fitz-william sat for Lostwithiel—one wonders how he lost his usual seat for Peterborough—and the Brounkers again represented Wiltshire and Devizes. It was the first Parliament since 1562 in which not one of the burgesses from Northamptonshire was related to Mildmay. Walsing-ham was returned for Surrey, but he seems to have been too busy at court to take an active part in the session; he was never a great parliamentary orator or organizer. Mildmay gained more support from Peter Osborne of the Exchequer, Member for Westminster.[29]

The session began with magnificent oratory from Hatton: his only opening address as Chancellor. Detailing the conspiracies of "the Pope (that wolfish bloodsucker) and of the Spaniard (that insatiable tyrant)," he rejoiced in their failure to build "a bridge of wood . . . over our seas." He exhorted both Houses to provide for continued defense of their country, sovereign, laws, and liberties; and, in passing, he gave notice that Parliament was not to meddle in causes of religion, unless it be to bridle the dissenting Catholics and Puritans. The Queen was firmly convinced that the Church, as it was, was good.[30]

In the Commons Mildmay heralded the defeat of the Armada in a speech of February 11. It was to be his last parliamentary oration, but, without a full text, we cannot regard it as his finest. Perhaps he was too ill, or too busy, to do more than draw up the outline which survives.[31]

He began by describing the "Spanishe entreprise against England." That fire, kindled and craftily nourished by the Pope and his ministers, had broken forth into "a terrible and dangerous flame," a conflagration intended to destroy the religion, liberty, lands, and lives of good Englishmen. The conspirators worked secretly, through "Jesuytes, Seminaryes, fugetyves, home Papistes, [and] traitors," as well as by overt means: "rebellion in the North, rebellion in Ireland; invasion there; two bulls; the great King, as they call hym, of Spayne; his last greate navy sent hither this somer; feare from the Duke of Parma owt of

---

[29] *Return of Members of Parliament*, I, 422–426.

[30] Neale, *Parliaments, 1584–1601*, pp. 195–201, quoting Petyt MS 538/10, fol. 54, Inner Temple, London; *LJ*, II, 145.

[31] F(M) P 147, probably written out by William Fitzwilliam.

Flaunders; ayde from the Duke of Guise owt of Fraunce; hope of a partye here [by] publishing of a late bull against the Queen."

But England had met the threat. His patriotic pride rising in a powerful crescendo, Mildmay listed "the meanes we had against them":

> The mightie hand of God;
> The providence of the Queens Majestie;
> Hir invincible courage;
> The magnanimitie and constancy of the nobilitie;
> The fidelity and readynes of the people;
> The Queens forces by sea;
> The forces by land;
> The goodnes of the quarrell;
> The defence of the Gospell and the Realme;
> The prayers of good people;
> The honorable and good dealing of the King and Realme of
> Scotland, tyed unto us with the bond of religion.

With these forces the Queen was victorious, while the Spanish had lost thirty-two ships and ten thousand men. "The hole enterprise [was] disappointed, and that so soone as hir Majesty may say, as Caesar did, *veni, vidi, vici.*" She had gained honor and fame while losing "not one ship . . . and veary few men." The great storm was over; calm and success reigned.

The clouds, nevertheless, were still dark overhead; another tempest threatened. "Aftre a daungerous storme," Mildmay said, "wise myndes . . . provide to resist another that may follow, doubting the second may be worse than the former. So we, having overcome this first attempt of our enemyes, . . . are to think uppon a second," and therefore to make provision of ships, men, and munition.

The need for new taxation followed naturally: "to prepare and kepe thees forces is requisite a greate masse of treasure, to be borne by the realme for the defence of hir Majestes and them selfes." The subsidy voted in 1587 had not covered half the necessary expenses, and the Queen had as usual supplied the deficit from her own revenues.

If the speech came to a stirring end we are denied it; our notes fade out with Mildmay's statement that preparation, "nedefull heretofore," was "most nedefull nowe or never." The great cause touched the Queen, her realms of England and Ireland, her whole people.

Mildmay and the other Councillors had decided that unprecedented taxation—two subsidies, with four tenths and fifteenths—were required to meet the desperate need. Hoping to promote acquiescence in committee rather than opposition on the floor, they primed the Speaker, Thomas Snagge, to delegate the matter to a large group of nearly a hundred Members, including one Knight from every shire. Precisely what occurred in the committee's meetings we do not know; apparently there was no real opposition to the subsidies, but considerable fear that a precedent might be established. Finally a preamble to the bill was drafted, setting out the unusual nature of the grant.

Mildmay, who must have presided over the committee, presented its report on February 17. The bill passed the first reading without dissent but was slow to reach its later stages: Members no doubt realized that the Queen would end the session as soon as the subsidy was passed, and they had other matters they wished to discuss. The second reading did not come until February 27, or the third—and probably a unique speech against the second subsidy—until March 10.[32]

The Parliament also witnessed abortive attempts at reformation in the Church and in the Exchequer. With the continuing Puritan onslaught, which came to nothing because of the Queen's prohibition, Mildmay does not seem to have been concerned, although he may have sympathized with a bill limiting pluralism and nonresidence.[33] He was, however, involved in the movement to reform the Exchequer. This began on February 14, when Sir Edward Hoby brought in a bill to limit the use of the ancient writ *quo titulo ingressus est* under which Exchequer officials were wont to vex landowners by inquiring into their titles. Hoby seems to have been rebuked outside the House, probably by Burghley, for attacking the tyrannous actions of Exchequer officials, but Mildmay and Osborne welcomed the opportunity to modernize the procedure of the Exchequer Court and gave their blessing to a new bill which emerged from committee on February 24. On Mildmay's suggestion the measure was immediately passed through two readings, and after the third reading on the twenty-fifth it was sent up to the Lords.[34]

---

[32] Neale, *Parliaments, 1584–1601*, pp. 205–206.
[33] On the religious maneuvers of Parliament see *ibid.*, pp. 216–232.
[34] *Ibid.*, pp. 207–208.

The Upper House had already passed a bill "to save discontinuance of writs of error upon errors in the Court of the Exchequer" when it received the Commons' measure.[35] The Lords seem to have been favorably disposed to the bill and would probably have passed it, together with a Commons' bill against purveyors, had not the Queen intervened. She would not have her prerogative touched; as Burghley told a delegation from both Houses on February 27, she would make due reformation herself but would not have Parliament legislate about such matters. This promise should have satisfied the Commons, but it did not. After considerable talk the Members agreed to send a delegation to the Queen with reasons why the bills should go forward. Elizabeth was not convinced, but she did sanction the appointment of committees, including Members of Parliament as well as Privy Councillors and officials of the concerned departments, to confer about suitable regulations for purveyance and the Exchequer.[36] It was a pleasing gesture, but it accomplished nothing: a bill to reform Exchequer procedure was again proposed in 1601 and passed both Houses only to be vetoed. The problems of purveyance were settled only by the Civil War.

With these and similar matters the Parliament dragged on until the end of March. By the seventeenth the subsidy bill had passed both Houses,[37] and the Queen, eager to send Members home before they overreached themselves, announced that the session would be terminated by Easter. So it was, but barely: the closing ceremonies took place on Easter Even, March 29. Elizabeth, after chiding the zealots who came to counsel but who were ignorant of what counsel meant, accepted twenty-four bills, vetoed three, and dissolved the Parliament.[38] Mildmay had taken little part in the second half of the session: hence, perhaps, its leaderless wanderings. His illness must have been growing upon him. Future Parliaments were to miss his eloquent speeches, his wise guidance, and his sympathetic mediation between the Commons and the Crown.

[35] *LJ*, II, 148–153.

[36] Neale, *Parliaments, 1584–1601*, pp. 210–215. We do not know if the committee for the Exchequer ever met; the only reference to it is a cryptic entry in the rough notes of the Commons' clerk.

[37] *LJ*, II, 161.

[38] Neale, *Parliaments, 1584–1601*, pp. 238–239.

On April 2, the Wednesday in Easter week, Mildmay wrote his last will and testament.[39] It is of unusual interest because of its detailed bequests and because of its long religious preamble. Although such confessions of faith are common in wills of the period they do not follow a standard form; rather they are expressions, in Mildmay's case unusually revealing, of personal conviction.[40]

"*In Dei nomine Amen,*" Mildmay began:

For as muche as all men livinge are subjecte unto deathe and that the time of their departinge houre is most uncerteyne, therfore I, Syr Walter Mildmaye of Apethorpe in the Countie of Northampton, knighte, callinge to my remembraunce the uncerteyne state of mans life that passethe awaye as a shadowe and fadethe as the flower or grasse of the feilde, and thinkinge it my dutie . . . to prepare myselfe in a redines agaynst the time that it shall please the Lord my God to call mee to himselfe, doe . . . make this my last will and testament.

He first bequeathed and commended his soul to God,

. . . beinge most certeynly perswaded that my synnes whiche be grevious and heavie are forgiven and myne election sealed upp in the onlye bloode and merittes of my Lord and Saviour Jhesus Christe, by whom and by none other meanes my redemption is made suer and certeyne accordinge to the unspeakable love of God towardes mankynde in his eternall and unsearcheable counsell and purpose before the foundations of the worlde weare laide, and whiche he hathe revealed in the latter age of the worlde for the comforte of his electe by his most holye Scriptures, the onlye waye to knowe his good will and pleasure.

Secondlye this tabernacle of myne earthelye bodye whearin it hathe pleased the Almightie Lorde that I shoulde walke here uppon th'earthe, created for his honor and mysused by me to his greate dishonor, I doe committ to th'earthe from whence it came. And the same to be buried and laide upp in suche place as it shall seeme good to my executors, ther to remayne untill the daye of resurrection of all fleshe when my sowle and bodye shall be joyned togeather in everlastinge incorruptiblenes and meetinge my most

[39] Prerogative Court of Canterbury, 51 Leicester, Somerset House, London. A copy is included in the Westm. MSS, 1, IX, 1.

[40] Cf. the comments on Tudor wills in W. K. Jordan, *Philanthropy in England, 1480–1660,* pp. 16–17.

mercifull Saviour in the cloudes shall continue withe him in endles joye suche as no eye hathe seene, eare hathe heard, nor harte of man conceyved.

He wished his executors to "avoyde suche vaine funerall pompe as the worlde by custome in the time of darknes hathe longe used, a thinge most unfitt for us Christians that doe professe sincerely the Gospell of Jhesus Christe." All superfluous cost should be spared and the money rather be bestowed upon poor preachers, poor scholars, and other needy people.

"Suche worldly goodes as it hathe pleased the Almightie Lorde withe his most gratius and bountefull hand to bestowe uppon me, most unworthie synner to receyve them," Mildmay wished to distribute "now whiles it hathe pleased the Lorde to give me perfecte memorie rather then to truble myselfe withe them at my latter time when it shall be most meete for me to forgett the worlde and all thinges therin and thinke only uppon my salvation in the Lorde Jhesus and uppon that heavenly Jherusalem wheare I am sure to remayne in joye, worlde without ende."

Mildmay's specific bequests, other than his lands, houses, and their furnishings, total the very large sum of £ 7,532.[41] Of this amount £ 5,723, or more than two-thirds, was left to relatives: sons and daughters, grandchildren, sisters, nieces, and nephews.

Anthony Mildmay, Sir Walter's older son, naturally received the bulk of the estate. His father bequeathed him £ 200 in money, £ 400 in silver plate, £ 340 worth of cattle and horses, £ 300 with which to purchase additional cattle, the house at Apethorpe with all its furnishings, half the "howsehold stuffe and utensilles" at London, two-thirds of Sir Walter's armor and ammunition, a new tent or "hall," a standish or writing stand of silver, and two large armorial seals. Anthony was to enjoy the lands surrounding Apethorpe and at Great St. Bartholomew's and to have the manor of Queen Camel at Charlton Musgrove

---

[41] Included in this sum are two estimates: Mildmay left rent charges and annuities of £ 16 per annum which I have multiplied by twenty years to give a capital value of £ 320, and he directed his executors to pay all his servants a year's wages, which I have, somewhat arbitrarily, put at £ 200. Fifty-one servants are listed in a schedule attached to the will.

in Somerset, which Mildmay had purchased in 1574. Grace, Anthony's wife, was given £ 100 in plate as well as a coach and two horses, a wagon, and a litter; their daughter, Mary, received £ 667, a gold chain, and a diamond ring worth £ 30.

Humphrey, the second son, inherited his father's lands in Essex, half of the household furnishings in London, a third of Sir Walter's armor and ammunition, a tent, a standish, a ring of gold set with a fair turquoise, two silver seals, all of his father's apparel and books, £ 200 in money, and £ 300 in plate.[42] Humphrey's wife, Mary, and his son, Walter, each received £ 50 in plate.

Mildmay's three daughters, Martha Brounker, Winifred Fitzwilliam, and Christian Leveson, each received £ 200 in money, and their husbands each £ 20 in plate. Mildmay gave Martha and Winifred each £ 220 in plate and Christian, his youngest and perhaps favorite daughter, £ 300. Sir Walter was also generous to his grandchildren: Martha's five children received a total of £ 461; Winifred's two sons and a daughter, £ 660; and Christian's four children, £ 720. Mildmay seems to have been especially fond of Mary Brounker, whom he gave £ 100 and a small diamond ring, and of Anne Barrett, whom he gave £ 100.

Sir Walter left his nieces and nephews a total of £ 340, mostly in sums of £ 20 each. He also remembered his sisters, including Lady Walsingham, Lady Paget, and Lady Dodington, and his son-in-law's parents, Sir William and Lady Fitzwilliam. Finally, he ordered his executors to distribute £ 100 to the poorest of his kinsfolk.

Friends in the government also figure largely in the will. Sir Walter gave the Queen, "as a remembraunce of my dutie to her Highnes, a jewell to be bought by myne executors of the price of one hundrethe poundes, most humbly besechinge her Majestie to accept the same in good parte, whiche ought to have byne farr greater in respect of her favour and goodnes ever shewed unto me." Hatton and the Earl of Huntingdon were to receive jewels worth £ 30 each; Burghley, "twoe guilte pottes withe covers whiche the late Earle of Sussex gave me"; Knollys, Buckhurst and his wife, Thomas Randolph and his son, Henry

---

[42] In 1586 Mildmay had revoked a feoffment of uses of the Essex lands, mainly near Danbury (ERO MSS, D/D Pl 19).

Killigrew, and Peter Osborne, £ 10 in plate each. Other associates were given rings as a remembrance, "whearof tenne of fortie shillinges a peece to be distributed to the barons of the Court of the Eschequire, judges, and other my frendes and neighbors at London and Apethorpe, and twentie and one of thirtie shillinges a peece to be distributed to the auditors and other officers of the Exchequire and to other my neighbors and frendes."

Mildmay's servants received £ 485 and a full year's wages, which probably amounted to something like £ 200. As executors Mildmay named his kinsmen Francis Walsingham, Edward Cary, and William Dodington, and he gave them and their assistants £ 210 for their "paynes to be taken in th'execution of my will and as a remembrance of frendshipp betwene us."[43]

It is somewhat surprising that charitable gifts do not account for a larger proportion of Mildmay's wealth; they amount to only £ 490, or about 6.5 per cent of all his bequests. He had, of course, already contributed heavily to Emmanuel College, and he may have realized that his sons were less able than he and needed strong support. The range of his charities is, however, interesting. He left £ 200 in money and £ 30 in plate to Emmanuel, £ 40 to Christ's Hospital, and £ 20 to Christ's College, Cambridge. He was also concerned for the poor, bequeathing £ 40 for relief at Apethorpe, £ 20 for the parish of St. Bartholomew's in London, like amounts for Danbury and Chelmsford, and £ 40 for poor prisoners in London and its suburbs. A further £ 20 was to be divided among poor preachers in Northamptonshire. In addition the parish of Apethorpe was given £ 40 "towardes the dischardge of the fifteenes whearwithe the saide parishe shall be from time to time charged and burdened to the Queenes Majestie, her heiers and successors."

A tabular analysis of Mildmay's bequests reveals the proportions in which he wished his estate divided.

---

[43] Walsingham seems to have borne the chief responsibility; his brief "memorial for the execution of Sir W. Mildemays wyll" survives among the state papers (SP 12/224/108). Cary and Dodington were probably brothers-in-law of Walsingham; Mildmay refers to them loosely as brothers. Both held offices in the government.

| Bequests to | Amount |
|---|---|
| Relatives | £ 5,723 |
| Friends and governmental officials | 424 |
| Servants | 685 |
| Executors | 210 |
| Charities | 490 |
| Total | £ 7,532 |

He had evidently endeavored to keep substantial sums in ready money, at least during his last years; £ 4,282 of his bequests are in cash and £ 2,000 in plate. One hesitates to estimate the value of his houses and their furnishings, but some figures from the Westmorland Papers do suggest the value of his holdings in real estate.[44] In 1578 Mildmay's lands yielded an income of about £ 550 or had a capital worth, estimated on the basis of twenty years' purchase, of about £ 11,000. Since he made no significant purchases in the following years and probably did little to raise his tenants' rents, this figure may approximate the value of his estates at the time of his death. His net worth must have been at least £ 20,000. Of this amount, Anthony received slightly more than half and Humphrey rather less than a quarter.

Sir Walter Mildmay died in London May 31, 1589.[45] His health had evidently deteriorated rapidly following his appearances in Parliament in February; he was probably not strong enough to travel to the country seat which he loved so well but saw so little. He was buried in Great St. Bartholomew's, his London parish church. We do not know whether his executors followed his typically Puritan order to avoid "funerall pompe," but they did erect "a very fair tomb"[46] over Walter and Mary Mildmay. Set in one of the sturdy Norman arches of the

[44] See especially Westm. MSS, 5, II, 1; 5, II, 2; 5, II, 10.
[45] The date is given in the Chancery inquisition post mortem (C 142/223/61) and appears on his tomb.
[46] The phrase is that of John Stow, *Survey of London,* ed. John Strype, Book III, p. 237.

chancel, it consists of an altarlike sarcophagus surmounted by two stages of carved marble. In a central plaque, flanked by Corinthian columns and surrounded by roundels and strap-work ornament, is a simple inscription:

Hic jacet Gualterus Mildmay, Miles, & Maria Uxor ejus.

Ipse obiit ultimo die Maii, 1589. Ipsa 16 die Martii, 1576.

Reliquerunt duos filios & tres filias.

Fundavit Collegium Emmanuelis Cantabrigiae.

Moritur Cancellarius & Sub-thesaurarius Scaccarii,

& Regiae Majestati a Consiliis.

Little needs to be said in summarizing Mildmay's life and evaluating its significance. His conscientious attention to the minutiae of financial administration, his skill in parliamentary manipulation, his concern for pure religion and good learning—all have been made obvious by his own actions. Mildmay's Puritan leanings, too, are clear. But his Puritanism was of a special type. He refused to join Cartwright's hotheaded followers, who denounced the established Church without comprehending the difficulties under which it labored. Mildmay wished to improve the Church—he founded Emmanuel College as his share in its reformation—but within its traditional framework. In religion, as in all else, his policies were responsible and constructive.

Several contemporary judgments are of interest, although they tend toward sycophantic flattery. All agree on Mildmay's integrity. John Harington, Elizabeth's godson and the translator of Ariosto, commented: "That wise and honorable counseller Sir Walter Mildmay, as in all other things he shewd himselfe an uncorrupt man to his end, so his writings and sayings were ever spiced with this reverent feare of God: for *ex abundantia cordis os loquitur* [the mouth speaks from the fullness of the heart.]"[47]

[47] John Harington, *Orlando Furioso,* p. 175. Harington mentions "a little volume" by Mildmay "which [he] himselfe gave me . . . when I was a boy of Eaton colledge"; it included this Latin verse:

Vltio peccatum sequitur delinquere noli,
  Nam scelus admissum poena seuera premit.
Quod si forte Deus, patiendo differat viam,
  Sera licet veniat, certa venire solet.

Grace Mildmay, Anthony's wife, described her father-in-law as "a pleasantly conceited man at his owne table"; he "continually would give wyse and profitable speeches, but would never suffer any man to be evill spoken of; neither would he suffer any, of whatsoever calling he were, to talke at his table of high matters of state . . . unreverently or prophanely. . . . The worst man that ever repayred unto him," she added, "would speake well of him and confesse that they had cause to love him." Her only complaint was that Mildmay made niggardly provision for Anthony's household; their allowance "could not by any means suffice in any competency to our necessities."[48]

Two commemorative odes contain more formal praises. The earlier, *Fames Trumpet Sounding* by Henry Roberts, is long-winded doggerel, but two stanzas are bearable:[49]

> Mildmay, by name, was milde in all his deedes,
> Pure was his thoughts, like gold his vertues shine,
> His upright justice fewe or none exceedes.
> To poore nor rich he never would encline,
> But right with right, as Lawes did him assigne,
> To every man he justice did impart,
> As cause required, and equitie of hart.

> For Princes cause, as his allegeance bound
> And duetie of that honorable place,
> He carefull was, his actions also sounde.
> With conscience pure he wayed every case,
> As well for Commons, as profit to her Grace.
> That Prince nor Subjects had just cause to say,
> Mildmay hath wrongd us any kind of way.

More sincere, as well as better verse, is the eulogy by Thomas Churchyard.[50]

[48] MS diary of Grace Mildmay in the Northampton Public Library, quoted in Rachel Weigall, "An Elizabethan Gentlewoman," *Quarterly Review,* CCXV (1911), 124.

[49] Henry Roberts, *Fames Trumpet Sounding,* fol. A iii^v. Another poem in the same volume eulogizes Sir Martin Calthrop, Lord Mayor of London, who also died in 1589.

[50] EC Lib. MSS, COL. 9. 14 (b), "The Epitaph of the right honorable Coun-

. . . few in Court gained more good will the wise grave Mildmay did:
In whose mild show and worthy skill were heapes of vertues hid.
In Court not only lov'd alone, but Country yeelds him fame:
And boasts, that there his bounty shone, & burnd with quenchles flame.
Like blazing torche on mountaine top, that could all blasts abide,
Yet seem'd but little twinckling Star, which is farre off espyed.
But every worde and sentence sweet he did in world let fall
Exprest an hye and noble spirit, and knowledge great withal.
His silence spake by stayed lookes, but when he moov'd his tongue,
Like tinkling bell of silver found, the Counsell chamber ronge.

. . . . . . . . . . . . . . . . . . . . . .

When pangues of death approch't apace, & would have clos'd his eyne,
He spake with milde and cheerfull face glad words that were devine,
Of eche degree as though some Saint were sent from God above
To showe how he should served be, in faith, in feare and love.
Wherat the hearers all gan weep, that then their Jewell lost:
Whiles Mildmay mildly fell asleep, and so gave up the ghost.
Not dead, death hath but broke the stamp; in Cambridg lives this knight,
Where he set up so faire a lamp, that gives all England light.

One returns with relief to the modest epitaph which Mildmay himself probably wrote for his tomb. "He left two sons and three daughters. He founded Emmanuel College, Cambridge. He died Chancellor and Under-Treasurer of the Exchequer, and a Councillor to her Royal Majesty."

He had devoted his life to serving the sovereign and his countrymen.

---

seller, Sir Walter Mildmay Knight," privately reprinted in 1913 from Thomas Churchyard, *A revyving of the deade.*

GENEALOGICAL TABLE

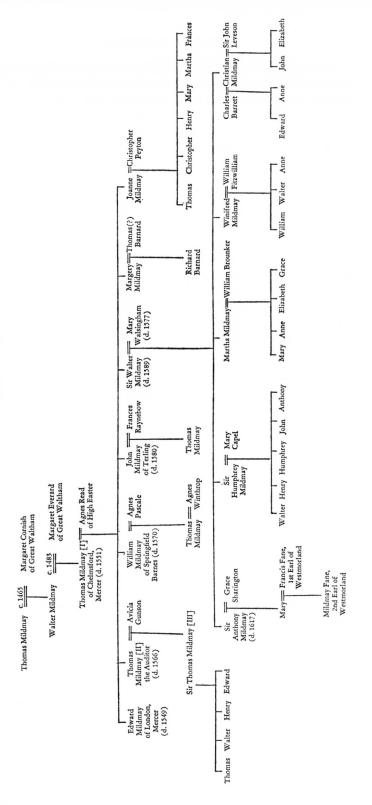

## A NOTE ON MANUSCRIPT SOURCES

As virtually none of Mildmay's letters and speeches have been printed, one must depend almost entirely on manuscript resources in writing his life. Most of Mildmay's own papers may be found in two collections at the Northamptonshire Record Office: the Fitzwilliam of Milton Papers and the Westmorland Manuscripts. The Fitzwilliam Papers which pertain to Mildmay appear to have been gathered by William Fitzwilliam, Mildmay's son-in-law, who probably acted as his private secretary throughout much of his later life; they include speeches, treatises, memoranda, and some letters, as well as Fitzwilliam's parliamentary diary of 1584–1585. The Westmorland Manuscripts, consisting of about 120 bundles, were removed from Apethorpe when Mildmay's heirs sold the house in 1904; deeds and financial records form the bulk of the collection, but some formal letters are included also, especially correspondence from Elizabeth and James VI. Indices of these collections are available at the Office.

The manuscript collections at the British Museum and the Public Record Office provide much supporting material. The most useful series at the Record Office are SP 12, State Papers, Domestic, of Elizabeth's reign, which includes many of Mildmay's letters, and SP 64/27–37, correspondence and memoranda on Exchequer affairs collected by Thomas Fanshaw, Remembrancer from 1568 to 1601. One may find some material on Scottish affairs in SP 59/14, Border Papers, and one may consult the Decrees and Orders of the Exchequer Court, E 123/1–15, although they shed little light on Mildmay's activities.

Mildmay's speeches in Parliament and the Star Chamber are available in two volumes at the British Museum, Harl. MS 6265 and Sloane MS 326. The latter, a late sixteenth- or early seventeenth-century compilation, was apparently intended as a text for publication of the orations, although no printed collection actually appeared. Among other important sources at the British Museum may be mentioned the following: Harl. MS 7033, manuscripts relating to Emmanuel College collected by Thomas Baker, an early eighteenth-century antiquarian; Harl. MS 7383 and Add. MS 30,198, copies of the 1552 report on the revenue courts; Sloane MS 3199 and Add.

MS 34,216, concerning Mildmay's embassy to Mary in 1570; Cottonian MS Caligula C. IX, on the negotiations with Mary, 1583, and the war with the Netherlands, 1584; Lansdowne MS 171, the papers of Sir Julius Caesar; Add. MS 15,891, Hatton's letter book; Add. MS 33,593, the correspondence of Sir Ralph Sadler; Add. MS 34,215, Exchequer accounts formerly among Mildmay's papers; Add. MS 4126 and Add. MS 24,459, volumes containing several of Mildmay's letters.

The parliamentary diary of Thomas Cromwell, at Trinity College Library, Dublin (MS N. 2. 12), includes considerable information about Mildmay's activities in the Parliaments of 1576–1585.

Mildmay's will is preserved at the Principal Probate Registry, Somerset House: Prerogative Court of Canterbury, 51 Leicester. The Essex Record Office, Chelmsford, holds genealogical materials, and some documents relating to the foundation and early years of Emmanuel College are to be found in the College Library.

# BIBLIOGRAPHY

## MANUSCRIPTS

Additional Manuscripts, British Museum, London.

Chancery Papers, Public Record Office, London.

Cottonian Manuscripts, British Museum, London.

Cromwell diary, MS N. 2. 12, Trinity College Library, Dublin.

Dean Piers Book, Peterborough Cathedral Library, Peterbrough.

Egerton Manuscripts, British Museum, London.

Emmanuel College Library Manuscripts, Cambridge:
BUR. 8. 1, COL. 9. 10, COL. 9. 14.

Essex Record Office Manuscripts, Chelmsford:
D/DM 6; D/DAV 14–16; D/DV 23/24–25; D/ABW 25/92;
D/DP/F240; D/DL 673, 687; D/D Pl 19.

Exchequer Papers, Public Record Office, London.

Fitzwilliam journal, Fitzwilliam of Milton Papers, Northamptonshire Record Office, Northampton.

Fitzwilliam of Milton Papers, Northamptonshire Record Office, Northampton.

Harleian Manuscripts, British Museum, London.

Lambeth MS 178, Lambeth Palace Library, London.

Lansdowne Manuscripts, British Museum, London.

MS Bodley e Museo 17, Bodleian Library, Oxford.

Prerogative Court of Canterbury, 51 Leicester, Principal Probate Registry, Somerset House, London.

Sloane Manuscripts, British Museum, London.

State Papers, Public Record Office, London.

Stowe Manuscripts, British Museum, London.

Tanner Manuscripts, Bodleian Library, Oxford.

Westmorland Papers, Northamptonshire Record Office, Northampton.

## PRINTED BOOKS

*Acts of the Privy Council.* Ed. J. R. Dasent. 32 vols. London: Stationery Office, 1890–1907.

*Acts of the Privy Council, Ireland.* SEE Historical Manuscripts Commission, *Fifteenth Report,* Appendix, Part III.

Anstruther, Godfrey. *Vaux of Harrowden.* Newport, Monmouth: R. H. Johns, 1953.

Ascham, Roger. *The Sholemaster.* Ed. Edward Arber. London: Muir & Patterson, 1870.

Bindoff, S. T., J. Hurstfield, and C. H. Williams (eds.). *Elizabethan Government and Society: Essays Presented to Sir John Neale.* London: Athlone Press, 1961.

Black, J. B. *The Reign of Elizabeth.* Oxford, Clarendon Press, 1936; second ed., 1959.

Brooks, Eric St. John. *Sir Christopher Hatton.* London: Jonathan Cape, 1946.

Burgon, J. W. *The Life and Times of Sir Thomas Gresham.* 2 vols. London: Robert Jennings, 1839.

Burnet, Gilbert. *History of the Reformation of the Church of England.* 2 vols. London: Richard Chiswell, 1681.

*Calendar of Patent Rolls, Edward VI.* 5 vols. London: Stationery Office, 1924–1929.

*Calendar of Patent Rolls, Elizabeth.* 3 vols. (1558–1566). London: Stationery Office, 1939–1960.

*Calendar of Patent Rolls, Philip and Mary.* 4 vols. London: Stationery Office, 1936–1939.

*Calendar of State Papers, Domestic, 1547–1625.* 12 vols. London: Longmans, 1856–1872.

*Calendar of State Papers, Foreign.* Edward VI and Mary, 2 vols.; Elizabeth, 23 vols. London: Longmans, 1861–1950.

*Calendar of State Papers, Ireland.* 11 vols. London: Stationery Office, 1860–1912.

*Calendar of State Papers, Spanish.* Henry VII–Mary, 13 vols.; Elizabeth, 4 vols. London: Stationery Office, 1862–1954.

*Calendar of State Papers Relating to Scotland and Mary, Queen of Scots, 1547–1603.* 13 vols. Edinburgh and Glasgow: General Register House, 1898–1952.

Camden, William. *Annales: The True and Royall History of the Famous Empresse Elizabeth.* London: B. Fisher, 1625.

Carrier, Robert. *The Vanished City.* London: Hutchinson, 1957.

Cassirer, Ernst. *The Platonic Renaissance in England.* Translated by James P. Pettegrove. Austin: University of Texas Press, 1953.

Churchyard, Thomas. *A revyving of the deade.* London: E. White, 1591.

Clapham, John. *Elizabeth of England.* Ed. Evelyn Plummer Read and Conyers Read. Philadelphia: University of Pennsylvania Press, 1951.

Cooper, C. H. *Memorials of Cambridge.* 3 vols. Cambridge: Macmillan, 1860–1866.

Cooper, C. H., and Thompson Cooper. *Athenae Cantabrigienses.* 2 vols. Cambridge: Deighton, Bell, 1858–1861.

Cowan, Samuel. *Mary Queen of Scots.* 2 vols. London: S. Low, Marston & Co., 1901.

Craig, Sir John. *The Mint.* Cambridge: Cambridge University Press, 1953.

Curtis, Mark H. *Oxford and Cambridge in Transition.* Oxford: Oxford University Press, 1959.

De Roover, Raymond. SEE Roover, Raymond de.

Dewar, Mary. *Sir Thomas Smith: A Tudor Intellectual In Office.* London: Athlone Press, 1964.

D'Ewes, Sir Simonds. *The Journals of All the Parliaments during the Reign of Queen Elizabeth.* London: John Starkey, 1682.

*Dictionary of National Biography.* Ed. Sir Leslie Stephen and Sir Sidney Lee. 22 vols. London: Oxford University Press, 1908–1909.

Dietz, F. C. *English Government Finance, 1485–1558.* University of Illinois Studies in the Social Sciences, No. IX. Urbana, Illinois: University of Illinois, 1920.

———. *English Public Finance, 1558–1641.* New York: Century, 1932.

———. *The Exchequer in Elizabeth's Reign.* Smith College Studies in History, No. VIII. Northampton, Massachusetts: Smith College, 1923.

*Documents Relating to the University and Colleges of Cambridge.* 3 vols. London: Longmans, 1852.

Ellis, Sir Henry. *Original Letters Illustrative of English History.* Second ser. 4 vols. London: Richard Bentley, 1827.

Elton, G. R. *England under the Tudors.* London: Methuen, 1955.

———. *The Tudor Constitution.* Cambridge: Cambridge University Press, 1960.

———. *The Tudor Revolution in Government.* Cambridge: Cambridge University Press, 1953.

Emmison, F. G. *Tudor Secretary: Sir William Petre at Court and Home.* London: Longmans, 1961.

Fanshaw, Thomas. *The Practice of the Exchequer Court.* London: T. Twyford and W. Place, 1658.

Feavearyear, A. E. *The Pound Sterling.* Oxford: Clarendon Press, 1931.

Fénelon, Bertrand de Salignac de La Mothe. *Correspondance Diplomatique.* Ed. Alexandre Teulet. 7 vols. Paris and London, 1838–1840.

Finch, Mary E. *The Wealth of Five Northamptonshire Families, 1540–1640.* Oxford: Oxford University Press, 1956.

Foster, Joseph. *The Register of Admissions of Gray's Inn, 1521–1889.* London: Hansard, 1889.

Foxe, John. *Acts and Monuments.* Ed. S. R. Cattley and George Townsend. 8 vols. London: R. B. Seeley and W. Burnside, 1837–1841.

Froude, J. A. *History of England from the Fall of Wolsey to the Defeat of the Spanish Armada.* 12 vols. London: Longmans, 1858–1870.

Fuller, Thomas. *The History of the Worthies of England.* 2 vols. London: F. C. and J. Rivington, 1811.

Gee, Henry, and W. J. Hardy. *Documents Illustrative of English Church History.* London: Macmillan, 1896.

*Genealogical Memoranda Relating to the Family of Mildmay.* London: Taylor & Co., 1871.

Giuseppi, M. S. *Guide to the Manuscripts Preserved in the Public Record Office.* 2 vols. London: Stationery Office, 1923–1924.

Goldsmid, E. and G. (eds.). *A Collection of Eighteen Rare and Curious Historical Tracts and Pamphlets.* Edinburgh: E. and G. Goldsmid, 1886.

Harington, John. *Orlando Furioso.* London: Richard Field, 1591.

Harrington, James. *Oceana.* London: Booksellers of London, 1700.

Henderson, T. F. *Mary Queen of Scots.* 2 vols. New York: Scribners, 1905.

Historical Manuscripts Commission. *Third Report.* London: Stationery Office, 1873.

———. *Fifth Report.* London: Stationery Office, 1876.

———. *Eighth Report.* London: Stationery Office, 1881.

———. *Fifteenth Report.* London: Stationery Office, 1897.

———. *Calendar of the Manuscripts of the Marquis of Salisbury.* 18 vols. London: Stationery Office, 1883–1940.

Hopkins, Samuel. *The Puritans and Queen Elizabeth.* 3 vols. New York: A. D. F. Randolph & Co., 1875.

Hughes, Philip. *The Reformation in England.* 3 vols. London: Hollis & Carter, 1952–1954.

Hurstfield, J. *Elizabeth I and the Unity of England.* London: English Universities Press, 1960.

Jordan, W. K. *Philanthropy in England, 1480–1660.* London: George Allen and Unwin, 1959.

*Journals of the House of Commons,* Vol. I (1547–1628). [London,] s.a.

*Journals of the House of Lords,* Vols. I–II (1509–1614). [London,] s.a.

Labanoff, Alexandre (ed.). *Lettres, Instructions et Mémoires de Marie Stuart.* 7 vols. London: C. Dolman, 1844.

Lambarde, William. *Archeion.* Ed. Charles H. McIlwain and Paul L. Ward. Cambridge, Massachusetts: Harvard University Press, 1957.

La Mothe Fénelon. SEE Fénelon, Bertrand de Salignac de La Mothe.

Leach, A. F. *English Schools at the Reformation, 1546–1548.* London: Constable, 1896.

Lee, Maurice, Jr. *James Stewart, Earl of Moray.* New York: Columbia University Press, 1953.

*Letters and Papers, Foreign and Domestic, Henry VIII.* 21 vols. London: Stationery Office, 1862–1932.

Mackie, J. D. *The Earlier Tudors, 1485–1558.* Oxford: Clarendon Press, 1952; second ed., 1959.

Mattingly, Garrett. *The Defeat of the Spanish Armada.* London: Jonathan Cape, 1959.

Maxwell Scott, M. M. C. *The Tragedy of Fotheringhay.* London: Black, 1895.

Mellows, W. T., and Daphne H. Gifford. *Elizabethan Peterborough.* Lamport, Northamptonshire: Northamptonshire Record Society, 1956.

Mildmay, Sir Walter. *A Memorial for a Son.* Ed. the Rev. Arundell St. John Mildmay. London: Griffith, Farrar & Co., 1893.

Mildmay, St. John. SEE St. John Mildmay.

Miller, Amos C. *Sir Henry Killigrew: Elizabethan Soldier and Diplomat.* Leicester: Leicester University Press, 1963.

Molinaeus, Carolus. *Tractatus commerciorum et usurarum.* Paris: R. Étienne, 1555.

Morant, Philip. *The History and Antiquities of the County of Essex.* 2 vols. London: T. Osborne, 1768.

Morison, S. E. *The Founding of Harvard College.* Cambridge, Massachusetts: Harvard University Press, 1935.

Morrison, N. Brysson. *Mary Queen of Scots.* New York: Vanguard, 1960.

Mulcaster, Richard. *Elementarie.* Ed. E. T. Campagnac. Oxford: Clarendon Press, 1925.

Mullett, Charles F. *The Bubonic Plague and England.* Lexington, Kentucky: University of Kentucky Press, 1956.

Mullinger, J. B. *The University of Cambridge.* 3 vols. Cambridge: Cambridge University Press, 1873–1911.

Neale, Sir John. *Elizabeth I and her Parliaments, 1559–1581.* London: Jonathan Cape, 1953.

————. *Elizabeth I and her Parliaments, 1584–1601.* London: Jonathan Cape, 1957.

Nichols, John. *The Progresses and Public Processions of Queen Elizabeth.* 4 vols. London: Society of Antiquaries, 1788–1821.

Nicolas, Nicholas Harris. *Life of William Davison*. London: John Nichols & Son, 1823.

————. *Memoirs of the Life and Times of Sir Christopher Hatton*. London: Richard Bentley, 1847.

Page, William (ed.). *The Certificates of the Commissioners Appointed To Survey the Chantries, Guilds, Hospitals, etc., in the County of York*. Durham: Surtees Society, Vols. XCI (1894) and XCII (1895).

Pevsner, Nikolaus. *The Buildings of England: Northamptonshire*. London: Penguin, 1961.

Pollard, A. F. *History of England from the Accession of Edward VI to the Death of Elizabeth*. London: Longmans, 1910.

Pollard, A. W., and G. R. Redgrave. *Short-Title Catalogue of English Books, 1475–1640*. London: Bibliographical Society, 1946.

Porter, H. C. *Reformation and Reaction in Tudor Cambridge*. Cambridge: Cambridge University Press, 1958.

Rackham, C. H. *Early Statutes of Christ's College, Cambridge*. Cambridge: Fabb & Tyler, 1927.

Read, Conyers. *Bibliography of British History, Tudor Period, 1485–1603*. Second ed. Oxford: Clarendon Press, 1959.

————. *Lord Burghley and Queen Elizabeth*. London: Jonathan Cape, 1960.

————. *Mr. Secretary Cecil and Queen Elizabeth*. London: Jonathan Cape, 1955.

————. *Mr. Secretary Walsingham and the Policy of Queen Elizabeth*. 3 vols. Oxford: Clarendon Press, 1925.

Read, Evelyn. *My Lady Suffolk*. New York: Knopf, 1963.

*Return of Members of Parliament*. 3 vols. London, 1878.

Richardson, W. C. *History of the Court of Augmentations, 1536–1554*. Baton Rouge: Louisiana State University Press, 1961.

————. *Tudor Chamber Administration, 1485–1547*. Baton Rouge: Louisiana State University Press, 1952.

Roberts, Henry. *Fames Trumpet Sounding*. London: Thomas Hacket, 1589.

Roover, Raymond de. *Gresham on Foreign Exchange*. Cambridge, Massachusetts: Harvard University Press, 1949.

Round, J. H. *Family Origins and Other Studies*. London: Constable, 1930.

Rowse, A. L. *The England of Elizabeth*. London: Macmillan, 1951.

————. *Tudor Cornwall*. London: Jonathan Cape, 1957.

Salter, F. R. *Sir Thomas Gresham*. London: L. Parsons, 1925.

Scott, M. M. C. Maxwell. SEE Maxwell Scott, M. M. C.

Shuckburgh, E. S. *Emmanuel College*. London: F. E. Robinson & Co., 1904.

Somers, John. *A Third Collection of Scarce and Valuable Tracts.* 4 vols. London: F. Cogan, 1751.

Somerville, Robert. *History of the Duchy of Lancaster.* London: Duchy of Lancaster, 1953.

St. John Mildmay, H. A. *A Brief Memoir of the Mildmay Family.* London: John Lane, 1913.

Stow, John. *Survey of London.* Ed. John Strype. 2 vols. London: A. Churchill, 1720.

Strype, John. *Annals of the Reformation.* 4 vols. Oxford: Oxford University Press, 1820–1840.

———. *The History of the Life and Acts of Edmund Grindal.* London: John Hartley, 1710.

Tanner, J. R. *Tudor Constitutional Documents.* Cambridge: Cambridge University Press, 1948.

Tawney, R. H., and Eileen Power. *Tudor Economic Documents.* 3 vols. London: Longmans, 1924.

Tytler, P. F. *History of Scotland.* 9 vols. Edinburgh: William Tait, 1828–1843.

Venn, John, and J. A. Venn. *Alumni Cantabrigienses.* Part I (to 1761), 4 vols. Cambridge: Cambridge University Press, 1922–1927.

*Victoria History of the Counties of England. Cambridge,* Vols. II–III. London: Institute of Historical Research, 1948, 1959.

———. *Huntingdon,* Vol. II. London: St. Catherine Press, 1932.

———. *Northampton,* Vol. II. London: Constable, 1906.

Waugh, Evelyn. *Edmund Campion.* London: Hollis & Carter, 1947.

Williamson, J. A. *Hawkins of Plymouth.* London: Black, 1949.

Willis, Robert, and J. W. Clark. *Architectural History of the University of Cambridge.* 4 vols. Cambridge: Cambridge University Press, 1886.

## ARTICLES

Archbold, W. A. J. "A Manuscript Treatise on the Coinage by John Pryse, 1553," *English Historical Review,* XIII (1898), 709–710.

Cross, M. Claire. "Noble Patronage in the Elizabethan Church," *Historical Journal,* III (1960), 1–16.

Dickinson, J. C. "Emmanuel College," in *Victoria History of the Counties of England, Cambridge,* III, 474–480.

Elton, G. R. "The Elizabethan Exchequer: War in the Receipt," in *Elizabethan Government and Society: Essays Presented to Sir John Neale,* ed.

S. T. Bindoff, J. Hurstfield, and C. H. Williams. London: Athlone Press, 1961, pp. 213–248.

Jack, Sybil, and R. S. Schofield. "Four Early Tudor Financial Memoranda," *Bulletin of the Institute of Historical Research*, XXXVI (1963), 189–206.

Johnson, J. H. "Chelmsford Grammar School," *Essex Review*, LIV (1945), 45–51.

Kirby, J. L. "The Rise of the Under-Treasurer of the Exchequer," *English Historical Review*, LXXII (1957), 666–677.

Lehmberg, Stanford E. "Gresham, Mildmay, and the Memorandum for the Understanding of the Exchange," *Notes and Queries*, CCVI (1961), 403–405.

Levy, F. J. "A Semi-Professional Diplomat: Guido Cavalcanti and the Marriage Negotiations of 1571," *Bulletin of the Institute of Historical Research*, XXXV (1962), 211–220.

Neale, Sir John. "Elizabeth and the Netherlands, 1586–7," *English Historical Review*, XLV (1930), 373–396.

———. "Proceedings in Parliament Relative to the Sentence on Mary Queen of Scots," *English Historical Review*, XXXV (1920), 103–113.

Oman, C. W. C. "The Tudors and the Currency, 1526–1560," *Transactions of the Royal Historical Society*, new ser., IX (1895), 167–188.

Read, Conyers. "Profits on the Recoinage of 1560–1," *Economic History Review*, VI (1936), 186–193.

Round, J. H. "The Mildmays and their Chelmsford Estates," *Transactions of the Essex Archaeological Society*, new ser., XV (1921), 1–16.

Simon, Joan. "A. F. Leach on the Reformation," *British Journal of Educational Studies*, III (1955), 128–143, and IV (1955), 32–48.

———. "The Reformation and English Education," *Past & Present*, XI (1957), 48–65.

T. "Apethorpe," *Country Life*, XXV (1909), 414–423, 450–459.

Weigall, Rachel. "An Elizabethan Gentlewoman," *Quarterly Review*, CCXV (1911), 119–138.

Wernham, R. B. "The Disgrace of William Davison," *English Historical Review*, XLVI (1931), 632–636.

# INDEX

Aldrich, Thomas: 117

Alençon, Francis, Duke of (later Duke of Anjou): marriage negotiations of, with Elizabeth, 108–110, 157–164; and revolt of Netherlands, 156–157, 261; death of, 164; mentioned, 107

Allen, William, Cardinal: 240

Alford, Francis: and Parliament of 1584–1585, 258

Alford, Roger: accounts of examined, 53

Alva, Duke of: governor of Netherlands, 63

Anderson, Sir Edmund: and execution of Mary, Queen of Scots, 278, 291

Angus, Earl of. SEE Douglas, Archibald

Anjou, Francis, Duke of. SEE Alençon, Francis, Duke of

Anjou, Henry, Duke of (later Henry III, King of France): marriage negotiations of, with Elizabeth, 105–108; and execution of Mary, Queen of Scots, 279; mentioned, 262, 266, 284

Apethorpe: acquired by Mildmay, 25; description of, 25–26; bequeathed to Anthony Mildmay, 304

apparel, excess in: discussed in Parliament of 1576, 136–138

Arran, Earl of: 210, 219, 221

Arscot, John: 23 n.

Arundel, Charles: and Throckmorton plot, 205

Arundel, Earls of. SEE Fitzalan, Henry, twelfth Earl; Howard, Philip, thirteenth Earl

Arundel, Matthew: 206 n.

Ascham, Roger: and *The Scholemaster*, 64

Association, Bond of. SEE Bond of Association

Audley, John: in Parliament of 1576, 135

Augmentations, Court of: establishment of, 9; Thomas Mildmay and, 9, 13; Walter Mildmay and, 11, 13; and reforms of 1547, 15–17; and reforms of 1552–1553, 33–35, 38–39; mentioned, 52

Babington, Anthony: executed, 271

Babington plot: discussed in Parliament of 1586, 274–276; mentioned, 221, 271–272

Bacon, Sir Nicholas: and Mary, Queen of Scots, 88, 99; and mint, 124, 125 n.; and Parliament of 1576, 145–146; and Edmund Grindal, 151; mentioned, 54

Baker, Sir John: as Chancellor of Exchequer, 51; death of, 48; mentioned, 45

Ballard, John: 275

Barnard, Richard: 6

Barnes, Richard, Bishop of Durham: 116–117

Barnes, Robert: 7

Barrett, Anne: 170, 305

Barrett, Charles: 170

Barrett, Edward: 170

Barwell, Edmund: 223 n.

Beale, Robert: and Mary, Queen of Scots, 212–213, 217, 277; and Parliament of 1584–1585, 236; and Parliament of 1586–1587, 273

Beaufort, Lady Margaret: 8

Bedford, Earls of. SEE Russell, John, first Earl; Russell, Francis, second Earl

Bell, Robert: and Parliament of 1576, 129, 140, 145, 146; death of, 172

Berkeley, Gilbert, Bishop of Bath and Wells: 116

Berry (a servant of Mildmay): 24

Bertie, Richard: 64

Bilney, Thomas: 7

Bingham, Richard: 209 n.

Blount, James, Lord Mountjoy: 166–167

Bond of Association: discussed in Parliament of 1584–1585, 242–244, 250, 256–257

Bothwell, Earl of. SEE Hepburn, James

Bowes, Sir Robert (d. 1554): and financial administration, 29, 31, 32; and Parliament of March 1553, 37

Bowes, Robert (d. 1597): as ambassador to Scotland, 154, 211, 213, 219

Bradshaw, Nicholas: 23 n.

323